The Best of
Social Anarchism

Edited by
Howard J. Ehrlich *&* a.h.s. boy

See Sharp Press • Tucson, Arizona

For information contact:
    See Sharp Press
    P.O. Box 1731
    Tucson, AZ 85702
    www.seesharppress.com

The Best of Social Anarchism / edited by Howard Ehrlich and a.h.s. boy (pseud.) –
        Tucson, Ariz. : See Sharp Press, 2013.
        ISBN 9781937276461
        Contents: Introduction / Jeff Shantz – Preface : Social Anarchism: An Editor's
History / Howard Ehrlich – THEORY: Anarchism and the question of human nature / Thomas
Martin – Reflections on the "New Anarchism" / Brian Morris – Toward a General Theory of
Anarchafeminism / Howard Ehrlich – Against The Law: Anarchist Criminology / Jeff Ferrell –
Economics for Anarchists - A Review / Frank Lindenfeld – Steps Toward a Post-Western Anarchism
/ Thomas S. Martin – A Critical History of Harrisonburg Food Not Bombs / Peter Gelderloos
– EDUCATION: On Scholars, Intellectuals, and Anarchists / Howard J. Ehrlich – The Role of
Anarchist Intellectuals / Jeff Stein – Anarchists in the Academy / Jeff Shantz – Anarchist in Academe
/ Kingsley Widmer – What Should Be Done About Higher Education? / Brian Martin – Ira Shor:
Critical Teaching and Everyday Life / Len Krimerman and Susan Corrente -- NOTABLE FIGURES:
Colin Ward's Everyday Anarchy / Jeff Shantz – An Interview with Colin Ward – Reading Political
Justice / Arthur Efron – Marie Fleming's The Geography of Freedom / John Clark – No Authority
But Oneself / Sharon Presley – Community in the Anarcho-Individualist Society / Richard P. Hiskes
– Against Everything That Is / Daniel Dylan Young – Chomsky's Contributions to Anarchism /
Robert Graham -- CONTEMPORARY VOICES: Poetry Like Bread / Neala Schleuning – Minding
Nature: The Philosophers of Ecology / Janet Biehl – Dear Social Anarchism... / Mitchel Cohen –
Burn Bibles not Flags! / Sam Sloss – Los Angeles, 1992- The Lessons Revisited / Howard J. Ehrlich –
Some Observations on the Oklahoma City Bombing / Howard J. Ehrlich – PRACTICE: Organizing
Communities / Tom Knoche – "Paying Taxes: It's Just Routine" / Jane Meyerding – Anarchy on
the Airwaves / Ron Sakolsky – Living in Community / SYD – The Roundhouse Co-op / William
F. Walker – Consensus / Caroline Estes – Fetishizing Process / Mark Lance – Democracy without
Elections / Brian Martin.
        1. Social Anarchism – History. 2. Anarchism -- Periodicals. 3. United States -- Social conditions
--1980- . 4. United States -- Politics and government -- 1945-1989. 5. United States -- Politics and
government -- 1989- . 6. Press, Anarchist -- United States -- History. I. Ehrlich, Howard J. II. boy,
a.h.s.
        335.83

www.socialanarchism.org
www.bestofsocialanarchism.org

Contents

Practice

Introduction: The Best of Social Anarchism
Jeff Shantz

To achieve any real lasting success, movements for social change require *infrastructures of resistance,* processes and institutions that provide a sustaining framework for creating and maintaining the struggle. Indeed, in the absence of such support, even lively and enthusiastic mobilizations can dissipate very quickly without much impact, as the Occupy encampments of 2011 vividly illustrate. Through common struggle and the pressing realities of meeting material, cultural, and social needs and desires, communities develop such infrastructures to sustain themselves and to provide the support necessary for ongoing struggles and the inspiration of the new world they seek to make. Infrastructures of resistance include a variety of institutions, organizations and practices, such as alternative media and publishing, shared spaces like social centers, bookstores, union halls and bars, workers campgrounds and medical clinics.

The building, maintenance, and nurturing of such infrastructures is a key part of social anarchist practice. For social anarchists, thoroughgoing social change — including what might be called revolutionary change — toward anarchist social relations involves the constant extension of spheres of mutual aid and solidarity until they make up the bulk of human social activities and relationships. These are processes of rendering the state obsolete — an obvious anachronism for all to see. At the same time, the community-based infrastructures of resistance provide bases of social defense against forces of reaction.

Part of this social transformation is imaginal or ideational — it involves advances in the struggles over ideas. In the words of *Social Anarchism*'s dedicated editor Howard Ehrlich, it requires the development of "anarchist transfer cultures," the perspectives and practices by which we sustain the move beyond state capitalism to anarchist social relations, building them as we go. Ehrlich describes anarchist transfer cultures in these terms:

> A transfer culture is that agglomeration of ideas and practices that guide people in making the trip from the society here to the society there in the future... As part of the accepted wisdom of that transfer

culture we understand that we may never achieve anything that goes beyond the culture itself. It may be, in fact, that it is the very nature of anarchy that we shall always be building the new society within whatever society we find ourselves.[1]

The journal *Social Anarchism* has long been a key resource in developing and nurturing this culture. It has played an important part in sustaining ideas and practices of anarchy against the dominance of archic ideologies. Art and literature, as well as economic and political analysis, have always found a home side by side in the journal's pages.

Unlike many movement publications of the last few decades, it has done so through thick and thin, high and low, surviving and even thriving both when movements have enjoyed an upsurge, as after the anti-WTO protests in Seattle in 1999, and during periods of demobilization or stalled growth, as during the early 1990s. With the renewal of anarchist movements in the twenty-first century, *Social Anarchism* continues to provide one of the most important forums of anarchist discussion and debate. Few journals can make this claim. As someone who has spent years working in anarchist free schools and infoshops, as well as community and workplace organizing, I can attest to the ongoing relevance of *Social Anarchism* and its significance as a resource for anarchism over decades. For much of the 1990s *Social Anarchism* was a primary intellectual resource, even *the* resource for those seeking thoughtful and incisive analysis of a range of social issues, theories and practices of social change. Many free school classes right up to the present have made use of articles from *Social Anarchism* as key readings and starting points for discussion. Combining theoretical depth with consistent accessibility and respectful exchange of ideas, *Social Anarchism* has made and continues to make a crucial contribution to anarchist ideas as well as offering a real venue for learning about anarchism. It is, quite simply, essential reading.

Social Anarchism has always displayed the strongest principles of anarchism in action. It has maintained and supported a commitment to honest and sincere engagement. Avoiding the sectarianism and exclusivity that mar perhaps too many radical and movement-based publications, *Social Anarchism* has always remained open to new and alternative ideas, and critical interchange with opposing viewpoints and perspectives. Thus in this collection the reader will see principled debates and discussions with ideas that are often posed as being outside the realm of social anarchism, and which are even hostile toward it. A few of the perspectives encountered in this collection include individualist, Randian objectivism, neo-primitivism, anti-civilization, and, well, sociology (I say as a sociologist).

Social Anarchism exemplifies the sometimes forgotten basis of critique. Critique is not about dismissal or ridicule of opposing views. Rather it is about indentifying and maintaining that which is useful and insightful, while moving beyond that which is inaccurate and ineffective in analysis. *Social Anarchism* always "gets this."

In truth, anarchism has always been social anarchism. Social concerns and commitments are the foundation of anarchist movements. This is so whether one talks about Peter Kropotkin and mutual aid or Emma Goldman's notion of individuality, the works of anarcho-syndicalists and anarchist unionism, or the active anarchy of Colin Ward. Even the prefigurative anarchism of infoshops and free schools or the countercultural approaches to communal living or food production, often derided as lifestylist, are social in character.

The history of anarchism is marked by the proliferation of significant journals. These publications provide venues for debate and discussion on a range of issues — social, political, economic, and cultural. Over time and space — particularly during lower periods of social struggle — these works have served to connect people and sustain movements while introducing new people to anarchism. *Social Anarchism* takes its place alongside the other great journals of anarchist history, such as *Mother Earth* in the early twentieth century, mid-century's *Anarchy*, and *Freedom*.

That *Social Anarchism* has survived and thrived over decades is a testament to the will and tenacity of its editors and to the continued relevance of its varied contributions. Producing and distributing a high quality thoughtful and informative anarchist journal over the course of decades is no small feat. As an editor of another decent social anarchist journal that had a good run but inevitably lost steam, the much lamented *Kick it Over,* which we put together out of Toronto for many issues, I can attest to the challenges and difficulties facing such projects. *Social Anarchism* continues to be an inspiration. Fueling capacities to understand and change social relations in the here-and-now of everyday life while firing the imagination to envision a better future, it remains a vital resource and a darn good read.

The *Best of Social Anarchism* is in many ways the best of contemporary anarchism.

Jeff Shantz
Surrey, B.C (Coast Salish Territory) / December, 2012.

Footnotes

1   Ehrlich, Howard J. "Introduction to Reinventing Anarchist Tactics." *Reinventing Anarchy, Again.* Ed. H. J. Ehrlich. Edinburgh: AK Press, 1996: 329-330.

Social Anarchism: An Editor's History
Howard Ehrlich

f I had thought we would ever publish a history of the magazine, I might have paid more attention to what we were doing. What we were doing was innovative and exciting, but we were too busy doing it to really reflect on the full meaning of our actions. As Fats Waller commented, "One never knows, do one?" (Fats Waller was otherwise not a contributor to SA.)

I guess it all started in 1979 when we completed assembling a considerable number of articles, magazines, pamphlets and so on about anarchism. Why we began this strange task I can't recall, but I do recall feeling like we discovered that we had been speaking anarchism all our lives. There were four of us: David DeLeon, a pack-rat radical historian whose enormous collection of materials gave us a jump start; Carol Ehrlich, an editor and feminist writer; Glenda Morris, a Jill of all trades; and me, a sociologist and social psychologist. Our antiwar and other political work had led David, Carol and I to a premature departure from our professorial roles. The four of us were also members of the Great Atlantic Radio Conspiracy. The Conspiracy produced a weekly radio program of public affairs and the radical arts, and over its career won seven national awards for documentary productions. Having spent years writing about political issues, and having established a solid collective work style, the idea of putting together an anthology of anarchist writings seemed actually a simple thing to do. And so we did. *Reinventing Anarchy,* as we called it, seemed appropriate at the time and we were able to get a solid mainstream publisher to put it out.

It all seemed so easy. So easy, in fact, that one day while sitting around our home studio I proposed to Carol, David and Glenda that we put out a magazine. It had been so easy to get writers for the anthology, we thought it would be just as easy to get them for our magazine. And so, armed with the latest in printing technology, an IBM Selectric typewriter, we began our work.

Our first obstacle was choosing a name. There were four finalists: *White Rose,* which was a knockoff of *Black Rose,* a Cambridge-based magazine and collective; *Broccoli,* just to reassert our New Age credentials; *The Radish* ("going to the root"); and *Social Anarchism.* We liked *Social Anarchism,* in large measure because it confused people. It was a deliberate contrast to the stereo-type of anarchists as violent and individualistic. And it worked. People even to this day ask what "social anarchism" means, giving us the opportunity for a brief political rap. More than that, the label social anarchism took on a life of its own.

We launched ourselves in the winter of 1980. We had assembled a group of 22 editors and put together a 55-page issue. The contents prefigured what was to come. At least in terms of content, it really was a solid issue. Graphically, we learned that we had a lot to learn about magazine production.

From the very beginning we made a series of decisions about the content. One, we were not going to publish reprints. Two, we would publish short works of fiction that had a political twist. Three, we would publish poetry that was accessible and had a political theme. Four, we would accept historical pieces, but try not to do more than one per issue. Five, we would try to have at least two editors review submitted articles, a practice that gave us extra credit with librarians and academicians since political magazines were almost never peer reviewed.

Sixth was our decision to emphasize reviews of new books of anarchist relevance. Especially when we started, anarchist books were hard to publish, and difficult to publicize. As a political matter, we tried, not always success-fully, to allocate 10% of the space to book reviews. And while the quality of the reviews was consistently high, we have been plagued over the years with reviewers who request a book to review and then never follow through with an actual review. The result? The book never gets reviewed and hundreds of people or more never even hear of it.

Seventh, we committed ourselves to editorial balance. That has been dif-ficult. Our intent in assembling and maintaining a board of editorial review-ers was to have, more or less, an equal number of men and women and an equal number of activists and intellectuals. By and large, we achieved those goals. Finally, we were politically and theoretically committed to a balancing of theory and practice: this anthology of our best reflects that commitment.

In issue one, we published a short story by Dan Georgakas. We were not successful in attracting other short story writers, in part, I believe, because short stories are difficult to write. Poetry was another matter. Over the years we have been inundated with poems, most of which were not publishable. Keeping up with all the poetry, especially the bad poetry, became so onerous that our first poetry editor, Susan White, left, because she felt she had to reply to all poets, and that simply was too much work. Here, for example, are the opening lines of what may well be the worst of what we received over the years.

"O wretched soul, what fowl
Have you provoked me to sallow?"

We have not included poetry in this anthology, but here is an example of a poem we enjoyed.

Warning label.
Phylis Campbell Dryden

Caution: the Federal
Food and Drugged
Administration
has found that
the active ingredients in this publication
may cause undue change
of attitude,
burning of the brain.
If symptoms desist, consult a physician
immediately.
For internal use only.
Keep this and all other
indoctrinations
out of the mouths
of babes.

The first two years were exciting. We produced four stimulating issues — our goal then and now was to produce two issues a year. Included in those issues were Peggy Kornegger, Kingsley Widmer, Elaine Leeder, Len Krimerman, Frank Lindenfeld, Jeff Stein, Leon Chorbajian, and Neala Schleuning. Not bad for a bunch of amateurs and first-time publishers. We were even able to move to a higher technology; we purchased an Olivetti typewriter that actually stored nine lines of type at a time. What excitement! Computers were still a long way off.

Despite this initial success, issue number five almost put us in the tank. I had come up with the idea, which everybody approved, to recruit other collective anarchist groups and literally rotate magazine production among them. The hope was to spur interest and strengthen connection among groups throughout the country. We started with Black Rose, which had been a fairly together collective, publishing a magazine of their own. The Black Rose people were enthusiastic, and received our go-ahead to run an interview with the anarchist and poet Philip Levine, along with some of his unpublished poetry, as their feature article.

I did not know at the time that the Black Rose collective was falling apart. There were, I believe, two factions: the artists versus the intellectuals. Although they kept assuring us they were working on the issue and that it would soon be ready, it became clear that we had just lost six months. By the time we wrestled the magazine back, they had procured the Levine interview but little else. We did not have enough copy to publish a new issue, since we were expecting them to do so. But we decided to publish what we had, if only to remind people that we were really a regularly publishing magazine. And so we printed number five — all 35 pages. It was demoralizing for us and we lost our momentum. Subscriptions expired and people forgot about us — just another transient anarchist magazine. But we continued to exist thanks to the support from the readers that stuck with us.

Over the next several years the magazine ran smoothly. We were getting to be reasonably well known and were able financially to always have enough to print the next issue, but not really enough to engage in advertising or other promotional activities. Then one day the phone rang. It was David Wieck, a long time activist, writer, editor and translator. He was a CO during World War II and was publishing anarchist and antiwar articles as early as 1938, as well as a professor of philosophy at Rensselaer Polytechnic Institute in Troy, New York. From the start, David had been a regular contributor to the magazine, both financially and intellectually. "Would you have a use for 2000 copies of Giovanni Baldelli's book *Social Anarchism?*" He had translated the book from the Italian and had helped Baldelli obtain an American publisher. The book was no sooner published than the publisher, Aldine Atherton, plunged into bankruptcy. Some 30 cartons went from the printshop to the warehouse. The book sat in storage for almost 10 years until the bankruptcy court offered it to David for the cost of shipping. We saw it as an opportunity to offer the book as a premium for new subscribers and to sell bulk copies to distributors and bookstores. As it turned out, sales of the book kept the magazine solvent for many years.

We were joined in issue number seven by Chris Stadler. Chris came to us through the Alternative Press Center and was in the process of building a magazine distribution firm in Baltimore. He immediately became our managing editor, seeing to all the fine details that kept the magazine running. He was an excellent editor and proofreader and established the *Chicago Manual of Style* as our style sheet, appearing at times to have memorized the 14th edition of that work. He remained active with SA from issues 7 to 20 and is on call still today, when needed. Joining us too was Mark Bevis (issues 10–25). He came to us through the Radio Conspiracy and left us in 1998 for Pacifica

National News. He became our first book review editor and subsequently our associate editor.

a.h.s. boy, a Baltimore writer and graphic artist also known as "Spud," took responsibility for the magazine's appearance and cover design in issue 17. He designed a unique database for subscriptions and sales, and a website where we plan to house all issues for free and easy access. Spud became editor at number 31, and in regard finally to both design and editorial content, we became a strong, creative, and productive team.

By issue 19, we were pretty well established. We had a European distributor, and regular outlets in Australia and England. Nevertheless, distribution was and is our major problem. Today there are fewer political bookstores than when we started. The costs of distribution have multiplied to the point where some issues cost more to distribute than to print. Distributors and bookstores demand a 50% discount. Payment in four to six months is not uncommon. Furthermore, individual subscriptions over the last several years have decreased, while our sales to distributors and bookstores have increased. Domestic postage rates have virtually doubled and our last mailing saw overseas rates tripling. As a result, our income today is considerably less than ever.

Over-the-counter purchases amount to almost half our sales. How people are moved to the point of purchase still eludes me. An attractive cover and interesting titles doubtless help, but there's no question that we have to overcome the stereotype and political stigma of anarchism.

By way of illustrating our uphill climb, I'll recount a story from my own experience. I had a contract to clean up the grant files of the Maryland office of the National Endowment for the Humanities. The office staff consisted of the director and her assistant. During the course of our many conversations, I let it be known that I published *Social Anarchism*. It was a very collegial setting and the director seemed genuinely curious, so I gave her a copy of the magazine. More than a month went by, and I received no comment on the magazine. I mentioned this to the director's assistant, who provided me with the details: the director had taken the magazine home with her and started to read it on the bus, but she felt like some of the other passengers were staring at her. Every day for a week, she would take out the magazine and try to read it, but people were watching what she was reading, and she was reading anarchism. A bit later she came to worry about what her husband's reaction might be, so she hid the magazine while at home, finally returning it to her assistant when the coast was clear. I sometimes wonder if we could have been more widely disseminated with another name. *Broccoli,* anyone?

In the 100th anniversary edition of the *Progressive*, the editor, Matthew Rothschild, wrote: "Magazines are fragile plants — magazines of dissent especially so. Only a few manage not to die from neglect or mishandling or poor planning." So far, so good.

Murray Bookchin had served a brief stint on our editorial board and I once asked him what he thought was the primary role of anarchists today. Without hesitation, he replied: "Making anarchists." That's the way we felt about the magazine. Our role was to put together for display and review the ideas and ideals of anarchism. Given that, I felt the strength of what we were doing lay in our diversity. If the magazine had a party line over the years, it was making anarchists across the spectrum of social thought.

Components/Principles of Social Anarchism

Social Anarchism "exists" as a personal philosophy, as a theory of organization, and as a theory of social change. The British anarchist, Brian Morris, characterizes SA as "an opposition to the state and all forms of power and oppression; recognition that the power of the modern state intrudes into all aspects of social life; a fervent anticapitalism; a rejection of the vanguard party, representation, and the notion that the transformation to socialism can be achieved through state power; a rejection of an abstract conception of human nature; and finally, the importance of creating alternative social forms of organization, non-hierarchic and independent of both the state and capitalism." To understand the full meaning of these principles we have broken them down into 22 principles and juxtaposed each anarchist component with a matching bureaucratic, capitalist component.

We live in revolutionary times recognizing that revolution is a process and not some arbitrary point in time when a mass of people fill the streets or tear down the ubiquitous wall hangings of some despot. The principles of social anarchism presented here are an integral part of this process.

BUREAUCRATIC, CAPITALIST	SOCIAL ANARCHIST
The organization has a clear hierarchy of power and authority.	Organizational power is diffused. The authority may be delegated on short-term basis.
Person or persons at the top carries final responsibility for work.	Responsibility is shared by all workers/citizens.
Decision-making follows established procedures in keeping with the formal organizational structures.	Decision-making is by consensus or some representative variation in which all persons participate.
Routine maintenance tasks (housekeeping, sanitation, etc.) are allocated to specialized roles. Persons performing those roles are at the bottom of the social hierarchy.	Routine maintenance tasks are shared by all persons.
Rewards are differentiated by office and by role performance in keeping with organizational hierarchy.	Rewards are, typically, equally distributed with some concern given the differences in need.
Jobs are allocated to people on the basis of their competency.	There is a regular rotation procedure across all jobs. Technical competency is treated with ambivalence.
Jobs are clearly defined, structured, and stable with individual achievement valued.	Job definitions are viewed as temporary, though they may be well-defined and structured. Collective action is valued.
Job methods should be carefully defined by engineers, systems specialists, and management.	How jobs get done is generally left to those performing the work.
Groups and individuals should be given specific information necessary to do their job, but no more.	All persons have open access to all organizational information.
There should be close supervision, tight controls, and well-maintained discipline.	Control mechanisms are normative and consensual, self-discipline is emphasized.
Files, rules, and written communications regulate organizational life.	Group meetings and informal communications predominate.
Role relations are designed to be formal, universalistic, and effectively neutral.	The personalization of social relations is encouraged. The personal is seen as the political.

BUREAUCRATIC, CAPITALIST	SOCIAL ANARCHIST
Equalitarian relations between people across statuses is discouraged. The components of societal stratification are generally accepted within the organization.	Equalitarian relations are self-consciously worked at, and external sources of stratification are viewed as improper if not divisive.
Play is seen as subversive of the organizational structure.	Emphasis on incorporating play into work.
The organization is viewed as autonomous — independent of the larger society.	The organization views itself as part of the larger community though its definitions and reciprocal obligations are variable
Education on social issues is seen as irrelevant. Released time may be granted for occupationally relevant education.	Internal education programs about the work of your organization, the community and its relation to the larger society are routine.
Growth through increasing the size of the organization is desirable.	Increasing size is devalued. The optimum size is seen as one which does not exceed members' comprehension of organizational structure or where social relations become depersonalized.
The effectiveness of the organization or community is generally assessed by economic criteria.	Effectiveness is assessed by citizen or worker-defined criteria in which satisfaction is given primacy or balanced against economic and political criteria.
Finance, banking and money management are generally concentrated among those in power and are typically managed in secret.	People are involved in those economic processes that concern their well-being, with financial management being participatory and transparent.
The basic elements — earth, water, and the air — are regarded as private property subject to those who own them.	The basic elements are held in common with everyone under a communal stewardship.
Technology, like the basic elements, is subject to private ownership and is most efficient when centralized.	Technology should be decentralizing and liberatory.
Successful organizations require a clear division of labor and system of consistent leadership.	Decision making is collective within an agreed-upon division of labor.

Theory

Thomas Martin's "Anarchism and the Question of Human Nature" is perhaps *Social Anarchism*'s most widely reprinted essay. Written in part as a response to Stephen Pinker's book *The Blank Slate: The Modern Denial of Human Nature,* this essay re-examines one of the core principles of modern anarchism: that human nature does not constrain our behavior, and therefore cannot explain (or restrict) the development and direction of human social evolution. Martin effectively argues that such a belief flies in the face of accepted modern science, but he also affirms that acknowledging the lessons of evolutionary biology or cognitive science need not fundamentally invalidate anarchist thought.

Originally published in issue 37.

Anarchism and the question of human nature
Thomas Martin

In these first years of the new century anarchism, as a philosophy and as an ongoing praxis, is faced with a number of disconcerting adjustments. Chief among these is the growing evidence that we, along with most other ideologies on the Left, have based our theory on a mistaken concept of human nature. We have learned over the years to distrust words like sociobiology, evolutionary psychology, cognitive science, and above all that dreaded buzzword, "hard-wired" — yet we can no longer ignore the fact that these sciences are probably right about human nature. It does exist; it has biological roots; and while it does enjoy a large measure of free will, its most basic drives and emotions are indeed hard-wired. The Left has long resisted and denied these facts, on the grounds that they might justify discrimination based on heredity, or that they militate against the possibility of radical social reform, or both. I hope to demonstrate that these fears are groundless.

The "hard-wired" concept is thoroughly anchored in evolutionary theory, and this is the first obstacle the Left runs up against when objecting to it. Evolution is a fact: we are animals, closely related to other primates and only a little more distantly to the rest of the mammals. We share many physical and emotional traits with them, and it is absurd to suppose that they are governed by instinct but that we are not. We don't know exactly how evolution works (in fact there are some serious alternatives even to Darwinism's most basic assumptions, like the central role of the gene); but it does work. Very few if any radicals or anarchists would disagree with that. But certain conclusions follow inevitably from that 'given,' and if we deny them, we put ourselves into very unsavory company. Biblical fundamentalists insist that we are a separate creation from the animals, our consciousness governed by a 'soul' which is in turn answerable to a 'God' — do any of us want that idea for a bedfellow? On the other hand, if we accept uncritically (as many on the Right do) the view of human nature suggested by today's neo-Darwinism, we wander into even more unsavory neighborhoods. The notorious Bell Curve is founded on those arguments, and so is neo-Nazism and other overtly racist movements.

This article is, in part, a response to the recent best-seller *The Blank Slate: The Modern Denial of Human Nature* (2002), by Steven Pinker of MIT. Pinker is that rare individual, a compassionate conservative (such creatures do exist, despite the oxymoronic nature of the phrase). He is neither racist nor sexist, and appears to believe sincerely in human equality and freedom, though he does not think we need to abandon capitalism or authoritarianism to achieve those goals. Much of the book is aimed at demonstrating the sources and ongoing project of what he calls the "blank-slate" hypothesis. Classical anarchism, with its origins in the work of Godwin and Proudhon, in the tumults of the French Revolutionary era, and — indirectly — in socialism of various hues, has always assumed that human nature is almost infinitely malleable. It is an idea shared by most philosophies of the Left, and was developed into scientific respectability by such left-leaning anthropologists, sociologists and psychologists as Boas, Durkheim, Mead, Kroeber, Jung, Reich and Goodman. Pinker traces it back to Locke and Mill, at least in its modern form (the idea actually goes back to classical Greece). It is still the dominant view of human nature in academia, and has usually been accepted unquestioningly by anarchists. Unfortunately (and I do mean 'unfortunately'), it is wrong.

The blank-slate hypothesis goes like this: humans, unlike all other animals, have evolved in such a way that we have almost entirely freed ourselves from the chains of instinct and biology. Very little, if any, of our behavior is hard-wired. We are essentially products of culture, which is not a biological phenomenon and is therefore capable of very wide variation. All differences among ethnic groups, so-called races, and even individuals are the result of nurture and life experience, not of genetic heritage. Consequently "social engineering" is possible: we can create a better world by manipulating culture. This conclusion has supported many experiments over the past century, ranging from the horrors of Stalinism to the liberal social welfare state, not to mention various anarchist communities. The "blank slate" is therefore associated with liberalism and radicalism generally — with civil rights, women's liberation, environmentalism, anti-globalism and queer studies, to name a few. But in recent decades, the sciences — notably cognitive psychology, genetics and brain research — have established that, while the human mind is flexible and creative, it is far from being a blank slate. Much if not most of our everyday behavior is in fact "hard-wired." (This term has become anathema to many academics on the Left.)

The evidence has given rise to several new fields of study, all of which have come under attack from the Left. The most notorious of these — known even to radicals who have no background at all in the sciences — is "sociobiology." Why do radicals oppose sociobiology? Because they see it as a possible prop for racist and sexist ideologies. It can be, of course, but that is too narrow and facile an interpretation. The idea derives originally from the work of Edward O. Wilson, a Harvard entomologist who noticed similarities between the social behavior of ants and humans, and developed a full-blown thesis of animal behavior as a product of evolutionary pressures. In his *Sociobiology* (1975, updated and expanded in 2000 as *Sociobiology: The New Synthesis*), Wilson argued that social behavior in all animals, including us, is primarily founded in our biology, which is in turn shaped by evolution. At no point does Wilson claim that nurture or environment play no part in human nature. Still, he and his followers have been attacked, not only in print but even physically in a few cases. In an attempt to bring these ideas more towards the political center, John Tooby and Leda Cosmides reformulated them as "evolutionary psychology," which has tended to focus on gender differences. The controversy continues, despite the recent death of Wilson's most prominent enemy, Stephen Jay Gould. The political problem with sociobiology is its association with neo-Darwinism, which has become a platform for many noisome reactionary academics like Charles Murray, Francis Fukuyama, and Richard Dawkins. The Right is certainly guilty of selective use of sociobiology's findings; but so is the Left, in its rejoinders. In his *A Darwinian Left: Politics, evolution and cooperation* (1999), Peter Singer attempted to find a middle ground, starting from a Left perspective; Pinker has done the same in *Blank Slate,* starting from the Right. Neither has entirely succeeded, probably because there is in fact no objective middle ground.

Sociobiology challenges the idea that society or culture, the whole collection of human behaviors, is somehow disconnected from the human organisms which practice it. Alfred Kroeber (father of the anarchist novelist Ursula LeGuin) once famously said, "Heredity cannot be allowed to have acted any part in history." (Degler, 1991, p. 84) I am a professional historian, and though I admire Kroeber, the fatuity of this statement astonishes me. Almost as soon as Wilson's book was published, the waters were irretrievably muddied by Gould, Waddington and other critics who linked him with such unpleasant doctrines as eugenics and Social Darwinism, not to mention racism. This was unfair, and took the debate off in an unprofitable direction. Matters were made worse by some of Wilson's supporters, like Richard Dawkins, Thomas Sowell, and the authors of *The Bell Curve,* all of whom have advanced selectively exaggerated versions of Wilson's ideas as backing for their own particular agendas. The end result has been to polarize the educated general public (which for the most part does not really understand the science involved) and to make them victims, in a sense, of an academic controversy (which, like all academic controversies, is really more political than intellectual). We in the West often laugh at Stalin's Soviet Union for wasting so much time and resources on Lysenko's crackpot theories — yet is this case so very different?

Sociobiology and its cognates depend for their scientific backing on neo-Darwinism, a set of facts and ideas represented in the popular press by the "selfish gene" metaphor. As the name suggests, this is only the latest version of mainstream evolutionary theory, which is itself still evolving. It pointedly rejects Kropotkin's claim that in evolution, cooperation is often a stronger driving force than competition. For this reason alone anarchists should question the motives of the neo-Darwinists. The fact that the sociobiological project is based on faulty (or at best, incomplete) biology does not necessarily invalidate its claims, but it does require us to look more carefully at the conclusions drawn from those claims.

No one with any sense really doubts that Darwin got the basics right. Evolution does happen; that is not a theory. But controversy still rages over the details of the process. The neo-Darwinists begin from a logical, reductionist and materialist standpoint. Their approach is sometimes called the "synthetic theory" because it combines Darwin's principles with the science of genetics founded by Mendel, a science that Darwin knew nothing about. The only possible selection is natural selection, and its mechanism is genetic. They are fundamentalists on this issue. The word "mechanism" is used advisedly. Neo-Darwinism is essentially Cartesian, a late branch of that world-view born in the Scientific Revolution of the seventeenth century. Nothing is real if it cannot be seen, touched, measured, accounted for objectively. The universe and everything in it is "mechanical" in the sense that it obeys certain simple laws of chemistry and physics. Given enough time and knowledge, we can figure everything out without recourse to emotional, intuitive, spiritual (that is, "unscientific") explanations. Moreover, this approach is reductionist: Darwin, but more so his followers, have believed that they can understand the world by examining minutely all the parts in isolation, and then putting them back together — not as they really are, in all their messy and illogical complexity, but in the form of a model that makes sense to the scientist. At the beginning of the twenty-first century, the neo-Darwinists are as yet undisturbed by the implications of subatomic physics, chaos theory, general systems theory and the like. The best simple way to describe their basic error is that they do not think holistically.

Neo-Darwinism's chief spokesman, Richard Dawkins, is unremittingly cold and "scientific" — in the negative sense of that word — when it comes to explaining what it means to be human. What it means is simply this: we are robots, mere machines built and programmed by genes whose only (and unconscious) goal is to replicate themselves. The genes too are machines, and therefore so is all of living nature. This extreme Cartesianism is at the heart of old-paradigm thinking, and a primary goal of post-Western science must be to hurry it off to its long-overdue grave. But, as Dawkins himself often points out, just because I can't or won't accept something as true, doesn't mean it isn't true. We cannot dismiss neo-Darwinism merely because it is unpleasant. We can, however, question the uses to which it is put.

Even if all other scientific proofs do not convince, this one should: our emotions, reflexes and senses all evolved in a world very different from the one we have made for ourselves, just in the last ten or twenty generations. This dissonance is no doubt the source of much of our malaise, psychological and physical. Fats and sweets taste good to us because, over several hundred millennia of scraping by on the African savannahs, we needed them to survive. Now, in a sedentary and over-technologized culture, they simply make us obese and diabetic. We evolved a "fight or flight" response to save us from predators; it now comes into play when we are stuck in traffic or on the carpet at work, and we turn it inward, causing ulcers and anxiety. If our slate were truly blank, we could fill it anew in every generation with responses and reflexes appropriate to the milieu, and everyone would be a great deal happier than they are now. The entire science of ecopsychology — an integral part of any post-Western paradigm — would be entirely unnecessary if we did not all have these deep-rooted evolutionary instincts.

It is no doubt true that genes 'want' to make more copies of themselves, and as many as possible. It does not follow that they 'want' to do so at the expense of other, dissimilar genes. This assumption goes back to one of Darwin's original errors: that living entities must always compete for scarce resources. This is where the great anarchist scientist, Peter Kropotkin, comes in. To make a connection between ecology, evolution and anarchism was a stroke of genius, to say the least — in my opinion it makes Kropotkin one of the greatest thinkers of the past thousand years, right up there with Aquinas, Calvin, Marx and Einstein. As all anarchists (but not many others) know, Kropotkin accepted Darwin's basic findings but disputed the Darwinist contention that competition rather than cooperation is the central mechanism of evolution. His Mutual Aid framed the idea, and it has been developed much further in the century since, with supporting input from general systems theory, the science of ecology, and other disciplines that Kropotkin himself did not live to see. Graham Purchase and Murray Bookchin, in different ways, have brought his theories up to date.

The other new field which has helped undermine the "blank slate" is usually called "cognitive science." The name falls a bit short of desirability.

Everything is "cognitive" in some sense, so the term is almost too vague to be useful. And the word "science" is tainted. But let's leave that alone and move on.

The philosophical roots of cognitive science are not very long: they reach down through time only so far as Maurice Merleau-Ponty and John Dewey. Merleau-Ponty was influenced primarily by Kojève and Husserl. Dewey, of course, is one of the best-known educators and philosophers in American life. His simple but profound epistemology, which challenges the traditional boundary between the inner and outer worlds of experience, is the philosophical basis of cognitive science.

Put simply, cognitive science argues that the way we construct our reality — the world we are conscious of, as well as its extensive unconscious foundations — is a product of our sensorimotor experience. The body interacts with its environment in certain ways that are severely restricted by its structure: we have two arms and two legs, eyes in the front of our heads, fronts and backs that are broader than our two sides, and so forth. We can see and hear only narrow frequencies of light and sound. Our eyes are a great deal more sensitive than our noses (we all realize that dogs smell the world much more than they see it). From birth, our bodies do certain things that produce certain more or less predictable results. This physical interaction with the world 'out there' establishes networks of neural connections that last a lifetime, and it is these same connections — not some disembodied 'mind' floating in the ether — that also generate our abstract ideas and our languages, that is, our culture. Every such interaction is unique, but they do fall into general patterns. When I push something I can expect it to move, unless it is too heavy or fixed in place. From this general truth I can formulate a definition of "push" that works over a wide span of time and space. All of these processes are more or less unconscious. But the conscious mind is very limited — it can concentrate only on a few things at a time, in a very small time/space region. Therefore it must oversimplify these patterns into metaphorical rules of logic that arise, but are disconnected, from the "real" world. Without this metaphoric ability, cognitive science argues, we could not learn or even function — each event or experience would be new, and we would have to start from scratch in reacting to it.

Currently the leaders in the field of cognitive science are George Lakoff and Mark Johnson of the University of California at Berkeley and the University of Oregon, respectively. Their short book *Metaphors We Live By* (1980) is the best introduction to the concept, and their rather-too-long *Philosophy in the Flesh: The Embodied Mind and its Challenge to Western Thought* (1999) extends their findings into every discipline imaginable. Like Dewey and

Merleau-Ponty, they start from the assumption, now pretty much proved by late-Western science, that there is no dichotomy between mind and body. In their words, these are the three central findings of cognitive science:

The mind is inherently embodied.

Thought is mostly unconscious.

Abstract concepts are largely metaphorical. (Lakoff and Johnson, 1999, p. 3)

The first and second points would now be accepted by all but the most retrogressive scientists, philosophers and psychologists, though they might argue about the meaning of certain terms like "mind" and "unconscious." The third point makes a statement about the nature of language, and the ways in which it generates our realities.

The most prized possession of Western philosophy has always been Reason: that capacity we supposedly have to look at the world, marshal and analyze what we see according to certain simple rules, and come up with an accurate representation in our minds of what is "out there." Cognitive science disposes of traditional "reason" rather easily, and undercuts the entire foundation of Western philosophy. The Western view, going back to the pre-Socratics and reinforced by Aristotle, Aquinas, Descartes and many others, is that "reason" is a edifice of thought — a set of rules for thinking — that exists quite independently of our physical selves. It goes on in our minds, but is not of our minds — this is another way of saying that the world is just as we perceive it to be, or that it would be just as it is now if we weren't in it to perceive it. This view underlies the blank-slate theory. Cognitive theory says, on the contrary, that our reason is a by-product of our neural, skeletal and muscular structures: we think the way we do because our bodies work the way they do. It is thus a product of evolution and is "universal" only in the sense that is shared by all human beings (and probably at least some other animals). Nearly all reasoning takes place at a subconscious level; all that comes to the surface is what we need for immediate action in a given situation. Because it is not conscious, it is metaphorical by definition: only a waking consciousness can think in concrete, explicit terms (and even then, only up to a point). And finally, cognitive science undoes the vast error of the Enlightenment, one we have suffered under for several centuries now: reason is not disembodied, following a set of universal rules "out there," but driven by the emotions and intuitions, just like everything else we do. As Lakoff and Johnson modestly point out, their theory brings down the whole structure of Western philosophy, with considerable collateral damage to science, psychology, sociology and history. This is not a bad thing. Of course, it also brings down anarchism as we have long understood it, but this is not a bad thing either: it gives us an opportunity to place our ideology on a sounder footing.

Reason as defined by Western philosophy is an impossibility, as even a little reflection will reveal. It is pictured as a sort of computer or calculating machine, housed in a container that insulates it totally from the "real world" — it is absolutely free and autonomous, not subject to any of the laws of nature, not even gravity or time. It is disconnected altogether from the lump of brain tissue it inhabits, yet somehow it can understand and exercise some control over the world outside its cocoon. Those readers who have some familiarity with formal Aristotelian logic will more easily get my point. This system of thought, while certainly very useful in limited areas, is a distillate of the whole vast idea of Reason into a small collection of rules for thinking. Formal logic — and even more so its latter-day mathematized descendants — is a world of absolutes, with no grey areas whatsoever. A is either B or it is not B, with no possibilities in between. We all know that the real world does not work like that. Worse, logic is never swayed by feelings or intuition: if all A is B, and all B is C, then all A is C, whether you like it or not. The new discipline known as "fuzzy logic" is just beginning to adjust the concept of reason to the findings of cognitive science, but it has a long way to go.

It should be clear by now that a fundamental cause of anarchism's shaky foundation (a problem it shares with most other products of Western philosophy) is dichotomization. In order to get past this problem we must, first of all, reject certain false dichotomies that contribute to our "blank-slate" fetish. The most basic is that between "nature" and "nurture," a dichotomy that goes back at least to Plato and Aristotle, but was first delineated in modern terms by John Locke and then developed to an absurd degree by psychologists and by philosophers interested in psychology. Dichotomy itself, as a concept, is a template example of why the nature/nurture binary is unsound. All human cultures have some notion of dichotomy, and it is easy to see why: the human body is bilateral. We have two eyes, two hands, two feet; a front and back; a left and right. Some basic dichotomies also exist in nature, such as night and day, or the somewhat different functions of the right and left brain hemispheres. It is therefore entirely natural to project other dichotomies onto the world around us, whether they are really there or not. In general, though, nature is not dichotomous, nor is the human mind. Cutting-edge physics, along with general systems and chaos theory, now posits that the world is a bewilderingly complicated network of interactions, in which everything is literally connected to everything else. Here is the way out of the conundrum set for us anarchists by cognitive science and evolutionary biology: because of the way our bodies and brains are organized, we see the world in a particular way (dichotomous, reified, logical), and this view has obvious survival benefits, otherwise we would not be here to talk about it. However, we project that model onto the world as a whole, onto vast regions of reality where it does not apply. This is the part of our behavior that is not hard-wired, and therefore, susceptible to learning and change. As Gregory Bateson said, evolution is learning — and we have the freedom of choice to direct that evolution, at least within the limits set by physical nature. Evolution may indeed predispose me to favor the survival of my genes over the survival of yours; but I can choose otherwise. My bilateral symmetry may predispose me to dichotomize society as Left or Right; but I can choose otherwise, and be Out In Front instead.

So we have, for more than a century, built our ideological edifice on shifting sands. But the news is not altogether bad. Predictably, critics on the right interpret the new findings as evidence in favor of their agenda. I do not refer to the crudely racist and sexist uses to which the "hard-wired" model has been put in the past. The conservative mainstream has learned to be more subtle than that. Here is how Steven Pinker summarizes the "blank-slate" fears about these findings:

- If people are innately different, oppression and discrimination would be justified.
- If people are innately immoral, hopes to improve the human condition would be futile.
- If people are products of biology, free will would be a myth and we could no longer hold people responsible for their actions.
- If people are products of biology, life would have no higher meaning and purpose. (Pinker, Blank Slate, p. 139)

Therefore, Pinker says, scientists on the "Left" reject the discoveries of evolutionary biology and genetics, all evidence to the contrary. From an anarchist perspective, we might reply that both sides are misstating the issue. Try this instead:

- whether people are innately different or not, oppression and discrimination are not justified, and need not be an automatic consequence of innate differences. Different means different, not "inferior" or "superior." Even the most hard-wired sociobiologist will admit that we have sufficient mental plasticity to make free choices about how we will deal with difference.
- "moral" and "immoral" are value judgments, subjective in regard to time, place and culture; and again, we are plastic enough to "improve

the human condition," regardless of whether our sense of right and wrong is biological in origin.

- "free will" and "determinism" are yet another false dichotomy. Even if our behavior is partly or even largely biologically determined, no one argues that it is 100% determined; we can choose to resist the biological imperative, and so of course people may be held responsible for their actions. The only question is what 'holding responsible' is to mean in terms of punishment or reprisal.
- whether people are products of biology or of culture is quite irrelevant to whether life has a "higher meaning and purpose." Aside from the subjectivity of that word "higher," life has the purpose and meaning we give it.

Let us look more closely at some of the social implications of the foregoing, especially as they relate to anarchism.

Recent studies of early childhood development seem to support the "hard-wired" theory, as indeed common sense tells us they should. Heredity establishes the basic personality: aggressive or shy; intelligent or not so bright. Socialization by the peer group is the main factor in how those basic traits are expressed: is the aggression played out on the football field, or in gang violence and rape? Is IQ developed to its full potential, or does it go to waste? Is attraction to the same sex (which nearly all children experience to some degree, at some stage in their development) suppressed, or encouraged by chance events and encounters to develop into homosexuality? The role of the parents is far less than most would like to think: they provide nurture and shelter (or they do not); they provide access to skills and knowledge, they have some part in choosing the peer group; it is largely up to them how 'secure' a child feels. But they do not seem to contribute much to the basic personality or intelligence, except through their genes. (Pinker, Blank Slate, ch. 19, esp. p. 392)

Is human nature essentially peaceful, or violent? Are we hard-wired to be aggressive? This is a crucial question for anarchists, because we are working towards a world in which artificial restraints are removed from human activity. If there is no government, no police, will we all (as one of my students recently wrote) "run wild and murder each other"? Every anarchist philosopher has addressed this issue. Almost all have assumed a blank-slate explanation for human nature: violence and aggression are learned, not innate. If we engineer our society in such a way that aggression is not rewarded, it will not happen. Peter Kropotkin's Conquest of Bread outlines such a society; the State is an "apparatus of violence." Even Darwin suggested that the "struggle for existence" is not necessarily violent; "As the mistletoe is disseminated by birds, its existence depends on birds; and it may metaphorically be said to struggle with other fruit-bearing plants, in order to tempt birds to devour and thus disseminate its seeds rather than those of other plants." (Darwin, *Origin of Species,* p. 63) Even Georges Sorel (who may or may not have been an anarchist, depending on whom you ask), in his *Reflections on Violence,* concluded that violence may be employed only to destroy violent institutions. (Sorel, *Reflections,* p. 195) What it comes down to is that we live in a dominative, patriarchal, hierarchic society in which violence is the chief instrument of policy, enshrined as an ideal in the schools and the media, studied extensively by scientists. Therefore we 'see' violence first; it is central to our consciousness; alternatives are rarely discussed or even thought about. (This is also, of course, why Darwinists "see" competition in nature rather than "cooperation.") We may in fact be hard-wired for violence, and we may have to accept that science has proved it. But we may also be hard-wired for many other behaviors and attitudes which have not been as well explored, because our science functions on behalf of our institutions of coercion. We do not need to accept the claim that, because violence is in our genes, we are therefore "violent beings."

Here, fortunately, Pinker's case is rather weak. In his chapter on violence, he gives many examples of apparently innate violent behavior, but all of them come either from our culture or from indigenous cultures under threat from Western civilization. The peaceful nature of most indigenous and matricentric peoples, before they ran up against the aggressive West, is well documented in the journals of early explorers and anthropologists. Still, recent studies do suggest that a tendency to violence and aggression is part of our biological heritage. This again is common sense: the most basic of all urges is that of self-preservation (including self-preservation through reproduction), and when faced with the classic "it's either me or you" situation, we are all going to choose "me." But that is an oversimplification, and oversimplification is one of the Right's oldest tricks. Aggression towards other species (such as hunting and killing for food) does not automatically translate into aggression towards one's own species, and violence in certain types of situation does not necessarily mean a "violent nature." Indeed the entire idea of "violence as natural" is undermined by Kropotkin's demonstration that cooperation is more fundamental to evolution than competition is. However, Kropotkin never denied that competition does exist in nature, and never suggested that it was anything other than "natural." It seems clear that some degree of aggression and violence is hard-wired into us. But biology is not destiny. The issue for anarchists should not be, "is violence innate?" but rather, "how is it directed?" In spite of what Pinker implies, we do not claim that violence is strictly a learned behavior. What we claim is that how we express our violent instincts is learned behavior.

A separate article would be required to explore the current status of "race" as a concept, but let us try to dispose of it briefly here. The Nazi era made racism and its fellow travellers (such as eugenics) unacceptable, and science has striven for the past half-century to demonstrate that race is not a rational basis for discrimination. Just since the 1990s, evolutionary genetics has begun to prove that "race" itself, as traditionally defined, does not even exist. Skin color, epicanthic eye folds and the like are very superficial and recent adjustments to environment, not in any way an essential part of what it means to be human. We are all very closely related, and the genealogical overlap among Africans, Europeans, Amerindians, and so forth is so extensive as to make any boundaries meaningless. Studies of DNA markers have produced some surprises: the Norwegians are not very closely related to the Danes; the Poles are more closely kin to many Pakistani tribes than they are to the Czechs next door; the predominant Irish Y chromosome has more in common with that of native Americans than it does with other European Y haplogroups. The closest relatives of today's Jews, both Sephardic and Ashkenazic, seem to be the Greeks. These findings relate only to mitochondrial DNA (from your mother's mother's mother and so on) or to the Y chromosome (father's father's father, etc.) and so do not even take into account the enormous mix that all of us can find in the other branches of our family tree. That being said, it must be added that race certainly does exist as an historical and social category, but that is not relevant to the present purpose.

But if much of our behavior is genetically rooted, and if differences can be shown in the genetic heritage of human groups, then scientifically-backed racial stereotyping is a real possibility. Here is Pinker's argument on stereotypes in a nutshell:

Categories and stereotypes may indeed be real, as long as we remember that 'real' is not a simple concept, but an interaction between our minds and the world, further complicated by the fact that our minds and the world are not independent entities. The bottom line is that it doesn't matter whether (for example) race and gender stereotypes are 'real' in some sense as opposed to socially constructed. What matters is that it is not moral or even logical to judge or rank individuals on the basis of membership in a category, or to judge or rank those categories themselves in some kind of value hierarchy based on our own admittedly subjective standards. It may be quite true, for example, that African-Americans as a group score lower on IQ tests than whites or Asian-Americans (leave aside, for the moment, the question of how valid the tests themselves are). It is probably even true that heredity plays a major role in IQ, though it is unlikely that this has much to do with race, as genetic diversity is greater within races than between races. It does not follow, in any case, that it is all right to discriminate against African-Americans because of IQ test results, or that all African-Americans are less intelligent than all whites or Asians. We cannot even replace all with some, since intelligence appears to be a strictly individual trait.

Pinker is right — but he doesn't go far enough. This analysis still emphasizes race (however defined) as a prime factor in human differences. What he neglects to consider is that in our culture, a hierarchy of power and privilege does determine many categories, and does rank those categories and stereotypes in a manner that legitimates discrimination. Race — given its usual definition some centuries ago, by privileged Europeans — has long been used as an excuse to cover up discrimination based on other criteria: gender, social status, and other hierarchic considerations. What we anarchists need to do is undermine that hierarchy, not just the categories themselves.

Many philosophers and scientists on the Left have condemned, sometimes on absurd and embarrassing grounds, the findings of cognitive science and evolutionary biology. Radical feminism, for example, sometimes goes to the extreme of arguing that all male/female differences are socially constructed. But even more moderate feminists sometimes ignore the scientific evidence. Countless studies have outlined differences in brain development, hormone balances, perception, and the like, most of them beginning in the womb. Many of the researchers conducting these studies, if not most, are women. The bottom line: it is simply not a matter of culture that little boys like toy guns and little girls like dolls. The general public tends to conflate "feminism" with its radical extreme, though in fact many radical feminists choose to emphasize and celebrate male/female differences. True, radical feminism has made some silly mistakes due to its reliance on the blank slate. And anti-feminists like Christina Hoff Summers or Camille Paglia have made equally silly errors because they are brainwashed by the dominant patriarchal paradigm. Both sides often miss the point: it doesn't really matter whether the differences between men and women are innate or imposed by culture. What matters is that we respect those differences (or deconstruct them, when appropriate) and refuse to use them as excuses for domination or discrimination. To his credit, Pinker recognizes this simple fact.

One brief article in one journal will not resolve this issue. But I hope that I have demonstrated the need for anarchists to take another look at the scientific evidence. We need not abandon Boas or Kroeber or the many other scientists and philosophers who have contributed to the anarchist stream of thought. But we do need to be critical when necessary, and we need to take cutting-edge science back from the right-wing ideologues who have commandeered it to their own uses. If there's one good thing we have learned from modern science, going all the way back to Bacon and Galileo, it's this: you can't pick and choose your evidence to fit your preconceived opinion. You can, however, choose how to interpret that evidence.

Pinker is no doubt correct that we will never achieve utopia, and the reasons he lists are quite valid. However, we need not accept his conclusion that the only alternative is a free-market economy under an authoritarian government. Each of his points can be reconciled with anarchism and a free society. Let's run through them:

> "The primacy of family ties in all human societies and the consequent appeal of nepotism and inheritance." What's the appeal of nepotism when there is no power to bestow, or of inheritance when there's nothing to inherit? What's to stop us from regarding the whole human race as our family?

> "The limited scope of communal sharing in human groups, the more common ethos of reciprocity, and the resulting phenomena of social loafing and the collapse of contributions to public goods when reciprocity cannot be implemented." This objection was answered by Kropotkin in chapter twelve of The Conquest of Bread: peer pressure, the innate need to be accepted by one's group, is sufficient to enforce communal sharing. Reciprocity may be hard-wired; how we implement it is not.

> "The universality of dominance and violence across human societies (including supposedly peaceable hunter-gatherers) and the existence of genetic and neurological mechanisms that underlie it." We have overwhelming evidence that dominance is not universal, but is a byproduct of patriarchy. As for violence—yes, we are hard-wired to use it, against the plants and animals we eat to survive; but we use it against one another only when there is some tangible payoff, or when we are threatened. Take away the payoff or the threat, and we are indeed peaceable. Pinker neglects to note that most indigenous people were in fact nonviolent before they were threatened by contact with aggressive, dominant cultures like ours.

> "The universality of ethnocentrism and other forms of group-against-group hostility across societies, and the ease with which

such hostility can be aroused in people within our own society." Here Pinker, like most rightists, confuses human society with the artificially created state. Yes, we are tribal by nature, but not statist. Violence and hostility are aroused in us when we try to put the tribal mentality to the service of the artificial state. Ethnocentrism is not dangerous; state politics is.

"The partial heritability of intelligence, conscientiousness, and antisocial tendencies, implying that some degree of inequality will arise even in perfectly fair economic systems, and that we therefore face an inherent trade-off between equality and freedom." This is a non-issue. We need not all be equal in all respects in order to agree that we all have equal rights. Inequality arises when we define certain characteristics as "superior," and reward their possessors with authority of some kind. And of course there is a trade-off between equality and freedom: this is the definition of "human society," and no anarchist denies it. What we deny is that we require some 'authority' to set the terms of the trade-off for us.

"The prevalence of defense mechanisms, self-serving biases, and cognitive dissonance reduction, by which people deceive themselves about their autonomy, wisdom, and integrity." Another non-issue. Of course we deceive ourselves all the time; the problem is that our society of domination and hierarchy encourages those particular traits, whereas a just egalitarian society would not. We are not so hard-wired that we must reward self-serving or self-deceptive behavior.

"The biases of the human moral sense, including a preference for kin and friends, a susceptibility to a taboo mentality, and a tendency to confuse morality with conformity, rank, cleanliness, and beauty." We are all kin, and if we could get that through our heads, we could all be friends, as well. As for morality: this is learned behavior. The fact that we do not all agree on what is 'moral' proves that morality is not hard-wired. Many of us believe that conformity and rank are immoral, that lack of cleanliness is a by-product of hierarchy, and that beauty is in the eye of the beholder.

Works Cited

Bookchin, Murray, *The Ecology of Freedom: The Emergence and Dissolution of Hierarchy*. Palo Alto: Cheshire Books, 1982.

Darwin, Charles, *The Origin of Species by Means of Natural Selection; or, The Preservation of Favored Races in the Struggle for Life*. London: John Murray, 1859.

Degler, Carl, *In Search of Human Nature: The Decline and Revival of Darwinism in American Social Thought*. New York: Oxford University Press, 1991.

Kropotkin, Peter, *Mutual Aid, A Factor of Evolution*. New York: McClure, Philips & Co., 1902.

Lakoff, George and Mark Johnson, *Philosophy in the Flesh: The Embodied Mind and its Challenge to Western Thought*. New York: Basic Books, 1999.

Pinker, Steven, *The Blank Slate: The Modern Denial of Human Nature*. New York: Viking, 2002.

Singer, Peter, *A Darwinian Left*. London: Weidenfeld and Nicolson, 1999.

Sorel, Georges, *Reflections on Violence*, trans. T.E. Hulme. London: Allen & Unwin, 1915.

Notes

The controversy touched off by Wilson has been admirably chronicled in Ullica Seger-stråle, *Defenders of the Truth: The Battle for Science in the Sociology Debate and Beyond* (Oxford: Oxford University Press, 2000).

The current state of mDNA and y chromosome research may be found in many places, but see especially the work of the Humane Genome researchers Luca Cavalli-Sforza and Peter Underhill at Stanford University. The best general work is Cavalli-Sforza's *The Great Human Diasporas: The History of Diversity and Evolution* (New York: Addison-Wesley, 1995).

With specific reference to some influential contemporary anarchist writers, Morris describes a series of modern variations on anarchism that have been garnering attention in recent years. From Ayn Rand's individualist capitalism to John Zerzan's anarcho-primitivism, Morris argues that the ideas being put forth are either patently inconsistent with anarchism, or are a thinly-veiled rehash of notions that Kropotkin advocated a century earlier.

There is a bit of an exasperated tone in Morris' writing, but not without cause. The almost hypnotic allure of postmodernism swept over most of the social sciences in the past few decades, and the intellectually radical theories of Derrida, Foucault, and Guattari probably served as the introduction to activist political philosophy for many students in recent generations. A reminder that not all of history need be jettisoned for the sake of (post)modernism is a welcome and refreshing read.

Originally published in issue 42.

Reflections on the "New Anarchism"
Brian Morris

This essay offers some critical reflections on the so-called "new anarchism," and poses the question: "What, exactly, is new about the "new anarchism?" With reference to the writings of Peter Kropotkin and other social or class struggle anarchists it concludes: precious little.

Prologue

No doubt you have heard about the coming "new age" and all about "New Labour." No doubt you have also read lots about postmodernism, poststructuralism, post feminism, post Marxism, and post humanism. There are even postanimals around, but they are not to be confused with the real badgers and dormice that inhabit the woods and fields. So you will not be surprised to learn that academic scholars have now discovered what is described as the "new anarchism" along with one of its variants, "post anarchism." (Day 2005, Kinna 2005, Curran 2006).

The suggestion is that anarchism as normally understood has become an "historical baggage" that needs to be rejected, or at least, given a "major overhaul" (Purkis and Bowen 1997: 3).

The anarchism of an earlier generation of anarchists is thus declared to be "old anarchism" and is perceived to be old-fashioned and out-dated; or as John Moore put it in the pages of the "Green Anarchist" (1998), just plain "obsolete." An historical relic of no relevance at all to contemporary radical activists (Holloway 2002: 21).

Embracing a crude linear, bipolar mode of understanding the history of anarchism — an approach that is facile, undialectical and lacking any sense of history — we are told by the academics that "old anarchism" is now antiquated and "outmoded" (Kinna 2005: 21). By "old" anarchism they essentially mean social anarchism or class struggle anarchism (mutualism, libertarian socialism, anarcho-syndicalism, anarchist communism) — which is, unbeknown to these academics, still the most vibrant strand(s) of anarchism around, judging by recent texts. (Sheehan 2003, Franks 2006).

Nevertheless, we are informed that "old" anarchism has been replaced by a new variety of anarchism — the "new anarchism." In fact, there has been a "paradigm shift" (no less!) within anarchism itself (Purkis and Bowen 2004: 5).

This "new anarchism," as the "new paradigm" appears to be an esoteric pastiche of poetic terrorism (otherwise known as Nietzschean aesthetic nihilism), anarcho-primitivism, the radical individualism (egoism) of Max Stirner, and an appeal to the oracular musings of post structural philosophers such as Jean-Francois Lyotard, Michel Foucault, Jacques Derrida, Gilles Deleuze and Jean Baudrillard. None of whom, it is worth noting, were anarchists.

We are also joyfully informed that no contemporary radical activist has ever read the works of Bakunin, Kropotkin or Malatesta, as they are deemed to be as old-fashioned as the novels of Charles Dickens (Purkis and Bowen 1997: 3). This is probably true, for the obvious reason that few people in the new social movements or in the recent anti-globalization protests are in fact Anarchists.

1.1 New Social Movements

Take the new social movements. Anarcho-feminists were in a distinct minority in the second-wave feminist movement. Most feminists were liberals, Marxists or republicans, embracing an identity politics that appealed to State power to enact reforms. There were also few anarchists in the American civil rights movement, though this movement was well represented by black nationalists and radical liberal pacifists.

And the ecology movement as I long ago indicated (1996: 131) embraces people right across the political spectrum. It includes liberals like Jonathan Porritt (now a staunch advocate of capitalism), members of the Green Party and other worthy liberals, outright authoritarian conservatives such as William Ophuls, Garrett Hardin and Rudolph Bahro, as well as German neo-fascists and the followers of the Nazi sympathizer Martin Heidegger, the darling of some deep ecologists and postmodernists. Within the ecology movement anarchists are therefore in a distinct minority, even though anarchism is the only political tradition that is fully consonant with an ecological sensibility — as Bookchin (1982) long ago argued. (Morris 1996, Hay 2002: 280–97).

1.2 Anti-globalization protests

Equally, anarchists form a minority in the anti-globalization protests, although their presence is invariably high-lighted by the media, especially when they destroy property. Most of the radical activists on the anti-globalization protests are reformist liberals who simply seek to humanize capitalism and make it more benign. Some like the late Pierre Bourdieu (1998) and the Brazilian Worker's Party (who hosted the first World Social Forum in Porto Alegre) merely want to bolster the economic power of the Nation-State, and thus curb the worst excesses of global capitalism. Some like Susan George and the French organization "Association for the Taxation of Financial Transactions to Aid Citizens" (ATTAC) simply advocate putting a tax on the movement of capital. Others still, like David Held, Arne Naess and George Monbiot — who has taken over Jonathan Porritt's mantle as the media radical on environmental issues — envisage some kind of "global democratic state" — heaven forbid!

[It is of interest that George Monbiot is always complaining about the "antics" of anarchists on the anti-globalization protests — for the anarchists lack discipline, destroy property and upset the police. Like a worthy liberal Monbiot seeks to uphold the sanctity of private property, and views the police as the benign custodians of "law and order" (see Monbiot 2000)].

To equate the anti-globalization protests with anarchism is therefore quite misleading. Even so, anarchists have made their presence felt — through the Black Bloc and with the politics of detournement — involving guerilla advertising and an emphasis on the aesthetic dimensions of protest. Such forms of protest are hardly novel. At the end of the eighteenth century Thomas Spence called his weekly periodical "Pig's Meat, or Lessons for a Swinish Multitude," precisely to parody Edmund Burke's derogatory opinion of working people. *Détournement* and symbolic protest did not begin with the Situationists; and even the concept of "multitude" is hardly a new idea (on Spence's agrarian socialism see Morris 1996: 112–122).

This is not to deny, of course, that there have been important anarchist tendencies in both the new social movements and the anti-globalization protests. These have been of particular interest to academic scholars (Day 2005, Curran 2006). One writer indeed suggests that the "soul" of the anti-capitalist movement is anarchist, in its disavowal of political parties, and its commitment to direct action. The movement is thus, he writes, firmly in the spirit of libertarian socialism — that is, the spirit of the "old anarchism" (Sheehan 2003: 12).

It is also of interest that in the wake of the anti-globalization protests, Purkis and Bowen seem to have revised their opinion about the "old anarchists." For they write that contemporary radical activists are seeking out the writings and quoting from the works of Kropotkin, Proudhon, Bakunin, Goldman and Malatesta — insisting that there are still issues and principles that are worthy of debate, despite a very different context (2004: 2). True.

2. The New Anarchists

The ideas and practices of contemporary mutualists and class struggle anarchists are, of course, just as "new" as those of primitivists, Stirnerite individualists and the self-proclaimed poetic terrorists. And certainly class-struggle anarchists—those who marshal under such banners as Class war, the Solidarity Federation, the Anarchist-Syndicalist Network, and the Anarchist (Communist) Federation—have been just as much involved in radical anticapitalist protest as have the likes of Hakim Bey, the Autonomist Marxists and the poststructuralists. Protest and radical activism have always been an essential part of class struggle anarchism (see Sheehan 2003, Franks 2006).

But who are these "new anarchists?" Well, according to Ruth Kinna, they essentially muster under six ideological categories, namely: Murray Bookchin's eco-socialism; the anarcho-primitivism of John Zerzan; the acolytes of the radical individualism of Max Stirner; the poetic terrorism (so-called) of Hakim Bey and John Moore, who follow the rantings of the reactionary philosopher Friedrich Nietzsche; the postmodern anarchism derived from Deleuze, Foucault and Lyotard; and finally (believe it or not), the anarcho-capitalism of Murray Rothbard and Ayn Rand.

Although admitting that there has been some antipathy between these various strands of the "New Anarchism" what they have in common, Kinna tells us, is that they have all repudiated the "struggle by workers for economic emancipation" (2005: 21). That is, they have abandoned libertarian socialism, or "leftism" (socialism), to use the current derogatory label (Black 1997). This is, of course, analogous to the politics of New Labour, as both Nicolas Walter and Graham Purchase suggested in their review of "Twenty-First Century Anarchism" (Purkis and Bowen 1997).

Two points need to be made initially regarding Kinna's depiction of this "new anarchism."

2.1 Bookchin's Eco-Socialism

The first point is that Murray Bookchin would undoubtedly refute being described as an advocate of the "new anarchism," or what he himself called "lifestyle" anarchism. Although Bookchin, like Bakunin and Kropotkin before him, certainly did not envisage the "industrial proletariat" as the sole revolutionary agent, he never repudiated class struggle anarchism. In his last years he may indeed have jettisoned the label "anarchist," as in the United States, anarchism had become virtually synonymous with anarcho-primitivism and aesthetic nihilism. And his strident advocacy of Municipal Socialism also found little favour among anarcho-communists and other class struggle anarchists. Nevertheless, Bookchin always acknowledged the need for serious class analysis, and affirmed the crucial importance of working class struggles in achieving any form of social revolution. What he attempted to do with his concept of hierarchy was to broaden existing conceptions of social oppression. Bookchin, therefore, always remained a revolutionary libertarian socialist, and had little but disdain for poetic terrorism, primitivism, technophobia, mysticism and anti-rationalism of the "new" or lifestyle anarchists. He was equally critical of the relativism, incoherence and nihilism of postmodern philosophers, who, he felt, tended to denigrate reason, the objectivity of truth and the reality of history (Bookchin 1995, 1999).

What is of interest is that Bookchin regarded Kropotkin as perhaps the most far-seeing of all the theorists he encountered in the libertarian tradition. Bookchin also emphasized — unlike the "new anarchists" — the need to respect an earlier generation of anarchists (Bakunin, Kropotkin, Reclus, Malatesta) not only for what they achieved in their own lifetime, but also for what they have to offer contemporary radical activists. But he also stressed the need to develop, to build on and go beyond their ideas, rather than arrogantly dismissing them as "obsolete" (Moore) or "irrelevant" to contemporary struggles (Holloway). (Bookchin 1993: 55–57).

The powers and intrusions of the modern state have undoubtedly increased over the past century, while capitalism has so expanded that it has turned virtually everything into a commodity; nevertheless the practices and theoretical perspectives of the early class struggle anarchists like Bakunin and Kropotkin still have a contemporary relevance. (On the continuing relevance of Bakunin, Kropotkin and Elisée Reclus, see, for example, Morris 1993, 2004, McLaughlin 2002, Leier 2006, Clark and Martin 2004).

2.2 Anarcho-capitalism

A second point is that the anarcho-capitalists are not by any stretch of the imagination anarchists — as this term is normally understood. Take Ayn Rand. Her political philosophy Ruth Kinna turns into another "ism," Aynarchism — adding yet another "ism" to the thirty or so that adorn her introductory chapter "What is Anarchism" (enough to bamboozle any "beginner" to the subject!) (2005: 25). But Rand, an early devotee of Nietzsche, explicitly repudiated anarchism, advocated a minimal but highly repressive state whose sole function was to support capitalist exploitation, and was a fervent promoter of free-market capitalism. She was in fact the intellectual guru of Margaret Thatcher. An egoist in ethical theory, anti-feminist and anti-ecology, Ayn Rand saw city skyscrapers as a positive symbol of American capitalism, and of the human conquest of nature. Her vision is thus the exact anti-thesis of John Zerzan's anarcho-primitivism. How on earth scholars like Kinna (2005: 35) and Simon Tormey (2004: 119) can consider Ayn Rand as "anarchist" is beyond my comprehension. She was essentially an elitist, liberal republican (on Rand's political philosophy see Morris 1996: 183–192).

3. What's New in the New Anarchism?

What is of interest and significant is that very little of this "new anarchism" is in fact new or original. Let us discuss each strand in turn.

3.1 Anarcho-capitalism

"Aynarchism," for a start, is just a re-affirmation of nineteenth century laissez-faire capitalism. The "egoism" embraced by Ayn Rand is, in fact, the very apotheosis of bourgeois thoughts on the individual, which go back to the classical liberalism of Hobbes and Locke.

3.2 Stirner's Individualism

The radical individualism advocated by the acolytes of Max Stirner is also somewhat antiquated. With Stirner, whose egoism is uncritically embraced by both Hakim Bey (1991 (aka Peter Lamborn Wilson) and John Moore (2004), the self becomes its own "property" and taking on the state form feels free to exploit and dominate others. "L'état, c'est moi," the state, it is me, Hakim Bey proclaims (1991: 67). This, surely, is not an anarchist sentiment, and is hardly conducive to mutual aid and voluntary cooperation.

Stirner was, of course, a left-Hegelian (not a poet!) and was critiqued by Kropotkin at the end of the nineteenth century (Baldwin 1927: 161–172).

Although acknowledging Stirner's historical importance, Kropotkin considered his amoral egoism limited and stultifying, in that Stirner repudiated neither property nor the state in his sanctification of the unique "ego." As Stirner puts it

> I do not want the liberty of men, nor their equality; I want only *my* power over them. I want to make them my property, *material for my enjoyment."* (1973: 318). Humans are thus not to be respected as persons, but seen only as an "object" for the ego's enjoyment (op. int., 311).

Interestingly, the anarchist critique of Stirner's egoism is completely ignored by his recent admiring devotees — Hakim Bey, in fact, tries to convince us that Stirner was not an "individualist" but embraced a joyous "conviviality" (1991: 67–71). Stirner certainly acknowledged an "association" of egoists, but as John P. Clark argued long ago, Stirner has little understanding of such values as community, solidarity, cooperation and mutual aid because he has such an *abstract* conception of the human individual (1976: 97).

Both Stirner's and Ayn Rand's egoism is merely an expression of bourgeois possessive individualism. To use a common expression : it is all "old hat." Although of course the "new" Stirnerite individualists like to appropriate the term "anarchy" for themselves, contrasting it with "old" fashioned class struggle anarchism or "leftism" (Black 1997, Moore 2004; for a useful, succinct critique of Stirner's individualism see Bookchin 1999: 125–26).

It is then quite ironic, if not perverse, to see academics like Saul Newman (2002) interpreting Stirner as an anti-essentialist thinker, when in fact Stirner was an essentialist *par excellence,* and was lampooned and critiqued as such by Marx and Engels long ago (1846/1965). Stirner's concept of the human individual as possessive, power-seeking, exploitative, amoral, competitive and atomistic is thoroughly abstract and Hobbesian (bourgeois), as Kropotkin indicated in critiquing Stirner's essentialism. Kropotkin, of course, like every other social anarchist, recognized that all humans have unique personalities; but articulating a social, non-essentialist conception of the human subject (unlike Stirner) Kropotkin stressed that the freedom, integrity and the self-development of the individual could only be achieved in a free society — what Kropotkin termed free communism.

3.3 Poetic Terrorism

The kind of radical "aestheticism" and "cultural elitism" that stems from Friedrich Nietzsche is also hardly "new," for it was fashionable among the avant-garde at the end of the nineteenth century. Now resurrected and labelled "poetic terrorism," "attentat art" (art as protest), "ontological anarchy" or "radical aristocratism" (take your pick!) it is again well represented by the "lifestyle" anarchism of Hakim Bey (1991) and John Moore (2004 C). Indeed, Hakim Bey's writings represent an incoherent esoteric pastiche of the following: anarcho-primitivism (while completely oblivious to the mutual aid and communist ethos of tribal hunter-gatherers); the asocial egoism of Max Stirner; the "psychic nomadism" of the poststructuralists Deleuze and Guattari (while completely ignoring their radical materialism); the aesthetic elitism and "poetic terrorism" of Nietzsche; new-age spiritualism, including the joyful embrace of Islamic mysticism; chaos theory (misunderstood!); along with Proudhonian federalism, cyberspace, the use of Black Magic as a revolutionary tactic (while denying the possibility of social revolution !); and — watch out! — "the psychic Paleolithic based on High-tech" (1991: 44).

In contrast to philosophers like Hegel and Whitehead, Hakim Bey makes a fetish of incoherence (as does Moore) and expresses his thoughts in the most pretentious, scholastic gobbledygook, designed by both to impress and intimidate the ordinary reader (Moore tends to follow in his wake). No wonder Murray Bookchin and John Zerzan both dismiss Hakim Bey's mystical blather as elitist, petty bourgeois and basically reformist.

Hakim Bey's concept of the "temporary autonomous zone" is likewise, hardly original, though it has provoked a bucket load of scholarly debate. Over the past century anarchists, as well as ordinary people, have been involved in autonomous activities: some fleeting, some enduring. They have thus created trade unions, affinity groups, communes, cooperatives, voluntary associations, and anarchist organizations, all of which have been independent of both the state and the capitalist economy. Some are work-place organizations; some community based. They have thus long ago been engaged in the creation of autonomous "zones" of social activity. As well, of course, as being involved in temporary events — sabotage, strikes, protests and demonstrations. In fact, for generations of class struggle anarchists " spontaneity" has always implied not just transitory events but rather the creation of non-hierarchical forms of organization that are truly organic, self-created and voluntary — as Bookchin expressed it long ago in his pamphlet: "spontaneity and organization" (1972/1980: 251–74). Thus there is precious little that is new or original in Hakim Bey's conception of a "temporary autonomous zone." It is what Colin Ward (1973) — also long ago — called "anarchy in action."

What *is*, however, new about Bey's concept is that it is purely fleeting and ephemeral, and is combined with the notion of a "nomadic individual," the archetype lone-ranger, who leaves to other mortals the care and upbringing of children, and the production of food and the other necessities of human life, all of which require some form of organization. Ignoring forms of social oppression and widespread inequalities, indeed abandoning any form of resistance to social oppression, Bey's liberal politics confronts neither capitalism or state power, but happily and joyfully coexists with them. All the while, indulging in disinterested aesthetic contemplation, blissful and ludic, along with occult practices and Islamic mysticism. All of which are thoroughly reactionary, and can hardly be described as either anarchism or anarchy. In fact, Hakim Bey's eclectic postmodern pastiche sits rather well with New Age Spiritualism and consumer capitalism. The choice that Bey (1994) offers us, that between Immediatism and Capitalism is, of course, thoroughly facile. (For useful critiques of Hakim Bey's liberal politics see Bookchin 1995 B: 20–26, Zerzan 2002: 144–46, Franks 2006: 266–67).

Contrary to what Giorel Curran (2006) suggests, the concept of TAZ "Temporary Autonomous Zone" has very little connection with the "carnivals of rebellion" or the "festivals of resistance" that have been part and parcel of such movements as Reclaim the Streets, the anti-roads movement and the anti-globalization protests. Indeed street carnivals and festivals have always been an integral part of class struggle, anarchism and revolutionary socialist movements ever since the French revolution.

Recent attempts by academic scholars to interpret Nietzsche as an "anarchist" (no less!) (Moore 2004 B, Sheehan 2003: 72) seem to me quite fallacious.

Although there is undoubtedly a libertarian aspect to Nietzsche's philosophy — for example, his solitary form of individualism with its aesthetic appeal to self-making; the radical critique implied in his "revaluation of all values;" his strident attack on the state in *"Thus Spake Zarathustra;"* and his impassioned celebration of the life-instincts and personal freedom and power. This is why Nietzsche had such an appeal to Emma Goldman and Guy Aldred.

But all this is more than off-set by Nietzsche's thoroughly reactionary mindset. This is illustrated by his elitist politics, his celebration of authority and tradition, his misogyny, his admiration of the Indian caste-system and dictators like Julius Caesar and Napoleon, and his complete lack of any progressive vision apart from the notion of an isolated, asocial nomad, the "overman" who will be the legislator of humankind. Reciprocity, mutual aid and equal rights for all were "poisonous" doctrines according to Nietzsche, for what he valued was a "good and healthy aristocracy" (his words). Nietzsche was, indeed, in many respects, as Richard Wolin argues, (2004: 52–63) a proto-fascist (see my critical review Morris 2007).

It is worth noting that although Kropotkin admired Nietzsche's poetic writings, and thought he was unequalled in his critique of Christianity, and was "great" as a theorist of "revolt," he nevertheless felt that Nietzsche always remained a "slave to bourgeois prejudices." For Nietzsche had little understanding of either socialism or anarchism, and his philosophy was not so much a repudiation or "refusal" of "modernity" as its apotheosis (Kropotkin 1970: 305).

3.4 Primitivism

Turning now to anarcho-primitivism this too is hardly "new." Primitivism is, of course, as old as the hills, and goes back to the beginnings of agrarian civilization. It is particularly associated with the Enlightenment philosopher Jean-Jacques Rousseau, and the concept of the "noble savage" John Zerzan (1988, 1994) and other anarcho-primitivists simply embrace this ancient idea, weld it to contemporary anarchism, and declare, in utopian fashion, that the "future" is primitive. This entails, one supposes, some kind of return to a tribal hunter-gathering existence?

John Zerzan presents an apocalyptic, even perhaps, a Gnostic vision. Our hunter-gatherer past is thus described by Zerzan as an idyllic era of virtue and authentic living. The last eight thousand years or so of human history after the rise of agriculture (the Fall) is seen as a period of tyranny and hierarchical control, a mechanized routine devoid of any spontaneity, and involving the anesthetization of the senses. All those products of the human creative imagination — farming, art, philosophy, technology, science, writing, urban living, symbolic culture — are viewed negatively and denigrated by Zerzan in a monolithic fashion.

The future, we are told, is "primitive." How this is to be achieved in a world that presently sustains around six billion people (for evidence suggests that the hunter-gatherer lifestyle is only able to support one or two people per sq. mile) or whether the "future primitive" actually entails a return to hunter-gatherer subsistence Zerzan does not tell us. Whether such images of green primitivism are symptomatic of the estrangement of affluent urban dwellers and intellectuals from the natural (and human) world, as both Roy Ellen (1986) and Murray Bookchin (1995: 120–146) suggests, I will leave others to judge.

But what is important about Zerzan's work is the affirmation that hunter-gatherers were, in many respects, "stone age anarchists." As Zerzan puts it; life in "primitive" society was largely one of leisure, gender equality, intimacy with the natural world and sensual wisdom. All this, of course, was emphasized by Peter Kropotkin long ago. Kropotkin stressed the close intimacy that existed between humans and animals in tribal society, that tribal people had an encyclopaedic knowledge of the natural world, and put a marked emphasis on sharing, generosity and mutual aid, which coexisted with an equal emphasis on individual autonomy and independence. But, unlike Zerzan, Kropotkin was not blind to the limitations of tribal life, the oppressive nature of certain traditions and the hierarchical aspects of tribal life (Kropotkin 1902: 74–101, Morris 2004: 173–190).

When John Moore embraced primitivism as a source of inspiration for contemporary anarchism he was not, then, suggesting anything new or original. Kropotkin had suggested this a century earlier. Indeed, having undertaken ethnographic studies among hunter-gatherers living in the Ghat Mountains of South India, more than two decades before John Moore penned his "primitivist primer" and having experienced the reality of hunter-gatherer social existence, I personally never contemplated any more than did

Kropotkin, becoming a permanent forager. Thus we need to draw inspiration and lessons from the cultural past of tribal peoples, as Kropotkin suggested, without romanticizing them, or trying to emulate the social life of the hunter-gatherers. (Morris 1982, 1986, 2005: 4–6; for critiques of Zerzan's primitivism see Bookchin 1995: 39–49, Shephard 2003, Albert 2006: 178–84)

It is of interest that Giorel Curran (2006: 42) outlines some of the criticism of Zerzan's eco-primitivism — as being misanthropic, as fanciful and hopelessly romantic, and as dismissive of the human potential for creativity and innovation, without ever indicating the source of such criticisms or whether in fact she agrees with them.

3.5 Postmodern Anarchism

Let me finally turn to so-called postmodern anarchism, otherwise known as poststructuralist anarchism, or simply post anarchism.

In the last decades of the twentieth century the academy was suddenly besieged by the rhetoric of the so-called "postmodernists," who, following in the footsteps of Nietzsche, Heidegger and Wittgenstein (all political reactionaries), have had a baneful influence on the social sciences. Now, somewhat belatedly, it seems that anarchists have also become infatuated with postmodernism — at a time when most social scientists are leaping off this particular band-wagon, and writing books like "*After Postmodernism*" (Lopez and Potter 2001).

Postmodernism is a diffuse, rather inchoate cultural movement or ideology that is difficult to define as it includes scholars with radically different approaches to social life. But as an intellectual ethos associated with such scholars as Baudrillard, Lyotard, Derrida, Foucault, Rorty, Laclau and Butler, it has been characterized by the following tenets, all presented in the most oracular fashion.

Firstly, as (supposedly!) we have no knowledge of the world except through "descriptions" (to use Rorty's term) the "real" is conceived as an "effect" of discourses. Anti-realism is thus in vogue, and we are informed that there is no "objective reality." As the anthropologist Mary Douglas put it: "all reality is social reality" (1975: 5). Or as Derrida put it "there is nothing outside the text" (1976: 158). (He was later to plead that he had been misunderstood (so meaning is not, as he always claimed, indeterminate!), and that he did not doubt the reality of the material world, but only wished to advance a "textualist" approach (Rotzer 1995: 45).

Postmodernism therefore tends to propound a neo-idealist metaphysic, and thus to repudiate REALISM — the notion that the natural world has an objective reality and existence independent of human consciousness.

Secondly, as our perceptions and experiences of the world are always to some degree socially mediated — acknowledged by generations of social scientists ever since Marx's reflections on Feuerbach's materialism — postmodernists take this insight to extreme and come to espouse an epistemological (and moral) relativism. Truth is either repudiated entirely (Tyler 1986), or seen simply as an "effect" of local cultural discourses (Rorty 1979, Flax 1990), or something that will be "disclosed" by elite scholars (Heidegger 1994). Truth as correspondence is thus repudiated, and as knowledge is always historically and socially situated, there can be, it is argued, no universal truths or values. Truth, we are told, is always subjective, indeterminate, relative and contingent. Both *objective knowledge* and empirical science are thus repudiated, along with universal values.

Thirdly, critiquing the transcendental ego of Cartesian rationalism (and phenomenology) together with the abstract individual of bourgeois ideology — which had, of course, been critiqued, indeed lampooned, by Marx, Bakunin and Kropotkin in the nineteenth century! — postmodernists again go to extreme and announce the "dissolution" of human subjectivity, the self being declared a "fiction." Human agency is thus repudiated, or the subject is viewed simply as an "effect" of "ideology" or "power" or "discourses."

Fourthly, there is a rejection of "metanarratives" (Lyotard 1984) (Marxism, Buddhism, human rights discourses, evolutionary biology, paleontology, universal history) and a strident celebration expressed of the "postmodern condition." The so-called postmodern condition — with its alienation, cultural pastiche, fragmentation, decentered subjectivity, nihilism — describes however, not so much a new paradigm or epoch, but rather the cultural effects of global capitalism.

Finally, there has been a growing tendency among post-modern academics — following Heidegger — to express themselves in the most obscure and impenetrable jargon, under the misguided impression that obscurity connotes profundity, and that a neo-Baroque prose style is the hallmark of radical politics It isn't! (Morris 1997, 2006: 8–10, Hay 2002: 321–22).

All this has led the acolytes of postmodernism to proclaim, with some stridency, the "dissolution" or "erasure" or the "end" of such concepts as truth, reason, history, class, nature, the self, science and philosophy — along with the Enlightenment "project" itself. Yet in their rejection of history and class, in reducing social reality to discourses, in their epistemic and moral relativism, in their dissolution of human subjectivity, and in their seeming obsession with the media, high-tech cyberspace and consumer capitalism, many have remarked that there seems to be an "unholy alliance" between postmodernism and the capitalist triumphalism of the neo-liberals (Wood and Foster 1997).

Postmodernism has, of course, been subjected to a barrage of criticism from numerous scholars, which makes one wonder why it is still held in such esteem by some academic anarchists. (For critiques, see, for example, Gellner 1992, Bunge 1996, Callinicos 1997, Detmer 2003, and from an anarchist perspective Bookchin 1995: 172–204, Zerzan 1994: 101–34).

Poststructuralism is sometimes described as the philosophy of postmodernism. Yet what is of interest is that the radical scholars that have most appeal to the post anarchists — Foucault, Derrida, Deleuze, Guattari — all expressed an opposition to postmodernism, or at least distanced themselves from it. Yet it also has to be recognized that few of the political ideas expressed by the poststructuralist philosophers are in fact new or original. For what they have done is simply to appropriate many of the basic ideas and principles of (social) anarchism, and wrapped them up in the most scholastic jargon — with little or no acknowledgement. These ideas, please note, include the following:

> opposition to the state and all forms of power and oppression; recognition that the power of the modern state intrudes into all aspects of social life; a fervent anti-capitalism; a rejection of the vanguard party, representation and the notion that the transformation to socialism can be achieved through state-power; a rejection of an "essentialist" (i.e. Cartesian/abstract) conception of human nature; and finally, the importance of creating alternative social forms of organization, non-hierarchic and independent of both the state and capitalism.

Kropotkin (and other social and class struggle anarchists over the past century) had, of course, expressed these ideas long ago — more concretely, and much more lucidly. Unlike most poststructuralists, from Bourdieu to Baudrillard and Derrida, Kropotkin (and Elisée Reclus) also expressed an ecological sensibility.

Here is a typical extract from Deleuze, discussing French capitalism:

> Against this global policy of power, we initiate localized counter responses, skirmishes, active and occasionally preventative defences. We have no need to totalize that which is invariably totalized on the side of power; if we were to move in this direction, it would mean restoring the representative forms of centralism and a hierarchical structure" (Foucault 1977: 212).

Deleuze seems singularly unaware that this strategy had been advocated by Kropotkin and the anarchist tradition for more than a hundred years.

All this is well illustrated in Dave Morland's (2004) suggestions about the *poststructuralist* anarchism supposedly being expressed in recent new social movements. He writes that such anarchism repudiates representational politics, advocates "autonomous capacity building" (what Kropotkin and early anarchists described simply as direct action!), is suspicious of vanguardism and revolutionary elites, and shuns the quest for political power. This is not some "new mode" of anarchism, and there is nothing "poststructuralist" about it: it simply reflects what social anarchists have been advocating and practising for the last hundred years. Social or class struggle anarchists have in fact always been a constituent part of *all* protest movements since the second world war, whether against fascism, nuclear power, the Vietnam war, the poll tax or more recently, global capitalism. Class struggle anarchists have always been around, and were in evidence long before the anti-globalization protests, when they received especial media attention as a "travelling circus" (Goaman 2004).

Likewise Saul Newman's definition of "postanarchism" simply regurgitates what anarchists like Kropotkin long ago emphasized: the repudiation of relations of domination; an ethic of mutual aid; the intrinsic relationship between equality and liberty; a commitment to respect "difference" (diversity) and individual autonomy within a collectivity; and an emphasis on community which is not equated with a "herd" mentality. But at least Newman, unlike his mentors, acknowledges his sources, namely the writings of Bakunin and Kropotkin! (2004: 123, see Morris 2004). Postanarchism is simply an exercise of putting old wine into new wine bottles! Richard Day (2005: 123) even describes Kropotkin as the "first post anarchist." Kropotkin wasn't "post" anything; he was an anarchist. He was part of an ongoing revolutionary movement and political tradition: namely, libertarian socialism (or anarchism). Day's "politics of affinity" and his advocacy of "structural renewal" simply exemplify the politics of "old" anarchism — the anarchism of Kropotkin and a host of social or class struggle anarchists from Goldman, Rocker and Landauer in the past to Bookchin and the Anarchist Federation in the present. Thus there is very little that is new or original in the so-called "post anarchism."

4. Conclusion

We can but conclude that there is nothing particularly "new" about the "new anarchism" and the anarchistic tendencies that are being expressed in the new social movements or in the anti-globalization protests is not some "new mode" of anarchism or some "new paradigm" but the kind of social or class struggle anarchism that had its origins long ago in working class struggles for libertarian socialism. This form of anarchism, as earlier indicated, is still the most vibrant form of anarchism around (see Sheehan 2003, Franks 2006).

References

Albert, M. 2006 *Realizing Hope: Life Beyond Capitalism*. London: Zed Books

Baldwin, R.N. 1927 *Kropotkin's Revolutionary Pamphlets* New York: Dover

Bey, H. 1991 *T.A.Z.: the temporary autonomous zone, ontological anarchy, poetic terrorism.* Brooklyn, New York: Autonomedia

———1994 *Immediatism*. Edinburgh: AK Press

Black, B. 1997 *Anarchy After Leftism*. Columbia: C.A.L. Press

Bookchin, M. 1980 *Toward an Ecological Society*. Montreal: Black Rose Books

———1982 *The Ecology of Freedom*. Palo Alto: Cheshire

Bookchin, M. et al. 1993 *Deep Ecology and Anarchism*. London: Freedom Press

———1995 *Re-Enchanting Humanity*. London: Cassell

———1995B *Social Anarchism or Life-Style Anarchism*. Edinburgh: AK Press

———1999 *Anarchism, Marxism, and the Future of the Left*. Edinburgh: AK Press

Bourdieu, P. 1998 *Acts of Resistance*. Cambridge: Polity Press

Bunge, M. 1996 *Finding Philosophy in Social Science*. New Haven: Yale Univ. Press

Callinicos, A. 1997 "Postmodernism: A Critical Diagnosis" in *Great Ideas Today pp.* 206–55 Chicago: Encyclopedia Brittanica

Clark, J.P. 1976 *Max Stirner's Egoism*. London: Freedom Press

Clark, J.P. and Martin C. 2004 (Eds) *Anarchy, Geography, Modernity: The Radical Social Thought of Elisée Reclus*. Lanham: Lexington Books

Curran, G. 2006 *21st Century Dissent: Anarchism, Anti-Globalization and Environmentalism*. Basingstoke: Palgrave

Day, R.F. 2005 *Gramsci is Dead: Anarchist Currents in the Newest Social Movements*. London: Pluto Press

Derrida, J. 1976 *Of Grammatology*. Baltimore: John Hopkins Univ. Press

Detmer, D. 2003 *Challenging Postmodernism: Philosophy and the Politics of Truth*. Amherst: Humanity Books.

Douglas, M. 1975 *Implicit Meanings*. London: Routledge and Kegan Paul

Ellen, R.F. 1986 "What Black Elk Left Unsaid" *Anthropology Today* 2(16): 8–12

Flax, J. 1990 *Thinking Fragments*. Berkeley: University of California Press

Foucault, M. 1977 *Language, Counter-Memory, Practice*. Ithaca: Cornell Univ. Press

Franks, B. 2006 *Rebel Alliances*. Edinburgh: AK Press

Gellner, E. 1992 *Postmodernism, Reason and Religion*. London: Routledge

Goaman, K. 2004 "The Anarchist Travelling Circus" in J.Purkis and J.Bowen (Eds.) (2004) pp. 163–180

Hay, P. 2002 *A Companion to Environmental Thought*. Edinburgh: Edinburgh University Press

Heiddegger, M. 1994 *Basic Questions of Philosophy*. Bloomington: Indiana Uni Press

Holloway, J. 2005 *Changing the World Without Taking Power*. London: Pluto Press.

Kinna, R. 2005 *Anarchism: A Beginners Guide*. Oxford: Oneworld Publications

Kropotkin, P. 1902 *Mutual Aid: A Factor in Evolution*. London: Heinemann

——1970 *Selected Writings on Anarchism and Revolution*. Ed., M.A.Miller. Cambridge, MA: MIT Press

Leier, M.2006 *Bakunin: The Creative Passion*. New York: St. Martin's Press

Lopez, J. and G.Potter (Ed's) 2001 *After Postmodernism*. London: Athlone

Lyotard, J-F. 1984 *The Postmodern Condition*. Manchester: Manchester University Press

Marx, K. and F. Engels 1965 *The German Ideology*. London: Lawrence and Wishart.

McLaughlin, P. 2002 *Mikhail Bakunin: The Philosophical Basis of his Anarchism*. New York: Algora.

Monbiot, G. 2000 "No Way to Run a Revolution" *The Guardian*, May 10, 2000

Moore, J. 2004 "Lived Poetry: Stirner, Anarchy, Subjectivity, and the Art of Living" in J.Purkis and J.Bowen (Eds) (2004) pp. 55–72

——2004B (Ed) *I am not a Man, I am Dynamite: Friedrich Nietzsche and the Anarchist Tradition*. Brooklyn, NY: Autonomedia

——2004C "Attentat Art: Anarchism and Nietzsche's Aesthetics in J. Moore (Ed.) (2004) pp. 127–142

Morland, D. 2004 "Anti-Capitalism and Poststructuralist Anarchism" in J. Purkis and J. Bowen (Eds) (2004) pp. 23–38

Morris, B. 1982 *Forest Traders*. London: Athlone Press

——1986 "Deforestation in India and the Fate of the Forest Tribes" *The Ecologist* 16: 253–57 in *Ecology and Anarchism Malvern Wells: Images*

——1993 *Bakunin: The Philosophy of Freedom*. Montreal: Black Rose Books

——1996 *Ecology and Anarchism: Essays and Reviews on Contemporary Thought*.

——1997 "In Defence of Realism and Truth: Reflections on the Anthropological Followers of Heidegger" *Critique of Anthropology* 17/3: 313–340

——2004 *Kropotkin: The Politics of the Community*. Amherst, NY: Humanity Books

——2005 "Anthropology and Anarchism: Their Effective Affinity" *Goldsmiths College: Anthropology Dept. Research Papers No.11*

——2006 *Religion and Anthropology: A critical introduction*. Cambridge: Cambridge University Press.

——2007 "Nietzsche and Anarchism Review, J. Moore (Ed.) *I am Not a Man, I am Dynamite.*" *Social Anarchism* 40: 54–57

Newman, S. 2002 "Max Stirner and the Politics of Humanism" *Contemporary Political Theory* 1: 221–38

——2004 "Anarchism and the Politics of *Ressentiment*" in J. Moore (Ed) (2004) pp. 107–126

Purkis, J. and J. Bowen 1997 (Eds.) *Twenty-First Century Anarchism* London: Cassell

——2004 (Ed) *Changing Anarchism*. Manchester: Manchester University Press

Rorty, R. 1979 *Philosophy and the Mirror of Nature.* Princeton, NJ: Princeton University Press

Rotzer, F. 1995 *Conversations with French Philosophers.* New Jersey: Humanities Press

Sheehan, S.M. 2003 *Anarchism.* London: Reaktion Books

Shephard, B.O. 2003 *Anarchism vs. Primitivism.* Tucson, AZ: See Sharp Press

Stirner, M. 1973 *The Ego and His Own.* NewYork: Dover Publications

Tormey, S. 2004 *Anti-Capitalism: A Beginners Guide.* Oxford: Oneworld Publications

Tyler, S. 1986 "Post Modern Ethnography" in J. Clifford and G. Marcus (Eds) *Writing Culture.* Berkeley: University of California Press pp. 122–140

Ward, C. 1973 *Anarchy in Action.* London: Allen and Unwin

Wolin, R. 2004 *The Seduction of Unreason.* Princeton University Press.

Wood, E.M. and J.B. Foster (Eds) 1997 *In Defence of History: Marxism and the Postmodern Agenda.* New York: Monthly Review Press

Zerzan, J. 1998 *Elements of Refusal.* Seattle: Left Bank Books

——1994 *Future Primitive and other Essays.* Brooklyn, NY: Autonomedia

——2002 *Running on Emptiness.* Los Angeles: Feral House

Building upon a number of essays that appeared in the *Reinventing Anarchy, Again* anthology, Ehrlich enumerates a list of feminist principles. Beginning with the fundamental tenets of any (e.g. liberal) feminism, he demonstrates that radical feminists have carried the logic of feminism beyond its simplistic beginnings to a point at which its critique of patriarchy merges with the anarchist critique of power.

Originally published in issue 19.

Toward a General Theory of Anarchafeminism
Howard Ehrlich

People who are familiar with theories of social anarchism and feminism are invariably struck by their similarities. Both sets of theories view social and economic inequality as rooted in institutionalized power arrangements; both stress the necessity of changing those arrangements as a precondition for liberation; and both work for the realization of personal autonomy and freedom within a context of community.

The essays of such writers as Elaine Leeder, L. Susan Brown, Peggy Kornegger, Carol Ehrlich, Neala Schleuning, and Jane Meyerding blend together in an extraordinary manner. While they all promote an anarchist feminist position, each uniquely grapples with the differences between that position and other varieties of feminism. This is where we have to start. I think we need to look at the basic statements of feminist theories and observe how people come to endorse some statements and not others.

All feminist theories start with a set of observations about women in society. These three statements represent the core of those observations.

1. *The social roles ascribed to women and men are primarily culturally determined.*
2. *Women are discriminated against in all sectors of society — personally, socially, occupationally, and politically.*
3. *Women are physically objectified and, as a consequence, routinely harassed and assaulted sexually.*

Given these observations, feminists have had to affirm that:

4. *Women and men are equal.*

Liberal feminists seek affirmation of their equality by means of modifying the existing power arrangements. Their objective is to eliminate discrimination, that is, the institutionalized forms of differential treatment. Their goal is not to change the basic structures of society. Further, they make no special claims about women as a class or about a women's culture. Their goal is to obtain equality in the access to resources of power.

The women's movement divided on the problems of existing inequalities *among* women, particularly those of social class, ethnicity and skin color. Both ideologically and from the standpoint of organizing a movement, these divisions proved as difficult for the feminist movement as they were for the larger society. For some feminists, these were not perceived as issues; while for others, they were seen as subordinate to the struggle for power. Still others, mainly radical feminists, split over the process by which matters of class, ethnicity and color should be incorporated into the women's movement.

For the varieties of radical feminists (and anarchists are one of those), there are additional belief statements that make up their theories. Central to all of the radical perspectives is an insistence on the consistency of means and ends, especially in one's everyday life.

5. *The personal is political.*

"Politics" are defined as extending beyond the narrow set of events relating to formal government. Politics involves everything we do in our daily lives, everything that happens to us, and every interpretation we make of these things.

Because cultures distinguish people on the basis of gender, females have a range of experiences that are different from those of males. Even similar experiences will carry different meanings. The consequence is that women (and men) have developed distinctive subcultures. Recognition of this cultural different is expressed in another belief statement of feminist theory.

6. *There is a separate, identifiable women's subculture in every society.*

The distinctive elements of that culture are usually those centered around activities involving maintenance, such as housework or subsistence farming, and activities involving interpersonal relationships such as nurturance, empathy and solidarity. (Some varieties of feminist thought include spirituality.)

Most radical feminists believe that the elements of women's culture are preferable to their male analogs in the dominant culture. Some radical feminists understandably stop at this point, choosing to live (and work, if possible) within a women's community. Some, claiming the superiority of women's culture, have argued that a society controlled by women would not have the oppressive characteristics of patriarchal societies. Some of them have developed matriarchal theories of past and future societies.

Like all political theories, radical feminism has a set of statements on how change is to come about. (Many of these are expressed in my essay "Building a revolutionary transfer culture" (*Social Anarchism*, 4, 1982). Central to the feminist transfer culture are two requirements:

7. *The individual working collectively with others is the locus of change.*

8. *Alternative institutions built on principles of cooperation and mutual aid are the organizational forms for this change.*

Meaningful social change does not come about by individuals working alone. Change comes through the organization of people in a setting of mutual aid and cooperation. In keeping with this, radical feminists and social anarchists have built an impressive number of organizations and networks: media collectives, clinics, theater groups, alternative schools, antiprofit business, community centers, and many others. The organizations built by radical feminists are often developed on anarchist principles although, as Peggy Kornegger points out in her essay "Anarchism: The Feminist Connection," this development is usually intuitive. In contrast, for the anarchist feminist the linkage is explicit. Freedom is an important concept in radical feminism, although it is not often explicitly or clearly articulated. One critical belief statement emphasizes what some anarchists have called a "negative" conception of freedom. It is a principle that asserts the necessity of a society to be organized in such a manner that people cannot be treated as objects or used as instruments to some end.

9. *All people have a right to be free from coercion, from violence to their mind or body.*

Perhaps one reason it is not often clearly articulated in radical feminist theories is because its implication moves beyond the bounds of most of those theories into an anarchist feminism. As L. Susan Brown says in "Beyond Feminism: Anarchism and Human Freedom": "Just as one can be a feminist and oppose power…it is also possible and not inconsistent for a feminist to embrace the use of power and advocate domination without relinquishing the right to be a feminist."

To be free from coercion means that one has to live in a society where institutionalized forms of power, domination and hierarchy no longer exist. For anarchists, power is the central issue.

10. *One should neither submit to nor exercise power over other people.*

Anarchists disavow the nation-state and see themselves as working for its delegitimation and dissolution. It is state managers who claim the right to define legitimate authority, including the authority to structure power arrangements and the monopoly rights to the mobilization of police and military force. Radical feminists work to end patriarchy, that is, the male domination of women through force and the institutionalized acceptance of masculine authority. To anarchist feminists, the state and patriarchy are twin aberrations. Thus, to destroy the state is to destroy the major agent of institutional-ized patriarchy; to abolish patriarchy is to abolish the state as it now exists. Anarchist feminists go further than most radical feminists: they caution that the state by definition is always illegitimate. For this reason feminists should not be working within the electoral confines of the state nor should they try to substitution *female* states for the present male states. Some radical feminists argue, as I have said, that a society controlled by women would not have the oppressive features of patriarchal society; anarchist feminists respond that the very structure of a state creates inequities. Anarchism is the only mode of social organization likely to prevent the recapitulation of social inequalities.

Anarchist feminists know what other radicals often have to learn from bit-ter experience: the development of new forms of organization designed to get rid of hierarchy, authority, and power requires new social structures. Further, these structures must be carefully built and continually nurtured so that or-ganizations function smoothly and efficiently, and so that new or informal elites will not emerge. If there is an underlying principle of action it is that we need to cultivate the habits of freedom so that we constantly experience it in our everyday lives.

Elaine Leeder points out the way in her essay "Let Our Mothers Show the Way," that it was anarchist women who extended the boundaries of male-dominated anarchist thought. To be sure, sexist anarchists existed then, as now, but as Susan Brown noted it is "only by virtue of contradicting their own anarchism."

Works Cited

The essays cited in text by Brown, Ehrlich, Kornegger, and Leeder all appear in Howard J. Ehrlich, ed., *Reinventing Anarchy, Again* (Edinburgh and San Francisco: AK Press, 1994).

Conflating criminology and sociology, Ferrell presents an anarchist vision of social justice. His two central concerns are the spiraling of laws (knee-jerk response legislation that leads to an even worse set of laws than it was meant to mediate) and the magnitude of state powers that leave people virtually powerless.

Originally published in issue 25.

Against The Law: Anarchist Criminology
Jeff Ferrell

To live outside the law, you must be honest.

— Dylan, "Absolutely Sweet Marie"

Anarchism is an orientation toward social life and social relations that is ultimately no orientation at all. In fact, anarchism might best be thought of as a *disorientation;* that is, an approach which openly values fractured, uncertain, and unrealized understandings and practices as the emerging essence of social life. What follows, then, is guaranteed to be an incomplete account of anarchism and anarchist criminology, a failed attempt at orientation. This failure certainly derives from the account's origins in the work of a single author, and from that author, like others, being caught up in the dementia of deadlines and daily work. But it also derives from the nature of anarchism itself. Like most all theoretical or practical models, anarchism incorporates a variety of limitations and contradictions (Feyerabend 1975). Unlike most other orientations, anarchism acknowledges and celebrates these failings, and doesn't bother to hide them behind cloaks of absolute certainty or competence.

Unlike most modernist intellectual orientations, anarchism and anarchist criminology don't bother pretending to incorporate reasoned or reasonable critiques of law and legal authority, either. In fact, to the extent that the legal and cultural machinery of the modern nation state, and the accumulated experiences of daily life under such regimes of power, construct "reason" and a sense of what is reasonable, anarchists and anarchist criminologists argue that progressive social change requires the "unreasonable" and the "unthinkable." In other words, to the degree that reason and "common sense" help keep us locked within present arrangements of authority and power, it seems in our interest to stop making sense, to imagine the unimaginable. Beyond this, as will be seen, anarchists and anarchist criminologists also launch aggressive and "unreasonable" critiques against law and legal authority because they see time and again that such authority undermines human community and constrains human diversity. Unlike some other critical or progressive criminologies, then, anarchist criminology stands not as a careful criticism of criminal justice, a "loyal opposition" to the state and state law. It stands instead as a disloyal and disrespectful (Mazor 1978) attack, a "counterpunch to the belly of authority" (Ferrell 1996: 197). As the Industrial Workers of the World (the *Wobblies*) — a free-swinging anarchist labor union of the early twentieth century — said: "We are not 'undesirable citizens.' We are not citizens at all. We are rebellious slaves....Therefore we are not respectable. We admit it and we are proud of it." (*Industrial Worker* 1912:2)

In promoting fluid and uncertain social relations, and attacking the sorts of legal authority which stifle them, anarchist criminology aims its disrespectful gaze both high and low. Anarchist criminology arrogantly assaults the structures of state and legal authority ensconced above us; but it also humbly encourages all those below and beyond this authority who invent ways of resisting it, and imagines with them a host of unreasonable and egalitarian alternatives. With H. L. Mencken, anarchist criminology seeks to afflict those comfortable with legal power and privilege, and to comfort those afflicted by its abuses.

Through the Past, Darkly

Anarchist critiques of law and legality, and thus the roots of contemporary anarchist criminology, trace as far as anarchism itself. Early anarchist writers and activists like William Godwin (1756–1836), Max Stirner (1806–1856), Michael Bakunin (1814–1876), and Peter Kropotkin (1842–1921) focused some of their most scathing and sophisticated attacks on state authority and legal control. Godwin (1971: 275, 276) for example argued that "whatever inconveniences may arise from the passions of men (sic), the introduction of fixed laws cannot be the genuine remedy," in that such laws tend "to fix the human mind in a stagnant condition," to inhibit lived solutions to human problems, and to promote state-administered "criminal justice" and punishment. Kropotkin (1975: 30, 31, 56) likewise critiqued the law's "tendency to crystallize what should be modified and developed day by day," but went further to call for the abolition of prisons — "monuments of human hypocrisy and cowardice" which promote rather than prevent criminality — and for the destruction of state law itself: "In place of the cowardly phrase, 'Obey the law,' our cry is 'Revolt against all laws!'" Similarly, Stirner (1971: 148, 157) called for "war... against establishment itself, the State" — for the state to be "abrogated, annihilated, done away with, not reformed" — and argued that crime in this context constituted a sort of individualistic rebellion against state law and authority. But perhaps Bakunin (1974: 58, 204), in calling for the destruction of the state and its replacement with "the spontaneous and continuous action of the masses, the groups and the associations of people," presented the twisted potential of the anarchist attack on state law most succinctly: "The passion for destruction is a creative passion, too."

Appropriately, anarchist critiques such as these have emerged not just as theoretical statements, but out of head-on confrontations between state legal authorities and anarchists attempting to construct alternative arrangements. Especially for Bakunin and Kropotkin, anarchist criminology was part of revolutionary activity against the Russian oligarchy and the emerging nation states of capitalism. In fact, Bakunin's notion of "the spontaneous and continuous action of the masses" referred to an actual case of anarchist revolt: the Paris Commune of 1871. In the U.S., anarchists like Emma Goldman (1869–1940) and Alexander Berkman (1870–1936) likewise mixed labor and social activism with insightful critiques — see for example Goldman's (1969: 109–126) essay "Prisons: A Social Crime and Failure" — and spent large periods of their own time in prison for their trouble. Most remarkable were the Wobblies. The Wobblies blended deceptive strategies to avoid legal prosecution with out-and-out defiance of the law; as their national newspaper, the *Industrial Worker* (1913: 2), put it: "Damn the laws of the ruling class. We will have none of them. Capitalist law and order means law forced upon the workers by order of the capitalists." But beyond deception and defiance, the Wobblies and their allied unions also invented strategies that could successfully turn the turgidity of the law against itself, and thus win for them labor and political victories. In the workplace, they at times obeyed every rule and regulation so precisely as to finally grind all work to a halt; in the streets, they systematically violated unjust laws in such great numbers as to overload courts and jails, and force dismissal of their cases (Ferrell and Ryan 1985; Kornbluh 1988; Ferrell 1991).

Anarchist criminology's uncertain trajectory of course continues into the present as well. In fact, the past few decades have seen an efflorescence of anarchist criminology. In 1974, the membership of the American Society for Political and Legal Philosophy for some odd reason "voted overwhelmingly for 'anarchism'" as the topic for their national meeting, and a book of essays on anarchism, law, and justice (Pennock and Chapman 1978: vii) followed in 1978. That same year, criminologist Harold Pepinsky (1978) published an article advocating "communist anarchism as an alternative to the rule of criminal law," and later transformed this approach into a "peacemaking criminology" (Pepinsky 1991; Pepinsky and Quinney 1991; see Pepinsky and Jesilow 1984) opposed to the violence inherent in the concept and practice of state law. Around this same time, criminologist Larry Tifft (1979; Tifft and Sullivan 1980) developed an anarchist criminology which argued for replacing state/legal "justice" with a fluid, face-to-face form of justice grounded in emerging human needs. More recently, Bruce DiCristina (1995; see Ferrell 1995a) has constructed a critique of criminology and criminal justice from the work of anarchist philosopher of science Paul Feyerabend (1975). And I (Ferrell 1994, 1995, 1995a, 1996; Ryan and Ferrell 1986) have developed an anarchist criminology aimed especially at examining the interplay between state/legal authority, day-to-day resistance to it, and the practice of criminality.

As before, though, contemporary anarchist attacks on state legality and control continue to emerge also out of non-academic realms. In 1968, a century after the Paris Commune, French "Situationists" spurred on an anarchist revolt against the centralized French governmental and economic system with slogans like "Work Is The Blackmail of Existence" and "Boredom Is Always Counterrevolutionary." Beginning in the late 1970s, and in the Situationist politics of its founders, the British and U.S. punk movement likewise promoted "DIY" — do-it-yourself — in place of outside authority and control. From bands like the Sex Pistols ("Anarchy in the U.K.") and The Clash ("Working for the Clampdown," "Guns of Brixton," "Know Your Rights") to Rancid ("11th Hour," "Time Bomb," "As Wicked"), the punks have continued to promote anarcho-critical understandings of state law and state injustice as well. During the 1990s, outlaw anarchist radio stations like Free Radio Berkeley (Ongerth and Radio Free Berkeley, 1995) have not only broadcast punk and other alternative music, but have defied FCC regulations to broadcast programs like "Copwatch" and "The First Amendment Show."

And there is more — more illegal "micro-power" stations hidden all around the country, more punks and prisoners with critical and "unwholesome" attitudes toward authority, more people whose day-to-day disavowals of state legality lie outside my knowledge and perhaps that of most others as well. This is, or course, exactly as it should be. Anarchism and anarchist criminology constitute less a closed intellectual system administered by a handful of experts than a critical undercurrent in which everyone may or may not be caught. And in this sense, anarchism and anarchist criminology exist as part of a long and dark "secret history" (Marcus 1989) of resistance, moving underground by force or by choice, and always flowing under and against state and legal authority.

The Spiraling Harm of Criminalization and Legal Control

Anarchist criminology certainly incorporates the sort of "visceral revolt" (Guérin 1970: 13) that characterizes anarchism itself, the passionate sense of "fuck authority," to quote the old anarchist slogan, that comes from being shoved around by police officers, judges, bosses, priests, and other authorities one time too many. Moreover, anarchists would agree with many feminist and postmodernist theorists that such visceral passions matter as methods of understanding and resistance outside the usual confines of rationality and respect (Ferrell 1997). But anarchist criminology also incorporates a relatively complex critique of state law and legality which begins to explain *why* we might benefit from defying authority, or standing "against the law."

Many contemporary critical criminologists agree that state law as practiced in the United States is so thoroughly lubricated by economic privilege, intertwined with patriarchal arrangements, and protected by racist procedures as to constitute a mailed fist regularly brought down on the heads of women, the poor, ethnic minorities, young people, and other outsiders to economic power or state authority. Anarchist criminologists agree as well, but go on to argue that the practice of centralized state law harms people, groups, and the social fabric which joins them even if not aimed directly at "the powerless." Put differently, the administration of centralized state authority and legality destroys community, worsens criminality, and expands the abusive power of the state throughout the contemporary social order — and then, through its discriminatory practices, doubles this harm for those pushed to the bottom of this system. Among the broad harms of state legality:

1. State legality operates as what Pepinsky and Jesilow (1984: 10) have called a "state-protection racket," extorting cash and conformity from those unlucky enough to be caught up in it. From speed traps to parking fines, from the plethora of licensing fees to the bureaucratized bungling of the IRS, the state operates as a vast revenue machine, an elaborate extortion device serving itself and those who operate it. And, as in any extortion operation or protection racket, state law provides for a host of state-sanctioned strong-arm tactics to enforce and enrich the fleece: impoundment, seizure, imprisonment, death. Clearly, such a system exists to perpetuate itself and to protect the powerful in and around it; the ideology that all of this occurs "in the interest of the community" seems at best a sort of cruel joke, or, to paraphrase the Wobblies, a cheap cologne sprinkled on the dunghills of state extortion. If you think otherwise, if you believe that this gigantic machine functions for us all, you might ask some frustrated middle class car owner trying to protest a parking ticket, some kid bankrupted and imprisoned for marijuana possession — or damn near any homeboy walking an inner city street.

2. Like a tangle of poisonous weeds, the labyrinth of state legality grows in the absence of human community, and once in place, further chokes possibilities for fluid and engaged human interaction. In a social world increasingly fractured by alienated labor and economic inequality, privatized leisure,

and the paranoia of the lonely crowd, police calls and civil suits proliferate — as does the sense that such disjointed, externalized tactics somehow constitute appropriate measures for solving disputes and achieving justice. But as parents file for (and are granted) restraining orders against three-year-old playground bullies (Thompson 1996), as suits and countersuits multiply, as the daily fear of crime is shadowed by a daily fear of legal intrusion, human communities continue to unravel. Ultimately, a reliance on state legality reinforces the power and authority of centralized control systems, disables the potential for human community and human justice outside their bounds, and increasingly reduces human interaction to a stale dichotomy of legality and illegality.

3. As the interactionist/labeling tradition in criminology has taught us, the confinement of people and groups within state-administered categories of criminality, and within state-administered systems of punishment and retribution, promotes not rehabilitative humanity but rather a downward spiral of crime, criminalization, and inhumanity. For the individuals and groups targeted by such a system, the spiral intertwines disassociation from non-criminal communities, constricted personal and professional identities, growing anger and resentment, and finally an amplification of criminality and criminal careers. For the larger society, this spiral interweaves state and media sponsored fears of crime, an ideology of state-sanctioned retaliation, and thus broad paroxysms of objectification, dehumanization, and legal retribution. In this way, a system of state law and state "justice" perpetuates, within individual lives and larger social relations, the very problems it claims, falsely, to solve.

4. Within this system, the "rule of law" continues to proliferate, to penetrate more and more corners of social and cultural life (Cohen 1979). As in a Weberian nightmare, state legality constitutes a sort of bureaucratic cancer that grows on itself, that produces an ever-expanding maze of legal control, and that in turn generates an ever-expanding body of bureaucratic and legal sycophants employed to obfuscate and interpret it. In 1886, Kropotkin (1975: 30) documented "a race of law-makers legislating without knowing what their laws are about…legislating at random in all directions;" a century later, that race continues to spew forth legal regulation at a remarkable rate. As such legal controls grow in number and coverage, they of course constipate the conduct of social life, forcing all of us into ongoing contortions within and around them. More troubling, the proliferation of legal controls finally suspends what little protection law once may have afforded. When every facet

of social and cultural life is defined by legal control, and thus by state definitions of legality and illegality, we all remain continually vulnerable to the egregious exercise of state power. So, in a typical example, a recent series of highway drug busts in Arizona were predicated on a single traffic offense by drivers: "unsafe lane usage" (Steller 1996). Finally, as state legality expands, we're all guilty — if not of "unsafe lane usage," then of another among the growing multitude of offenses. And finally, as the modern state and its many subdivisions make more and more of social and cultural life against the law, we must choose to stand against the law as well.

A Note on the Situated Politics of Crime and Resistance

Anarchist criminology's profoundly radical critique of state law as a system of inherent inhumanity, and its sense of therefore standing "against the law," leads to a criminology of crime and resistance as well. Labor historians and sociologists of work have long documented the pattern by which systems of authoritarian, alienating work generate among workers incidents of sabotage — of intentional rule-breaking and disruption — as a means of resisting these systems and regaining some sense of humanity and control. Anarchist criminologists suggest that this pattern may likewise be found in the interplay of state legal control and criminality. Rather than dismissing criminality as mindless misbehavior, or worse, simply accepting the state's construction of legality and illegality as definitive of good and bad human conduct, anarchist criminologists seek to explore the situated politics of crime and criminality. Put more simply, anarchist criminologists argue that the political (and politically inequitable) nature of state law and state criminalization means that acts of crime under such a system must also carry some degree of political meaning. And so, as with Foucault and Genet (Simon 1991: 31), anarchist criminologists seek to blur and explore the boundaries between crime and political resistance. This exploration neither assumes *a priori* that all crime constitutes resistance to state authority, nor ignores the often (but not always) negative consequences of criminality for people and communities. It does, though, call for paying careful attention to various criminal(ized) activities — graffiti writing, "obscene" art and music performances, pirate radio broadcasts, illegal labor strikes, curfew violations, shoplifting, drug use, street cruising, gangbanging, computer hacking (Ferrell 1995, 1996; Ferrell and Sanders 1995) — as a means of investigating the variety of ways in which criminal or criminalized behaviors may incorporate repressed dimensions of human dignity and self-determination, and lived resistance to the authority of state law.

Anarchist Criminology and Anarchist Community

As implied in its critique of centralized state authority, and its embracing of various alternatives to it, anarchist criminology calls for human communities which are decentralized, fluid, eclectic, and inclusive. Moreover, anarchist criminology proposes that this sense of inclusive, non-authoritarian community can benefit critical criminology itself. Clearly, anarchist criminology shares much with the epistemic uncertainty and situated politics of feminist criminology; with the decentered authority and textual deconstruction of postmodern and constitutive criminologies; with the critical pacifism of peacemaking criminology; and of course with the broader critique of legal injustice common to all critical criminologies. Even left-realist criminology, though coming in some sense from a "direction polar opposite" (Einstadter and Henry 1995: 232) to that of anarchist criminology, shares with anarchist criminology a concern with identifying and exploring the situated consequences of crime and crime control. In the spirit of eclectic inclusivity, then, anarchist criminology argues against partitioning critical criminology into a series of small intellectual cubicles, and then closing one critical cubicle to the occupants of another (Pepinsky 1991). Instead, anarchist criminology calls for an ongoing critical conversation among perspectives, for a multi-faceted critique of legal injustice made all the more powerful by its openness to alternatives. Cohen (1988: 232) speaks of his "lack of commitment to any master plan (such as liberalism, left-realism, or abolitionism), a failing, I would like to think, not of my own psyche but of the social world's refusal to correspond to any one theory." Anarchist criminology shares this lack of commitment to master plans — including its own — and embraces instead fluid communities of uncertainty and critique.

A Footnote on Failure

Perhaps an anarchist criminology, and an anarchist vision of justice or community, won't ultimately work. Perhaps, in its "pure" form — whatever "pure" might mean to an approach which embraces particularity, confusion, and adulteration — anarchism incorporates too much fluidity and disorder to ever construct itself fully. And perhaps so with anarchist criminology: as an approach which acknowledges no set boundaries, which claims no pedigreed intellectual heritage or exclusive scholarly turf, anarchist criminology may ultimately constitute no more than a defiant sensibility, an outlaw orientation and analysis, which floats around and against criminology (Cohen 1988). From an anarchist viewpoint, of course, so much the better; for anarchists, nothing succeeds like uncertainty, nothing fails like success. And from this viewpoint, an anarchist criminology which fails to reach full fruition, which fails (and refuses) to "win out" over other perspectives, remains for this very reason an important thread in the larger project of critical criminology. For in a criminal justice universe of centralized and constricting authority, in an academic universe still largely fouled by mythologized standards of truth and imposed hierarchies of credibility (Becker 1967), anarchist criminology functions if nothing else as a useful corrective to encrusted certainty and the desire for domination. And in this way, it undermines the tendency to embrace our own intellectual authority, or the exterior authority of the state, as appropriate — or worse, inevitable — frameworks for social order and social change.

In the 1600s British poet John Milton (1958: 91), in his "Sonnet On His Blindness," reminded us that "they also serve who only stand and wait." Three hundred years later, the new wave of British film makers sharpened this notion's anarchic edge. In the film *The Loneliness of the Long Distance Runner* (Richardson and Sillitoe 1962), lead character Colin Smith has been packed off to the harsh controls of the reformatory, where the headmaster manipulates him into running an importance race against a rival school. By the last few yards, Smith has the race won — and with it, approval of the headmaster, glory for the reformatory, and most importantly his own release from its confines. But just short of the finish line, Smith stops. While the rival school's runner passes him to win the race, Smith stands, stares, and smiles straight at the headmaster. And in his stopping, in his willful failure, he undermines his own hope for freedom — but at the same time undermines the labyrinth of rules and regulations, the daily degradations of obsequiousness and obedience, the phony ideologies of competitive loyalty to the institution and the state, through which his freedom and that of others has long been bought and sold.

So it is with anarchist criminology. Complete or incomplete, as intellectual critique or failed moment of visceral defiance, anarchist criminology serves if only by standing outside the law, by stopping short of the seductive ideologies of obedience and conformity which undergird it. And in this stance, in this disavowal of legal authority and it destructive effects on social and cultural life, anarchist criminology serves to remind us that human relations and human diversity matter — and that, in every case, they matter more than the turgid authority of regulation and law.

Author's Note: I thank Mark Hamm for ideas, inspiration, and the Dylan quote; and Harry Lyrico, who by word, deed and art, and despite his claims to the contrary, sketches the dangerous and honest beauty of life outside the boundaries of legality and privilege.

References

Bakunin, Michael. 1974. *Selected Writings.* New York: Grove Press.

Becker, Howard S. 1967. "Whose Side Are We On?" *Social Problems 14:* 239–247.

Cohen, Stanley. 1979. "The Punitive City: Notes on the Dispersal of Social Control." *Contemporary Crises 3:* 339–363.

Cohen, Stanley. 1988. *Against Criminology.* New Brunswick, NJ: Transaction.

DiCristina, Bruce. 1995. *Method in Criminology: A Philosophical Primer.* New York: Harrow and Heston.

Einstadter, Werner and Stuart Henry. 1995. *Criminological Theory: An Analysis of Its Underlying Assumptions.* Fort Worth, TX: Harcourt Brace.

Ferrell, Jeff. 1991. "The Brotherhood of Timber Workers and the Culture of Conflict." *Journal of Folklore Research 28:* 163–177.

Ferrell, Jeff. 1994. "Confronting the Agenda of Authority: Critical Criminology, Anarchism, and Urban Graffiti." In Gregg Barak, ed., *Varieties of Criminology: Readings from a Dynamic Discipline,* pages 161–178. Westport, CT: Praeger.

Ferrell, Jeff. 1995. "Urban Graffiti: Crime, Control, and Resistance." *Youth and Society 27:* 73–92.

Ferrell, Jeff. 1995a. "Anarchy Against the Discipline" *Journal of Criminal Justice and Popular Culture 3:* 86–91.

Ferrell, Jeff. 1996. *Crimes of Style: Urban Graffiti and the Politics of Criminality.* Boston: Northeastern.

Ferrell, Jeff. 1997. "Criminological Verstehen: Inside the Immediacy of Crime." *Justice Quarterly 14:* 3–23.

Ferrell, Jeff and Kevin Ryan. 1985. "The Brotherhood of Timber Workers and the Southern Lumber Trust: Legal Repression and Worker Response." *Radical America 19:* 55–74.

Ferrell, Jeff and Clinton R. Sanders (eds.). 1995. *Cultural Criminology.* Boston: Northeastern.

Feyerabend, Paul. 1975. *Against Method.* London: Verso.

Godwin, William. 1971. *Enquiry Concerning Political Justice.* London: Oxford.

Goldman, Emma. 1969. *Anarchism and Other Essays.* New York: Dover.

Guérin, Daniel. 1970. *Anarchism.* New York: Monthly Review.

Industrial Worker. 1912. (Editorial). Spokane, WA: IWW. October 24: 2.

Industrial Worker. 1913. (Editorial). Spokane, WA: IWW. June 26: 2.

Kornbluh, Joyce (ed.). 1988. *Rebel Voices: An IWW Anthology.* Chicago: Charles H. Kerr.

Kropotkin, Peter. 1975. *The Essential Kropotkin.* New York: Liveright.

Marcus, Greil. 1989. *Lipstick Traces: A Secret History of the Twentieth Century.* Cambridge, MA: Harvard.

Mazor, Lester J. 1978. "Disrespect for Law." In Roland J. Pennock and John W. Chapman, eds., *Anarchism,* pp. 143–159. New York: NYU.

Milton, John. 1958. "Sonnet On His Blindness." In Roy J. Cook, ed., *One Hundred and One Famous Poems*, p. 91. Chicago: Reilly and Lee.

Ongerth, Steve and Radio Free Berkeley. 1995. "Challenging the Manufacture of Consent." *Z Magazine 8:* 18–22.

Pennock, Roland J. and John W. Chapman (eds.). 1978. *Anarchism*. New York: NYU.

Pepinsky, Harold E. 1978. "Communist Anarchism as an Alternative to the Rule of Criminal Law." *Contemporary Crises 2:* 315–327.

Pepinsky, Harold E. 1991. "Peacemaking in Criminology." In Brian D. MacLean and Dragan Milovanovic, eds., *New Directions in Critical Criminology*, pp. 107–110. Vancouver: The Collective Press.

Pepinsky, Harold E. and Paul Jesilow. 1984. *Myths That Cause Crime*, 2nd ed. Cabin John, MD: Seven Locks.

Pepinsky, Harold E. and Richard Quinney (eds.). 1991. *Criminology as Peacemaking*. Bloomington: Indiana.

Richardson, Tony (dir.) and Alan Sillitoe (screenwriter). 1962. *The Loneliness of the Long Distance Runner*. Great Britain: Woodfall Film Productions.

Ryan, Kevin and Jeff Ferrell. 1986. "Knowledge, Power, and the Process of Justice." *Crime and Social Justice 25:* 178–195.

Simon, John K. 1991. "Michel Foucault on Attica: An Interview." *Social Justice 18:* 26–34.

Steller, Tim. 1996. "Busted." *Arizona Daily Sun*. March 24: 1, 4, 5.

Stirner, Max. 1971. *The Ego and His Own*. New York: Harper and Row.

Thompson, Carolyn. 1996. "Sandbox 'bully,' 3, hauled into court." *The Arizona Republic (Associated Press)*. March 8: A1, A22.

Tifft, Larry. 1979. "The Coming Redefinition of Crime: An Anarchist Perspective." *Social Problems 26:* 392–402.

Tifft, Larry and Dennis Sullivan. 1980. *The Struggle to be Human: Crime, Criminology, and Anarchism*. Orkney, U.K.: Cienfeugos.

This is a review of four books, all of which are focused on alternative community systems for the distribution of money. Lindenfeld, a long time activist in the movements for workers' control, applies his experience in judging the adequacy of new monetary systems. He presents thirteen anti-capitalist principles by which he assesses an alternative currency. Each of the books reviewed shares a focus on localism in both production and consumption.

Originally published in issue 23.

Economics for Anarchists—A Review
Frank Lindenfeld

Barbara Brandt, *Whole Life Economics*
Susan Meeker-Lowry, *Invested in the Common Good*
Edgar Cahn and Jonathan Rowe, *Time Dollars*
Thomas H. Greco, Jr., *New Money for Healthy Communities*

The contemporary postindustrial era extends the promise of material abundance and a good life for all in the U.S. In reality, however, there is widespread poverty, homelessness, and unemployment, a growing gap between the rich and the poor, and continuing destruction of the natural environment. Corporate capitalism is a major cause of these evils. To maximize profits, corporations cut costs by replacing workers with automated machines or by moving to low wage countries, and expand sales through advertising that persuades people to buy things they don't need. Corporate capitalism is based on greed, hierarchy, and domination—of employees by bosses and capitalists, of women by men, of poor countries by rich ones, of blacks by whites. The major ideology in capitalist societies is a belief in progress and economic growth based on mass markets and global trade. The major religion, practiced daily and reinforced by mass media and educational institutions, is the worship of money.

From its very beginnings, capitalism has been challenged by socialist, anarchist and cooperative movements and critiques. The decentralist/cooperative tradition, into which I place the books under review, includes general agreement on most of the following principles, quite antithetical to those of capitalism:

- All humans are equally valuable and should be treated as ends, not means.
- All members of society are entitled to share in its wealth and to have access to adequate food, shelter, and other necessities.
- Income should be distributed equitably.
- Workers should have a say in the decisions that affect them.

- Worker and community ownership and control of businesses is desirable.
- Workers should share equitably in the profits they help create.
- Small economic units are preferable to larger ones.
- Communities should be self reliant, emphasizing local production for local and regional consumption.
- Instead of maximizing profits, economic organizations should balance profit with providing high-quality goods and services, meeting the workers' needs for job security, income, and personal growth, and sustaining the natural environment.
- Economic organization should be based on mutual aid and cooperation; people should care for and help one another, and work together for common benefit.
- Work should be useful and empowering.
- "Normal" work week should be as short as possible to afford all of us more leisure and to spread the available work around.
- Unpaid, voluntary and caring activities are as valuable as paid jobs.

Can corporate capitalism be reformed or replaced with a cooperative system embodying these values, and if so, how? There are no easy answers, though these five books offer many useful ideas. A common thread running through them is their discussion of community barter networks and local currencies. Such currencies are not guaranteed by the state; they rest upon voluntary agreement by the members of a community to accept them in trade. Local exchange systems strengthen local communities by increasing their self-reliance, empowering community members, and helping protect them from the excesses of the global market.

Barbara Brandt reminds us that capitalist workplaces are designed to degrade workers and disempower them. To accumulate short term profits, businesses destroy real wealth — in the form of healthy individuals and communities and a sustainable natural environment. Such commonly used economic measures as the gross domestic product do not include what people produce within their homes for their own use, barter between friends, nor community volunteer services. If a family pays someone to provide child care, that is counted; but it a mother takes care of her own child, it is not counted. The total value of informal, unpaid, economic activity in postindustrial societies is at least as large as that of the paid side. Brandt reminds us that it generally those with the greatest need for care (such as children and the elderly) who lack money, and are thus particularly dependent on informal and volunteer efforts.

What is needed, says Brandt, is a new outlook that balances work and leisure, the economy and the rest of life, one that ends our addiction to jobs and money. The existing economic paradigm based on the belief that money represents value, devalues women, nature, and caring activities because these are treated as economically invisible. Brandt sees the emergence of a new and empowering paradigm, "whole earth economics," based on a sustainable relationship between people and the Earth, increased social responsibility of businesses, a greater valuation of traditionally female activities, and better-paid work opportunities coupled with a reduction in work time.

Susan Meeker-Lowry's vision is similar to that of Brandt. In place of the existing economy, she proposes instead an Earth-centered, sustainable economy. Its core would be strong, diverse, locally controlled economies that use local resources and recycle money locally instead of having it leak out to metropolitan centers. Meeker-Lowry sees support for "green" businesses — those that are socially and environmentally responsible — as a transition strategy that can help move us toward a more sustainable society. She also mentions the Coalition for Environmentally Responsible Economies (CERES) which encourages corporations to accept a greater social and ecological responsibility. Its principles include sustainable use of natural resources, protection of the biosphere, energy conservation, etc. CERES members include social investors, environmental and religious organizations, public interest groups, and public pension trustees, who together represent more than 10 million people and $150 billion in invested assets.

I am not as optimistic as Meeker-Lowry and Brandt, however, about the prospects for internal reform of corporations, A better approach can be found in community organizing to limit corporate power and to build up local economies. A strength of *Invested in the Common Good* is its inclusion of profiles of a number of such organizing projects and alternative institutions. They include:

- Community development financial institutions like Community Capital Bank, the Self Help Credit Union, and the Lakota Fund
- Community organizing and boycotts
- Taking back corporate charters
- Direct action for the Earth
- Barter and work exchange networks
- Community land trusts
- Community supported agriculture and local food systems

Very upbeat in its enthusiastic support for community volunteering and the power of love is *Time Dollars*. Volunteer service credit networks advocated by Edgar Cahn and Johathan Rowe have been organized in dozens of localities primarily as an additional way to provide services to the elderly. They function as communities instead of as charities. Volunteers provide care in return for "time dollars," service credits they can redeem at a future time when they may need help, or donate to someone else for their use. Each hour volunteered earns the same credit, and credits are generally redeemable only within a defined local community. There are some costs of organizing, publicizing and maintaining service credit systems, donated by sponsoring organizations. The programs are limited to those who join as members; there is no guarantee that credits earned will be redeemable in the future, except trust in the members of the network and the sponsoring organization(s). As of 1995, there were about 80 programs operating in 31 states. Thousands of people have given and received personal care through this system, many of them people who could not afford to purchase care services.

One of the pioneer service credit systems, *Womanshare*, is a network of women in New York City, limited to 70 members. Womanshare encourages the formation of friendships among members. All member's hours are counted equally, regardless of skill level. Womanshare publishes a newletter for members, holds monthly meetings, and sponsors educational workshops. Credits and debits of members' work hours are kept by one of the organizers. In contrast with many service credit systems that restrict both provision and receipt of services to those 60 or over, Womanshare includes women of all ages.

In common with the other books, *New Money for Healthy Communities* emphasizes the role of local production for local consumption. Healthy local economies, says Thomas Greco, are based on a diversity of skills and resources as well as on a large measure of self reliance. Economic empowerment of local communities will require the use of local, democratically controlled trading systems and least partial withdrawal from the global exchange system. The advantages of local exchange networks and local currency, according to Greco, are that they promote community cohesion and local economic development. Such currencies are created locally, can be spent only locally, and encourage local people to patronize one another rather than buying from outside. They also help to protect the community from the global market's extreme effects.

Greco provides an excellent overall analysis of conventional and alternative currency systems. Money, he reminds us, is a convenient medium of exchange designed to overcome the limitations of barter between two parties. Money is based on a social agreement to accept a piece of paper that does not necessarily have any value in and of itself for goods and services that are valued. The existing money system has numerous flaws. Money is misallocated, going not to those who need it most to purchase necessities, but to political power centers and to those who already control large pools of wealth. Moreover, there is a constant flow of money from the poor to the rich. Greco discusses several types of local exchange systems that overcome these limitations and promote community development, including LETS and local currency systems such as *Ithaca Hours*.

Local Employment Trading Systems (LETS) enable members to trade goods and services with each other through the use of a newsletter that lists services offered or desired, as well as phone numbers of members so they can contact each other to make exchanges. LETS members go into debt by accepting services from other members; they pay by providing services to others. Debits and credits are posted electronically to each individual account maintained on a computer in the LETS offices. Members of a LETS agree to accept payment for their services in some combination of official and alternative currency. In contrast to Womanshare, most LETS accept exchanges where more highly skilled persons receive a greater number of credits per hour than less highly skilled ones. LETS have spread in Australia, New Zealand, and England, though they nave not gained a foothold in the U.S. The largest LETS network, in Auckland, New Zealand, has 2,000 members.

There are also local barter exchange networks that make use of scrip or alternative local currency. One of the most developed systems is Ithaca Hours, described by Paul Glover in *Hometown Money*, an informative if slightly disorganized how-to-do-it manual based on excepts from the newspaper, *Ithaca Money*. Organized by Glover in 1991, Ithaca Hours has continued to print a newspaper listing goods and services offered and wanted and to distribute and maintain a local currency called the Ithaca Hour. The currency is issued in two hour, one hour, half hour, quarter hour and eight hour notes, each with its own serial number. The free bimonthly newspaper is distributed locally, Those who list their services in *Ithaca Money* and agree to accept payment for at least part of their services in the form of Ithaca Hours receive two Hours for the first ad; if the ad is repeated four times they receive two additional Hours. Those who sign up for or renew their membership at one of the periodic potluck meetings receive one Hour. Ithaca Hours donates 10% of its Hours to local nonprofit organizations chosen at the meetings. As of 1995, Ithaca Hours has been able to attract 80 stores and 150 other local businesses as members, which greatly increases its acceptability as a local currency. The local credit union accepts the payment of loan fees in Ithaca Hours; some restaurants accept 100% payment in this local currency. Hours paid by customers buying goods and services from a merchant can be spent by buying supplies from other local vendors. Some employees have agreed to accept part of their wages in the form of Ithaca Hours. Each Hour is considered the equivalent of about $10 in U.S. currency, the average for regional hourly wages in that area. As of 1996, some $50,000 of spending power has been added to the local economy of Ithaca, and the cumulative volume of trade in Ithaca Hours now exceeds $500,000. The idea has been successfully copied in dozens of other U.S. communities.

The organization of local currency systems does require resources to pay for materials and for the time of an organizer. Expenses can be paid for partly with alternative currency, partly in official currency derived from a membership fee and from advertising in the network publication.

Volunteer and service credit systems and alternative currencies by themselves may not be enough to replace the corporate capitalist system. Nevertheless, they can help build the economic strength of local communities, empower local residents, and mitigate some of the consequences of poverty and unemployment. At the point where a substantial minority of the trade in a local community is conducted through an alternative currency or service credit system, we would expect a significant improvement in community cohesion and in the quality of life. By the time a majority of a community's goods and services are traded through a local exchange or currency system or provided by volunteers, that community will be well on its way to becoming a living embodiment of many anarchist ideals.

References

Whole Life Economics by Barbara Brandt. 256 pp. Gabriola Island, British Columbia: New Society Publishers, 1995. $14.95 paper. (P.O. Box 189, Gabriola Island, B.C. Canada VOR 1X0)

Invested in the Common Good by Susan meeker-Lowry. 272 pp. Gabriola Island, British Columbia: New Society Publishers, 1995. $16.95 paper.

Time Dollars by Edgar Cahn and Jonathan Rowe. 288 pp. Emmaus, PA: Rodale Press, 1992. $19.95 cloth.

New Money for Healthy Communities by Thomas H. Greco, Jr. 213 pp. Tucson: Thomas H. Greco, Jr, 1994. $15.95 paper. (P.O. Box 42663, Tucson, AZ 85733)

Hometown Money by Paul Glover, 82 pp. Ithaca, NY: Ithaca Money, 1995. $10 paper. (P.O. Box 578, Ithaca, N.Y. 14851).

In this provocative and forward-thinking essay on the future of anarchism, Thomas Martin begins to address the challenges of anarchist praxis as it comes to terms with the social and political equivalents of the so-called "paradigm shifts" already witnessed in physics. Our understanding of reality itself is changing, he argues, and while anarchism is perhaps the best-suited political philosophy to adjust to these changes, it is nonetheless requires a radical transformation in our thinking.

Originally published in issue 23.

Steps Toward a Post-Western Anarchism
Thomas S. Martin

One of anarchism's shortcomings is its unwillingness to consider new and radical ideas outside the rather narrow field of political philosophy. Even feminism had a hard time "breaking in," though it is essentially political. The movement has now incorporated a sincere ecological outlook, thanks to the untiring work of Murray Bookchin and a few others, but this is only a beginning. Anarchists tend to ignore or denounce vast regions of human endeavor — the hard sciences, mysticism and religion; many are not even very comfortable with literature and the arts. Such parochialism would be a problem even if Western civilization were not heading into a terminal crisis. But all signs say that it is, and very little of the old order can be expected to weather the transformation. It is not possible, and probably not desirable, to make predictions about the shape of human culture a century from now. It will be largely unrecognizable to us, but not entirely so. The new is already a-building within the shell of the old. Anarchists have always claimed that we have a coherent and humanistic vision for the future of humanity; but if we do not start paying attention to the other streams of consciousness that are running parallel to ours, we may not have the opportunity to help shape that future. The intent of this essay is to suggest a few of the tentative steps that should be taken, with a view to encouraging further research and bridge-building. What follows will be unfamiliar to many anarchists, and may even seem a bit incoherent, but that is in the nature of first steps.

The post-Western world, whatever it may look like, will not be a clean break with the past; history after all is dialectical. New systems structure themselves out of their predecessors. We can assume that the anarchist critique, addressing as it does the constitutional flaws in Western civilization, will carry over in some form. This essay will hazard some predictions about what that form might be. As the shift is still in its early stages, and as futurology is notoriously inaccurate, these predictions will probably be wrong. But we have to start somewhere.

What I propose is that anarchists begin to re-think at least some of our positions in light of current ideas and research in the areas of post-Einstein physics and general systems theory. Plenty has been written in the last decade or two about both these cutting-edge fields. Much of it is New Age garbage, or (at the other extreme) is accessible only to specialists; but some of it speaks directly to radicalism. What physics and systems theory now suggest about the nature of reality is so totally outside the everyday experience of Western thinking that we should not be surprised if it sounds like nonsense. Some of it probably *is* nonsense. But there can no longer be any doubt that the Western worldview, in which anarchism is embedded, is based on an outrageously false set of premises. The fact is that the physicists and cosmologists are dragging us willy-nilly across a frontier that few people really want to cross. By now Thomas Kuhn's *Structure of Scientific Revolutions* is well known as the paradigmatic description of "paradigm shifts"—those periodic transformations of worldview that punctuate history, installing new fundamental premises that are "incommensurable" with the old. The word "paradigm" has become a buzzword, and its arrogation by the multinational capitalists to describe the next stage of their global conquest is especially galling. Still, it is the right word, and we radicals need to take it back. What Kuhn describes are actually secondary shifts: the fall of the Roman Empire, the collapse of the medieval synthesis, the eponymous Scientific Revolution of the seventeenth century. They were profound, but not fundamental; they all happened within the basic context of Western culture as established in the Fertile Crescent some thousands of years ago. In systems language, they were "confirmatory" rather than "innovative," meaning that they strengthened rather than weakened the underlying worldview. What we are looking at today, however, is perhaps the beginning of the first *primary* paradigm shift since the Neolithic Revolution. Not many fundamental paradigms have existed in human history. That of China is more persistent and stable than ours; the holistic-animistic paradigm shared by indigenous peoples all over the world may yet help save us, if we don't obliterate it first. Paradigms are dynamic systems of human consciousness, inherently conservative and self-sufficient; when we find one that works, we stick with it. In fact our sanity, our very survival, depends upon our particular paradigm being true. This is why paradigms are so hard to dislodge, even when they are patently unwholesome. The crises of the twentieth century— most notably the ecocidal compulsions of late capitalism—have pushed the Western paradigm to the very brink. Everything is about to tumble over, including anarchism. Assuming that we survive to forge a new paradigm, anarchism as we know it will seem as antiquated and useless as cuneiform.

Anarchism, Systems Theory, and the New Physics

The first step toward a post-Western mindset is the study of physics as it has developed since Albert Einstein opened a most unexpected door. More than one observer has noted that physics, religion, psychology and even linguistics are converging toward a general explanation of the universe that will little resemble the model we all still learn in school — the worldview crafted centuries ago by that unholy trinity of Bacon, Descartes, and Newton. The ingredients are holism and process philosophy, as developed by Bergson, Whitehead and many others; quantum mechanics, with its eerie paradoxes — Heisenberg's uncertainty and Pauli's exclusion principles; and a few other models so radical as to defy classification: especially the work of Gregory Bateson, Rupert Sheldrake, and Ilya Prigogine. A few anarchists have already begun to address the implications. Murray Bookchin stands far above the crowd, not least because he ferrets out the anti-libertarian potentials in the work of scientists who are not much interested in political theory.

A full discussion of quantum mechanics, systems theory and their dialectic is not obligatory here. The radical implications can be glimpsed in the work of Fritjof Capra, Morris Berman, Timothy Ferris and others. We can go straight to the cutting edge, the recent theories of David Bohm and Geoffrey Chew and their implications for post-Western anarchism. The idea that reality can be reduced to a "field" of some kind (in which objects shape, and are shaped by, their surroundings) is not new, but David Bohm has suggested that the field is "holographic"— that is, any sector of it contains the whole of the field. Our idea (drawn from classical mathematics) that everything can be located at a "point" in space and time thus becomes meaningless. According to Bohm the order and chaos we perceive in the physical realm are epiphenomena of the "implicate order," a structure that underlies all structures and systems and is not directly accessible to our minds. The implicate order is transcendent, holographic, and inclusive of all potential objects and events. Above all it is *real*, whereas our own "real world" is only the surface effect of that reality: objects are abstractions, "relatively independent subtotalities," like eddies in a stream. The twin great and deadly errors, which anarchism shares with all other Western philosophies, is what I will for convenience call "dichotomy"—the chopping-up of the world into pieces that exist only in our minds, and "reification"—believing that those pieces have a fundamental reality. Our habit of seeing discrete entities where there is only unbroken wholeness is the source of many of Western civilization's problems and may indeed be the death of us all.

Geoffrey Chew's bootstrap theory is so revolutionary that we may place it over the paradigmatic line as the first post-Western model of physics, rather than the last Western one. It is based on S-matrix theory, a mathematical model of the universe first proposed by Heisenberg in 1943 to explain the strong interaction of hadrons at the subatomic level. S-matrix suggests that the patterns exhibited by particles aren't really fundamental; they arise from tendencies of those particles to act in certain ways. The only possible explanation for the success of S-matrix theory, Chew said, is that matter does not exist at all: the universe is "a dynamic web of interrelated events. None of the properties of any part of this web is fundamental; they all follow from the properties of the other parts, and the overall consistency of their mutual interrelations determines the structure of the entire web." In this model all laws — of physics, of chemistry, of history — are purely human constructs imposed by our minds on a reality beyond our comprehension. Structures and processes must be "self-consistent" and consistent with one another, but not with any fundamental principles that lie "outside" the processes themselves. The bootstrap hypothesis destroys the entire project of Western philosophy, whose purpose is to reveal underlying principles for how and why things work as they do. Such an inquiry is now exposed as a dive into a bottomless well. Rather than waste our time trying to figure out "fundamental" postulates, we would be better off following the lead of the mystics, who strive for direct intuition rather than rational understanding. This insight must be adopted by post-Western anarchism: to grasp directly and intuitively the place which we occupy in the world.

The new physics is, as everyone knows by now, far more in tune with the "primitive" opinions of indigenous people than with anything that ever came out of a university seminar or a particle accelerator. The Pueblo shaman in his dusty *kiva* knew more about the world's workings than did Oppenheimer in his Los Alamos laboratory a few miles away. The Western obsession with murdering, dispossessing, converting, and otherwise obliterating native peoples is now easier to understand: they knew the truth, and we were determined to live a lie; we could not look them in the face. The post-Western world, whatever shape it may take, will have to go humbly as a supplicant to that mescal-eating, painted savage it once despised. Most anarchists rightly scorn New Age "philosophy" as a confused and shallow babble of late-capitalist egocentrism, but we must not throw the baby out with the bathwater. Indigenous people do indeed have something profound to teach us, but it isn't quite what the channelers and the Celestinomaniacs want to hear.

All these assorted ideas come together in a compelling fashion in general systems theory, a consensus product of cybernetics, quantum physics, chaos theory and several other new disciplines. Systems theory is not new, but has only very slowly won acceptance, for reasons that are more political than scientific. A "system" is an aggregate of related elements which takes its identity, not from the nature of the components, but from the nature of the dynamic relationship among them. The theory also assumes that no element of a system is autonomous; all are "holons" (the word is Arthur Koestler's), phenomena that are simultaneously parts and wholes. This is another way of saying that the whole is greater than the sum of its parts, a very ancient concept. It will be objected by many anarchists that systems theory is inherently flawed by its habit of describing interconnections in terms of hierarchy. The point is well taken, though it is based on a conflation of two rather different phenomena that share the same name. A social or political hierarchy is an artificial human creation, doing violence to the natural order of things. Systems hierarchies are natural by definition, but probably it would be better to think of them as networks or webs. They can be visualized as horizontal rather than vertical — eliminating the values implied in terms like "higher" and "lower"—without compromising the substance of the theory. Another valid objection arises from the origins of systems theory as a mechanical, cybernetic viewpoint. Systems language still tends to talk of social and cultural phenomena as though they behaved like chemical or physical structures. It reminds us of the reductionism and mechanization that we are supposed to be fighting. Unfortunately, systems theory is largely a product of World War II weapons research. Like computers and game theory, it was invented to facilitate the more efficient killing of larger and larger numbers of people. The idea is now in the process of escaping its unsavory childhood, but in the popular mind the word "system" still carries this scientific and capitalist connotation. Both these criticisms can probably be overcome with a careful attention to terminology and an awareness that systems theory, like so much else, can be used for good or for evil.

General systems theory began to take shape in the 1920s, when physicists proved that the Newtonian view of the universe as a collection of discrete objects is false. The inauguration of the "quantum age" was the first great crack in the foundation of the Western paradigm. It required philosophers, mathematicians, biologists, and many other scientists to reconsider their view of the world as a great machine which could be understood by analysis into its constituent parts. What had once been absolute dogma became mere "mechanism" and "reductionism" as we grasped a deeper truth: phenomena must be apprehended as dynamic wholes; when we reduce them to their constituent parts we cannot get an accurate picture of them. All traditional sciences were now seen to be useful only in describing the structure of phenomena; a new methodology was required to explain their *function*. We have had to replace the "world as machine" with the "world as system." From this preliminary shift grew a cluster of new disciplines which fit only with some discomfort into the old categories: semiotics, various forms of structuralism, game and decision theory, cybernetics, fuzzy logic, and the like. Perennial philosophical questions now ceased to have meaning: the mind/body problem, objectivity, determinism versus free will, mechanism versus organicism. We are coming to understand that when no suitable answer can be found, there is probably something wrong with the question.

Without belaboring the point any further, it is by now obvious that our entire worldview is based on a stupendously bogus answer to the question, "What is reality?" How could Western philosophy, grounded as it is in a successful and all-consuming science and technology, have made such a profound error? And how could primitive indigenous people — shamans, dancing about bonfires and wearing silly masks — be so *right* about the way physics and cosmology work? The answer is not difficult or arcane. A proper understanding of the nature of the universe— its systems, its indeterminacy, its holism— is an adaptive trait, a concomitant of the successful evolution of the human race. If our ancestors *hadn't* understood such things, we would never have swung down out of the trees. By the same token, our modern civilization has established its hierarchies and learned to control nature (including people) precisely because some humans *forgot* what evolution taught them. Thanks to the remarkable flexibility of our brains (and hands) we have been able to make this aberration work for several thousand years now. But like everything else in physics and evolution, a countervalence of some kind is required, a redressing of the balance. Syntropy is paid for by an increase in entropy. We took out a loan, and the mortgage is now due.

The price could be very high indeed: the annihilation of our species. The first installments have already been paid, in the form of this century's totalitarian systems with their policies of genocide and ecocide, not to mention the most destructive wars in human history and the current unprecedented extinction rate. Anarchists have not adequately confronted the meaning of twentieth-century history. Based on new understandings of how the world works, however, we can now come to some decision about what anarchists must embrace — and abandon — if we are to move forward. The Western worldview has left us with a great deal of unnecessary baggage; we are very attached to some of it. Nevertheless it will have to go.

First Steps: Dichotomy and Reification

So what is it, exactly, that anarchists need to re-think in light of the new physics and general systems theory? The list is already very long, and promises to get longer. Here we will consider just two of the Western delusions that need correcting: dichotomy and reification. They are, I think, the two most significant, and they are connected. "Dichotomy" comes from Greek words meaning "cutting in two," and is now often used to denote the drawing of false boundaries to separate two or more things that are really unitary. The most dangerous Western dichotomy, already identified by the social ecologists, is that between *physis* and *nomos*. Western thought separates human beings (at least the better sort) from the rest of nature. This convention probably goes back to the invention of agriculture and domestication, but it was not described in philosophical or theoretical terms until the late pre-Socratic period in Greece. In Sophocles' *Antigone*, the theme concerns a conflict between human law and the demands of the gods. The sophist Antiphon, sometimes claimed as a proto-anarchist, declared that self-interest was the basic law of nature. The laws of society require us to submit to the good of the community, and are therefore against nature. Plato took up this interesting dichotomy in the *Republic* and in several of his dialogues, making it a permanent and central feature of Western philosophy. We are not sure who first used the terms *physis* (nature, physical reality) and *nomos* (law, human-established order) in opposition to one another, but all the great philosophers of the classical age had something to say about it. One set of rules (*nomos*) applies to us, another (*physis*) to the rest of the cosmos. This is a good example of what the Greeks called *hubris*, though they did not understand the irony. The pre-Socratic dichotomy of *physis* and *nomos* was probably the first major confirmatory shift within the Western paradigm, and the strongest. By setting itself apart from the world, Western culture took on the right to command, manipulate, exploit, and perhaps ultimately destroy that world. In science, it produced Newton's clockwork universe. The end result was Robert Oppenheimer's famous remark: "The hell with your ethics. The thing is superb physics!" In religion, it created Augustine's ethereal City of God alongside the cesspool called the City of Man. In fact it took God right outside the universe, though before he left he gave Adam and Eve (who were of course white Europeans) permission to do what they liked with it. Until very recently, no Western ethical system seriously questioned this basic dichotomy. Even the classical anarchists believed "man" must conquer "nature." The biocentrism (or better yet, the ecocentrism) of deep ecology is the first clear sign that the *physis/ nomos* assumption is undergoing reversal.

To argue that all dichotomies are false immediately involves one in all sorts of paradoxes and contradictions. If we say, "all dichotomies," we imply the opposite of dichotomy (holism, unity?) and *that* is a dichotomy. And "false" presumes "true"—yet another dichotomy. It is not difficult to see why these incongruities arise. The structure of Western logic and reason, embedded in our Indo-European languages (Greek and Latin, especially), leaves us unable to talk or think about anything in a manner that is not dichotomizing. This logical structure is one of the prime ingredients of our cultural paradigm, perhaps even its foundation stone. Trying to operate without it is nearly impossible for us. So far only the quantum physicists, some mystics and a handful of remarkable philosophers employing dialectical reasoning have been able to do so, and even they cannot convey their thoughts to the rest of us in language that everyone can understand. This writer is not so vain as to think he can do any better.

The hopelessness of the task is no excuse, however. We must reject dichotomy and all its works. We could opt to be pure philosophers, and talk about this on a cosmological level; but it might be more worthwhile to forget that for the time being and focus on our own planet and species. The ecosphere is One, and that's all there is to it. No social or political system that fails to recognize this can be genuinely libertarian. All dichotomies are false, including the dichotomy between dichotomy and holism. Here again anarchism has an advantage: it is inherently dialectical, opposed to boundaries and barriers, and it is flexible. As with all Western philosophies there is a tendency to dogmatism, but anarchists at least recognize the dangers. We must begin to take seriously what Tolstoy meant when he said that the Golden Rule is the only law humanity needs. We must listen to Kropotkin about the advantages of cooperation over competition; to Bookchin about the unity of humans with nature. We have already absorbed much from ecology, feminism, and the non-Western traditions; this trend must continue. What we have not yet done is to look at new developments in the "hard" sciences, and in the realm of psychology. We do not have to fall into the traps of New Ageism or ecofascism. The strategy is to keep the falseness of all dichotomies firmly in mind.

Next, and more difficult from a theoretical standpoint, is noncompliance with the central Western project of reification. The world consists of processes, not things; let's get used to it, and adjust our anarchist strategies accordingly. I suggest that a thoroughgoing anarchist analysis of language is the place to start. We should all learn something about non-Western languages and how they organize reality in the minds of their speakers. This is not to say that anarchism will save the world if we all learn Nootka, but an awareness of the primary role of language in cognition and consciousness is essential. We will not change the world until we change the way people think, and this will not happen unless we change the language they think in. At the simplest level, much work has already been done: we now understand the sexism inherent in English and its cousins. We know that the negative connotations of the word "black" have contributed to racism. At the other end of the scale, Noam Chomsky has explored the deep grammar common to all linguistic expression; it is no coincidence that the world's leading philosopher of language is also an anarchist. But there are many other avenues to explore. Etymology is relatively accessible to everyone. An example: the word "consciousness" has a great variety of contradictory uses, both everyday and technical. The root is Latin *scire*, "know," which doesn't help much until we look further back to the IE *skei-*, "to cut, split". This verb appears to concern objects that are cut off from some larger parent body. Irish *scían* "knife" is cognate, but so are *schism, schizoid, shed, ski, shield, sheaf*, and even *shit*. If *skei-* is related to *sek-*, as paleolinguists believe it is, then some other cognates include *scythe, sword, skin*, and the large family of Latin words from *secare*, as well as *Saxon*, a "warrior with a knife." The deep unconscious connection between "knowing" and "cutting" is of vast significance for Western thought: from the very beginning, to "know" something was to "cut it off" from the undifferentiated mass of reality, to separate it, isolate it, tear it from its place in the holistic order. Given this deep unconscious connotation of knowing, how could our culture have avoided dichotomy and reification?

In short, the banishment of reification will be promoted if we all become more aware of the great fluidity and power of language. I need to be able to look at the coffee mug on my desk and realize that its discrete object-ness is largely a product of the fact that I employ a reifying noun to describe it. Failure to properly understand reification is perhaps one of the prime reasons for the failure of anarchism to catch the world's attention. Our ideology opposes exploitation and domination, the putting of price tags on everything, generalization and stereotyping. It supports cooperation and interconnection, respect and acceptance. However, it is largely unable to explain *why* it holds these values. If it is our purpose to end the domination of one person by another, or of nature by humans, we must demonstrate the fallacy of reification. By snatching a handful of process out of the great flux and naming it, we create the Other. Reification is the error of pointing to "that" or "him" or "her," by which we imply that the Other is not Us. Here is the foundation of all ideology, all dichotomy, all our false beliefs that We are Not-Them. Here is also the justification for all forms of domination.

Praxis

What are the implications for anarchism as a living, dynamic project? Even in its present very early stages the post-Western paradigm implies some very difficult concessions. First, and most painful, is the concept of individual autonomy and all its accoutrements. What we once thought of as individual rights will have to be recognized as ecosystemic rights, owned by us because we are participants in a holistic universe, not because we are individuals. Anarchism is better equipped to handle this change than other systems arising from nineteenth-century liberalism or socialism. Other ideologies focus either on the autonomous individual or on the undifferentiated community; only anarchism comes close to a model that allows for a free individual within an authentic community. We can improve this model, both in theory and praxis, if we incorporate post-Western concepts. At present the most promising approach is that of philosophers like Kenneth Goodpaster, Christopher Stone, Tom Regan, and Peter Singer, whose primary interest is the "rights" of animals and other entities in non-human nature. The idea that individuals have certain indefeasible rights is clearly a human notion, both incomprehensible and irrelevant to cows, sea slugs and petunias. Yet it is equally clear that all living things share certain interests with us — survival, reproduction, freedom from pain — and that we base our definition of rights on those interests. The resulting conundrum has no solution within the limits of Western thought, and we are beginning to look elsewhere for radically new answers. Where this will lead is unpredictable, but anarchists had better pay close attention.

Second, we must strive to make anarchism post-ideological as well as post-Western. A large body of literature already exists to address the question of what it means to be post-ideological, and we can begin with that. Most of it stems from deconstructionism, and is therefore highly opaque and pretentious, but it is still perhaps on the right track. We can also consider the principles of bioregionalism, mediation and conflict resolution, cooperatives, identity politics, holistic medicine, even computer hacking and other such concepts aimed at improving the quality of life in practical everyday ways without the "help" of government. The most promising non-ideological strategy, however, already has deep roots in the history of anarchism. This is the principle of *scale*. If we think of human societies (whether neighborhood food co-ops or empires) as systems in dynamic equilibrium, it quickly becomes apparent that for their long-term survival, the way in which they are organized is less critical than their size. The Diggers and William Godwin understood this principle, and so did most classical anarchists. Even today we give much thought to the ideal size of a commune, or collective, or whatever we choose to call the basic unit of anarchist society. If you have to raise your hand to speak, is the group too large? One of the basic rules of Western civilization is that "bigger is better," and we anarchists long ago rejected that rule. But anarchism is itself an ideology, and it has always tackled the question of scale as an ideological problem. That is, we worry more about whether the political unit is capitalist or Marxist or fascist than we do about whether it is too big or small. In a post-Western world we may well find communities of Nazis or Satanists or Republicans— and where's the harm in it, as long as no one is coerced into membership and they are too small and decentralized to threaten the rest of us? Hakim Bey (Peter Lamborn Wilson) has even suggested that monarchy is not necessarily incompatible with anarchism. This sort of talk will no doubt set off alarm bells in most anarchists, but we have to be open-minded. General systems theory will help. All systems are embedded in and interconnected with other systems, in a dizzyingly complex network that stretches unbroken from the ecology of a tidal pool to the furthest boundaries of the universe. Individual or primary systems, however, tend to be quite simple. If they consist of too few elements they do not last long; if too many, they eventually collapse under their own weight, often doing considerable damage. There is an optimum size that produces the greatest possible stability and longevity. Systems are destabilized by the presence of "chaotic attractors," wild-card elements that do not harmonize with the rest of the system and tend to throw it off balance. A sufficient number of such attractors can destroy the system altogether. The larger and more complex a single system is, the more prone to this sort of disruption. The current disintegration of Western civilization is a prime example. This is not an argument against diversity or in favor of uniformity. In fact the more diverse a system is, the more stable — this insight is the great contribution of the science of ecology to political theory. We are talking here about quantity, not quality. The next generation of anarchists will have to sort out this rather perplexing set of ideas. We are puzzled because we cannot help thinking in terms of dichotomy and reification; perhaps they will do better.

Third, we must start taking seriously the idea of equality. This means opposing any tactic or movement aimed at separating or alienating people from one another — racism, sexism and bigotry in all their guises, both male and female chauvinism, all forms of elitism from executive washrooms to college fraternities. Even to distinguish anarchists from non-anarchists must be recognized as a fallacy. Governments and power elites know they would vanish like dew on a summer morning if we all suddenly started thinking of ourselves as truly equal. "Divide and conquer" is Rule Number One in the Establishment's handbook. We must see through and challenge all class distinctions, and eschew whatever artificially sets one person apart from another. Ask a Cadillac owner why he drives such an uneconomical and pretentious car in a world of poverty and dwindling energy supplies, and he will probably answer "comfort" or "dependability," as the advertisements have instructed him to say. Bringing the *real* motive to everyone's consciousness is our challenge. Going to Harvard is great, but don't get to thinking it makes you "better" than a freshman at Podunk State. Read Thorstein Veblen on the "leisure class." His style is turgid and his wit too subtle for most, but he was *right*.

Of course many other issues must be addressed. How can post-Western anarchism incorporate systems thinking into its practice of education, sexuality, art and music, direct action, grassroots democracy, alternative states of consciousness? It can be done, if anarchism will accept the task of explaining why the nature of reality and consciousness do not allow for the domination and oppression of one human being by another. Its praxis will be to define human relationships so as to ensure cooperation, productivity and growth without the exercise of power and authority. In order to achieve its purpose, anarchism will need to adapt to and integrate with other fields — not just ecology, but also physics and psychology. Complex dynamic systems work better when the whole choir is singing from the same hymn book. This does not mean grey conformity, as it would under the hierarchic, mechanistic Western paradigm. Rather, it means a vigorous dialectic of ideas on a level playing field. To this end anarchists must support the breakdown of traditional boundaries among intellectual disciplines; this is already happening, and we have lagged behind. The anarchism of the future will be, as Kropotkin envisioned, a complete and coherent ecological and scientific world-view, not just a political ideology. Let us make sure that it is we, and not the physicists and ecologists, who establish what this means.

Although much of the work of anarchists is centered about the building of alternative and oppositional movements, relatively little attention is given to the evaluation of such movements, in part because such research is difficult for even the trained social scientist. In this report, Gelderloos sets his sights on a food co-op in a relatively small community. The research focused on three dimensions of anarchist organization: the equality of roles, mutual aid, and decentralization.

Originally published in issue 39.

A Critical History of Harrisonburg Food Not Bombs
Culture, Communication, and Organization in an Anarchist Soup Kitchen
Peter Gelderloos

Every Friday at 4pm, a motley group of people come together at a Mennonite Church in Harrisonburg, Virginia, and eat a free meal cooked from dumpstered and donated food. They are young and old; black, white, and latino; workers, students, and unemployed. The event is called Harrisonburg Food Not Bombs. Some people think of it primarily as a free meal, others think of it as social time, some experience it as a duty, and others consider it a radical act. Amid all these varying perceptions lies an experiment in anarchist organizing that has succeeded roughly as much as it has failed, and if we dig deeper, a veritable dumpster-full of lessons for anarchists trying to organize with one another and with their communities.

This critical history will paint a background portrait, for those not familiar with Food Not Bombs or the Harrisonburg chapter thereof, and then examine three episodes that shed light on difficulties and developments experienced by the Harrisonburg activists, which will hopefully be instructive for anarchists elsewhere.

Background

Food Not Bombs started in Cambridge, Massachusetts, in 1980 and has since grown "hundreds" of autonomous chapters across the country and across "the Americas, Europe, Asia, and Australia" (www.foodnotbombs.net, 2005). Essentially, the group is a sort of soup kitchen with four major modifications. Meals are vegan, to draw attention to the violence of industrial meat production and its role in exacerbating global poverty and hunger, and also, though not admittedly, to cater to the white punk/anarchist subcultures from which most chapters draw their activists. Meals are served in the open, to resist the shame and obscurity with which poverty is made invisible, to make a visible, political act out of serving free food, and oftentimes to meet homeless people on their own turf, in the urban parks where they congregate. Thirdly, Food Not Bombs sets itself in opposition to charity, ideally avoiding the paternalism of traditional soup kitchens and striving for the ideal of cooking and eating meals together, to blur the distinction between the giver and receiver of charity. Finally, Food Not Bombs is anti-militarist. This orientation manifests in the name, in the distribution of literature by many chapters portraying militarism as a drain on social resources and a cause of poverty, and in the location of Food Not Bombs within anti-war, anti-globalization, and other left-wing opposition movements (either through the other affiliations of Food Not Bombs activists or the collaboration between Food Not Bombs and other protest groups, whereby a Food Not Bombs chapter might cook meals for a protest or conference).

Harrisonburg Food Not Bombs began in Fall 2001 in conjunction with a new anarchist community center, which city authorities later shut down. A group of fewer than a dozen activists, predominantly young, white students from James Madison University, assembled the bare minimum of cooking supplies and began serving meals. The group initially served meals downtown, on the sidewalk in front of the community center once that opened. After the anarchist space got shut down, Food Not Bombs moved its weekly meals to Court Square, and eventually shut down for about a year due to lack of help. It restarted in 2003, serving out of a park on the northeast end of town, but by the end of the year moved into a small, progressive Mennonite church in an old working class neighborhood, and began serving its meals indoors. Harrisonburg Food Not Bombs has served meals at this location every Friday for over two years now.

The majority of materials used by Harrisonburg Food Not Bombs are taken from grocery store dumpsters, and the rest is acquired through donations. Seldom, staples, spices, or cooking oils are purchased out-of-pocket.

There is a high degree of regularity to who eats and prepares meals every week at Food Not Bombs, though the group is dynamic and fluctuating. If a particular Food Not Bombs chapter successfully achieved its ideal, everyone involved would be considered a Food Not Bombs member, as membership is open and informal, and everyone is intended to cook, eat, and clean up together, regardless of whether they are a homeless person, a full time activist, or a student. Harrisonburg Food Not Bombs does not meet this ideal, and neither does any chapter I know of.

Those who do nearly all the planning and preparing for the meal are far more homogenous than the total pool of people who come out for any given meal. The people seated around the plastic tables every Friday are black, white and latino; they include children and septuagenarians; students, social workers, taxi drivers, the homeless, disabled, and unemployed. But the Food Not Bombs members, those who hold power and responsibility in the outcome of the weekly meal, are on average younger, whiter, wealthier, better educated, and more politically active. Harrisonburg members struggle to make the appropriate distinctions to describe the divisions within the group. Generalizations regarding age or socioeconomic background are accurate, but imperfect. Not all older people and working-class/homeless people remain external to the group, and many younger people and middle-class people do not become members. Though it is not defined, membership in Food Not Bombs is observable, and the barrier between membership and non-membership is most certainly cultural. But it is not an impassable barrier, and membership exists in degrees, or shades of grey, in Harrisonburg Food Not Bombs. One old, disabled curmudgeonly man with little sympathy for anarchist activism has won a firm social niche over the years, and he regularly carries out multiple responsibilities, though he declines to partake in meetings. To avoid generalizing either group, I will make my distinction functional, between "activists" and "participants." The latter term is not simply euphemism. Anyone who comes to Food Not Bombs often enough will eventually participate in some way other than simply eating. After all, the meal is not treated like charity and everyone is encouraged to help out. However, most people will never become involved in decision-making, planning, or other regular responsibilities fulfilled by the "activist" core. It should be understood that participants are a diverse group, while activists are predominantly young and white, and mostly students, though with limited variation.

Pass the Salt, Share the Work

For most of its history, Harrisonburg Food Not Bombs distributed work in such a way as to encourage burn-out among activists. For several months at a time, two or three activists would be responsible for nearly all the work each and every meal, including dumpstering the night before (I'll refer to these people as "leaders," though the only authority they had stemmed from the fact that they did all the work). They would carry out these duties as best they could, and just when they were ready to give up, another two or three people stepped forward, and the former leaders faded into the background, sometimes never returning to the group, sometimes filling the thankless leadership role again down the road. I personally have played this role three or four times throughout the history of Harrisonburg Food Not Bombs. There were a few exceptional periods in the group's history when large numbers of people shared and rotated work, but these were rare. In Fall 2005, the current leaders were suffering from burn-out, and other activists who had already had experience as the leaders did not want to step forward again. There were few people coming to the meal who would actually go hungry without free food, and morale was low. Food Not Bombs activists discussed ending the weekly meal and devoting their energies to other projects. We realized, after all, that Harrisonburg's Food Not Bombs chapter had originally been founded, and restarted, not based on any strategic decisions regarding local organizing or the needs of the community (which has a small homeless population relative to other cities), but because Food Not Bombs was something anarchists in other cities did, so...

In response to our impending end, one community member who did rely in part on our meals began searching for restaurant donations for us, to spare us some of the work of dumpstering, and several younger student activists began recruiting their friends to come help out. Morale boosted, we began to figure out how we could share the work and make Food Not Bombs sustainable. In the past we had tried dividing tasks between volunteer coordinators (e.g. dumpstering, prep, cleanup, outreach). Each coordinator was supposed to coordinate their particular field of work and recruit volunteers to help them cook, or clean-up, or dumpster, each week. But every time the system fell apart after a couple months. Coordinators would pass on their responsibilities to other activists, or would take on all the work themselves and not look for other volunteers to help out and learn the skills that would be necessary for them to take on more responsibilities. No one held themselves or other activists accountable to their obligations.

This time around, we met and came up with a new structure for sharing work. We set out coordinator positions again, but stipulated that they be rotated every month. We also emphasized and agreed to make criticisms and compliments of one another, and actively hold other activists accountable. So far, creating a visible power structure has allowed more people to take on responsibilities within the group, though time has yet to tell whether we will keep ourselves accountable or lapse again in fulfilling and sharing the duties involved in making the weekly meal.

The Four Hardest Words: "Hello, My Name Is..."

A recent academic article on the anarchist movement, co-authored by a retired police chief, speculates on how the movement funds itself. One hypothesis is that networks of Food Not Bombs chapters across the country provide free food for anarchists (Borum and Tilby, 2005). Though the article is laughably haphazard, the observation that Food Not Bombs exists to cater to a subculture is worth taking seriously. Numerous outside observers, and even most of us who are integrally involved with Harrisonburg Food Not Bombs, have remarked that the group is welcoming to activists who fit in with any of the white anarchist subcultures (politically radical punks, hippies, and indy kids) and varyingly lukewarm or uninviting to all other people, whether they be visiting college students who dress conventionally, or older homeless people with few cultural reference points in common. Most of the Food Not Bombs activists are very nice to newcomers, but if a group consists of a core group of friends, and then various other people, no amount of politeness will prevent divisions from arising.

An ongoing challenge for the Harrisonburg chapter, and from what I have seen other Food Not Bombs chapters, is to be truly welcoming to people outside the dominant clique, and in fact to destroy that clique. Activists have to constantly remind themselves and one another to make an effort to talk to and get to know other participants, especially the people who rely on the free food that we serve. Otherwise, during a meal all the young activists sit, eat, and talk loudly at one table, and the poor people eat quietly at another table. People from privileged backgrounds especially fail to grasp the importance of building real relationships as a basis for their activism. We need to prioritize getting to know people from different social circles and cultural backgrounds, beyond politeness and to the point of establishing a real rapport. Once we know someone well enough to socialize and joke with them, we have a basis for working with them, asking them to take on responsibilities, and respecting and listening to their input. This is a necessary goal if Food Not Bombs, or similar projects, are to be anything but charity by another name.

An Unorthodox Chapter of an Ostensibly Unorthodox Organization

How does a decentralized organization evolve? Is a chapter that deviates from the original principles of the organization still a part of the group, if there is no central committee to kick it out? Perhaps more so than most chapters, Harrisonburg Food Not Bombs stretches the common traits that foster unity in the absence of centralization, hierarchy, or even regular communication between the chapters.

The Harrisonburg chapter serves its meals indoors, and we are not vegan — though there are always vegan options we usually have food with eggs or dairy (usually dumpstered) and we often serve donated meat dishes. Many of the people involved in the Harrisonburg chapter have been Food Not Bombs activists for years, several of us having been active with chapters in other cities, and we only broke with these two norms (outdoor meals and veganism) after years of doing it by the book. I would argue to any orthodox Food Not

Bombs die-hards that our two acts of deviance violate the form of Food Not Bombs, but uphold the underlying principles more effectively, given the particular local conditions we in Harrisonburg have to face.

Harrisonburg's homeless population is small enough that they do not congregate in parks; so by serving meals outside we were bringing them out into the elements, often in bad weather, when they would otherwise be indoors or in cars. Especially through the winter, we were faced with the choice of getting food to those who needed it by moving to an indoor location, or making a point about poverty by giving free food to college students. By moving indoors, we prioritized the needs of economically disadvantaged participants, and looked for other ways of making a point about poverty. Serving food in a comfortable location in a working-class neighborhood, we are working to destigmatize poverty and portray free food in a good light, accessible and enjoyable to the homeless, the working poor, and the middle-class alike.

The shift away from veganism was much more painful. The majority of lower-class participants strongly preferred us to provide non-vegan food, and several even used their food stamps to buy us meat to cook — a couple of these people stopped coming after vegan members of the group responded in an icy, exclusionary, or condescending way. Many participants appreciated our healthy food, but without any protein or fat it wasn't much of a meal. The lack of appetizing food and the major cultural barriers created by enforcing a vegan space on a mostly omnivorous population caused consistently low turnout from the very populations we were trying to provide with free food. Some activists insisted we couldn't be a Food Not Bombs if we weren't vegan (though they had not brought up the same orthodox objection to our move indoors), and they also refused to recognize that vegan food is not culturally neutral, or even constitutive of a meal to people from some cultural backgrounds. No one was suggesting that we stop serving vegan food. And by adding non-vegan food to our menu, we would not be supporting the meat industry, as any meat we served was not purchased, and would have ended up in the trash. In the end, we decided to allow for a menu catering to non-vegans as well as vegans, and a couple activists who wanted to preserve the vegan comfort zone stopped coming. On several occasions, additional people from the neighborhood have come to eat because of the availability of meat dishes, though our reputation for unsatisfying food will take time to overcome, especially given lingering difficulties making nourishing, appetizing meals with consistency (though this is more often the fault of limited resources than of the efforts of our group).

Because Food Not Bombs has no hierarchy or centralized administrative body, we changed our group in opposition to these founding principles without getting permission from any other chapter. I have a good deal of apprehension about how the often clique-ish Food Not Bombs milieu would respond to the unorthodoxy of the Harrisonburg chapter. At regional Food Not Bombs gatherings in the past I have brought up the deviance of the Harrisonburg chapter and the reasons for it, but nobody responded; I am not sure if this is because they were fine with it or they wanted to stifle discussion. In any case, the autonomy of Food Not Bombs chapters is meaningless if they are ostracized for adapting to local conditions. Flexibility and autonomy are necessary, but so is communication, to foster growth and coordination between far flung autonomous chapters. Decentralized networks such as Food Not Bombs need to develop means for communicating and discussing innovations, such as those developed and employed by the Harrisonburg chapter. Regional conferences, that give greater focus to group conversations structured to trade and evaluate skills and lessons, or help particular groups brainstorm solutions to their particular problems, would be invaluable. Magazines, newspapers, and other periodicals would also help encourage discourse, as well as recruit or educate those outside the movement. Recently, email listserves have come into limited use, though the medium does not encourage well thought-out analysis or the participation of the many people with limited computer and internet access and literacy.

The ideals that anarchists assert to be possible — horizontal organizing, mutual aid, and decentralization — are indeed. But these possibilities do not become realities without a great deal of work. In a capitalist system, it makes perfect sense that people are either used to slacking off and avoiding responsibility, or taking individualistic leadership roles and toiling like martyrs. To share power and responsibilities, consciously crafting horizontal organizing structures is as important as the informal activities that no structure will automatically guarantee — like holding ourselves and each other accountable with a healthy mix of compliments and criticisms. We also need to be conscious and deliberate in overcoming the barriers of race, class, and culture if we are to create meaningful networks of mutual aid, not just self-serving cliques. Finally, our necessary emphasis on decentralization and autonomy must be complemented by developing and perfecting anti-authoritarian methods for communicating and coordinating over large areas and large populations. Without this, local groups will stagnate, or remain at the mercy of the bureaucratic, elitist coalitions that currently exploit the grassroots and dominate large-scale organizing within the anti-war and anti-globalization movements, and other movements in which decentralized networks like Food Not Bombs could play an important role if they overcame certain habitual deficiencies.

Notes

"The Food Not Bombs Story," [internet] www.foodnotbombs.net/firstindex.html Viewed December 13, 2005.

Randy Borum, Chuck Tilby, "Anarchist Direct Actions: A Challenge for Law Enforcement." *Studies in Conflict and Terrorism*. No.28, 2005.

Education

In these two short essays, Stein and Ehrlich explore the various functions and forms of the intellectuals, academics, scholars, and anarchists, including the follies and failings in the performance of their roles. Both Stein and Ehrlich exhibit a strong belief in the capacities and duties of engaged intellectuals to help form a new society through the promotion of clear, reasoned thought.

Originally published in issue 29.

On Scholars, Intellectuals, and Anarchists
Howard J. Ehrlich

Years ago, in one of those moments I am not allowed to forget, I told a dear friend that I regarded her as anti-intellectual. I had confused "intellectualism" with the printed word. You see my friend seldom reads anything or, for that matter watch television or listen to the radio. She talks, she questions, she observes, she listens. Most of what she learns she learns interpersonally. She listens to new ideas, entertains conundrums, and is unafraid of complexity or ambiguity. In these behaviors she is an intellectual.

For some time, I thought of myself as a scholar. I did so mainly because the professors I was surrounded by were so superficial that I searched for a label that would set us apart. As I progressed through graduate school, I recognized my scholarly impulses, but I came to realize that I was transparently "an intellectual." I say transparently because even as I worked at service and blue collar jobs, I often was labeled as the "professor." It seemed that all I had to do was speak and people recognized that I had a different status.

An experience I had — and as a transparent intellectual most of it was in my head — brought home to me what being a scholar meant. For an anthropology course, I was searching for data about a (since forgotten) tribe that settled on the west bank of the upper Mississippi. In my search, I came upon a book review. The book was about the growth of Indian corn on the west bank from 1819 to 1845. (I confess that I no longer recall the exact dates.) I remember at the time feeling admiration for such scholarship. Imagine the work that must have gone into the research! And while I knew I was unlikely to write anything like that, deep down I actually thought that maybe some day I might. *The Rise of the Bagel in Brooklyn, 1900–1901* — I could hear my father, "For this you went to school all those years?" My father was not a scholar.

The reviewer was an obvious practitioner of what in those days we called "one-upmanship." Obviously he was himself a scholar, also expert on the growing of Indian corn on the west bank of the Mississippi, 1819–1845. He proceeded to reduce the book and the author to corn husks. I noted this to my anthropology professor who told me that these two men, the author and the reviewer, were the only two scholars of this recondite subject and that they hated each other. That image of two scholars living out their days uncovering more and more obscure information on a subject of such triviality and ripping each other's scholarly efforts apart, perhaps for their entire careers in academia, has never left me.

The scholar, I have come to understand, is dedicated to the specialized study of objects or events. S/he may do other things, though this is typically not so. The scholar's primary, and primarily obsessive concern is with their (usually narrow) domain of study. If you have never obsessed over getting the details for a footnote or to find a reference in an obscure out-of-print journal, you may not be able to regard the scholar with empathy. I have and I do.

Where do the scholar and the intellectual part? I believe that an intellectual is a person who likes to play with ideas. All ideas, any ideas: playing with ideas through discussion, observation, reading, writing are the intellectual's obsession. Discussion and the acquisition of knowledge are ends in themselves. There are three types of intellectuals — the monkeywrencher, the disengaged, the engaged.

The monkeywrencher, typically male, uses his intellectual skills in macho displays. He is the person who will invariably sabotage discussion by articulating counter-arguments to the consensus. Often his counter-arguments are directed at his own arguments. Discussion for him is a zero-sum game. It is winning that really counts. The content is of lesser significance. Such persons are typified by their willingness to work for or support any political regime. They commonly harbor the belief that since they are free to pursue their lives as intellectuals, they can get by. As one gay intellectual once told me during a discussion we were having about fascism, "I could survive in any political regime." Of course he couldn't, and his narcissism defies history. Most authoritarian regimes reject the role of intellectuals precisely because they can't be trusted. The monkeywrenchers are free riders trying to ride the political currents wherever they go.

The disengaged intellectual avoids politics and social issues. These are domains of ambiguity and often strong feelings. The disengaged intellectual is intolerant of ambiguity and is seldom a passionate actor. The disengaged live in a world of ideas populated by a small circle of significant others. They can be good sources of information and great foils for exploring or rehearsing arguments. They are not political allies. In temperament they are alienated from themselves, living in an alien nation.

The unique characteristic of the engaged intellectual is that of bringing passion to their intellectual concerns. Many engaged intellectuals are not political in the narrow sense of trying to change society, but they are "political" in their engagements in their personal sphere. The clinical psychologist who works to empower her clients, the art historian who does battle with the curators and critics over their interpretations, the teacher who drills students in critical thinking— these are people living passionately in a world of ideas.

The politically engaged intellectual can live anywhere on the political spectrum. They fall out in two distinct categories, the authoritarian and the antiauthoritarian. The authoritarians generally represent the dominant ideas or intellectual currents of the society. They tend to be conservative and are likely to identify themselves as part of an intellectual elite. As such, their role is to articulate the often inchoate ideas of the political elite. This is obviously not so for the anti-authoritarians. They are the voice of the opposition, and they see their role as that of undermining the legitimacy of the governing regime if not the idea of "government" itself. While the poet may express the soul of movements for change, the antiauthoritarian intellectuals are the map makers for the movement. They help people see where they have come from and they help to chart the course to a new society.

The Role of Anarchist Intellectuals
Jeff Stein

Before answering the question of the role of intellectuals, one needs to define the term "intellectual". The simplest definition would be to compare an intellectual to an athlete. An athlete is a person who engages in sports to a much higher degree than most people, whether or not one gets paid for it. There are amateur athletes just as there are highly paid professionals. An intellectual is someone who engages in intellectual activity, reading, researching, writing, editing, and discussing ideas, all to a much higher degree than most people, whether or not one gets paid for it. Thus I would include someone like the late Sam Dolgoff, a house painter by profession and author of numerous books and articles as an intellectual, although he never completed high school and never held a teaching position in any college or university. This is not to deny the value of formal schooling and intellectual training. One of the problems with self-education is that one's reading habits can reinforce one's prejudices, leading to dogmatism. Having a teacher, or a mentor, who introduces a one to a broad range of sources can help a person avoid these pitfalls. Dolgoff had the good fortune to be mentored by the exiled Russian anarchist, Gregory Maximoff.

What then is the proper role of intellectuals? Certainly it is not to control or dominate the anarchist movement, to make themselves the self-appointed "general staff". Intellectuals are subject to the same temptations as anyone else to put their own interests ahead of others. Just because one has read more, done more research, or is more articulate, does not make one more altruistic or objective, any more than being an athlete makes one a good sport or a non-biased referee (not to mention a "role model"). The appropriate role of intellectuals is to contribute according to their ability, to do what intellectuals do already: to research, write, debate and educate on behalf of the anarchist movement. To engage in anarchist intellectual activity is to help other anarchists discover what they need to know to build an anarchist movement, and eventually, help discover what we all need to know to create a more libertarian society.

So far what I have written should probably be obvious. A more difficult question would be, are anarchist intellectuals presently playing such a role? With a few notable exceptions, I would have to say that they are not. To be an intellectual means one must think rationally. The present anarchist movement does not place value on rationality or science. The tendency in our movement since the 1960s has been to equate rationalism with the horrors of modern warfare, police surveillance, and ecological destruction. One could argue just as well that all of these things are due to the irrationality of our social institutions, but this would quickly degenerate into a circular argument. If one uses rational methods for irrational ends, is it rationality or irrationality that is to blame? This misses the point that without some method for determining what is objectively true, it is impossible to choose between one person's opinion and that of another. In the absence of logic, effective democratic decision making becomes an impossible struggle between the prettiest face and the loudest voice. Anarchist intellectuals should be defending rationality and science, but with the present exceptions of people like Noam Chomsky and Murray Bookchin, they are not. Instead many anarchists quite seriously extol the virtues of ignorance and superstition, which have the advantage of being low tech.

Another failure of our anarchist intellectuals has been not to rise above the latest fads of both the capitalist media, and of the so-called Left, and expose them. I grimace each time I read an anarchist article that speaks of "post-modern" or "post-industrial society". How can a society be more "modern" than modern, more new than now? It is like an ad for laundry detergent which claims to make your bed sheets "whiter than white". As for "post-industrial", have we all stopped using manufactured goods, regardless of who makes them? If we now live in a "post-industrial society" shouldn't all our environmental problems have been solved instead of getting worse? Rather than mimic the capitalist media (whose real objective seems to be for us to accept that declining living standards for workers are inevitable), our anarchist intellectuals should collect facts and figures, and determine what is really happening to industry and to workers. That is what Kropotkin did a century ago, but where are our "Kropotkins" now?

Our intellectuals have failed in their greatest task, encouraging people to think clearly. I remember my own experience as a young anarchist, when I met Sam Dolgoff. I had recently graduated from a large university with a Bachelor of Science degree, but like many anarchists of that time and now, I was heavily influenced by the latest political fads. I had fallen into the common misconception that to be "radical" is to be "extreme", to be "revolutionary" is to believe the most unsubstantiated conspiracy theories and wildest speculations. It took only a few minutes for this true anarchist intellectual, who never graduated from high school, to demolish all my arguments and show my mistakes. What Dolgoff showed me was that the intellectual training I had received was not all bourgeois nonsense, but a valuable tool which could help me solve problems and find my own answers.

Is the growing presence of anarchist academics on university faculties a success to be celebrated? Jeff Shantz supports this development while urging us to proceed with caution, noting academia's tendency to take ideas away from the people whose struggles inspired them and isolate them into inaccessible, impracticable theories. While occupying space in the academy is important, Shantz warns against the assumption that it will be enough to alter institutions towards an anarchist path, and while some are theorizing, the work of organizing continues.

Originally published in issue 41.

Anarchists in the Academy
Concerns and Cautions
Jeff Shantz

narchist academic David Graeber devotes the first section of his book *Fragments of an Anarchist Anthropology* to his attempt to answer the question, "Why are there so few anarchists in the academy?" For Graeber, this is a pressing question, given the veritable explosion of anarchist theory and lively debates over anarchism outside of the academy, especially within the numerous social movements which have emerged recently. Despite the blossoming of anarchist thought and practice, David Graeber is perplexed that this flowering of anarchism has found little reflection in the academy. Graeber seems to long for the type of success that Marxists have enjoyed in their move into the academy following the rise of Marxist theory among the students of the New Left. As he notes in his disappointed comparison of anarchist successes with those of the Marxists: "In the United States there are thousands of academic Marxists of one sort or another, but hardly a dozen scholars willing openly to call themselves anarchists" (2004: 2). In his view this is something that should be a cause of concern for anarchists.

Yet it would seem that Graeber's fears are quite unfounded. A glance across the academic landscape shows that in less than a decade, since Seattle in 1999, there has been substantial growth in the numbers of people in academic positions who identify as anarchists. Indeed, it is probably safe to say that unlike any other time in history, the last ten years have seen anarchists carve out spaces in the halls of academia. This is especially true in terms of people pursuing graduate studies and those who have become members of faculty. Several anarchists have taken up positions in prominent, even so-called elite, universities, including Richard Day at Queen's University in Canada, Ruth Kinna at Loughsborough University in England, Jesse Cohn at Purdue University and, for a time, David Graeber at Yale. Indeed the Politics Department at Loughsborough has actively recruited graduate students for a program of study that focuses specifically on anarchism. The flourishing of anarchism in the academy is also reflected in other key markers of professional academic activity. These include: academic articles focusing on varying aspects of anarchist theory and practice; the publication of numerous books on anarchism by most of the major academic presses; and growing numbers of courses dealing in some way with anarchism or including anarchism within the course content. There have also emerged, perhaps ironically enough, professionally recognized associations and networks of anarchist researchers, such as the Anarchist Studies Network of the Political Science Association in Britain. Suddenly it's almost hip to be an anarchist academic.

At one time, not so long ago in fact, this would have been a curious situation for anarchists to find themselves in. There was once among anarchists a rather healthy suspicion of the academy as an elitist institution fully bound up with the reproduction and extension of power structures within capitalist societies. Yet the growing enthusiasm among some anarchists over their newfound acceptance within the academy, and the encouragement this gives growing numbers of anarchists to consider academic programs, has not been matched by critical reflection on the limitations of a turn to the academy by anarchists. This piece offers the beginnings of such a reflection and raises certain cautions.

I should be clear that I am in no way criticizing individual anarchists for choosing to pursue academic work. I am certainly not suggesting that anarchists stay out of school or leave the academy in the manner of earlier generations of socialists who abandoned universities to take up industrial work. For sure the more places in which anarchist thought might develop and flourish the better. The advances made by neo-conservative academics in shifting economic and social policies, providing the intellectual capital for neo-liberal capitalism and imperialism, while making post-secondary education even less accessible for working class students, shows what can happen when we abandon or are defeated in any field of struggle.

At the same time it is important to contextualize anarchist academic activity in relationship to other types of anarchist activities. If anarchists are to be effective in waging struggles in the academy, and even more importantly, if academic anarchism is to contribute anything to struggles outside the academy, then we need a clear discussion of the matter, one which does not tilt towards uncritical celebration or an envious longing for something we could as well do without. I write this as someone from a blue collar background, the first in my extended family to go to university, who has also spent perhaps way too much time in school, so I've seen the view from multiple perspectives.

Academic Anarchy?

David Graeber describes his recent work *Fragments of an Anarchist Anthropology* as "a series of thoughts, sketches of potential theories, and tiny manifestos — all meant to offer a glimpse at the outline of a body of radical theory that does not actually exist, though it might possibly exist at some point in the future" (2004: 1). The theory, the non-existence of which is of such concern to Graeber, is, primarily, an anarchist current within academic anthropology. I say primarily because Graeber also asks similarly why there is no anarchist sociology, anarchist economics, anarchist literary theory or anarchist political science. In posing these questions, and in failing to acknowledge that on some level anarchist versions of each of these "disciplines" do in fact exist, Graeber betrays what is really at the root of his concern. That is the existence of academic or professional versions of anarchist thought in these areas and the acceptance of anarchist theories within established academic disciplines and institutions.

Indeed in asking the question, "why is there no anarchist sociology?" Graeber entirely overlooks the significant sociological works of people like Colin Ward, Paul Goodman and John Griffin, to name only a few. One could make the same point in identifying significant contributors to an anarchist economics, such as Tom Wetzel and Larry Gambone. Notably, these writers, while extremely important in the development of contemporary anarchist thought and influential within anarchist circles, occupy only marginal places, if any, in academic sociology or economics circles. So the problem is not so much the existence of anarchist sociology, but its recognition, acceptance and legitimation among academics or professional sociologists. Curiously, Graeber even overlooks the contributions of anarchist sociologists who have succeeded in bringing anarchist theory into the academy such as Lawrence Tifft and Jeff Ferrell, again, to name only a few.

The case is the same when one returns to anthropology. Graeber (2004: 38) claims that "an anarchist anthropology doesn't really exist" and then sets it as his task to lay the groundwork for just such a body of theory and practice. Yet to make this claim, and even more to set himself up as the person to correct the situation, Graeber does a disservice to people like Harold Barclay who have been working tirelessly for decades to establish an anarchist anthropology within accepted academic circles. Curiously, Barclay is a name that appears nowhere in Graeber's writings.

At this point, however, I would point out, in light of Graeber's desire to see anarchism recognized within the academy, that many anarchists have been quite good at developing analyses that go beyond mainstream social science. Indeed, such has been the invaluable work contributed by what I call constructive anarchist *theorists* from Gustav Landauer to Paul Goodman to Colin Ward. Again, the problem has not been the absence of anarchist theory or theorists, low or high, but rather the acceptance of those theories and theorists within the academy. This is what concerns Graeber deeply, but I have to ask whether such a concern might be overemphasized, if not misplaced.

"Academonization:" Knowledge Becomes Technology

Of course to advocate unproblematically the move of anarchist theory into the academy is to present an uncritical rendering of the perils and processes involved in academic knowledge production. Beth Hartung, in a much earlier, and less optimistic account of the engagement of anarchy with the academy, sounded this cautious note: "Once a theory is taken from the streets or factories and into the academy, there is the risk that revolutionary potential will be subverted to scholarship…; in other words, knowledge becomes technology" (Hartung, 1983: 88). As Murray Bookchin (1978: 16) has similarly argued, academic works often subject social movement perspectives and practices, as in anarchism, to a reformulation in "highly formalized and abstract terms." Almost thirty years after Bookchin's observation, it seems that the recent academic works on anarchism, produced by self-identified anarchists such as Newman and Day, have indeed continued this practice of making anarchist thought conform to the style and substance of the academic discourse of the day.

Even with graduate training in social theory and familiarity with the language used in such texts, I find these works to be rather inaccessible. They are texts directed primarily at other academics, addressing issues almost exclusively of concern to academics in a specialized language that is most familiar to academics. Such approaches contradict the anti-vanguardist commitment shared by most anarchists.

Some try to excuse this use of language by arguing that the complexity of ideas being addressed requires a complex language, beyond the grammar of more down-to-earth expressions. While this might be a fine position for mainstream academics, I think that anarchists have to work harder to break the exclusivity of academic discourses.

Approaching the Academy: Not Another "Long March through the Institutions"

For anarchists, as Graeber (2004) points out, the role of intellectuals is in no way the formation of an elite that attempts correct political lines or analyses by which to lead the masses. Graeber (2004) suggests that academia might benefit from an engagement with anarchist approaches to knowledge production and sharing. Such an engagement would, in his view, allow social theory to be refashioned along the lines of direct democratic practice. Such an approach, drawing on the actual practice of the newest social movements, would encourage a move beyond the medieval practices of the university, which sees "radical" thinkers "doing intellectual battle at conferences in expensive hotels, and trying to pretend all this somehow furthers revolution" (Graeber, 2004: 7). An approach taken from social movements, beyond its rejection of "winner take all" attempts at conversion, might also allow for a move beyond a "great thinkers" approach to knowledge.

Yet I'm not convinced that anarchists' energies are best spent in trying to reform the academy in this way. The real problem is the existence of a hierarchical and inegalitarian social structure that separates and elevates knowledge production in such a way as to reproduce the existence of universities as exclusive and privileged institutions. Over the last two decades, largely through the hard work of feminist and anti-racist researchers, there has been a move to more participatory and community-based research. This has certainly been an improvement over the days of grand theory, conjured in an armchair, and the social science of surveys, statistics and social subjects. At the same time, all of this new research, no matter how "community-based," still takes place within, and is conditioned by its existence within, an authoritarian and unequal political economy of knowledge production. The presence of a hundred or a thousand more anarchist professors within the hallowed halls is not going to change this much more than the presence of a few thousands Marxist academics has over several decades. This approach, what an earlier generation of radical academics referred to as the "long march through the institutions" has been revealed as rather a failed strategy.

My concern is that rather than tearing down the walls between town and gown, head and hand, academic and amateur, the move of anarchists into the academy may simply reproduce, reinforce, and even legitimize the political and economic structures of the academy. It definitely lends a certain shine to the claims of those conservative academics who like to crow about academic freedom and the openness of the neo-liberal university. "Look, we don't exclude anyone. We even allow anarchists a place at the table."

More than this, of course, is what happens when anarchists, through the "publish or perish" pressures of promotion and the pursuit of tenure, begin to mold anarchism to fit the language and expectations of academic knowledge production rather than the other way around. This has been one of the fatal flaws of academic Marxism. Taking a language of the people, born of their struggles and aspirations, and turning it into something distant, abstract and inaccessible to the people, who have now been turned into little more than passive subjects of study or "social indicators" where they appear at all. Much of academic Marxism has become yet another variant of grand theory, something of a parlor game, exciting for its ideas perhaps, but of little social concern. Could the same not happen to anarchism? Some critics of the academically inspired "post-anarchism," which has tried to meld anarchist theory with the esoteric philosophies of post-structuralism, might suggest it is already happening.

There is certainly something of value in drawing upon the works of social science, for example, to inform anarchist thought. Even mainstream social science can provide important information and analysis that might aid anarchists in examining, understanding, critiquing and changing society. The works of anarchists from Kropotkin and Reclus to Paul Goodman and Colin Ward have shown the beneficial aspects for anarchist theoretical development of an informed engagement with academic research. Similarly, there have been a number of amazing works provided by historians providing insights on anarchist movements that might otherwise have been lost to time. For sure the works of historians have made the greatest and longest term contributions to anarchist movements recently.

Conclusion

Overall, the emphasis should remain on using the academic work to inform and enrich anarchist analysis rather than using anarchist analysis to bolster academic disciplines or theoretical positions that have little connection with people's lives. In terms of social theory, I would suggest that the work done by theorists such as Paul Goodman, Colin Ward, Murray Bookchin and Howard Ehrlich, people who may have been trained in universities but who have consistently offered complex analyses in engaging and accessible terms, offer more for anarchist movements "on the ground." This is the case both in terms of the applicability of their analyses and in terms of the issues and concerns to which they devote their attention.

The primary orientation of anarchist academics must remain the anarchist movements actively involved in struggles against capitalism and the state. In some senses, anarchist academics are subsidized by the movement activists who are doing the day to day work of building movements while the academics are pursuing their own, often very personal, interests. Anarchist academics need to recognize that while they're doing academic work, much of which is involved in "departmental work" or "professional development" which contributes little to social struggles, someone else is taking care of the organizing work (that they may be theorizing or analyzing). This is not to say that anarchist academics are not able to contribute to organizing at the same time as getting their work done; it's more a call to remember the division of labor.

I want to point out that I am in no way criticizing those anarchists who have taken work as professors for their choice of employment. Arguments that this represents some sort of sellout or compromise are ridiculous. There are worse jobs under capitalism — trust me I've had them — and there's no shame in taking a job that offers good pay, benefits and generally decent working conditions. As long as one does not become an academic boss with teaching and research assistants working for you, of course. My concern, rather, is the extent to which creating a space within the academy is taken as a priority for anarchist organizing, when active and thoughtful anarchists might put such time into activities that take place in less exclusive contexts.

References

Bookchin, Murray. 1978. "Beyond Neo-Marxism." *Telos.* 36: 5–28

Graeber, David. 2004. *Fragments of an Anarchist Anthropology.* Chicago: Prickly Paradigm Press

Hartung, Beth. 1983. "Anarchism and the Problem of Order." *Mid-American Review of Sociology.* 8(1): 83–101

Kingsley Widmer was one of the most prolific contributors to the magazine. His essays were almost always a blend of the personal and the political. He railed against authority, hypocrisy and the vapidity of the elites. In this essay, quite typical of his approach to education, he begins with a diatribe against the mundanity of Creative Writing, proceeds to an analysis of three major critics of the current state of education, and concludes that—at best—the very scale and format of the university needs to change.

Originally published in issue 14.

Anarchist in Academe
Notes from the Contemporary University
Kingsley Widmer

Most current American universities, of course, are hardly appropriate places for anarchists. For among the obvious criteria for libertarianism of almost every shade would be opposition to hierarchy, to large bureaucratic organization, to direct service of the state, to exploitative corporate subservience, to systematic mediocrity, to elaborate inequalities and controls, among other abuses. The university, middling or massive, public or quasi-private, fancy or ordinary, is undeniably all of these anti-libertarian things. And considerably more. An anarchist who endures in such institutions must be defined as not a little of a social-moral hypocrite. *Mea culpa.*

But, if I can self-indulgently assume that my corruption of character is not unique, there may be several other issues of possibly larger interest from an anarchist perspective. (It is not my purpose here to make an apologia for nearly for decades of trailing, however iconoclastically, through a dozen academic institutions out of whatever mixture of naivete, incompetent greed, and other-than-anarchist social and intellectual motives.) That there are some anarchists in universities (including a considerably number of contributors to *Social Anarchism*) may be related not only to our corruption but to the expansive muddle of universities (rather more than their thin tolerance). It also usually requires considerable professional costuming. A now fully dead dean: "You're an anarchist! If you weren't such an energetic teacher an much-published scholar…. Why don't you go someplace else where they appreciate your sort?" — but he never explained, nor has anyone else, where that libertarian someplace may be found. The costuming takes its toll, and not just in the nastily cliquish and obscurantist-styled academic neo-Marxists. (I have never heard of any institution eagerly tenuring an anarchist, though there is a current more-liberal-than-thou fashion for doing so in several fields with the more pretentious Marxists.)

In considering how the academic undermines libertarian sensibility, it might be helpful to remind ourselves of some of the things the contemporary university is about, as well as not about to allow. Start with the obvious bureaucratization. The petty corruption is pervasive. Clinging-the-greasy-pole (to use an old definition of hierarchical careerism), the pursuit of positions, tenure, rank, prestige, and assorted paltry goodies, permanently bends most backs. And puckers most mouths.

But I assume that everyone knows such institutional corruption is standard stuff all over our society. There are, of course, earnest, decent, concerned people not altogether crippled by assuming the academic position. But the majority pretty much behave as would be expected in such structures. The character deformations from competitive hierarchy, however, are not the whole story, even for that minority (say, one out of ten, at generous most) who have some intellectual engagement and quality. The problem also must include that the academician is a "professional" (generally taken as an accolade), a prostitute inclined to proneness. And what (to use a no-longer fashionable phrase) has one sold out to? Often simply to institutionalization, that is, endless processing. But that processing expresses one of the more extreme styles of the division of labor — division of thinking — that fundamental source of hierarchical sensibility and its falsities.

With much reason, considerable libertarian theory sees professional specialization as a root distortion of human equality and fullness. One ends up thinking, and acting, in terms of specialisms and their pyramidal structures. Consider a not usually sited academic example, the frequently sleazy and anti-intellectual supposed subject euphemistically called "Creative Writing." It is not a major, and increasingly expansive, subdivision of English (usually the largest custodial unit of the humanities area, a main packaging for what remains of the traditional cultural role of the university). One of uncreative writing's specialties is "narrative prose." That is often subdivided into courses in "short narrative prose" and "long narrative prose," which, of course, are further specialized into introductory, intermediate, advanced and graduate levels (the last also further repetitiously divided into different levels, mostly numberings). In practice, there are also alternative versions of, say, short narrative prose to reflect various personality and ideological conflicts. (One often really looks to order courses and fill hiring slots at that level.) Creative Writing becomes not only its own competitive bureaucracy but its own cliques, publications, aggrandizements, and hermetic styles of bad prose. Al that, however, is rather separate from other teaching of "prose writing," as in the "Composition" or "Rhetoric" program (usually with its own director, policy committee, regulations, courses, progression, recruiting, etc.). Its subdivisions include the officially remedial (though sometimes that is organized into a separate "remediation" program or department for patently inappropriate students). And compositions for the beginning, the intermediate, the advanced, plus further specialties, such as composition courses for majors, for non-majors, for technical writers, for would-be teachers, for advanced remediation (for would-be graduates who have failed a how-level writing competency test), for graduate courses (such as Advanced Rhetorical Theory) for those who would teach those already composition teachers to teach composition, and so on. Like Topsy, it just grows and grows — but overdevelopment is the American way, in academia as well as other suburbia. (I recently taught an authorized "experimental" course, partly to teach literature teachers to teach appropriate composition to literature classes, paralleling efforts to teach composition teachers to teach literature to composition classes, little of either being standard.) One accelerating absurdity in both Composition and Creative Writing is to separate intellectual reading from writing, as part of the very specialization. That results even at best in a semi-literacy with little content. The general lunacy takes on piquancy when an administrator most responsible for the local proliferation solemnly assures me, "I'm not at all the bureaucratic sort." Just a usual academic.

Surely people do not take this seriously, literally? Not altogether, for the same specialist in rhetoric (by definition, usually one with little literary or other intellectual engagement) is expected to teach several types and levels of composition (depending on the various manipulations of numbers), though not the ostensibly quite different "creative" parallels (as if they were somehow a different language, culture and intelligence), and vice versa. And a good bit of earnest time and effort is spent in developing and redeveloping such programs, and myopically attempting to work within them. The other results include, as is well known, increased problems of literacy, cultural and social as well as literal writing. In this ornate, multi-leveled, however muddled, fucking-over of semi-literacy, few come out writing well, and even fewer with much critical perception of the culture and society in which they live.

The bureaucratic proliferation of the divisions of writing is something more than institutional dressing. It reflects, and encourages, the fracturing of the awareness and thinking which is much of what writing is truly about. The dehumanization of writing into denatured specialisms and skill levels and hierarchies of ordering becomes a cast of mind. We can see such fracturing even in the more intellectually open theorizing about "composition" (such as that of the noted an influential Robert Scholes, author of *Textual Power*). Composition even around literature becomes a complex hierarchy of levels in which one has to, with appropriate reductiveness, move gradually through "textuality" into "context" and then fearsome "interpretation" and only with trepidation toward "criticism." More bluntly put, fuller meanings and judgments and purposes about reading-writing can only be reached for at the end of a labyrinthine classroom trail up the pyramidal expertise. Even at best (and I will grant that Scholes is arguably better than many) that result seems to be an institutional stroking to culminate in intellectual coitus interruptus. More often, no cultural and social hard-on is even allowed. The resulting composition and thinking is mostly flaccid and impotent, which must be considerably the real purpose of academic writing programs.

One doesn't have to be a radical libertarian to conclude that the proliferation of academic writing programs under the aegis of skittish if not castrated theorizing produce little good writing, or much else other than the expansive professional bureaucracy. So earnest/ambition academics come up with yet another supposed system for teaching composition, or more "creative" alternatives, or redundant committees and programs for "Writing Across the Curriculum" (to pretend to get it where it actually belongs), or workshops and conferences for indoctrinating the lower orders in how they should better prepare high school students, or elementary pupils, or nursery school charges — no doubt genetic engineering in creative prose is next. The reformist endless regress. Probably such pseudo-subjects as Composition and Creative Writing — about what? — should not be in universities. Though most know that, they are unwilling to admit the simply obvious: The state of public prose is indeed bad; academicizing it does not much improve it; hence, abolish all academic writing programs, courses, orderings. In good old anarchist terms: Down with the state of English.

Quite probably the more genuine kinds of writing would improve, following more directly their own purposes. Official, commercial, professional writing might not. Good. Let literacy or its substitutions more closely express their real functions. Encourage political prose to follow its lying bent, and the decent to reject it. The styles of advertising are mostly false and glitzy? Of course. Don't disguise them with the normative niceness taught by we English teachers. Professionals, from utility technocrats to literary theorists, go in for a prose of pretentious obscurantism? They should, and we should contemptuously ignore them. The attempt to impose a hierarchy of prose manners is mostly more counterfeit social reality. Basically, official academic writing efforts aim to coat on a normative semi-literacy. It should be resisted by both the illiterate and the truly literate.

I don't mean to suggest that "composition" and its frosted-up parallel, "creative writing" — probably the single largest university "liberal arts" area, however paltry in subject matter, intellectual engagement, or other literate purpose — provide the nastiest absurdities. That might plausibly be reserved for the more eye-on-the-paper-bill professional criminalities of, say, such booming academic fields as Entrepreneurship, Recreation, Real Estate Management, Communications, Athletics, Education, and the like. To pretend to teach the composition of would-be "creative prose" in such a context may seem slightly more decent, even with forlorn iconoclastic and subversive possibilities (every composition program has a few radical-in-spirit sorts), and hence more "real."

But is it really? The current common wisdom is that universities have lost even minimal cultural literacy. That is, again, from all sorts of perspectives, not just the libertarian. I have at hand three recent (1987) touted books about intellectual literacy by academics attempting to reach beyond mere professionalism: Alan Bloom, *The Closing of the American Mind*, E.D. Hirsch, Jr., *Cultural Literacy: What Every American Needs to Know*; and Russell Jacoby, *The Last Intellectuals: American Culture in the Age of Academe*. I give them in a kind of ascending political order: neoconservative (Bloom), quasi-liberal (Hirsch) and leftish (Jacoby). That is also in declining order of popularity: Bloom's reactionary nastiness has been a longtime bestseller: Hirsch's bland reformist simplicities have had a shorter hyped run; and Jacoby's arch radicalish analyses seem to be rather marginal in the marketplace. But that itself may suggest a paradigm of the market pathology of intellectual life in contemporary America.

On a natural libertarian bias of reverse order (let the last be first), my brief responses start with *The Last Intellectuals*. Its theme is the "impoverishment of public culture" in the current generation, a good part of which must be blamed on academicization and its "excessive professionalism." In a sophisticatedly knowledgeable way, and in a hard-edged understated style (much the best of the three), Jacoby surveys the past and present generational scenes treed with American intellectual critics. The forefront of past, broadly critical writers of all shades — H.L. Mencken, Edmund Wilson, Lewis Mumford, Dwight Macdonald, Paul Goodman, I.F. Stone, and others — have no adequate counterparts in the present. Just professors mostly writing for professors, in proper specialist style and narrowness. New Left dissidents of the 1960s professionalized and "became radical sociologists, Marxists historians, feminist theorists, but not quite public intellectuals." The reasons, he grants, are not solely academicization. The vociferous neoconservative takeover of intellectual organs and fashions, the showbiz debasement of mass media, the specialist fragmentation of even the broad culture (whether for buffs of computers, environments, rock music, guns, causes, or other sports), leave no common audience or commonly effective criticism. Even the ones we have are "celebrated intellectuals whose status is often due more to luck and friends than to intrinsic talents." Patently.

But the academicization is crucial, Jacoby holds, in undercutting the breadth, style, and critical spirit. His examples include the neo-Marxists theoreticians of *Telos*, whose ineffectiveness over several decades illustrate that the philosophy "profession is armed against critical inquiry." However, he has the detachment to also rightly skewer (though from an oblique angle) one of the more pretentious obscurantists of neo-Marxist literary theory and its academic gamesmanship (Fredric Jameson) who "exemplifies the failings of a new academic Marxism" in its social obtuseness as well as bad style. He accords rather positive treatment to his two avowed anarchist examples, Noam Chomsky and Murray Bookchin (though both belong to an older generation than hi these calls for, and neither is an academic professional in social criticism). However, the majority of his examples come from the professional social sciences (he quite abstains from most aesthetic areas), never much known for other than obtuseness in style, intelligence, and critical function. In sum, the younger radical intellectuals, in their march through the institutions, which are of course dominated by conservatives, show that "the institutions are winning."

Since I never thought (or much experienced) otherwise, nor have any of my radical friends, I am puzzled as to whom or at what the argument is addressed — at the smugness of some young would-be radical academic intellectuals? While it is nice to have some of Jacoby's informed and acute observations, it is hardly adequate critique of the academic, and certainly not sufficient footing to take off against exploitative American culture and its considerably contemptible intellectuals. The mild hatcheting is mostly academic in several sense, but at least carries some larger critical spirit.

That is only ostensibly so with Hirsch's *Cultural Literacy*. What "every American should know" is an incoherent mishmash of identifications of historical, literary, scientific, artistic, political, etc., figures, events, and notions, culminating in a silly sixty-page list. A kind of earnest super-trivia game given academic sanction. Sort of liberal — it goes out of the way to make qualifications for minorities, etc. — it also even lists rock stars and bits of mildly dissident culture, trying to include every mainstream professorial-acknowledged canon in the pretense of a common culture. It has one belabored commonsense premise: what is taught in schooling should have some more substantial subject matter and consensual reference. Sure.

But it doesn't much probe how to get rid of the majority of administrators, teachers, and purposes of the schools nor of the universities, nor of the showbiz media, nor of the other institutions whose styles and ends demand a rather different sort of cultural consent. There are considerable purposes of subservience served by American anti-intellectualism and cultural debasement. The fallacies of misplaced concreteness — confusing intellectual engagement and critical spirit with names, events, and denatured concepts — is, of course, mostly just the old pedantry updated. Shaping up the curriculum a bit with these terms seems not only paltry but an irrelevant critical response to the cultural malaise.

That something has gone grievously wrong with the higher hired learning seems insistent in quite different views, as with Alan Bloom's tract slogan: "How American Higher Education Has Failed Democracy and Impoverished the Souls of Today's Students." Bloom's own impoverishment includes a style mixing the trite ("feet of clay," "two birds with one stone," etc., and many of his details and laments) with pretentiousness (misused passages from Plato, Flaubert, Tolstoy, Nietzsche, and others). But grant him the courage of his confusions in expressing high dudgeon against feminism (women's nature is really against easy sex and for staying home nurturing children), the loss of traditional orderings ("deformity of the spirit, in the students....whose parents are divorced"), sexual popular music (as if it had not been so from jazz through swing to rock for three generations), radicalism (the penultimate chapter indignantly focuses on a minor student disruption of the sixties which paid no attention to Bloomism), and on the "relativism" and "nihilism" of radical intellectuals which encouraged all this. Reverse compliment — I had not thought we had been so successful!

And we probably haven't, given the popularity of Bloom's closed mind. Of course this self-caricature of the resentful, traditional-humanistic academic in the elitist university does not represent the whole enterprise. He even has some condescending kindness for we lesser sorts: "Teachers of writing in state universities, among the noblest and most despised laborers in the academy, have told me that cannot teach writing to students who do not read, and that it is practically impossible to get them to read, let alone like it." The condition is true but he blames it on "the sixties and...the pallor of university-level humanities." That is dumb about the larger conditions of the culture, which is not, contrary to arrogant professors, just the creation of universities. But not matter, for he concludes that we common cultural laborers "have all but disappeared."

Perhaps we should have if we had the quaint priestly bigotries of Bloomism, and his pomposity, and his dedication above all, he concludes, to the "teaching of moderation and resignation." If that is what he got from twisting the Great Books (his near-exclusive definition of serious teaching), then it is just as well to forgo that mind-closing and life-impoverishing tradition.

I came out of that tradition, and teach and write around many of the books Bloom misreads (though I long ago moved away from the parochial and piously retarded definitions of the canon, as have most of my better colleagues, and realized that our critical and other intellectual purposes could be well served by a variety of materials). But on the next (and final) page Bloom has a much larger claim, without the resigned moderation he imposes on students: "Just as in politics the responsibility for the fate of freedom in the world had devolved upon our regime, so the fate of philosophy in the world has devolved upon our universities, and the two are related as they have never been before." Academic imperialism. Certainly in its arrogant resignation to what is, and its lack of larger critical response to a dubious sociopolitical order, it makes no case for the academic intellectual except as a symptom of political as well as cultural pathology.

My starting point was *not* to suggest the total abolition of the universities (after all, I have, in however oppositional ways, imbedded my life for nearly two generations in them), but, given the justified mockeries of Jacoby, the earnest trivialization of Hirsch, and the vicious identifications of Bloom, I am not so sure. If these three different current views represent a fair span, then there is very little to be said for the current reign in America of academe.

Universities are horrendously overblown, not only as individual bureaucracies for low-level processing but as cultural and social institutions. The majority of academicians (as Richard Mandell argued a decade ago in *The Professor Game*) "are under worked and overpaid." The society is paying a disproportionate price for a few small intellectual potatoes in a rotting hill.

Obvious logic: To the degree that academicians can teach, they can also misteach. Learning is not a one-ways street. And we misteach millions of inappropriate students the low arts of semi-literacy, trivialization, and uncritical spirit. That dominating vocation tends to denature the few things, the humanities and sciences, that the universities might be able to do well. As for the rest, from semi-pro sports to cultured marketing, from reinventing hierarchical sleaze to reblooming the ancient pomposity of resignation, from dull poets to deadly technocrats, bury them. Long live the university....

But let me conclude with a constructive note. With far more authentic moderation then that announced by the likes of Bloom, we might consider alternatives. I am assuming that the appropriate libertarian attitude toward the universities — after all, we don't pretend to determine such institutions (or, like some presumptuous power-ploy neo-Marxists, take them over) — might be to hold that they should be scaled down in most every way. Meaning not only drastically smaller in size and claims but in their roles in the society which they largely replicate. (But my friends who want to see them as intellectual refuges, sexy monasteries, for a saving remnant are probably being too optimistic.) For those who hold to the contrary, a modest proposal also: Simply rename every American city over one million The University of _____ (Mayor as Chancellor, Big Developers as Deans, everyone else as Student, except for the socially and culturally literate who would be labeled Anarchist and ordered out of town). While it might be hard to notice much difference, it should be more thorough, fair, appropriate, and properly academic in the contemporary sense.

Should one disengage from the institutions involved in the promotion and maintenance of capitalism, or try to change them from within? Applying this frequently asked question to academia, Brian Martin acknowledges the rationale behind both approaches, then argues ultimately for active partnership and collaboration between activists and academics. While he acknowledges that there is no easy formula for developing these "collective strategies," he urges us to focus our attention towards building them.

Originally published in issue 14.

What Should Be Done About Higher Education?
Brian Martin

A friend of mine recently completed his Ph.D. He prefers to remain anonymous; I'll call him Fred. Fred's thesis was a study of capitalism in a particular industry, based in part on interviews with workers. In a rare integration of theory and practice, Fred circulated the texts of the interviews to the workers themselves, in acknowledgment of their role in the production of knowledge. This may also help them to understand better their relation to their bosses.

Fred plans to prepare a more accessible book out of his thesis. It will provide valuable, if rather unpalatable, lessons to social activists. If they will read it, they will learn how industry has turned its workers into its supporters against outside activists, instead of workers and activists uniting against the owners.

On completion of his thesis, Fred exited from academia. He believes in the "reuniting of practical and theoretical consciousness" which is virtually impossible in universities with their intellectual division of labor. He has chosen to work for community organizations, aiming to empower oppressed groups.

Does this sound like an anarchist? Perhaps, but Fred acts on the basis of a highly developed Marxist, nonanarchist theory of society.

On the other hand, two other friends of mine, Val Plumwood and Richard Sylvan (formerly Val and Richard Routley), are two of the most prominent and prolific anarchist theorists in Australia. Each holds an academic position. They have produced numerous scholarly papers as well as activists writings for many years.

I present these examples to illustrate that there is no automatic connection between anarchist beliefs and action in relation to higher education. What should be done about higher education? On the one hand there is the argument for "deinstitutionalization." The idea here is that higher education is part of the problem. It provides training and research results to the state, military, big corporations and professions. It reproduces the class structure by providing credentials to children of the upper and middle classes. In its own structure it incorporates hierarchy, patriarchy and elitism. Following the lead of Ivan Illich, the solution should not be to reform formal education but to get rid of the need for it altogether. Learning and research would instead be integrated into the life of the community. The way to achieve this is by building up alternative forms of learning and research outside the ossified bureaucracies of educational institutions. Another argument accepts this picture but reaches a different conclusion. Yes, the goal should be learning controlled by learners and teachers outside the large credentialing bodies. But this is a long term goal. In the meantime there is much that can be done from the inside of academia. Seldom are activist workers, such as members of the IWW, criticized because they work for a capitalist firm, even if their aim is to transform these firms into self-managed operations. Likewise, it makes little sense to advocate a mass exit from academia, so long as some activists do useful things there, either as part of their job or in their spare time. I doubt Noam Chomsky would become more effective in promoting anarchism were he to resign from MIT.

I think both of these arguments have merit. There is no single best path for everyone.

What I plan to do here is outline some of the strategies for action concerning higher education, and point out their strengths and weaknesses. Before doing that, I list some of the problems with academia. These are likely to be familiar, which is why I can be brief.

The Problems

From the point of view of the classical ideals of higher education, which can be summarized by the phrase "the pursuit of truth," the failings of modern higher education are many.

- Knowledge is treated as a commodity, passively accepted and absorbed by student consumers.
- Classroom experience is organized around the premise that learning results only from being taught by experts.
- Knowledge is divided into narrow disciplinary boxes.
- Original, unorthodox thoughts by students, and nonconventional choices of subjects and learning methods, are strongly discouraged.
- Competition prevails over cooperation.
- Knowledge and learning are either divorced from social problems or channeled into professional approaches.
- Credentials, the supposed symbols of learning, are sought more than learning itself.
- Performance in research has precedence over commitment to teaching.

- Most research is narrow, uninspired and mediocre, useful only to other experts or vested interests.
- Scholarly openness and cooperation take second place to the academic rat race and power struggle, which involves toadying, back stabbing, aggrandizement of resources and suppression of dissidents.
- Original or unconventional thoughts by staff, or action on social issues, are penalized, while narrow conformist thought and action are rewarded.

Thorstein Veblen in 1918 argued that universities in the United States are controlled by or subservient to business interests. Business influence has a thoroughgoing impact on the staff hired, the curriculum taught, which departments are introduced, expanded or contracted, and the type of research supported and published. In earlier years big business influence was exercised directly through university governing bodies. Today there is greater reliance on grants, the promise of jobs, and the setting of social agendas concerning what is useful knowledge.

There are two additions that can be made to this analysis. Another major force involved in controlling higher education and being served by it is the state, including government bureaucracies, the military, the police, judiciary and welfare bureaucracies. The state provides most of the funding for higher education, including large amounts for so-called private universities.

Second, higher education also serves the interests of elites within the academic hierarchy. The interests of politically powerful educationists are closely linked with corporate and state patrons, who provide the basis for funding, prestige and jobs. But inside tertiary institutions (that is, colleges and universities), powerful figures have independent interest in building up administrative empires, increasing centralized control and laying claim to decision making over areas of the curriculum and research. Although students often see staff as the enemy, it is the steady acquisition of power by academic administrators over both students and staff that is a key feature of tertiary education over the past few decades.

So far I have focused on the content of higher education, such as the subjects in the curriculum and the types of research undertaken. Since the late 1960s the form of education has come under scrutiny. The "hidden curriculum" the structure of the learning/teaching situation reflects and reproduces aspects of wider society. The dependent, passive relation of students to teachers and administration is similar to the relation of employees to management. Acceptance of the frameworks in which social questions are put by major institutions. Certification of satisfactory performance, and implicit certification of acquiescence to standard procedures, is similar to the reward system in state or private employment. Emphasis on intellectual analysis and actual avoidance of practical action reflects most academics' own avoidance of action on social issues.

One of the most insightful critiques of higher education is *The Credential Society* by Randall Collins. Collins documents that most job skills are learned on the job, not in formal education. The reason that credentials are required to enter certain occupations is more to raise professional status than to guarantee skills. The main content of schooling is middle class culture; this helps perpetuate class divisions. The expansion of higher education in the United States is a result of competition for lucrative professional and managerial jobs, a competition which has led to enormous inflation in requirements for credentials.

Collins concludes that the best way to address these problems if by abolishing credentials. But he doesn't say how. Nor is it obvious that this would really challenge occupational inequalities in a fundamental way.

Alternatives

One of the ways to respond to the problems with higher education is to develop alternative systems. An excellent example is Abbs and Carey's *Proposal for a New College*, which is based on the following features:

- small size;
- curriculum based around aesthetic education;
- equality of staff salaries and status;
- internal democracy (staff and students);
- work as an integral part of learning;
- practical use of skills for self reliance, for example, production of food;
- sharing of all routine tasks such as cleaning and preparing meals.

Abbs and Carey find the basis for their proposals in many vintage ideas and movements, such as Fountains Abbey, the Bauhaus and Gandhian schools, and also draw inspiration from more recent developments.

A more political approach to learning has been espoused and adopted in Paulo Freier's approach to combining development of literacy and political awareness, which has mainly been applied in nonindustrialized countries. There are also a number of inspiring programs in rich countries, and a host of small scale experiences and experiments showing the value of freedom, direct democracy and social relevance in promoting learning. Especially worthy of not is learning "at home," advocated for children by John Holt, which can even more easily be applied to learning at the tertiary level.

These efforts at building alternatives are vitally important. But it is also essential to ask, are they enough to challenge the dominant tertiary institutions? Is it also useful, or even necessary, to work from within?

Campaigns

There are various campaigns inside academia. It is worth examining to what extent they challenge the basic directions of present higher education. Here I use Australian examples in many cases because they are familiar to me. Many of the conclusions apply more widely.

Fees. In the mid 1970s, the Australian government abolished tuition fees for all tertiary students, after a major campaign by student organizations. (All Australian higher education is funded by the federal government.) In the following years there were some attempts by politicians to reintroduce fees, but the political outcry from students and parents of students was enough to block this. In 1987, though, a $250 annual "administrative fee" was introduced. This is seen by many students as the thin edge of a wedge for much higher fees, such as those already charged to overseas students.

The aim of free tertiary education was to enable disadvantaged groups such as immigrants, Aborigines, women and working class and disabled students to gain access. Some groups, such as mature age women, have undoubtedly benefitted. But the effect of the abolition of fees on the class, ethnic and gender composition of student bodies has not been all that large. The problem is that fees are only one barrier. Other crucial factors are home environment, secondary schooling, and peer expectations.

Nor have fees campaigns challenged other aspects of higher education, such as the links between teaching and research and the interests of corporations and the state, or the hierarchy and competitiveness within academia itself. The abolition of fees has meant that a somewhat wider cross section of the population is enabled to compete for places in an otherwise unchanged tertiary education system.

Representation On Committees. In the aftermath of the student movement in the late 1960s and early 1970s, there were concerted efforts around the world to "democratize" higher education. What this meant in practice was that previously exclusive clubs of professors and community elites who sat on powerful academic decision-making bodies had to open up some positions for students, junior faculty and non-academic staff. This has had a moderating influence on academic hierarchies, but has seldom altered the channels through which power is exercised. Students are almost never given more than token representation. Being on committees and councils can provide an insight into how things happen, but seldom much influence on what does happen. This is because the setting of agendas, the detailing of options and the labor of negotiating courses of action through complex systems of committees is still carried out by academic bureaucrats (whether members of faculty or administration). Students simply do not have the time nor the inside connections to become key players in this sort of system. Another problem is that representation on committees can serve to legitimize the committees while draining off the energy of the more active students.

Equal Employment Opportunity (EEO). One of the greatest challenges being mounted against present power structures in higher education has grown out of the feminist and minority group movements. The most common expression is EEO and affirmative action, which officially means providing everyone a fair chance in the competition for academic degrees and posts. This is a sever threat to the dominant privileged group, white middle class men, who occupy the bulk of top positions in academia. These men have long been serviced by wives, secretaries, research assistants, and others. Some of these people are now demanding a chance to join the academic elite.

There are problems with the EEO strategy. For example, it does not directly challenge the gender division of labor in the home, and women are still heavily disadvantaged by their disproportionate share of the tasks of housework and child rearing. But even if EEO efforts were to be ultimately successful in considerably enlarging the number of women in elite positions in academia, it is worth asking, would this really change the nature of higher education very much?

In one area it would: the role of higher education in preparing men and women for jobs normally considered to be masculine and feminine (male engineers, female primary school teachers). But otherwise it is possible that things would be much the same. Teaching and research could still be geared to the interests of corporations and the state. The hierarchy and competition within academia could remain just as entrenched. The role of credentials in justifying status and inequality could persist as before. My conclusion is that EEO is vitally important but not enough.

Assessment. Until the 1970s, most Australian students were assessed by massive end-of-year exams. There were many complaints about this, such as the lack of feedback during the year and the intense pressure at exam time. One of the key student demands was for a change in the assessment system, with more student choice over assessment methods.

The net result of student agitation over this issue was a move toward so-called "continuous assessment." This means giving less weight to final exams and more weight to assignments, exams and participation throughout the course. However, students now complain about continuous assessment. It ties them down to lots of work. Some argue that the old system, while strenuous, nevertheless allowed leeway during the year. Students could choose how and when to study, or could devote large chunks of time to political issues. Lost in the shuffle was the objective of student influence over the form of assessment. What happens in many cases is token consultation by teachers with students about assessment, or choice between some very similar options.

In any case, changing assessment does not challenge the basic structure of higher education.

Curriculum. Campaigns for a broader, more socially relevant curriculum definitely hold the potential for changing course content away from direct service to corporations and the state. Many programs in women's studies, environmental studies and peace studies provide critical perspectives and stimulate political action. But such programs are vulnerable. They are often attacked if they are conspicuous or radical. They have few allies because most disciplinary departments find interdisciplinary programs a threat to their monopolies over subject matter. In the process of avoiding attack and just surviving, many such programs lose their critical edge. They may end up simply providing credentials and experience more suitable for modern styles of open management.

Another way to the change the curriculum is for teachers to do "critical teaching" in any class. Teachers often do have a considerable degree of freedom in how they run their classes. This path is admirably presented by Ira Shor in *Critical Teaching and Everyday Life*. Shor describes how he used methods inspired by Paolo Friere for promoting learning through dialogue and for promoting critical literacy.

Personally, I recommend Shor's book to all teachers, and indeed to students who would like to know what is possible. But Shor's initiatives are difficult to implement in many situations. There are two main obstacles: teachers and students!

Many teachers are not given the freedom to alter teaching methods that Shor used so effectively. In some cases the restraint comes through peer pressure, in others through formal requirements for covering certain subject matter in certain ways. While Shor's approach could be adapted to teaching science, it would require a highly sympathetic departmental environment.

Students can also thwart Short type initiatives. While some students will respond well to learning based on dialogue, others demand traditional methods. This is especially the case when students want credentials with the minimum amount of work and learning. Some of these students may be won over. The problem is that no lasting structures for critical teaching are established. When the Ira Shors of academia retire, burn out or move on to some other activity, curriculum is likely to revert to the usual methods and materials.

It is still worth making educational innovations, and persisting with previous innovations. I strongly believe this. But that should not blind us to the limitations of even the most exciting of initiatives in critical teaching—limitations built into the overall structure of higher education.

What to do?

After this series of criticisms of campaigns within higher education, it is reasonable to ask, is it worth putting effort into any of them at all? Or is it better to avoid wasting energy on them? I should make it clear that I support all the campaigns I've described and criticized. It is "progressive" at some level for tuition fees to be abolished, for students to be represented on academic committees, for equal employment opportunity measures to be implemented, for students to help decide on assessment methods, and for the curriculum to be made more critical and socially relevant. Compared to the old (and continuing) authoritarian systems, moves in these directions open up opportunities for further action. At the same time it is important to realize the limitations of campaigns in such areas.

One key limitation to many present campaigns is that they are organized almost entirely within educational institutions themselves, for example, by students who push staff or administration for changes in curriculum. The key feature of educational institutions which is not challenged by this approach is their monopoly over certification of knowledge.

To overcome this problem I think it is vital for efforts from within educational institutions to be linked with social campaigns outside the. Groups on the outside, such as trade unions and feminists, can help challenge the hierarchy, monopolization of knowledge and the service to vested interests found in educational institutions. Groups on the inside can help those on the outside to develop and strengthen self-reliance in knowledge, both learning and research. The interaction of efforts in these two directions is a combination of action and learning/research, relevant both for social action and education.

To illustrate the possibilities here, I will describe some of my experiences in the campaign against nuclear power and uranium mining in Australia. In the late 1970s this was one of the foremost social issues in the public eye, and certainly the most prominent environmental issue. A large number of activist groups took up the uranium issue, initially Friends of the Earth and then later groups such as Movement Against Uranium Mining. There were anti-uranium groups of all sorts, including suburban groups and university students. Many trade unions led the struggle by holding short strikes to publicize the issue and by refusing to handle goods or perform services that could help the uranium industry. The Australian Labor Party and the Australian Council of Trade Unions in 1977 each adopted stands against uranium. (The Labor Party has since virtually abandoned its platform.)

In Canberra, where I worked at the time at the Australian National University, there was a student anti-uranium group. Many academics privately opposed uranium mining but only a tiny number took a conspicuous public stand (by, for example, writing a letter to the newspaper). The people at the university who most actively supported the anti-uranium struggle were, first, undergraduate students and, second, a small number of others low in the hierarchy: graduate students, tutors and research assistants. The professors who took the most active public roles were pro-uranium. So far this may seem to confirm the worst analysis of academia. Most faculty members avoided being involved in a highly controversial issue. The uranium issue did not stimulate curriculum changes to make it a focus of study. Academics did not rush to do research which might bear on the crucial issues being raised.

Nevertheless, there were some useful interactions. The strength of the environmental movement helped sustain the Human Sciences Program, an innovative set of courses in environmental studies with a critical perspective on science and social institutions. Human Sciences had been attacked by traditional academics from its inception, although it was highly regarded by students. Human Sciences offered a course of study which provided the intellectual tools for examining the full dimensions of the uranium issue, and many other issues. Human Sciences did not formally campaign against uranium. But it did encourage the sort of study and critical thinking which led quite a few students (and faculty) to support the campaign. Conversely, the strength of community concern about uranium helped legitimize Human Sciences by showing the importance of the issues it addressed, and helped stimulate resistance to attacks on Human Sciences from the more traditional, discipline bound parts of the university.

Another useful interaction was the contribution of some academics and scientists to the arguments used by anti-uranium campaigners. There was a tendency in the movement to rely on emotional appeals, typified by cartoons showing two headed animals caused by radiation. While emotion is an important force in campaigning, it can be counterproductive if poor arguments are used.

Speakers for the Canberra anti-uranium movement were offered practice and training in the arguments by some of those in the university. A number of people had studied the arguments and read some of the technical literature, for example on nuclear reactor safety, proliferation of nuclear weapons and treats to Aboriginal culture from uranium mining. Much of this literature was written, in Australia or overseas, by academics and scientists. Many of those in Canberra who studied this literature were themselves academics or scientists, with the training and inclination to develop rigorous and effective arguments.

This moderately organized effort in Canberra to study the literature and encourage a range of people to learn the arguments and be able to speak on them was not duplicated everywhere. In some places the campaign had a much more "hippie" flavor, with more "spontaneity" and less concern for rigorous argument. This style, whatever its advantages for its participants, is not effective in convincing some audiences and on occasion was disastrously counterproductive.

In 1983 a Labor government was elected and suddenly there was hope that uranium mining could be stopped. In Friends of the Earth in Canberra we perceived that after these hopes were dashed, an anticipation soon confirmed there was a danger that the anti-uranium campaign would languish again. It so happened that most of our small group had some connection with the university. When we set out to collectively write about strategy for the anti-uranium movement, it might almost be said that this was simply a group of academics. But there was a vital difference in our experience in Friends of the Earth and our usual academic experiences. We were writing to encourage dialogue and promote a cause, away from the competition and highly critical atmosphere of the university. But without our academic backgrounds, we might not have been as well prepared to address the issue using the tools of anarchist, feminist and Marxist analysis.

I am acutely aware that our intellectual stimulation in writing about uranium mining is what should be happening in academia routinely. Indeed, the lack of such experiences is an indictment of the way universities are structured. What is to stop a group of activists, with no connection with academia, doing just what we did? In theory, nothing. In practice, it is the monopoly over intellectual skills and resources by educational institutions which often discourages intellectual activity on the "outside." The unfortunate tendency in many environmental groups to disdain critical analysis and to rely exclusively on feelings is a symptom of this monopoly. They reject critical thinking along with the structures which have institutionalized it.

I think it is precisely the interaction between those "inside" higher education and those "outside" given that many people are in both places at the same time which provides the best opportunity in the long run to challenge the division between inside and outside itself. Activists inside academia need to realize that there is more to politics than academic infighting. There are useful things students and faculty can do in support of social movements. There are also a lot of things they can learn. Activists on the outside should not "write off" all of higher education, rejecting the good along with the large amount of bad. Remember that student protest has stimulated the toppling of regimes.

The issue here is not simply one of choosing whether to work on the inside or the outside. It is also one of developing collective strategies which can help remove control over intellectual resources from the hands of academics and their patrons. It won't be easy but I think it is worth trying.

References

Abbs, Peter and Graham Carey. *Proposal for a New College.* London: Heinemann Educational Books 1977.

Collins, Randall. *The Credential Society.* New York: Academic Press, 1979.

Dixon, Marlene. *Things Which Are Done In Secret.* Montreal: Black Rose Books, 1976.

Friere, Paolo. *Pedagogy of the Oppressed.* Harmandsworth: Penguin, 1972.

Friere, Paolo. *Cultural Action for Freedom.* Harmandsworth: Penguin, 1972.

Friends of the Earth, Canberra. "Strategy against nuclear power," *Social Alternatives*, vol. 5. no. 2, April 1986, pp. 916.

Goodman, Paul. *The Community of Scholars.* New York: Random House, 1962.

Graubard, Allen. *Free the Children.* New York: Random House, 1972.

Holt, John. *Teach Your Own.* New York: Delacorte Press, 1981.

Illich, Ivan. *Deschooling Society.* London: Calder and Boyars, 1971.

Kozol, Jonathan. *Free Schools.* Boston: Houghton Mifflin, 1972.

Lewis, Lionel S. *Scaling the Ivory Tower.* Baltimore: Johns Hopkins University Press, 1975.

Martin, Brian, C.M. Ann Baker, Clyde Manwell and Cedric Pugh (eds). *Intellectual Suppression.* Sydney: Angus and Robertson, 1986.

Shor, Ira, *Critical Teaching and Everyday Life.* Montreal: Black Rose Books, 1980.

Smith, David N. *Who Rule the Universities?* New York: Monthly Review Press, 1974.

Spring, Joel. *A Primer of Libertarian Education.* Montreal: Black Rose Books, 1975.

Veblen, Thorstein. *The Higher Learning in America.* New York: B.W. Huebsch, 1918.

The question of critically engaging students whose experience in the education system has been one of marginalization and oppression is addressed in this mainly enthusiastic review of Ira Shor's book. Krimerman and Corrente, educators themselves, discuss Shor's techniques, assess him as promoting unorthodox and nondogmatic anarchism, and actively promote the book's application for a broad audience.

Originally published in issue 2.1.

Ira Shor: Critical Teaching and Everyday Life
Len Krimerman and Susan Corrente

Dear Carol and Howard,

You asked for a review of Ira Shor's *Critical Teaching and Everyday Life*, and instead you're receiving a letter. But it's a long one, and besides, this format seems ideally suited to Ira's book. For ultimately *CTEL* is a very long letter from one comrade to others, a kind of participant's personal report from a combat zone. It's a hope-giving book — it tells of successes we can all duplicate, achieved under improbably and soul-grinding conditions much like those we all confront. Specifically, *CTEL* relates how damaged learners at Staten Island Community College, tracked into "remedial" classes, began first to externalize and then to transcend oppressive socialization and self-deprecation. Virtually any teacher or organizer will find practical resources and theoretical insights in every chapter — especially perhaps those persons engaged in the delicate struggle to initiate and nurture growth away from programmed acquiescence and towards increasing self-determination. But on to the details.

To begin with, as practical pedagogy *CTEL* is unsurpassed. Its final five chapters proved a storehouse of techniques, models, exercised, etc. — original and battle-testes tools that should be useful in many diverse kinds of teaching situations. If our students can act better than they can read or write, we can turn to Chapter 8, "Reflection Through Drama," for help: It depicts how to build the latter skills from the former. If sexist attitudes are undercutting classroom communication, we may be able to confront them openly and creatively through the process of "renegotiating marriage contracts" (Chapter 7). One of us (Len) has used the "social inquiry" model (Chapters 5 and 6) to organize learning with both university undergraduates and urban high school dropouts: It moves from students' collective observations of everyday items such as hamburgers or classroom chairs to a sharpened understanding of the social relations behind these objects (why do school cafeterias provide such standardized and hopeless food?), and from there to imagining alternative arrangements of social life. (Would worker - and/or student-managed cafeterias furnish better food mor cheaply?) These are just a few out of the dozens of tools Ira describes in rich, personal, and painstaking detail. And he is faithful to the ambiguities and perplexities of actual class room activity: We are occasionally allowed to see a tool malfunction.

What is the point of all these concrete pedagogical techniques? There are, it seems, two answers to this question — a short one, and a long one. The short answer is that they are designed to salvage learners crippled by formal schooling, in particularly, those Ira describes as "worker-students." These are first generation college entrants, forced to support themselves and find tuition by holding miserable part-time jobs, and thus "under-employed while being under-educated" at "debased and manipulative" community college campuses. They arrive in Ira's "remedial English" classes having

> already experienced twelve years of mass education, so they know what's going on, and carry over from high school much resentment and defensive hostility…Non-attendance, non-performance and blank agreement with the teacher fare the limits of their pacifism. Vandalism, fights, con games, drugs and alcohol, theft, and challenges to the teacher's lectures and methods comprise their active sabotage. (p. 20).

They arrive, in short, with more than two strikes against them, for they believe that they will swing and miss whatever else is next thrown their way. At the least, Ira's pedagogical tools subvert this defeatist and self-destructive attitude. And they do so in a novel way, one which goes beyond offering guidance or support — though it is clear from every page how very much Ira is in his students corner. He relies here on a kind of pedagogical cunning: that is, each of the tools can succeed only because the students are *already* competent and articulate in a way they did not previously recognize or validate. When this is realized, it nullifies self-approved limits on their own learning potential, and readies them for the next pitch.

But there is more to Ira's tools, much more, that brings us to *CTEL's* original, indeed ground-breaking *theoretical* perspective. That is, Chapters 2 and 3 develop what we see as a "new paradigm" for educational theory. Though it may seem a detour, we want to discuss this new paradigm in some detail before examining the way it illuminates Ira's practical pedagogy.

On the whole, educational theorists have oscillated between two extremes. On one hand (e.g., Skinnerians), they devise supposedly value-free accounts of how most efficiently to program learning responses. On the other hand (consider Whitehead's *Aims of Education*) the offer purely normative or conceptual analyses of what constitutes optimum learning or the ideal curriculum. Thought the clash in many ways, these two types of theories are strangely alike in their rigid focus on a singularly abstract and socially isolated learner. They think of "the learner," in short, as devoid of any discernible class or occupational or ethnic background, as shielded from cultural influences that obstruct learning or distort it, and as cut off from or in competition with others in the search for understanding and development.

And there is yet another respect in which this rarefied learner remains unreal within almost all received educational theory. The (often implicit) conception is of someone placed at one end or the other of the educational process. In Skinnerian frameworks, s/he is viewed as a *pre-learner*, i.e., as just entering upon, or as uninfluenced by, prior educational/cultural activity. In classical philosophies of education, we are asked instead to concentrate upon *fully developed learners* who exhibit human learning in its most distinctive or perfected forms. In both cases, these theories have little or nothing to tell us about "mid-stream learners" (our phrase): ones damaged by prior learning situations, submerged in counter-educational institutions, but still coping with strengths and powers which, if cultivated, can repair much of the damage and surmount many of the obstacle (Ira's conception).

In contrast to all of this, *CTEL* discards the rarefied learner. Instead — and this is Ira's paradigm shift — it gives us a framework for educational theory in which culturally shaped, mid-stream, and damaged learners occupy center stage. It is in this sense that Ira's title invokes "everyday life" as a chief concern for both teachers and educational theorists. For he sees everyday life as what both disables, and can be used to re-empower, damaged learners. It is the mixed bag in which we must locate (a) our learners' culturally induced and incapacitating habits of mind and (b) their largely hidden aptitudes and strengths. Thus, at Staten Island Community College the "cultural interferences to learning" included *vocationalism* with its "machinification of character" and reduction of work to sterile routine, and *"acceleration*, the frenzied pace of commercial media and of urban lives split between family, school, a job or two, freeway traffic, subway rushes, fast food, fast sex... a pace which preempts thought and debases mental life. (See also pp. 47–81.) And Ira's students bring with them such "skills, strengths, and sensitivities" as a "popular dislike of arbitrary power," a " strong suspicion of organized authority," "savvy about life's nitty-gritty demands," and "a diversity of work skills (that is) awesome." (See here also p. 53 and pp. 84–87 and almost any chapter in which Ira describes how his students developed in response to his pedagogy.)

We have illustrated the (a) and (b) of "everyday life" with examples drawn from Staten Island community College, but it is clear that Ira wants his new paradigm to be understood and applied quite generally. No matter who or where we teach, the learners we face will be "damaged" and in "mid-stream." Their learning will be stunted by a certain *specific* set of "cultural interferences"; they will possess powers in common (often unknowingly) which can be used to offset those obstructions. The implications for teachers and organizers are clear:

> Anti-critical mass culture is the first and largest learning problem of the general population. Thus, the interferences to critical thought must be conceived as social and pervasive, not as personal problems or as isolated pedagogical ones…Faced with this threat, the designers of an empowering pedagogy *have to study the shape of disempowering forces*…(they) need a working knowledge of the anti-critical field in which a critical pedagogy develops. The systematic investigation of mass reality prepares the teacher for using daily life as subject matter (pp. 48, 47; our emphasis).

Further:

> Faced by all the social interferences to critical thought,…the teacher and students need to use popular strengths to undo the damage of mass culture…Without recognizing and using these resources, a critical teacher would be unable to begin a liberatory process(p. 87)

Let's return, then, to the purpose of Ira's practical pedagogy. The long answer is that these concrete techniques help fulfill his new paradigm for educational theory. They move us beyond the rarefied, socially isolated learner into the mid-stream of everyday life. Through their use, everyday life becomes a subject for critical reflection, rather than a set of hidden obstacles and latent (or unrecognized) aptitudes. The tools, then, take on a more radical dimension.

> By critically studying the lives they live uncritically and the culture which eclipses reason, students begin changing their powerless place in society…The struggle for critical consciousness in nothing less than a battle for a new social design (pp. 48, 82).

So what does all of this imply for the readers of *Social Anarchism*? Would this book of Ira's be seen as another in the long anarchic tradition from Godwin and Warren, Francisco Ferrer and Tolstoy, to Paul Goodman and George Dennison? In some ways, no doubt. But these good anarchists receive no mention in *CTEL*; and though it's just a word, "liberatory rather than "libertarian" is the one Ira selects to describe his classroom and his pedagogy. He draws not only upon Freire but on recent Marxists such as George Lukacs who analyze popular culture and its role in producing "reified" (frozen, stunted) thought. Ira is a libertarian educator, but with some important and instructive differences.

For one thing, anarchist or libertarian educational theory has rarely, if ever, taken "everyday life," in Ira's sense, seriously. Certainly it's there, and certainly in *practice* we work with mid-stream rather than rarefied learners. But no systematic study of the shape of disempowering forces, of the socialized patterns internalized by different groups or subcultures (white working class, black female, rural poor, etc.) is undertaken. Our contact with damaged learners is largely personal, anecdotal, intuitive, pre-theoretical (e.g., Tolstoy, Dennison). Or where theory does appear, it tends to be spaciously abstract (Goodman, Illich, A.S. Neill), attacking such generalizations as "authoritarian teachers," "compulsory miseducation," and "dead schools." Treating all damaged learners alike, we assume that creating non-authoritarian and self-governing environments, providing resources and encouragement for learning, enabling learners to move at their own pace, providing models of successful self-directed learning — that these very *rarefied* remedies by themselves will nullify cultural interferences, root out specific forms of false consciousness, and bring to life hidden collective strengths. These blanket and blithe assumptions are challenged by Ira's new paradigm. Freedom, *CTEL* insists, cannot develop within a cultural vacuum.

There is a second way in which Ira's educational theory collides with libertarian orthodoxy. For on many pages and in many different ways, he sees the teacher as "indispensable." (See here pp. 84–87, 98–104.) In large part, this indispensability arises from and is justified by the initial gap between wheat teachers and learners grasp about everyday life and about its implications for personal development and social transformation. For Ira, this gap is explicitly a temporary and progressively diminishing one; the teacher should work at becoming expendable. Nonetheless, at the outset and for some time thereafter, the damages/mid-stream learner is neither able nor willing to be self-directed. If this is to change, the teacher/organizer (Ira Believes, and we agree) cannot step back and wait for the natural juices of self-initiated learning to flow, or count on the redemptive magic of collective deliberation or consensus decision-making. (As he wisely notes, "the liberatory ideas of communal life or cooperative action surface as *more* threats to freedom. As far as worker-students can tell, they need to be accountable to *fewer* people, not more." False consciousness wears many guises.) We thus arrive at a point Dewey raised in criticism of "progressive education": Where teachers fail to exercise pedagogical authority, and shy away from making most of the key decisions, they may only strengthen those very cultural interferences which have distorted or suppressed critical learning. (See here *Experience and Education*, pp. 8–10, 96–100.)

It is in these two ways that Ira sets himself apart from the tradition of libertarian pedagogy: He would have us understand our students *collectively*, as products of *specific cultures* each having its own set of internalized and disempowering social myths, and its own set of latent or untapped resources for transformation. And he would preserve pedagogical authority in order to initiate the "long march" against these diverse cultural interferences and towards the "active transcendence of domination." For these reasons, we believe, Ira can be seen as a "liberatory" rather than a libertarian educator.

Moreover, Ira's deviations here also mark out his position as a clear illustration of what one of us (Len), in "Anarchism Reconsidered," published in the last issue of *Social Anarchism,* called "unorthodox anarchism" For Ira, it is almost self-evident that there are situations (everyday life is full of them) that require us to retain a form of authority, albeit of a transitional and transitory sort. Our ultimate goal or final end (full equality between teacher and learner, the latter taking charge of his/her own learning) is simply *not* our means written large or elaborated in more detail. The two are distinct; indeed, somewhat at odds. Ira's circumstances at Staten Island Community College hardly allow him to *start from* "prior consensus" or "political commitment," or with comrades "who know anarchist principles" and "band together...to apply (them)"!! (Quotes are from Glenda's and Howard's *commentaries* on Len's article.) To do so would be to abandon, rather than aid in, the liberation of his worker-students. Instead, as a good "zig-zag anarchist," Ira "dives into the wreck," continually shaping and reshaping his role, remaining alive to sporadic needs for his direction and...leadership.

CTEL makes other contributions to unorthodox anarchism. In the first place, given the rampant false consciousness at Staten Island Community College, Ira's retention of unequal authority seems to us quite legitimate. Anything else, *from an anarchist point of view,* would be irrational: It would perpetuate authoritarian tendencies in the college, in his students, and in their everyday lives. But if unorthodox anarchism makes good sense in education, why not elsewhere as well- wherever the victims of oppression are disabled by their own beliefs, disempowered by the mass culture within them, agents of their own enslavement? Secondly, how should the boundary between libertarian and liberatory educators be understood? We see it as a gap to be bridged rather than a territory to be fought over and then appropriated, zero-sum fashion. The main issue for us ins not who is right and who wrong, or whether to develop libertarian or liberatory environments. (Why not both?) The real issue is how to bring about the fullest sort of intellectual and practical collaboration. What's to be gained by rejecting one another as allies? The issues that separate us are *not* that critical; they can be left dangling while we form an active coalition. Only in this way can the entire range of oppressive conditions and forms of domination be effectively countered. And once again, what is true within education would seem to hold generally; what is most needed between orthodox and unorthodox anarchists is not disputation, but collaboration.

Despite our praise and admiration, *CTEL* does contain some major flaws. We'll conclude by discussing what we see as three of these, and, in the spirit of comradely criticism, by indicating how the book could be modified or strengthened to offset them. First, though Ira certainly achieves some real gains at Staten Island Community College and does so within a liberatory classroom, how do we know that the former *resulted* from the latter? He assumes this, and is confident of it, but no evidence is given to substantiate it. Perhaps some other factor, e.g., the sheer *amount* of attention Ira bestows on individual students, is really at work. (Non-libertarian educator such as Bruno Bettelheim and Terry Borton also report dramatic successes.) A related problem: How *durable* are the gains Ira achieves in conscientization? Do they last when his students move back into less liberatory settings? For us, the absence of follow-up data undercuts Ira's faith in his pedagogy:

The process of reconstructive learning fulfills a prophetic cliche — big things can grow from small beginnings, extraordinary changes can be provoked from scrutiny of the ordinary features of mass life (p. 233).

We call this first group of problems *effectiveness/durability.*

A second problem is whether *CTEL* will be found accessible and whether it will be fruitful and multiply adherents of Ira's pedagogy. (This can be called the *accessibility/reproducibility* problem.) We have two different worries here. For one thing, the book continually buzzes with Freirean and neo-Marxist terms ("dialogic," "problematize," "mystification," "reified culture," etc.). These are probably clear enough to those who have already read or discussed the originals, but may well frustrate and distance mainstream teachers/organizers less familiar with radical pedagogy and politics. This would be a doubly great loss: Ira has much to offer non-radicals, and without their active support, his pedagogy will remain a marginal one, without much influence. Secondly, Ira spends a good bit of time attacking "vocationalism," and much of this is sound and sorely needed criticism of "Narrow skills-training…which sends worker-students into the bottom levels of the job market." But his case is overdrawn, as is his bias for the "liberatory humanities" (see pp. 23–33, 50–54). There are forms of "vocational," "career," and "professional" education that outshine the liberal arts in liberatory potential. And there is a wide and increasing number of educators in such areas (e.g., health care, agriculture, nutrition)who find their fields in creative flux and have themselves begun to challenge rigid vocational and professional training. There is room here for fertile coalitions, but Ira's dichotomy between "humane liberal arts" and "inhumane voc-tech" can only close off communication.

Our last problem is a familiar one for anarchists. We call it the problem of *abuse-ability*. Thus, granted a (transitional) right to pedagogical authority, how can we tell when this right should be relinquished or when it has been overstepped? One very familiar answer sweeps us back into a Platonic or Leninist classroom: The teacher determines how to move her/his learners through pre-fixed stages of development deemed necessary for the ascent to autonomy. Ira steers clear of this, but into an equally familiar part of the dilemma:

> When the liberatory process is working well, the learners themselves assume more responsibility for the class…This internal, organic test of development — assessing how much direction the teacher is responsible for — is a means for determining the progress of humanization (p. 100).

A means, certainly — but the only one? It looks as if the boot of arbitrary authority has here simply been shifted to the other foot. Students can misuse authority and misjudge their capacity to learn (and let others learn) freely as much as teachers. (What if, thought fired up for self-determination, they are still racist or sexist, or have no interest in anything beyond pinball or video games?)

As for modifications of *CTEL*, we can think of some that are fairly straightforward and easy to implement and others that are more complex and long-range. The simpler ones would include providing follow-up information on students after they leave the liberatory classroom: How do they see themselves after a year or more of traditional instruction? Do they find or create space for increased empowerment in the workplace? And it would help to have a glossary of Freirean and other key terms, as well as concrete illustrations of their use as soon as they appear. If this is done with care, it will open the book more fully to a wider audience. In addition, it will show how notions such as "conscientization," "externalization of false consciousness," and "transcendent possibilities of dialogic learning" can be substantiated and thus shed light on how to test the effectiveness and durability of Ira's liberatory pedagogy.

The longer-range suggestion would be for Ira to transcend the false opposition he draws between humanities and voc-tech education, by incorporating the single "liberatory humanities classroom" within problem-oriented and work-connected programs and to combine liberal arts with professional or career education. A single classroom, however innovative, is bound to be a lonely and fragmentary experience for both teacher and students. But an entire "mosaic program," drawing on different disciplines and colleges, could offset this. (We have helped begin one such mosaic at UConn which spans seven disciplines and four colleges; an article about it will appear in the Fall, 1981 issue of *Radical Teacher*.) Students would not be split up between one "alternative" and four or five traditional classrooms; teachers could be released from rigid and/or single-department publishing demands. In the midst of growing talk of a "crisis in the liberal arts," such mosaic programs should be attractive to administrators as well as to student sand teachers.

No doubt, to bring off this sort of mosaic development (like any venture in unorthodox anarchism) will prove enormously difficult and tricky. But the potential gains are immense. Such programs could provide a strengthened way of initiating the liberatory process and of keeping it alive. And they would make Ira's paradigm substantially more accessible and reproducible than the narrow form it takes in *CTEL*. (We spoke to Ira a few months ago about the virtues of mosaic liberatory programs linked to fields of work rather than to particular jobs. He agreed that professional/vocational education need *not* be an enemy of critical learning and invited us to think of a name for programs which combine the two. Our first ideas: *HOPE* Humanistically-Oriented Professional Education, and *COPE*: Critical Options in Professional Education. We're still thinking.)

Can HOPE or COPE help with the problem of abuse-ability? Possibly so, thought the issue is too large for us to dig into very deeply here. But there is such a thing as "professional development," and it can be measure with some *objectivity* — despite being linked to a professions's broad social values, to how it should connect with other fields and parts of the same field, to personal development goals of individual professionals, etc. (Objectivity here means that judgments about "professional development" — one's own or another's — are never infallible or indisputable.) If this is true, professional development might provide an additional criterion for the acceptable use and scope of pedagogical authority; such authority should aim at augmenting professional development, should also manifest it, and should be progressively curtailed as students exhibit more and more of such development. With a great deal of elaboration, then, mosaic programs might point a way out of the hoary dilemma of pedagogical authority. They might, that is, help indicate how otherwise arbitrary and incontestable decisions by either teachers or students can be evaluated and kept from excessive forms of abuse.

Well, that would seem more than enough for now. We've gone on at such length because we're excited about *CTEL* and in order to convey fully its usefulness for front-kine teachers and organizers, its contributions to how we think about education, and what it has to offer (undogmatic) anarchists. A last precautionary note: Chapter 1, a history of Open Admissions at CUNY, should probably be read *last*, as an appendix; it doesn't lead very well into the remaining, and most central, portions of the book.

Heterodoxical solidarity,
Len Krimerman and Susan Corrente

Critical Teaching and Everyday Life by Ira Shor. $15 cloth; $6 paper. Boston, MA: South End Press, 1980.

Notable
Figures

In the genealogy of contemporary anarchist writers, Colin Ward is the grandfather. His writing has been recognized world-wide not just because of the ideas he presented but also the simplicity with which he has been able to express his ideas. Shantz, like Ward's major biographer David Goodway, appropriately directs the reader to Ward's insistence that even the most complex of anarchist issues can be expressed in everyday terms. More than that, they must be expressed in everyday language if anarchism is to develop as a coherent and persuasive theory.

Originally published in issue 40.

Following that is an earlier interview with Colin Ward himself, conducted in 1991 with the editors of *Social Anarchism.*

Originally published in issue 16.

Colin Ward's Everyday Anarchy
Jeff Shantz

Colin Ward may be one of the few anarchist writers to have a larger readership outside of anarchist circles than within them. This is a testament both to his writing (and the issues he addresses within those writings) and to the rhetorical preferences of contemporary anarchist readers — especially at a time when highly abstract and theoretical postmodern/anarchist hybrids have provided some footing for academic anarchists and their publishers.

Colin Ward is perhaps best known, at least to anarchists, through his third book *Anarchy in Action* which was — until his 2004 contribution to the Oxford Press "Short Introduction" series, *Anarchism: A Very Short Introduction* — his only book explicitly about anarchist theory. Longtime anarchist George Woodcock identified *Anarchy in Action* as one of the most important theoretical works on anarchism and I would have to agree. In the pages of that relatively short work, Ward makes explicit his highly distinctive version of anarchism, what might be called an anarchy of everyday life or, more simply, everyday anarchy.

Ward describes his approach to anarchism as one that is based on actual experiences or practical examples rather than theories or hypotheses. Ward's anarchism, "far from being a speculative vision of a future society...is a description of a mode of human organization, rooted in the experience of everyday life, which operates side by side with, and in spite of, the dominant authoritarian trends of our society" (Ward, 1973: 11). While having no formal background in sociology he argues for the importance of taking a sociological approach to the world. Taking this approach has consequences simultaneously liberatory and practical since "once you begin to look at human society from an anarchist point of view you discover that the alternatives are already there, in the interstices of the dominant power structure. If you want to build a free society, the parts are all at hand" (Ward, 1973: 13). As David Goodway suggests, this approach also addresses two seemingly insoluble problems that have long confronted anarchists and socialists alike (Ward and Goodway, 2003: 11).

The first is, if anarchism (or socialism) is so highly desirable as well as feasible, how is it that it has never come into being or lasted no longer than a few months (or years). Ward's answer is that anarchism is already partially in existence and that he can show us examples "in action". The second problem is how can humans be taught to become cooperative, thereby enabling a transition from the present order to a cooperative society to be attained. Ward's response here is that humans are naturally cooperative and that current societies and institutions, however capitalist and individualist, would completely fall apart without the integrating powers, even if unvalued, of mutual aid and federation. Nor will social transformation be a matter of climactic revolution, attained in a millennial movement, but rather a prolonged situation of dual power in the age-old struggle between authoritarian and libertarian tendencies, with outright victory for either tendency most improbable (Ward and Goodway, 2003: 11).

The primary historical influences on Ward's everyday anarchy are Peter Kropotkin's anarcho-communism and the libertarian socialism of Gustav Landauer. In *Mutual Aid* Kropotkin documents the centrality of cooperation within animal and human groups and links anarchist theory with everyday experience. Ward has suggested that *Anarchy in Action* is merely an extended contemporary footnote to *Mutual Aid* (Ward and Goodway, 2003: 14). As Ward (2004: 29) reminds us: "A century ago Kropotkin noted the endless variety of 'friendly societies, the unities of oddfellows, the village and town clubs organized for meeting the doctors' bills' built up by working-class self-help." Still, Ward goes beyond Kropotkin in the importance he places on cooperative groups in anarchist social transformation. In this Ward's anarchism openly draws on Landauer's exhortation that militants prioritize the formation of producers' and consumers' cooperatives. At the same time Ward follows Kropotkin in identifying himself as an anarchist communist.

The Propagandist

Ward was won to anarchism through his contact with Glasgow anarchists Eddie Shaw, Jimmie Dick and, especially, Frank Leech, during a posting, ironically, with the Army School of Hygiene in 1943. Leech encouraged the young Ward to put together some articles for the London publication *War Commentary — for Anarchism* published by Marie Louise Berneri of the Freedom Press Group and the material appeared in December of 1943.

Ward notes that this was a time when most of the British left was swept up in a torrent of what he calls Stalin-worship, in which there was a tacit agreement not to utter criticism of the Soviet Union. Ward suggests that it is difficult for later generations to fully appreciate how deeply the assumptions of the British and Western European intellectuals were constrained by Marxist and Stalinist ideas. Ward explains the left's infatuation with Stalinism during that period as a result of the search for ultimate certainties in sociology and politics. Ward has spent much of his life working against similar tendencies to search for ultimate certainties within anarchism.

Ward began his long publishing career in 1946 with a series of nine articles on the postwar squatters' movement in the long-standing anarchist magazine *Freedom*. In 1947 Ward was invited to join *Freedom's* editorial group. By the early 1950s the characteristic preoccupations that Ward would emphasize over the next five decades of his writings had emerged: housing and planning, workers' control and industrial self-organization (Ward and Goodway, 2003: 5).

Ward was deeply impacted by the squatters' movements that emerged during the 1940s as homeless families seized empty military camps. Yet his anarchism was so outside of the parameters of mainstream anarchism that in the 1940s, when Ward tried to convince his Freedom Press Group colleagues to print a pamphlet on the squatters' movement "it wasn't thought that this is somehow relevant to anarchism" (Ward and Goodway, 2003: 15).

In March 1961, in a compromise response to his arguments that *Freedom* move from weekly production to become a monthly, Ward was assigned the editorship of *Anarchy*, a monthly complement to *Freedom*. Under his editorial guidance *Anarchy* produced 118 issues until its closing in 1970, with a circulation of more than 2000 copies per issue. Less well known is the fact that Ward often wrote much of each issue of the great journal himself, under a string of pseudonyms or in unsigned articles (Ward and Goodway, 2003: 8). Again the journal reflected Ward's major preoccupations, focusing on housing and squatting, progressive education and workers' control.

One of the major contributions of the journal *Anarchy*, under Ward's editorship was to take anarchist writing from the status of fringe or marginal commentary and to encourage a broader audience to take anarchist ideas on a variety of topics seriously. By intervening in a credible and engaging manner, beyond easy cliches or prefabricated responses, on matters of public concern *Anarchy* showed that anarchists could offer coherent and relevant responses to key social questions.

For three decades Ward also disseminated this approach to anarchy as a regular contributor to the sociological journal *New Society* and its successor *New Statesman and Society*. For almost a decade, beginning in 1988, Ward contributed a weekly column to that publication. Through this work he was able to spread anarchist ideas more broadly, and among more diverse readerships than most anarchists are able to achieve.

The challenge, which Ward met mostly successfully, was to keep routine and ready-made formulas from intruding on his writings, especially as they gained in longevity and scope.

> I am convinced that the most effective way of conducting anarchist propaganda through the medium of a monthly journal is to take the whole range of partial, fragmentary, but immediate issues in which people *are actually likely to get involved*, and to seek out anarchist solutions, rather than to indulge in windy rhetoric about revolution. A goal that is infinitely remote, said Alexander Hezen, is not a goal at all, but a deception. On the other hand, these preoccupations led to a neglect of a whole range of topics which *Anarchy* has ignored. Where, for example, is a thorough anarchist analysis of economic and industrial changes in this country (Ward and Goodway, 2003: 59).

Through the responses of readers to articles published in *Anarchy*, Ward found that for many people anarchy aptly described the "organized chaos" that people experienced during their daily lives, even at their workplaces. It was this convergence of peoples' everyday experiences and their responses — whether active or in terms of thoughts and feelings — to these experiences with anarchism that informed Ward's work throughout. Recognizing and respecting the fact that many people understood the world in an anarchistic way, even if they had no contact at all with explicitly anarchist theory or with anarchist movements encouraged Ward to write in a straightforward manner on a variety of issues that were often overlooked within anarchist publications. It also taught him that anarchist ideas were more important than attachment to a specific theoretical body or tradition and that the anarchist writer would find a ready audience, indeed a diversity of audiences, willing to engage with anarchist perspectives if they were presented in a clear language and if they dealt, not necessarily with the "big picture" issues anarchists thought were most important, but with the daily concerns people face in going about their lives.

In one of his earlier articles Ward, in reflecting on the condition of anarchist politics, suggests that "it was 'Because we have failed to formulate anarchist alternatives in the most prosaic as well as the most important fields of life, that the very people who could bring to life our own activities cannot bring themselves to take us seriously" (Ward and Goodway, 2003: 57). Taking this approach Ward, more than most anarchists, has come to have an impact well outside of anarchist or even leftist circles. His views on issues ranging from education to architecture to children's activities to planning have been sought after by people seeking alternatives to government initiatives or business mandate cutbacks. As Ward himself suggests: "My aim was, as always, to make the anarchist approach a point of view that was taken seriously in every field of social life. I want anarchist attitudes to be among those that citizens everywhere know about, and cannot dismiss as an amusing curiosity of the political fringe" (Ward and Goodway, 2003: 123).

As one example Ward has become an important influence within planning circles. He has gained recognition as a credible advocate for anarchist approaches to planning and has been credited with launching a movement in planning that has revived the anarchist visions of planning pioneers such as Ebenezer Howard and Patrick Geddes. In his inventive and widely influential paper "The Do-it-yourself New Town," Ward advocated "a new concept of building communities, in which the residents themselves would be involved directly in planning, designing and building their own homes and neighborhoods. The role of local authorities would be limited to that of site provision and basic services" (Hardy, 1991: 173). Ward suggests that "squatters' campaigns, as well as providing a roof for homeless people, are significant as a symbolic challenge to the concept of property, and for their effect on the participants" (Ward and Goodway, 2003: 73).

The Anarchist Sociologist

The anarchist and popular sex educator Alex Comfort was one of the first to argue that anarchists had much to learn from sociologists. In his work *Delinquency* (1951) Comfort called for anarchism to become a libertarian action sociology.

Ward took this call to heart and he draws much of his inspiration from the sociology of autonomous groups. His readings of the now out of print sociology bulletin *Autonomous Groups* contributed to understandings of capacities for influencing social change within informal networks such as the Batignolles Group, founders of Impressionism and the Fabian Society. Notably these groups were incredibly effective, exercising an influence well beyond their numbers.

Autonomous groups that he has studied or participated in are characterized by "having a secure internal network based on friendship and shared skills, and a series of external networks of contacts in a variety of fields" (Ward, 2003: 44). Such autonomous groups are marked by a high degree of individual autonomy within the group, reliance on direct reciprocities in decision-making, for decisions affecting all group members, and the temporary and fluctuating character of leadership. Autonomous groups are distinguished from other forms of organization characterized by "hierarchies of relationships, fixed divisions of labour, and explicit rules and practices" (Ward, 2003: 48). Among these groups Ward includes the Freedom Press Group, A.S. Neill's Summerhill School of alternative education, Burgess Hill School and South London's Peckham Health Centre which offered approaches to social medicine.

As Ward (2003: 48) notes, anarchists traditionally "have conceived of the whole of social organization as a series of interlocking networks of autonomous groups." Thus it is important that anarchists pay serious attention to the lessons to be learned from successful ones.

Anarchists address the key issues of "who provides and who decides." Everyday anarchism is about developing ways in which people enable themselves to take control of their lives and participate meaningfully in the decision-making processes that affect them, whether education, housing, work or food. In a contemporary, post-Fordist context, Ward notes that changes in the structure of work, notably so-called lean production, flexibalization and the institutionalization of precarious labour, have stolen people's time away from the family along with the time that might otherwise be devoted to activities in the community (Ward and Goodway, 2003: 107). Of course this has always been a central part of class struggle under capitalism: the struggle over everyday life and the time spent in activities of capitalist value production against the time spent in taking care of ourselves (what some call self-valorization). Ward finds resonance in the findings of industrial psychologists who suggest that satisfaction in work is very strongly related to the "span of autonomy," or the proportion of work time in which workers are free to make and act on their own decisions.

Ward has made some important contributions to analyses of the welfare state and its role in the deterioration or destruction of mutual aid in capitalist societies. In discussing the welfare state, Colin Ward sums up its positive and negative aspects in short: "The positive feature of welfare legislation is that, contrary to the capitalist ethic, it is a testament to human solidarity. The negative feature is precisely that it is an arm of the state (Ward and Goodway, 2003: 79). Ward focuses on recent examples, such as holiday camps in Britain, "in which a key role was played by the major organizations of working-class self-help and mutual aid, the cooperative movement and trade unions" (Ward and Goodway, 2003: 17). A significant theme in the perspectives of everyday anarchy is "the historic importance of such institutions in the provision of welfare and the maintenance of social solidarity" (Ward and Goodway, 2003:

17). Ward points out that the provision of social welfare did not originate from government through the "welfare state." Rather, it emerged in practice "from the vast network of friendly societies and mutual aid organizations that had sprung up through working-class self-help in the 19th century" (Ward, 2004: 27). Sam Dolgoff makes the same point with reference to the importance of mutual aid groups for the provision of education to elder care within the labour movement in the US. Ward notes that "the only thing that makes life possible for millions in the United States are its non-capitalist elements… Huge areas of life in the United States, and everywhere else, are built around voluntary and mutual aid organizations." (Ward and Goodway, 2003: 105).

In numerous works Ward has illustrated how, since the late nineteenth century, "'the tradition of fraternal and autonomous associations springing up from below' has been successively displaced by one of 'authoritarian institutions directed from above'" (Ward and Goodway, 2003: 17). As Ward suggests, this displacement was actively pursued, with often disastrous results, in the development of the social citizenship state: "The great tradition of working-class self-help and mutual aid was written off not just as irrelevant, but as an actual impediment, by the political and professional architects of the welfare state…The contribution that the recipients had to make…was ignored as a mere embarrassment" (quoted in Ward and Goodway, 2003: 18). From his research on housing movements Ward comments on "the initially working-class self-help building societies stripping themselves of the final vestiges of mutuality; and this degeneration has existed alongside a tradition of municipal housing that was adamantly opposed to the principle of dweller control" (Ward and Goodway, 2003: 18). Ward's work is directed towards providing useful "pointers to the way ahead if we are to stand any chance of reinstituting the self-organization and mutual aid that have been lost" (Ward and Goodway, 2003: 18).

> It is still an anarchism of present and permanent protest — how could it be anything else in our present peril? But it is one which recognizes that the choice between libertarian and authoritarian solutions occurs every day and in every way. And the extent to which we choose, or accept, or are fobbed off with, or lack the imagination and inventiveness to discover alternatives to, authoritarian solutions to small problems is the extent to which we are their powerless victims in big affairs. We are powerless to change the course of events over the nuclear arms race, imperialism and so on, precisely because we have surrendered our power over everything else (Ward, 2003: 55).

Rather than falling into the trap of excessive enthusiasm, Ward is also aware of Errico Malatesta's reminder that anarchists are only one of the forces acting in society and history will move according to the resultant of all the forces. Thus, it is necessary for anarchists to "find ways of living among non-anarchists as anarchistically as possible" (Malatesta quoted in Ward and Goodway, 2003: 85) This, beyond being a reflection on the difficulties facing anarchist organizers in overcoming authoritarian social relations, is a warning against being satisfied only with subcultural or lifestyle approaches to carving out spaces of anarchy within archic society.

Ward has little time for artsy anarchists concerned with producing avant-garde works "intended to shock the bourgeoisie, without regard for the fact that artists of all sorts have been shocking the bourgeoisie for a century, and that the rest of us find it hard to suppress a yawn"(Ward and Goodway, 2003: 124). At the same time he has avoided the trap of sectarianism. His criticisms of other anarchists and their perspectives has always played a minor part in his writings and he has publicly offered the view that squabbling among anarchists tends to lessen their relevance to non-anarchist readers. "To the outside world, anarchism, like Trotskyism, makes itself ridiculous because of its ideological subdivisions" (Ward, 2003: 41). Similarly Ward is critical of anarchists' preoccupation with anarchist history and in his own works prefers to emphasize the here-and-now and the immediate future (Ward and Goodway, 2003).

This does not mean that he avoids debate on anarchist strategy, tactics or theory, however. Ward's concern that anarchism develop practical, real world alternatives in the here-and-now has left him with little patience for the emergence of primitivism and anti-civilizationism within anarchy. He comments, with some disdain, on the "sentimental and privileged idealization of 'wilderness' and the natural environment" that has led many anarchists to abandon involvement in social issues in favour of adopting a stance of "misanthropy towards their fellow humans" (Ward and Goodway, 2003: 97). In his view Deep Ecology became fashionable among those affluent enough to "get away from it all" and pursue a variety of esoteric and mystical beliefs "as long as the cheques kept flowing into their bank accounts" (2004: 93). Ward suggests that "as ecological awareness spread among the children of the affluent, the national guilt over the genocide of indigenous peoples led to an exaltation of the Noble Savage, and a distaste for ordinary mortals who hadn't got the Message (Ward and Goodway, 2003: 98).

Ward joins Murray Bookchin in repudiating these approaches and seeking instead "to confront the abandonment of social concerns in an increasingly divided America" (2004: 94). This, in turn, requires challenging the hierarchical, racist, sexist, class-based state apparatus and its histories of militarism, conquest and occupation. It is not enough to cheer on the supposedly impending collapse of civilization, as primitivists are wont to do.

The Reformist?

Some critics might dismiss Ward's work as being "non-revolutionary." To do so is to repeat the mistake, common in much thinking on the left, of conceiving of revolution narrowly as a specific moment of upheaval or seizure of power (usually in terms of the state). Under this sort of narrow view, which insists on a rather abstract opposition between revolution and reform, Ward would be conceived as a reformist. Ward's work recognizes that revolutions do not emerge fully formed out of nothing. His perspective emphasizes the need, in pre-revolutionary times, for institutions, organizations and relations that can sustain people as well as building capacities for self-defence and struggle. As Ward notes: "The pathos of oppressed people, however, is that, if they break free, they don't know what to do. Not having been autonomous, they don't know what it's like, and before they learn, they have new managers who are not in a hurry to abdicate" (Goodman quoted in Ward, 2004: 69). Taking a more nuanced approach to revolutionary transformation one can understand Ward's work as concerned with the practical development of what Howard Ehrlich calls revolutionary transfer cultures. Anarchist organizing is built on what Ward calls "social and collective ventures rapidly growing into deeply rooted organizations for welfare and conviviality" (2004: 63). Colin Ward refers to these manifestations of everyday anarchy as "quiet revolutions."

Conclusion

When people have no control over, or responsibility for, crucial decisions over important aspects of life, whether regarding housing, education or work, these areas of social life become obstacles to personal fulfillment and collective development. Yet when people are free to make major decisions and contribute to the planning and implementation of decisions involving key areas of daily life there are improvements in individual and social well-being (Ward and Goodway, 2003: 76).

The perspectives and practices of everyday anarchy, in addressing immediate day-to-day concerns, provide an important reminder to revolutionary anarchists that anarchists must offer examples that resonate with people's experiences and needs. Or as Herzen has remarked: "A goal which is infinitely remote is not a goal at all, it is a deception" (quoted in Ward, 2004: 32).

References

Ward, Colin. 1973. *Anarchy in Action*. New York: Harper Torchbooks

Ward, Colin. 2004. *Anarchism: A Very Short Introduction*. Oxford: Oxford University Press

Ward, Colin and David Goodway. 2003. *Talking Anarchy*. Nottingham: Five Leaves

An Interview with Colin Ward

SA: What makes an anarchist different from other kinds of political people?

W: Well, there was the woman who ran that library in Amsterdam that was started by Max Nettlau and has a great deal of anarchist material from the past. She always said, "I'm a socialist but the anarchists are nicer. You can have more fun with the anarchists." And this is my view. There are plenty of politicos you cannot have fun with.

SA: What is it about anarchism that makes the anarchist more fun?

W: Anarchists by my definition are liberated people and the politicos seem to me to be enslaved to all sorts of social illusions.

SA: When did this idea of anarchism start? When did it come about?

W: It started with Even in the Garden of Eden.

SA: And you're going to leave us hanging there?

W: Yes, indeed! No, I think its an aspect of human thought and behavior that crops up, not of course under the name of anarchism, all through history. Some anarchists delight in going back and saying the Greeks has a word for it. They talk about Zeno of Kitium whom they say was the first anarchist, but unfortunately not a word of his utterances truly survives. I think the best way of seeing it is that there are libertarian and authoritarian tendencies in human life which are always in battle and have been all through the centuries.

SA: If you, as an anarchist and a man who has given a lifetime of thought to changing social arrangements, were to write a blueprint, what would your anarchist society look like?

W: I don't really know. I imagine it would look exactly like our present society because I am quite fond of conserving buildings and would not like the present lot to be swept out of the way. I never think about the picture of an anarchist society as such because I think this is unhistorical thinking.

I think all societies are mixed societies and the example that I always use and the only thing that makes life tolerable in capitalist America is the huge unacknowledged socialist element in American life. Similarly, it is quite obvious to everyone that the only thing that makes life tolerable in communist Russia is the enormous capitalist element which means that people like me can buy razor blades and things of that sort. In other words, all societies that we can truly imagine are mixed societies, if you like, plural societies.

SA: Kropotkin, a writer you are quite fond of, argued that what anarchists have to do is have a vision of the future.

W: I prefer not to have a vision of the future. I think its self-indulgent. How far do you take it? To tastes in music? In a free society will comrades like Mahler? In having a vision of the future what we are doing is projecting personal predilections on the rest of humanity.

SA: Can we interpret your remarks as being hostile to utopian writers?

W: No, I enjoy utopian writers just as you might enjoy science fiction because they are dealing in fiction, aren't they?

SA: We are going to try again because we are not giving up on this point. You have studied and written about housing, urban planning and community design. Now, if the mayor of Baltimore, whom you recently interviewed, had asked your opinion as to how to go about redesigning the City of Baltimore, what would you have told him?

W: I would have told him, "expropriate the landlords and leave it to the tenants."

[Laughter]

SA: Let's talk about that for a while. You have a faith that if we turned the housing over to the tenants something would emerge from that. Other people would say that even if they were willing to concede that people had that potential, they do not yet have that knowledge and skill. How would you reply to that?

W: On every block there will be the community technical aid sector where all those worthy people with architectural or plumbing skills could make them available to members of the group. This, after all, is what the People's Homesteading movement is about, isn't it? Sharing and expanding people's own skills.

SA: Having done this, having expropriated the land and turned it over to the tenants, what kind of society do you think they would organize?

[Laughter]

W: Well, it would mean that one of these problems which has been with people ever since Adam and Eve left the Garden of Eden — this question of landlord and tenant — would have been solved. No tenant ever loves his landlord and no landlord ever loves his tenant. We would have, at one go, got that out of the way and then we could think about other things. We could think about diet and education and pollution and love and topics of that sort. One very crucial issue would have been got our of the way by this perfectly simple little task of expropriating the expropriator.

SA: Sitting at these microphones, we once asked Murray Bookchin what he thought was the single most significant problem preventing the realization of anarchist community and he replied, without any hesitation, "autonomy — of helping people to grow to be autonomous." How would you reply to that question?

W: Well, I'm glad that Murray has found the answer for me. I think he is right. Now, if I were rich I would fund research to look into the libertarian personality. We have all met some absolutely liberated people who are autonomous without anybody having given them autonomy; they have taken it. And so it would be nice to know what made them tick. In the same way we need to look at this human characteristic of resourcefulness. We rejoice at it when we find it in other people. What makes people resourceful? Why are some children resourceful and independent from a very early age while others are timid and unimaginative? This is a marvelous field for research, so thinking about it, I think Bookchin is right.

SA: You have given some though children in the city. What are some of the things that make for a libertarian personality for the growing child?

W: There used to be a slogan in the progressive school movement — have them, love them and leave them alone. It is an anti-child-abuse slogan and there is a lot of sense in this. Progressive thinkers in education of the most liberal sort, as opposed to anarchist, have had the same conclusion. There isn't an anarchist patent on this. Dewey would have said the same thing, wouldn't he?

SA: Again, if you were helping to design a city of tomorrow, how would go about making the conditions of that city for liberated children?

W: Well, it would be one in which they weren't, for example, herded into child ghettos like schools and playgrounds. I believe a play pundit called Herman Mattern had this slogan: "Down with playgrounds, free the child." Meaning that a good urban environment would be as useful and acceptable to children as to adults and all of those small environmental changes which we can think about for the sake of the old would similarly be valuable for the young. You remember Paul Goodman's novel, *The Empire City*, this great shambling, hulk of a book. Buried in there are all sorts of useful information where his hero, Horace (named after Horatio Alger) is using the street and the environment as a learning device. This is what cities are for as far as children are concerned. I think that the future city will be a much more dispersed city; it will be a city region simply because those very forces which have brought people together in the compact overcrowded city have been dispersed — the industries are no longer there and the technical means for decentralized, dispersed industry are there. So probably the city will be very different in that sense. It might even be Ebenezer Howard's garden city, Now there are some people who can't stand this because they want the drama of the street and the excitement of downtown New York or something of this sort. But I think that during the family life cycle there are appropriate cities for everybody and certainly I think that, despite the notion of the streetwise urban child who exploits the whole thing, the dispersed city with a front garden and backyard, is the right childhood environment. But when children come to be 14 or 15 they want to be in the thick of the exciting city where all the action is. Alright, they move off to the city commune. The parents back home worry just as they would if the daughter went into service in the 19th century or the boy ran away to sea. Those city kids having worked through their teens in the city themselves become parents and they very soon want the space and so on of a suburban or a rural environment. So there is an appropriate city for most people's different age groups. The dispersed regional city, the sort of thing that people like Lewis Mumford have been ruminating about for years, seems to me to be the pattern for the future city.

SA: Would these cities be fairly autonomous? Could they feed themselves, for example?

W: Well, now once again, the medieval city was like that. Kropotkin envisaged, as you know, that every city would have all around it its market gardening area. I'm very interested in the community gardening movement. In England such gardens are called allotments because they are land which was allotted to the poor after the enclosures of common lands. They have a very long history. The allotment movement of the "community garden" or "liberty garden" or "victory garden" movement in the United States was diminishing for years after the Second World War when people were more affluent and less interested in growing their own vegetables. Suddenly, in the 1970s came a new generation of people who put a particular value on organically grown vegetable or fresh vegetables, and saw a particular virtue in growing them for themselves. With the emptying of the cities comes the greening of the cities and the possibility for food production on a very large scale within the city region itself. You have only to think about cities like Singapore or Hong Kong in the Far East where they are surrounded by what are, in effect, community gardens — tiny, highly productive vegetable patches. Yes, the autonomous, self-sufficient city like the city-state of the Middle Ages which so appealed to Kropotkin, certainly appeals to me.

SA: How do you deal with issues of technology? I know that many anarchists seem hostile to technology and others, again to use an example from Murray Bookchin, talk about a liberatory technology.

W: Yes, a liberatory technology is precisely what we want and the decision about what kind of technology people will use will obviously be individual. We all have our romantic notions about craftsmanship in the past and there will always be, no doubt, people who want to make their own household crockery or their own tables and chairs and others who will be only too pleased to have them made of plastic extrusions they can put together. I think it was Goodman, once again, who put this beautifully in the book *Communitas* where, as you remember, he has his three possible cities of the future — the City of Efficient Consumption, which is exactly like Victor Gruen's plan for Fort Worth, Texas, in the 1950s — a sort of dome over one great shopping mall. Or there is the New Commune, as Goodman puts what is his hobbyhorse, which is the small-scale community of parents and children doing their own thing. But he and his brother's most interesting thought about the future city, I thought, was the one which he calls "Maximum Security with Minimum Regulation." (I believe that was the title.) And what he meant was the kind of social welfare that came about in Britain during the Second World War and afterwards as well as some of the programs in America for social security. How can that be achieved with minimum regulation of people's lives? The answer, says Goodman (it's a non-anarchist solution) — there is a form of industrial conscription just like military conscription — everybody at 18 does their two-years on presumably the maintenance of the assembly line, turning out the plastic cups and saucers or the blue jeans or the canned whatever it is — the ordinary, basic things of life. And having spent two years in that ordinary mass production economy, the rest of their time is their own. They are entitled to the products of those machines and this double decker civilization which the Goodmans envisage answer a whole lot of the kind of questions that you might be coming on to me about.

How do you cope with the problem of luxury in an anarchist society? Answer: That is in the free market; yes, a market economy on top of the basic economy that supplies all of our needs. So the question now of who has or hasn't got a Renoir or a 1922 Deusenberg car is something we just don't have to worry about because that is in this free market economy. But we are concerned that basic needs are met. And there are certain Puritans, probably anarchists might be amongst them, who will take pride in wearing the basic clothes that came off that machine and not the beautifully hand-stitched, hand-woven Sea Island cotton blouses which come in the luxury economy. Using the liberatory effects of ordinary mass robotic production, our basic needs are met and then pushed out of the way simply for a couple of years of conscription. As I said, that is a non-anarchist view. We can disguise it. We can say, "No, it's really our social obligations which make us do this. It will be the done thing. The young person who avoids it will be shunned as peculiar." I think this is a thoughtful use of utopianism rather than a blueprint for a free society.

SA: If we have a mixed market economy, how can we be sure that we won't once again develop a maldistribution of wealth?

W: There isn't any guarantee about this. I think this is the whole tragedy of politics — the juggling act between liberty and equality. Probably socialists put more importance on equality than on liberty, while anarchists give much more importance to liberty than to equality. So, of course, do right-wingers and right-wing libertarians. Trying to eliminate inequality wastes a terrible amount of human effort. I don't believe there are any political guarantees at all. I think the final struggle, as it says in the words of "The Internationale," is really a myth. I think it was Martin Buber (of all people) who said that the day after the revolution is really the day before the revolution for all those except the ones who got bogged down in some particular point in history. And we all know, don't we, all too well about the Iron Law of Oligarchy — the way every institution, however libertarian it is, hardens into something which then has to be rebelled against.

SA: You don't then envision any structural means by which to break that iron law.

W: Well, a whole lot of bodies, bodies like the IWW, I would say, attempted to do this — to have temporariness and impermanence built into the system. You can make efforts to avoid oligarchy, but there is no indication that they are going to be successful. And I am not worried about this. You think of all of those institutions in our society which go on and on simply because once a thing has been started it is very hard to stop. And yet in most of the fields that I can think of it always becomes necessary to abandon the old institution and start a new one. Beside which, of course, everybody in every generation ought to have the joy and delight of starting something.

SA: Since you're working in architecture, what is an anarchist architect?

W: (Chuckles) I don't know. Architects are interesting people. They are more interested in people than, let's say, structural engineers. You don't hear structural engineers endlessly discussing the morality and ideology of their profession. I am quite fond of architects because of that. There have been anarchist architects, including some celebrated anarchists, even though their names escape me for the moment. Your real question is: Could you tell from their architecture that they were anarchists?

SA: Yes, and what do anarchist architects concern themselves with?

W: I think, if you regard architecture in that sense as a fine art, you might find that the most anarchist architects were those who adhered most rigorously to a bizarre style of architecture just as, amongst artists (there are anarchist artists) think of Courbet; there is nothing about Courbet which suggests that he had an anarchist ideology. Or Pissaro, this famous and delightful character, was an anarchist artist but you would be belittling him if you suggested that his art reflected his anarchy or else you would be sentimentalizing about it. But, quite obviously, there are architects who are primarily not concerned with externals of the building. They are concerned with who their client is and in providing a genuine service to their client. There was a very, very interesting Anglo-Swiss architect who died a year or two ago in his late seventies. His name is Walter Segal and he was brought up on an anarchist commune in Switzerland in the Ticino. It was a great embarrassment for him to be brought up amongst these free-thinking people. The other children used to laugh at the funny clothes that his mother sent him to school in and he told me he always had a double feeling about this. One was pride in that he wasn't like all the rest of these kids and, of course, the other was desperately wanting to be like the rest of the kids. He spent years and years of his lifetime gradually simplifying his work until he designed very cheap, simply-built structures. He claimed this which would enable any poor man to build his own house much more cheaply than it could be done by anyone. And he disclaimed the title of a community architect. He simply regarded himself as a good professional providing a service to his clients. I am afraid that's a terribly long answer to a simple question.

[Laughter]

W: Yes, there are a whole lot of topics on which it would be very nice if we had our anarchist pundits. From this point of view, Chomsky is a useful man, isn't he? Chomsky is really an example of somebody who has made a big reputation in one field and consequently, because we're always so willing to have our thinking done for us by a pundit, we all think that if he's a big boy in linguistics, therefore he's a big boy in everything else. It's the Einstein or the Bertrand Russell syndrome, isn't it, really? And that's not anarchistic; that shows how we all value expertise.

SA: But you think…

W: Before we start recording again, what do we feel about Chomsky?

SA: I have very mixed feelings about Chomsky mainly because from much of his writing you would not know that he was an anarchist. There is nothing in most of his essays that would lead you to believe that this man was anything more than an angry liberal critic. So when an anarchist writer doesn't use that frame of reference in a critique or analysis of his subject, then what is it that makes him an anarchist? Wouldn't you feel angry or embarrassed if somebody read one of your works on housing and said, "I can't discern any anarchist orientation or perspective in it." Isn't that precisely what you do — bring to bear your own anarchist ideas when you write about issues of housing and urban planning?

W: Yes, it is. But on the other hand I don't say that every anarchist writing on housing has to refer to what Kropotkin said in *The Conquest of Bread*, like every Marxist writing about housing is obliged to refer to Engels on *The Housing Question*, nor do they have to genuflect to the Red masters of the past.

SA: Yes, but you are still applying an anarchist perspective.

W: Yes.

SA: So now let us ask you how you regard Chomsky's writings.

W: I feel, as a matter of fact, between ourselves [chuckles] a little same about Chomsky as about Murray Bookchin. I think that they (I may be libeling them come rather late in life to anarchism and have a view of anarchism that is very much shaped by a socialist, Marxist path. But we all bear the stigma of our previous experiences so I wouldn't criticize either of them on that account. Chomsky did, I think, write about anarchism specifically in some pamphlet or other and it seemed to me a rather poor explanation of anarchism. Though I have spoke to him on a radio hookup and he seems to me to be a very nice, engaging sort of man.

SA: How did you come to anarchism?

W: Well, I was in the army in the Second World War for over five years and that's enough to make anybody an anarchist, I think. [chuckles]

SA: Alright. You left the army and then what happened? Surely you were an anti-authoritarian before then.

W: Well, I was young. I'm very fortunate in never having been anything else. My parents were ordinary Labor Party socialists but I was a late developer and I didn't start thinking until I came out of the army or rather, I did start thinking when I was in the army. As soon as I came out of the army I was asked to join the editorial group of *Freedom* (that was in 1947) and I always make people laugh by saying that I thought that paper was at its absolute best just before I joined the editorial group.

SA: So you had encountered people from *Freedom* while you were still in the army?

W: Yes, indeed.

SA: You're going to tell me they were in the army too?

W: They weren't in the army, no. This really will amuse you. The *Freedom* press group, whose journal during the war was called *War Commentary for Anarchism*, was one of the very few political groups in Britain to be opposed to the war. Others were pure pacifists and there were presumably a few Nazis, although there was no real right-wing opposition to the war in Britain. The anarchists published their journal unscathed all through the war, but right at the end they were arrested and charged with inciting or rather "seducing" the members of the forces from their duty. A case was brought against them because of raids on the personal belongings of various people in the army. Five or six soldiers were brought at great expense to the Old Bailey, the central criminal court in London, to give evidence for the prosecution against the editors of *Freedom*. Naturally, we all swore on oath that we hadn't been seduced from our duty to the army by reading Freedom Press publications except one of our number (we were not known to each other) conscientiously thought, yes he had been seduced and a jolly good thing, too. That was his particular line. And out testimony provided no evidence for the prosecution — much more for the defense. But my first contact with those people who for years became my dearest friends was as a prosecution witness against them in 1946. They were sent to prison for 9 months on charges which, in English law at the time, they could have been given 14 years. It wasn't altogether a laughing matter.

SA: So, they still let you be on the editorial group or they were all in jail and you took over?

[Laughter]

W: No, they were out of jail by that time. In fact, when they were in jail, the paper was put together by those who were not — Marie Louise Berneri and George Woodcock — who later emigrated back to Canada in 1949.

SA: Didn't Orwell work on Freedom Press?

W: He did write for it occasionally. He was very active in a body called the Freedom Defense Committee which was set up to provide a defense for the editors of *Freedom*. Orwell was very sympathetic, very friendly with the then editors. The normal body for such things was called the National Council for Civil Liberties, the equivalent of the American Civil Liberties Union. It so happened that at that time in the 1940s, it was controlled by our friends in the Communist Party who weren't going to use their resources to defend a bunch of anarchists. As you know, the Communists were a fiercely patriotic party after 1941. So the Freedom Defense Committee received a very great deal of help from George Orwell, including the very typewriter he used to write *Animal Farm* which has long since gone into the typewriter junk shops. It hasn't become a holy object amongst the Orwellians.

SA: We published an article by Ruthann Robson, one of our editors, which is a satiric piece was a serious understructure — "How to Lead an Anarchist Life." I know that when I have given talks and workshops people ask me questions of this kind and so without any embarrassment, I am going to ask you the same questions, namely, how should an anarchist live? How do you maintain your principles as an anarchist in a repressive, capitalist society?

W: Oh, I think we betray our principles every day. If I was really cynical, I would say that is what principles are for. Of course, unless you are going to be a martyr, you pay income tax. If you are actually an employed person in Britain your taxes are deducted from your pay by your employer under the PAYE (pay as you earn) system introduced during the war. Many an anarchist that I know have worked in the very margins of the economy for the usually reasons of making a living while devoting their real time, so to speak, to the production of anarchist propaganda. I have always very much admired them for it. I would suggest myself that you and your group are precisely that kind of persons who have got the work issue in perspective. I for a long time was not able to do that because I am not very clever and not very adaptable. I worked for years on the drawing board in architecture. I then, at the age of 40, took a one-year teacher training course. I actually left school when I was 15 and my teacher's certificate is the one qualification in anything that I have ever got. I then left teaching in 1970 to work for a voluntary body producing the journal called *BEE*. This was the *Bulletin of Environmental Education* which was aimed toward showing school teachers, whatever their subject was, how the environment came into their teaching. All my friends used to laugh because they used to say that *BEE* was indistinguishable from *Anarchy* which I edited in my spare time in the 1960s.

And then finally, I gave up working for anybody and became a full-time writer. Needlessly to say, I have never been so financially insecure in my life. But, on the other hand, our eldest children had left school and the young one was making the transition from the primary to the secondary school (as we call it in England) so nowadays I work harder than ever before. I am an absolute slave to my typewriter doing journalism for pay in order to produce my books which, unfortunately, don't pay. That's not really the way an anarchist should live. Think of Malatesta. Malatesta determined at a very early age that he was going to be an anarchist propagandist so he learned a useful trade which would always be in demand. He became an electrical engineer just at the time when houses were first being wired for the most primitive form of electric lighting. Thus, he could travel in any country in the world, pursuing his metier as an anarchist propagandist — and he did. He was here in the United States, he was in London, he was in Latin America, very often being turned out by the police. So he was self-supporting. He wasn't being dependent on patrons or charity or welfare handouts. He was self-supporting. His time was his own. He determined his own life.

SA: Actually, an anarchist prostitute friend advised me to take up watchmaking and told me that being a watch repair person would make me totally independent and I could travel wherever I wanted and there would always be work for me. I never took her advice.

[Laughter]

W: I do think that the attitude of the younger generation is changing shortly in this respect. While we always hear about yuppies, all the young people I know (my own children and their friends) never have any notion of actually going to work from 9 to 5. They happen to be musicians and so have been self-employed from a very early age. I live now deep in the country where the boys and girls leaving school very frequently are either with their families, friends or relations in the informal economy and have no intention of submitting to the discipline of employment in an office — still less in a factory. But as the factory system is dying they would never get the opportunity to do that. I think that young people are making these decisions themselves.

SA: One of the things you have talked about is the necessity, and I think that is a fair word to use, for anarchists to have an area of expert knowledge — punditry you call it. And you regard yourself as a housing pundit. Talk about that a little bit. Why do you think that is so important?

W: Well, because, when you say "anarchist" you almost imply anarchist propagandist because every anarchist, or every anarchist I know, is a propagandist. And they can be very bad propagandists, but nevertheless, that's what they are and that's what I see myself as and this means that they are using the media, whether the good, old-fashioned newspaper or books or, of course, radio and television. And because anarchism to many people's mind is an absolutely outlandish, weirdo belief, my intention has always been to make it respectable. And by that I don't mean respectable in the bourgeois sense, I mean worthy of respect. And the topics we have to discuss nowadays and that we continually hear about and are talked about in legislatures are immensely complicated subjects and we do need to have an alternative mastery of them than the political left and the right. In Britain, as you know, we have the Conservatives and the Labor Party. Even though from the anarchist point of view we can say they are exactly the same. I think that the human motivations that give rise to their attitudes are very different. In the case of housing, they have particular views which are sort of individualist and collectivist, And the anarchist view is, so to speak, at a tangent to all of these and I, and others like me, always say that the first principle of housing is dweller control. It is a notion which is much associated with me and John Turner and it is also quite obviously an anarchist position on housing just as workers' control would be in industry. As a propagandist, what I want to find in British anarchist press, what we lack, are people who have the same kind of specialist but simple anarchist approach to other topics. The whole business of social medicine and the health services in most countries are in crisis and I would like somebody who had mastered this and could talk back to the free marketeers or the socialists on equal terms. I think that would make anarchism worthy of respect and would get away from the utopianism. The idea that there are no solutions to anything except one big solution has made as all anti-utopian, I think, especially in the century of Hitler and Stalin. So *applications of anarchy are really what I am about.*

SA: What does that mean in architecture?

W: Well, the secret is that I'm rather bored with architecture as such. I think it is a big, pompous word for the art of building and I'm one of those people who is more interested in shacks and shanties and all these poor peoples' housing. I even have, and it sounds a bit sordid, an aesthetic of the shanty town. But this is precisely like everybody else in the architectural world. They were classic, then Gothic and then revivalist and then came along the modern movement which browbeat them all into a sort of Stalinist puritanism and gradually people said, "but we don't like it." Concrete isn't a beautiful material so we have all these neo-vernacular revivalisms, postmodernisms, and so on. And the shanty style will come in and we can say that's anarchist architecture. If anarchist architecture implies a kind of absolute randomness, well, there's plenty of that. Isn't there a chain of out-of-town supermarkets in America whose feature is the bricks permanently tumbling down or things of that sort. When you have what, in the pejorative sense, you'll call anarchy in architecture, design doesn't matter any more. It's a matter of choice. I personally like a period when there is anarchy in design like that. So in that sense I think that what architects can give to community groups is nothing at all to do with design, which is what they are trained to do, but that purely technical knowledge of building, which they have, the stuff about U-values, vapor barriers and that kind of thing, which you cannot expect a layperson to know but which is an important contribution to the lay environment. So, in fact, as somebody said, a long time ago, let's abolish architecture and start building.

SA: What do anarchist builder have to offer to community design?

W: Do you mean by community design, housing? The sort of thing done by self-build or homesteading movements or are you thinking about the whole layout?

SA: I was thinking about the whole layout.

W: I believe, like Walter Segal, that what they have to do is give a genuine professional service to that community. This implies, in terms of our previous conversation, that they help create an environment for all of the citizen, including the old and the young, and this probably implies that it will be a pedestrian environment just for safety's sake. And it may very well be that there will be some reflection of anarchist ideology about the place. Maybe the place that in the medieval village was held by the parish church and will now be held by the community hall where everybody goes to anarchist meetings on a Saturday night. [chuckles] But maybe it shouldn't be. Maybe it won't be that at all.

SA: What do you tell people who ask you what to read to learn more about anarchism?

W: Well, it's a very funny thing. Many of the books which I find most sympathetic in persuading people to become anarchists are not anarchist books at all. One of my favorite books from that point of view is a book called *Paths in Utopia* by Martin Buber. Buber was a theologian, if anything, but with some very close and interesting links with anarchism. As you know, having done a radio program about Landauer, he was Gustav Landauer's literary executor. I find Buber's book a survey of what is known of utopian socialism — alternatives to the Marxist tradition — a very sympathetic and persuasive book. Another of the books which I am very fond of is the book by Leopold Kohr which is called *The Breakdown of Nations*. It is an argument for the small state, the small scale world, and is very witty. In fact, a whole number of books which seem very, very persuasive to me and tend not to be specifically by anarchists. This is very interesting, I think, how people adopt some political idea. Someone becomes a Marxist and then has to read *Capital* and all these great works — it's a terrible penalty for them.

SA: But having paid that penalty, they have to stay a Marxist for the rest of their lives.

W: And similarly, someone who has converted to Catholicism is converted and then receives instruction in the faith and reads the right books. And when somebody says to me, "What should I read about anarchism?" the most obvious works are not extraordinarily valuable. Suppose we say, Kropotkin's *Mutual Aid*. This is a very long argument to show that mutual aid is effective in evolution because Kropotkin was preoccupied not in making anarchism respectable but in making it scientific. He was convinced that his 19th century approach to science was correct. So very often Kropotkin is not the best introduction to anarchism. His work which obviously did appeal to the young in the 1890s will make the young double up with laughter by the 1990s. Good, new introductory books are not being written today. But a serious person, slightly aware of the different currents in social thought would find that book of Buber's most interesting — and it is not even directed toward making people anarchists.

William Godwin is often recognized as the godfather of modern anarchism, and his 1793 work, Enquiry Concerning Political Justice, is an acknowledged classic of anarchist literature despite its age. In this essay, Art Efron attempts to re-evaluate Godwin's work with a contemporary eye. He finds that, while not without some short-sighted flaws, Godwin's work still provides "an extensive terrain" in which we can retrace the fundamental tenets of radical political philosophy.

Originally published in issue 24.

Reading Political Justice
A New, Experiential Anarchist Approach
Arthur Efron

A year ago, while reading *Political Justice*, I happened to see a bumper sticker a 4-wheel drive pick-up truck, of the type now so popular in the U.S.A. The sticker read: "We Live, Eat, Sleep, and Love on Our Cycles." I also glimpsed two motorcycles loaded on that truck. In that bumper sticker, I recognized the typically American assertion of freedom: the truck's owners were saying "This is the way we choose to spend our lives, and that choice may not be criticized by others, no matter what anyone else thinks of it." I was about to shrug this off as harmless when I involuntarily thought of something I had been reading in *Political Justice*. Some of Godwin's arguments about that which he terms "duty" came to mind. Godwin is a moralist, but he is not being simply moralistic in stating that duty is necessarily central to our lives. He is not claiming that we all have duties to parents, spouses, or children, simply because those are our relatives. It is Godwin who claimed that in some circumstances, it would be necessary to rescue a non-kinsman philosopher from a fire rather than our own brother or even mother. For Godwin, duty is more like a contextual principle of our effects on other people: it tells us, for example, that when we know people we encounter are destitute, then we must expend some of our energies in helping them — and that we have to give them that help *instead of* selfishly riding our bikes night and day.

Although I hope I have a grasp of what Godwin might have in mind by the term "duty," I still have my suspicions about the notion. I am not entirely sure that if we were all to help others in need, rather than engaging in the many activities we have an interest in doing, the world necessarily would become a better place. I don't know that much; Godwin thought he did know that much, and that is one of the problems of reading *Political Justice* today. Still, when I look inside my own mind and feelings, when I more deeply consider what it is I value and what I distrust, then these doubts about Godwin, while retaining their validity, become far less important. I find I am actually more sympathetic to what Godwin has to say about duty than I am to the kind of sentiment of freedom I see emblazoned upon that bumper. In fact, if I think about it, I realize that Godwin's principle of duty is too vital to be denied. Lacking his assurance, as I lack his certainty throughout *Political Justice*, I find myself nonetheless in the position of affirming his principle. I would call duty, in his sense, as I would call several other of his principles, "back to the wall" societal propositions. They are principles which, if denied, would leave us with a world of authoritarian order and its inevitable chaos. If everyone in the world were content with the free disposal of their energy in the manner of the cycle riders, I do know that the world would be even worse than it is now. It is not a matter, as Max Stirner was to argue, of each of us having an ego that we must not and in fact cannot give over to the collective social self (which term is a mere illusion for Godwin as well as for Stirner). But a world of selfish egos would be an extremely bad world. I know that because I have seen plenty of that kind of world, and have been part of it. For me as a reader in the 1990s, Godwin's principle of duty, like most of the principles he announces in *Political Justice*, must be questioned and restated so that it would lose its ring of certainty. But could I really reject it? When I reached the roots of the matter, I realized that my back was to the wall, and I could retreat no further: I could throw out duty, in his sense of the word, only if I were willing to accept a perfectly loathsome world.

Let us hear this in some of Godwin's own words. We will quote him from a later passage on "virtue," where duty has now become implicit.

> If self-love be the only principle of action, there can be no such thing as virtue. Benevolent intention is essential to virtue. Virtue, where it exists in any eminence, is a species of conduct modelled upon a true estimate of the different reasons inviting us to a preference. He that makes a false estimate and prefers a trivial and partial good to an important and comprehensive one, is vicious. (Godwin, 1985; p. 385)

These few sentences bring out major aspects of Godwin's thought.[1]) There is qualification as well as firmness: virtue has to reach some eminence or degree, or as we might say, it has to reach a level of critical mass, in order to be worth talking about in this context. It is not virtue in the abstract. Godwin takes pains to support his positions, not only by piling up reasons and assertions in their favor, but also by carefully attending to the scope and precise meanings of his terms. This quality can easily be missed if one notices only those statements which appear to be given as absolutes.) Second, virtue even in its "eminence" is contextual, that is, it is based on a true estimate of the different reasons inviting us to develop a preference. 3) That we can and do make such estimates is a function of our capacity for reason, but, 4) furthermore, human reason is integrally related to "benevolent intention." As Chris Jones has shown, this is part of a common argument for universal benevolence in late 18th century; it is one that Godwin states coherently. Here we are far away from Freud's understanding that the intellect is grounded in sadism, or, for that matter, from Jacques Lacan's notion of the ego as basically paranoic. 5) Finally, we have to absorb the force of Godwin's concluding word in the brief passage I have quoted: those who settle for "a trivial and partial good" when they know that there are important and comprehensive goods to be had instead, are not merely mistaken: they are ''vicious." What could that mean?

Let me tackle that question by pointing out two basic approaches we might take. One of these is simply to chalk up the word "vicious" to Godwin's moralist bias, in which he had been well schooled. Motorcycle riders, after all, are not usually "vicious," and it is hardly desirable that we be led into thinking of them as such. On the other hand, if we search for Godwin's meaning in more empathic ways, we can see that the huge aggregate of human devotion to trivial pursuits is indeed what vitiates social improvement. The reason is that we thoughtlessly channel so much of our constructive energies into activities that make no contribution to lifting any of humankind's burdens, such as the continual resurgence of famine, the prevalence of displaced people, or the use of torture by governments. Such displacement can well be called "vicious."

This approach to Godwin is experiential in John Dewey's sense of the term. I seek to validate Godwin's principles by appealing to all that I know, and by trying to understand his own experience in so far as it bears on his argument. In the mass of argumentation that makes up his 750-page text, I propose that we each start again, and that we ask what is valid now? But we must ask this about basic principles that matter to us, rather than give this text primarily an historical reading. This is the opposite of the validation performed recently by George Crowder, in his book *Classical Anarchism*. Crowder assures us that Godwin, Proudhon, Bakunin and Kropotkin all make very good sense, and that they basically agree with one another. But, we can say this only if we notice the underlying premise of their thinking, which was in each case a form of scientism, or the faith that scientific progress would sooner or later bring us into an enormously improved, virtually utopian world. But while the great classical anarchists may have thought that, that cannot be what makes them important for us now. Scientism is a rightly discredited faith.

Fortunately, even if *Political Justice* is indebted to scientism, the book is not all of a piece. Even the assurance of the triumph of reason is sometimes tempered with realization that it may never happen: "It may be to a certain degree doubtful," writes Godwin in a chapter on obedience, "whether the human species will ever be emancipated from their present subjection and pupillage, but let it not be forgotten that this is their condition" (p. 248). We are not obliged to accept or reject the book's arguments as a whole, and we have good indications within it that we need not do so. What *Political Justice* is, is a mass of arguments as well as one overall massive argument. Godwin may have believed that he had systematically laid out his case, but despite the form of the book, with its carefully counterpoised arguments and their opposing viewpoints, and despite its systematic division into 8 sequential "books," *Political Justice* has an undeniable experimental quality. As Godwin recalls in the preface to the first edition, the book was not fully planned out. He only came to see what he was saying while writing it. The major revisions for the second edition of 1796, he admits, are not completely satisfactory, and in the third edition of 1798, he made further minor and major changes and deletions. All of this is well-discussed by Peter H. Marshall, in his biography of Godwin. Marshall also shows us a Notebook entry where Godwin planned still further important changes which he did not have opportunity to write (Marshall, 1984; p. 199), and other modifications were included in a book of essays Godwin published in 1797 but did not incorporate into his text (Marshall, pp. 163–68). Rather than apologizing for the book's rough edges, Godwin says that he did not think it wise to "suppress any opinion because it was inconsistent with the prejudice or persuasion of others" (p. 72). Marshall also states, correctly, that the summary Godwin added in the 3rd edition is inconsistent with the text, and that he realized this. The book was intended to exhibit "perfect explicitness and unreserve," and if this purpose turned out to be "an improper one," no reversal was possible. For one thing, any impulse to reverse that experimental quality came too late into the writing process, and for another, the work would lose all integrity if the author "rescinded sentiments originally advanced as true," as long as those statements could still be presented with their "original evidence" (p. 72).

A major dissonance that Godwin allows to remain in the book is its absolute faith in the certainty of truth alongside a recognition that human situations are immensely varied. Godwin greatly honors the "immutable" quality of truth (p. 117, etc.) and at the same time makes the strikingly modern statement that "Everything in man may be said to be in a state of flux; he is a Proteus whom we know not how to detain." (p. 186). These claims may not be in formal contradiction, but they point to different intellectual worlds: the first toward the Age of Reason, and the second to an acceptance of change so inclusive that it must deny anything immutable, including truth. It is as if Godwin is saying that Reason, the greatest of human powers, and our only way of determining truth, is itself unchanging and not in flux; yet everything human is in flux. A number of students with whom I have read *Political Justice* are troubled by this disjunction.

But this is where I am going to draw a line of resistance to our modern preoccupations. It would be too easy to `"deconstruct" *Political Justice*, showing that its arguments are undercut by its own admissions. That would be sterile; and instead of accepting the book's experimental quality and responding to it accordingly, we would only be reading it from a safe observational station. That the book undercuts its own propositions is a conclusion we would be foredoomed to reach anyway, given the assumptions of deconstruction. What would be valuable to do, however, is something quite different: to *reconstruct* (the term is John Dewey's) this book's central anarchist arguments by clearing our own pathways within it, and linking them, selectively, to the trails of reasoning that Godwin has provided. Based on my own thirty-five years of reading in this work, I am willing to predict that if we adopt such a procedure, we will find that lines of Godwin's arguments will first seem to collapse — and then will be reconstructed.

The only major aspects of his thought that I think must be unequivocally rejected, insofar as these are critical for anarchist thought, are the two obvious ones which have been pointed out many times by Godwin scholars: one, that he falls into authoritarianism in his uncritical confidence that the opinion of one's peers will form a non-coercive kind of pressure to control our tendencies toward anti-social behavior; and two, that we need not undertake any action "in concert," that is, in cooperative consultation with other people. I have found that these strands in his argument tend to be written in a manner that betrays their unsoundness. The arguments for the fine effects of social pressure exerted by one's fellows tend to be given in flat, confident declarations, lacking the usual density of consideration that Godwin gives to other topics.

As for his suspicions about more than two people managing to work together in a rational manner, his assertions tend to slip by without being properly argued. At one point Godwin asks, theoretically, why "men in a collective capacity" cannot be just as fully entrusted to follow the discipline of reason as men in their individual existences (p. 692), but this uncharacteristic admission is quickly passed over. Then later, Godwin seems to be anxious and impatient about the whole topic of cooperative reasoned action, and reaches for the easy answer that this may not even be necessary: "We ought to be able to do without one another" (p. 761). In the context of the many vigorously considered problems in the book, this vacuous "ought" is a low point, Godwin's equivalent of mumbling under his breath.

Locating these major weak points is not difficult; what is interesting about them is their conjunction with weak writing, as if Godwin himself could not identify adequately with what he was trying to say. The real problem for readers sympathetic to anarchism, is how best to deal with the many strong points of the argument, points which often need to be restated, qualified, reconstructed and — if there is to be any anarchist future — defended.

I propose that a creative method for accomplishing such a reading is to do what I was beginning to do in my example of the motorcycle riders: consider the various propositions put forth and ask, by bringing to bear our own fullest experience and knowledge, if we dare to reject what Godwin is saying. I have found that very often, I could not reject: my back was put to the wall, and I had to take my stand with Godwin.

Here then are a few such examples, which I focus upon for their value in thinking in anarchist ways about the future of social relations.

Veracity: "That the Motives to Deceive Can But Rarely Occur"

Here we are dealing with Godwin's apparent naivete. In a comment on Part IV of *Gulliver's Travels* Godwin is more than eager to take the satiric text at face value, while regretting that "its mere playfulness of form" prevented it from instructing mankind effectively (p. 552). From the example of Swift's Houyhnhnms, Godwin draws support for his belief that after government is abolished, it will become feasible to persuade people, solely by means of "reasonableness," to cooperate for their common benefit (pp. 552–53). No coercion will be necessary; truth will triumph — although not immediately. It is much easier to assume such a thing if you believe, as Godwin apparently did, that "the obvious use of the faculty of speech is to inform, and not to mislead" (Godwin, p. 217), and that deception seldom would be attempted if people were to recognize what they owe to one another. Of course he knows that in political matters, deception is rampant and inevitable, but this does not prevent him from claiming that we know human beings enough to be sure that "the motives to deceive can but rarely occur, while the motives to veracity will govern the stream of human actions" (p. 217).

That is a wonderful wish, but can it be any more than that? In reading *Political Justice*, we will encounter such claims for the invincibility of truth. It is virtually mandatory to doubt them, but it is also necessary to not surrender the values which they hold. The undefended generalization that speech exists to inform rather than mislead must rouse our doubts, but when the process of doubt has run its course, will we actually reject the principle? In Godwin's favor, we can try to support it genetically. Lying, widespread as it is in society, is not something people do at birth. The infant prior to language knows nothing of such use (or of irony, wit, or double meanings) and in the early stages of language acquisition, I venture to say that lying plays no part. Lying is learned behavior, and authoritarian society encourages such behavior by pressuring people to pretend that they are in compliance with society's mores and its political presumptions. Godwin knows all about such things. I suppose that we will be unable to assert, with Swift's noble horses, that it is unimaginable why anyone would "say the thing which is not," but the high position of veracity in human motivation might be supportable after all. If not, maybe we should forget about social anarchism, which depends on being able to trust people to communicate honestly.

The Emulation of Excellence

The term "equity" for Godwin counters the apparent exception to the "moral equality of mankind." For while we all "partake of a common nature," the great benefactors of mankind appear to be so exceptional that their equality with the rest of us is not apparent. But this is only an appearance, because we all have some "equity," meaning some human share, in their accomplishments. We identify with the great liberating minds not because we feel we are their equals, but because as reasoning human beings, we share something with them. The important claim for an anarchist future is that equity "is calculated to infuse into every bosom an emulation of excellence" (pp. 183–84). As readers coming to this book 200 years after its publication, we can easily confute this claim of the emulation of excellence by pointing to the many instances of slavish, fanatic following, by masses of people, of some of the worst leaders in history. But can we afford to rest with this refutation? To do so would be to accept that humans have such a large, innately irrational principle built into their behavior that the only way to preserve society would be through authoritarian trickery, as Godwin, alluding to Edmund Burke's faith in "salutary prejudices and useful delusions" (p. 118), has already pointed out. This would mean that human reason, since it could not be used for the regulation of life, had discovered the most rational principles of society only to find them all "abortive" efforts. Thus the mind itself would have been some huge evolutionary error. The latter, in fact, is a thought Godwin wants us to face: if we become aware of the "havoc" that the human species exhibits under the rule of its political institutions, and if we assume that such chaos is "the unalterable allotment of our nature," then "the eminence of our rational faculties must be considered as rather an abortion than a substantial benefit…" (p. 88). No doubt by now Nietzsche has considered that possibility for us. If we are satisfied with that line of inquiry, we can forget about any genuine connection between human reason and "benevolent intention."

But for the anarchist as well as for the democrat, or for anyone else who hopes for a more humane and genuinely free society, these are speculative, misanthropic conclusions not to be adopted. The emulation of the excellence of those who have benefited mankind, such as those who realized that slavery is wrong, is not guaranteed. But such emulation has happened some of the time, and it is our constructive task to find reasoned ways to encourage it.[2] Otherwise we allow the realization to go to waste.

Godwin's Value for Us, His Current Readers

There is of course much more in Godwin's great book, but it has not been my aim to provide a commentary upon it. That has already been well done by such scholars as Marshall and John P. Clark. What I have tried to convey is a way of reading *Political Justice* for our own time. Reading it over a period of time, taking within our selves some of its massiveness, is a very different experience than reading about it, or reading excerpts drawn from it. Reading *Political Justice* provides an extensive terrain in which to encounter and reconstruct a huge range of anarchist thinking about the basic relation between uncompromising intellectual freedom and non-authoritarian social organization. As far as I am aware, there is no other work in the anarchist tradition that can offer us this opportunity. By accepting both the labors and the delights of reading this book, we can still join with Godwin in his love of the "universal exercise of private judgment" (p. 208), a principle which he finds "unspeakably beautiful." It is also one that remains central to anarchism.

Endnotes

1 As for the motorcycle lovers, we could quote this Godwin statement: "According to the usual sentiment, every club assembling for any civil purpose…has a right to establish any provisions or ceremonies, no matter how ridiculous or detestable, provided they do not interfere with the freedom of others. Reason lies prostrate at their feet…" William Godwin, *Enquiry Concerning Political Justice and Its Influence on Modern Morals and Happiness*, ed. I. Kramnick, Harmondsworth: Penguin Books, 1985; p. 196. All further page references to *Political Justice* refer to this edition.

Here Godwin is incautiously denying the sacredness of what has come to be called "negative freedom," although he even more strongly defends as the last fortress of reason, the right of individual private judgement. Undoubtedly there would be grave dangers in attempting any prohibition of the silly or mystifying conventions of various voluntary groups, and as anyone involved with anarchism would say, coercion must not be used for such an end. Godwin would be the last to deny each person his or her "sphere of discretion" (p. 198). But he is also saying that humanity will continue to pay a huge price for the waste of energy that goes into uncritically accepted activities.

2   Godwin would hardly have dreamt that today "the emulation of excellence" has become abstracted from its benevolent base. Thus every American child is encouraged to emulate the great professional athletes or/and the body-constructs of the advertising world, even though these have no value in alleviating the pressing problems of humanity and could well be harmful to such. I think of the "game-playing" mentality of the populace during the Gulf War, which treated the killing as a kind of sports contest; and, with regard to the emulation of advertisements, of the undergraduate student born in India who said that only in the past year had she come to accept that she would never look like those "ads." For Godwin, emulation is properly based on the admiration due to humane reasoning, not to hero-worship or mindless following.

Works Cited

Clark, John P. 1977. *The Philosophical Anarchism of William Godwin.* Princeton: Princeton University Press.

Crowder, George. 1991. *Classical Anarchism: The Political Thought of Godwin, Proudhon, Bakunin and Kropotkin.* Oxford: Clarendon Press; New York: Oxford University Press.

Godwin, William. 1985. *Enquiry Concerning Political Justice and Its Influence on Modern Morals and Happiness* ed. I. Kramnick. Harmondsworth: Penguin Books.

Jones, Chris. 1993. *Radical Sensibility.* London: Routledge.

Marshall, Peter H. 1984. *William Godwin.* New Haven-London: Yale University Press.

Priestly, F. E. L. (ed.). 1946. *William Godwin's Enquiry Concerning Political Justice.* Toronto: University of Toronto Press.

St. Clair, William. 1989. *The Godwins and the Shelleys: A Biography of a Family.* Baltimore: The Johns Hopkins Press.

John Clark, by way of a book review, introduces us to
Elisée Reclus, the 19th century French geographer, and
"by far the greatest scholar in the history of anarchism."
While Reclus has long been neglected in the anarchist
canon, Clark opines that his theories and work deserve
substantially more attention than they have garnered.
Having lived through the Paris Commune, worked with
Bakunin, and established himself as a pioneering geog-
rapher (as well as precursor to modern social ecology),
Reclus left us with a legacy of neglected riches.

Originally published in issue 22.

Marie Fleming's The Geography of Freedom:
The Odyssey of Elisée Reclus
John Clark

This biography by Marie Fleming is highly recommended as a comprehensive, readable survey of the life and ideas of Reclus. The book is a revised and improved edition of Fleming's earlier *The Anarchist Way to Socialism: Elisée Reclus and Nineteenth-Century European Anarchism*, which was already the best source of information on Reclus in English. While the only other extensive study in English, Dunbar's *Elisée Reclus: Historian of Nature* is useful for those interested in Reclus as a geographer, Fleming's work is far superior as a presentation of Reclus as a complex human being and a fascinating historical figure. She gives the events of his life a rich context in nineteenth-century European history, in the radical milieu of that period, and, most particularly, in the events and ideas of the anarchist movement of the epoch. Where the work is weakest is in the area of theory. Fleming hardly mentions Reclus' most important work of social theory, *L'homme et la terre*, an impressive six-volume study, and she makes only a few brief references to other theoretical discussions.

Yet, Elisée Reclus is without doubt one of the greatest theorists in the history of anarchism. Unfortunately, his theoretical contributions receive little notice today, and he has been known more as a great geographer who happened to be an anarchist, or as a moderately important figure in the anarchist movement. Fleming notes the failure of Reclus to make the "list of major figures" of anarchism. (p. 20) She blames this on a lack of appreciation of his importance by historians. However, the failure of mainstream historians to appreciate his contributions does not explain the surprising degree of neglect of Reclus by anarchists and writers on anarchism. He was certainly a better person, a better thinker, and a better anarchist than major "canonical" figures like Proudhon and Bakunin, who remain in the anarchist pantheon despite qualities like sexism, anti-semitism, vanguardism and occasional megalomania — not to mention their theoretical incoherence. He also had the intense political engagement and the concern for issues of personal life of an Emma Goldman, while lacking her sense of self-importance. And he was a more profound thinker and a more consistent anarchist than even Kropotkin, perhaps the most deserving of the revered few.

The neglect of Reclus as an anarchist has resulted, I think, primarily from the fact that his major writings are extensive geographical studies (often running to thousands of pages) in which his political philosophy appears either in widely dispersed commentary and analysis or, more significantly, as an underlying theoretical orientation that is not intruded conspicuously into every discussion. To appreciate his insights, one must read carefully his quite extensive works concerning human society and nature. Anarchists have usually been in a hurry to change the world, and a tract by Bakunin or Kropotkin has been a more convenient source for a quick injection of ideology. And strangely, Reclus' most profound and striking social and political analysis does not appear in his more explicitly political works, which are rather heavy on inspiring rhetoric, stirring exhortation and vague generality. Thus, those few of his works that have been reprinted as movement tracts do not reveal his qualities as a major thinker.

Yet, in the totality of his work Reclus towers above most figures who are accorded vastly greater attention and recognition as anarchist theorists. His discussions of social and political issues have a depth and breadth unequaled in anarchist thought, and he is by far the greatest *scholar* in the history of anarchism. Furthermore, his ideas are of much more than historical interest. Above all, his synthesis of anarchism and social geography makes him an important precursor of ecological anarchism and social ecology — a thinker from whom all who are interested in these currents have much to learn.

The Exemplary Life of an Anarchist

It is said that Reclus once exclaimed to the Dutch anarchist Ferdinand Domela Nieuwenhuis, "Yes, I am a geographer, but above all I am an anarchist." (p. 20) This describes him well, for though his life work encompassed magnificent achievements in social geography, the pursuit of the anarchist ideal was his life itself. At an early age he developed a deep faith in freedom and equality that later received full expression in his anarchist political theory.

Reclus was born into a Protestant family on March 15, 1830, in Sainte-Foy-la-Grande, a small town on the Dordogne in southwestern France. His independence of thought and his quest for the ideal, just community were no doubt influenced by his heritage of religious dissent. Indeed, his anarchism can be seen as the ultimate Protestant revolt against the dominant religions of the Modern Age: capitalism and statism. He studied at the Moravian School in Neuwied, Germany, the Protestant College of Sainte-Foy, from which he received the Baccalauriat, and the Protestant University in Montauban. By age 17, he had already developed an interest in radical political ideas and was becoming increasingly rebellious against his conservative Calvinist environment. Despite his restlessness, he managed to return to the school at Neuwied, where he taught briefly, after which he completed his formal education with a short period of study at the University of Berlin, where he attended lectures on geography that stimulated greatly his enthusiasm for the subject.

Already, during his student years, Reclus' political ideas were quite advanced. In an essay of this period entitled "Développement de la liberté dans le monde," the 21-year old summarizes a view which defined his future anarchism and its underlying basis. "For each particular man," he asserted, "liberty is an end, but it is only a means to attain love or that which appears to be its equivalent, to attain universal brotherhood." (p. 34) His lifelong concern with the ideals of freedom and solidarity is already evident, and he has already reached an anarchist position in regard to the state. He describes the "destiny " of humanity as "to arrive at that state of ideal perfection where nations no longer have any need to be under the tutelage of a government or any other nation. It is the absence of government; it is anarchy, the highest expression of order." (p. 36)

By this time, both Elisée and his brother Elie had become interested not only in advanced ideas but also in radical political politics. They were enraged by Louis Napoleon's *coup d'état* of December 2, 1851, and participated in an apparent plan to seize the *mairie* (town hall) of Orthez. Though the affair was a fiasco that threatened nothing, the reaction by the authorities led the Reclus brothers to flee France for the greater tolerance then prevailing in England. For Elisée, this flight began over five years of foreign travel, and affected profoundly his future vocation as a geographer.

By early 1853, Reclus had crossed the Atlantic and was living in Louisiana. He spent several years as a tutor at a plantation fifty miles up the Mississippi from New Orleans. One of the strongest impressions that he gained from his experience of the much romanticized plantation society of the Old South was of the cruel inhumanity of slavery. His repulsion by the slave system was largely responsible for his decision to leave Louisiana and helped form his views concerning racism and domination in general. Reclus saw racism as one of the most pernicious forms of oppression and domination. He believed that the resulting problems of social conflict and exploitation could only be solved ultimately through the intermingling of races. Racism, he concluded, was based on a false view of social hierarchy and division that contradicted his fundamental principles of human equality and the acceptance of social diversity. In his view, humanity is always strengthened by the creative diversification resulting from the blending of cultures and races.

Another consequence of Reclus' visit to Louisiana was the strengthening of his belief in the inhumanity of capitalism. While his experiences in Europe led him to abhor the evils of economic inequality and exploitation, he discovered in America an economistic mentality that far surpassed that of more traditionalist European cultures. He concluded that the spirit of commerce and material gain had deeply infected American culture and poisoned it. As he wrote to his brother Elie, he believed the country to be a "great auction hall where everything is sold, slaves and owner into the bargain, votes and honour, the Bible and consciences. Everything belongs to the one who is richer." (p. 44) His loathing for the virtues of free enterprise continued throughout his lifetime.

When Reclus returned to France, his beliefs concerning the blending of races and cultures were put into practice in his personal life when he married Clarisse Brian, the mulatto daughter of a French father and a Senegalese mother. The marriage was a happy one, but ended after only a few years with Clarisse's death shortly after the birth of their third child, who also died. A year later, Reclus married an old friend, Fanny L'Herminez, according to anarchist principles, without the sanction of either church or state. This alliance proved to be his closest and most valued relationship, profoundly affecting him for the rest of his life. Although no other relationship ever reached the depth of that with Fanny, after her death he entered into another "free" and happy marriage with his third wife, Ermance.

In general, Reclus' biographers have agreed that his egalitarian and cooperative ideas were practiced admirably in his personal life. His fundamental principles of solidarity and mutual aid were much more than political slogans. This is true of his relationship not only with his wives, but also with other members of his family and his wide circle of friends. He was noted for his great sense of humility. While he became well known as both a scientist and a political writer and activist, he vehemently rejected the idea of having *followers* or of placing himself in a position of *superiority*. As he once wrote to a young woman who presented herself as a would-be disciple: "For shame.... Is it right for some to be subordinated to others? I do not call myself 'your disciple.'" (p. 192)

During the 1860s, Reclus published a great many articles on geography in the *Revue des deux mondes* and other journals, and he completed the first of the three great geographical projects of his life. This vast work, *La Terre: description des phénomènes de la vie du globe*, established him relatively early in his career as an important figure in the field of geography. Several other geographical works followed, but Reclus' scholarly work was interrupted abruptly in 1871 by the events of the Paris Commune and its aftermath. He participated both in the politics of the Commune and in the defense of Paris. His column of the Paris National Guard was taken prisoner by the Versailles troops and he spent the next eleven months in fourteen different prisons. He was sentenced to deportation to New Caledonia, but despite his refusal to submit to the new regime, and largely because of his prestige as a scientist and intellectual, his friends and supporters succeeded in having his sentence reduced to ten years' exile. As a result, he was allowed to emigrate to Switzerland, where he began his association with the anarchists of the Jura Federation and developed close ties with the major anarchist theorists Bakunin and Kropotkin.

Reclus' views concerning social transformation were profoundly affected by his participation in the First International, and by the influence of Bakunin. Bakunin, the foremost figure in the international anarchist movement for many years, was a great admirer of the Reclus brothers. Reclus' admiration for Bakunin was also great, although he was in no sense a "follower" of the charismatic and often manipulative Bakunin. While Reclus and Bakunin opposed one another at various times on several issues, including the role of secret societies, the influence of the latter was responsible in part for Reclus' development of a firm belief in the necessity of social revolution. He participated in such Bakuninist revolutionary organizations as the International Brotherhood and the Alliance for Social Democracy, and in Bakunin's efforts to move the nonrevolutionary League for Peace and Freedom in a more radical direction. Reclus was also a member of Bakunin's International Brotherhood — the secret society of dedicated Bakuninist revolutionaries — from 1865 on. He attended the meetings of the General Council of the First International in 1869 and defended the anarchist (majority) position in the world's first great working-class organization.

It was also in Switzerland that he began his greatest geographical work, the *Nouvelle géographie universelle*, consisting of nineteen volumes published between 1876 and 1894. Reclus remained in Switzerland until 1890, heavily occupied with both scholarship and political activity, after which he returned to France. In 1894 he began a new phase of his career when he accepted an invitation to become a professor at the New University in Brussels. He had some reservations about this undertaking, having remained outside the academic world until quite late in life. However, he was a great success, achieving renown as a teacher and winning the enduring admiration of many students. During this period he also completed his last great work and his most important work of social theory, *L'homme et la terre*. This impressive study ran to six volumes and reinforced his reputation as a major figure in the history of geography.

Reclus died in the countryside at Thourout near Brussels on July 4, 1905. It is reported that his last days were made particularly happy by news of the popular revolution in Russia. He expired shortly after hearing of the revolt of the sailors on the battleship *Potemkin*.

The Enduring Importance of Reclus' Ideas

Reclus made a number of important contributions to anarchist thought. Though Fleming does not devote much attention to the details of his theoretical analysis, one can gain from her book an idea of some areas of theoretical importance. She points out that he devoted some attention to anarchist organization, and that he was highly skeptical of such approaches as utopian communalism and the establishment of cooperative enterprises. His arguments on these topics often seem rather weak, since he dismissed such forms of organization without much analysis as destined to either irrelevant marginality or voluntary cooptation. But though Reclus focused primarily on opposition to institutions of domination, he also made an important contribution to discussion of immediate, creative forms of self-organization. In his view, the anarchist should "work to free himself personally from all preconceived or imposed ideas, and gradually group around himself friends who live and act in the same fashion. It is step by step, through small, loving and intelligent societies that the great fraternal society will be established." (p. 20) Reclus was thus, as early as 1895, arguing for the centrality to the process of personal and social transformation of what became widely known in anarchist practice and theory as the "affinity group." Though he fails to offer a vision of how anarchist values could be expressed through a growing community of cooperative groups and institutions, he has an unusual grasp of the importance of transforming the closest personal relationships.

In addition, Reclus made some significant contributions to defining the anarchist goal for the future. Fleming points out that Reclus' vision of a cooperative society goes beyond both the collectivist principle of distribution according to labor (advocated by Bakunin and his followers) and the communist principle of distribution according to need (supported by Kropotkin and others). For Reclus, the concept of distribution according to each person's need still preserves a somewhat backward, egoistic view of the individual and society. According to Fleming, his principle of solidarity implied a concept of social need, "the fulfillment of one's own needs within the context of the needs of others," and it therefore "represented a harmony between the individual and society, and consequently a higher level of humanity." (p. 175) He thus began to move beyond the simplistic concepts, rooted in the ideology of economistic individualism, that limited the outlook of most of the classical anarchists.

An area in which Reclus' ideas have had some continuing importance in anarchist thought has been on the topic of revolutionary and evolutionary change. He saw certain slowly developing but pervasive changes in society moving it toward a future of freedom and justice. While he argued for the need for periodical violent revolutions, he believed that these events only marked the culmination of gradual changes that were taking place over long periods of time. He notes the (apparent) decline in belief in certain scientific absurdities and religious superstitions, and the waning power of traditional hierarchical and deferential attitudes. In effect, he argues (contrary to Marxist materialism) that changes in consciousness can precede and give rise to changes in the "material base" of society as long-term evolutionary transformations produce more apparent revolutionary upheavals.

One of the most controversial of Reclus' principles was the right of the workers "to partial recovery of the collective products" by means of the individual's "personal recovery of his part of the collective property." (p. 151) Reclus means, of course, the kind of activity that is usually labeled "theft." While some were shocked by this gentle man's advocacy of such actions, he argued that their horror is misplaced. He asks why we should echo the dominant culture's hypocritical condemnation of the efforts of the oppressed to improve their miserable position in society through such reappropriation. To him, the truly abhorrent form of theft is that practiced by the rich and powerful, who much more successfully confiscate the product of the labor of others. The troubling question of the possible corrupting effects of this "reappropriation" process on those who carry it out in sovereign moral isolation was apparently not pondered very deeply by Reclus. Furthermore, his contention that "everything is theft" (p. 152) has rather disturbing implications. On the one hand, it demonstrates an admirable awareness of one's own implication in a system of domination and injustice. On the other hand, it implies a moral equivalency of all actions "before the revolution" that threatens to create a nihilistic rather than an anarchistic ethos. If all is theft, all is deceit, all is exploitation (since we participate in corrupt systems in which these evils are ubiquitous), then "everything is permitted." This is a *laissez faire* that unfortunately implies unfettered egoism as much as liberatory social practice.

Perhaps even more upsetting to Reclus' critics was his apparent approval of acts of "propaganda by the deed." During the 1880s and 1890s, attacks on political officials, bankers and industrialists, and even any random *bourgeois,* became increasingly common. The names of terrorists such as Ravachol, Vaillant and Henry became well-known to the public. Many of the enemies of the established order began to invoke anarchist principles in defense of their violent deeds, causing a crisis of conscience for anarchist theorists. While some disassociated themselves from these acts, and others, like Kropotkin, adopted an ambiguous position, Reclus refused to condemn the terrorists. In his opinion, violence is a necessary result of a cruel and inhumane system of oppression, and blame should not be focused on those victims who act out of desperation. Reclus has been justly criticized for overlooking several crucial points, such as the fact that the terrorists' victims were also innocent to varying degrees, not having personally created the social system and all its injustices, and the fact that such actions were, in any case, a disastrous failure that did not promote authentic social transformation and often only created reaction. However, Reclus did have one quite valid argument on this topic: those who hasten to condemn the occasional violent acts of desperate individuals while complacently accepting the enormous system of violence embodied in unjust social institutions, are guilty of the worst form of hypocrisy. While Reclus' ideas sometimes remain within the narrow limits of nineteenth-century revolutionary optimism and oppositionism, there are areas in which his thought transcends its age and has an enduring relevance. One of the strengths of anarchism is that it has often diverged from the mainstream of Western thought and practice in being more conscious of the place of humanity in the natural world. While the anarchist tradition has been profoundly affected and, indeed, distorted, by humanity's alienation from nature and the quest to dominate nature, it has also had some notable success in seeking to uncover the roots of that alienation and in beginning to see beyond the project of domination. It is instructive that anarchist theory at the beginning of this century was strongly influenced by the social geography of Kropotkin, while at the end of the century it is often inspired by the social ecology of Bookchin. What is not often noticed is that it is *Reclus*, much more than Kropotkin, who introduced themes later to be developed in social ecology.

George Woodcock, in his introduction to Fleming's book, notes that "modern environmental concerns are eloquently anticipated" in Reclus' statement that a "secret harmony exists between the earth and the people whom it nourishes, and when imprudent societies let themselves violate this harmony, they always end up regretting it." (p. 15) However, Reclus' greatest contribution to ecological thought concerns not these "secret harmonies," but rather his laborious analysis of the complex interrelationship between human society and the rest of the Earth, with which we are in constant and intimate interaction. Reclus sounds most strikingly in accord with modern ecological thinking when he not only depicts nature as a delicately balanced whole, but also proceeds to explore the detailed relationship of economic, political, technological and cultural institutions to this larger context. Like contemporary social ecologists, he emphasizes the importance of humanity's integral place in nature and its responsibility for maintaining or upsetting the balance of nature.

Reclus also touches on topics of contemporary ecological relevance when he writes of our relationship to other species. His approach goes far beyond a limited "animal rights" or moral extensionist perspective. He believes an understanding of our relationship to other animals to be important for us both theoretically and morally. He contends that a greater understanding of animals and their behavior "will help us penetrate deeper into the science of life, to increase both our knowledge of the world and our capacity to love." (p. 191) His ethical vegetarianism testifies to his belief in the unity of knowledge and moral judgment. It also shows once again the centrality of the concept of love (not as an abstract ideal but as a *practical* reality) to his worldview and forms an integral part of his pursuit of a morally coherent life.

For Reclus, greater knowledge of the earth and its inhabitants offers an expanded scope for identification: identification with our own species, identification with all the inhabitants of the planet, and finally, identification with the planet itself. As Reclus expressed at the beginning of *L'homme et la terre*, humanity is "*la nature prenant conscience d'elle-même*" — nature becoming self-conscious. In this insight, Reclus anticipated the most profound dimensions of contemporary ecological thinking.

Voltairine de Cleyre was a 19th century American anarchist feminist and major advocate for women's liberation who fiercely opposed marriage, the church, the state and any other social institutions that infringed on individual autonomy. She lived her life according to her principles, and believed that independence for women would only come "by making rebels wherever we can." In this article, Presley explores de Cleyre's writings, with a focus on her most radical essay, "Sex Slavery." Presley makes an argument for de Cleyre's relevance today, noting that many of her observations and critiques still apply to today's society, despite what equalizing advances have been achieved.

Originally published in issue 27.

No Authority But Oneself:
The Anarchist-Feminist Philosophy of Autonomy and Freedom
Sharon Presley

"Why am I the slave of Man? Why is my brain said not to be the equal of his brain? Why is my work not paid equally with his? Why must my body be controlled by my husband? Why may he take my children away from me? Will them away while yet unborn? Let every woman ask…"There are two reasons why," answered in her and these ultimately reducible to a single principle — the authoritarian supreme power GOD-idea, and its two instruments — the Church — that is, the priests — the State — that is, the legislators… These two things, the mind domination of the Church and the body domination of the State, are the causes of Sex Slavery."

—Voltairine de Cleyre in "Sex Slavery"

Voltairine de Cleyre's passionate yearning for individual freedom was nowhere more evident than in her writings on feminism (then called the Woman Question) and nowhere more at home than the anarchist movement. The anarchist feminist movement of the late 19th century was truly a haven in the storm for women who longed to be free of the strictures of the stifling gender roles of that time. Unlike most women in socialist and mainstream feminist organizations of the time, the anarchist feminists were not afraid to question traditional sex roles. Anticipating the 20th century feminist idea that the "personal is the political," they carried the anarchist questioning of authority into the personal realm as well. "The women who embraced anarchism," writes historian Margaret Marsh, "worked to restructure society as a whole, but they also wanted to transcend conventional social and moral precepts as individuals, in order to create for themselves independent, productive and meaningful lives."

Today it is hard to imagine how difficult and stifling the lives of women were a century ago. Without the right to vote, women had few legal rights. Married women could not dispose of their own property without the husband's consent, could not sign contracts, sue or be sued, nor did they have any custody rights. The father's right as a parent superseded the mother's, violence against the wife was sanctioned; marital rape was an unheard of concept. Sentimentalized Victorian attitudes about the role of women as keepers of the hearth who must put the needs of husband and children above their own kept most women limited almost exclusively to the roles of wife and mother.

Since few economic opportunities existed for single women, let alone married ones, there was tremendous economic as well as cultural pressure to get married. The few job opportunities that existed were poorly paid, often with unpleasant conditions. While middle class women might be able to obtain jobs as teachers or nurses, most working class women were relegated to dismal sweatshops and grim factories where they worked 10 to 12 hours a day in harsh conditions.

Puritanical sexual mores also conspired to keep women in their place. Sex outside of marriage was considered shameful and the idea that women might actually like sex was simply not even imagined outside of radical and bohemian circles. Access to birth control and abortion was virtually illegal and very limited.

It was in this context that the anarchist feminists rebelled against conventional American culture as well as government, demanding not the vote as did the more mainstream feminists, but something far more sweeping and radical — an end to sex roles, the right to control their own lives and destinies completely, the right to be free and autonomous individuals.

Voltairine de Cleyre's Role

Though Emma Goldman is the anarchist feminist best remembered today, Voltairine's role as an advocate of liberation for women was second only to Emma's in the turn-of-the-century American anarchist movement. From the 1890s till her death in 1912, Voltairine spoke and wrote eloquently on the Woman Question in individualist anarchist journals such as Moses Harman's Lucifer and Benjamin Tucker's Liberty, as well as communist anarchist journals such as The Rebel and Emma Goldman's Mother Earth. These writings on feminism were among Voltairine's most important theoretical contributions.

Voltairine's feminist writings began in 1891, a year after the birth of her son Harry, a child she did not want and did not raise. Adamantly in favor of women's reproductive rights but unable to have an abortion because of her precarious health, her experience as a reluctant and unmarried mother sharpened her feminist consciousness and helped impel her exploration of the Woman Question. Her ambivalent relationship with Harry's father,

James Elliot, ultimately unhappy and embittering, was another experience that no doubt significantly colored her views on marriage, motherhood and childbearing.

Voltairine de Cleyre's Social and Psychological Legacy

Questioning traditional marriage

Voltairine's importance as a feminist rests primarily on her willingness to confront issues such as female sexuality and the emotional and psychological, as well as economic, dependence on men within the nuclear family structure. Though a few other writers, most notably socialist feminist Charlotte Perkins Gilman, dealt with issues of the family and women's economic dependence, much of the organized women's movement of that time was far more wrapped up in the issue of women's suffrage. Mainstream documents such as the Seneca Falls Declaration had raised important issues about the nature of marriage and several prominent feminists, including John Stuart Mill and Harriet Taylor, even entered into written marriage contracts to repudiate existing law and custom, but Voltairine's radical anarchist individualist philosophy took the analysis of marriage a step beyond.

Voltairine and the anarchist feminists did not just question the unfair nature of marriage laws of that time, they repudiated institutional marriage and the conventional family structure, seeing in these institutions the same authoritarian oppression as they saw in the institution of the State. Though some, like Lillian Harman, daughter of anarchist publisher Moses Harman, were willing to participate in non-State, non-Church private wedding ceremonies and others, like Voltairine, denounced even the concept of a private ceremony, all were united in their opposition to State-sanctioned and licensed marriage.

Voltairine, while not rejecting love, was among those most vehemently opposed to marriage of any kind, a theme best explicated in "Those Who Marry Do Ill." In an age when men had almost total control over the family as well as the wife, when most women were economically dependent on men, and when women's chief duty was to her husband and family, even to the point of self-sacrifice, Voltairine understandably viewed marriage as slavery, a theme she developed further in "The Woman Question."

Voltairine's fierce advocacy of individual autonomy, "the freedom to control her own person," was the cornerstone of her denunciation of marriage, an institution that she saw as crippling to the growth of the free individual. "It is the permanent dependent relationship," Voltairine writes in "The Woman Question", "which is detrimental to the growth of individual character to which I am unequivocally opposed." This advocacy led her to a position more radical than all but the most radical of contemporary women — a call for separate living quarters. Seeing dependency as a sure way to lose one's individuality, she even advised against living together with the man one loves in a non-marriage love relationship if it means becoming his housekeeper.

This desire for autonomy, "a room of one's own," a separate space to grow and explore one's own individuality, though appearing as early as the late 18th century writings of Mary Wollstonecraft, is a theme still being examined today among mainstream feminists. However, though many feminists may now eschew formal marriage in their love relationships (at least till children come along), relatively few of them have been willing to emulate the example of feminist icon Simone de Beauvoir when she decided not only not to marry her livelong lover, philosopher Jean Paul Sartre, but to live separately from him as well. Voltairine would have understood her motivation very well, not only because of the issue of individual autonomy but also because she believed that love could only be kept alive at a distance. Though many feminists have thought about the potentially negative psychological effects of living together in a love relationship, the issue is still very much alive, often unresolved in individual women's lives, and certainly deserving of more consideration.

Opposition to the economic dependence of women

An integral part of the anarchist feminist opposition to institutional marriage was the belief that the chief source of women's oppression within marriage was economic dependence on men. This was a theme explored frequently by many anarchist feminists in the pages of anarchist journals such as Benjamin Tucker's Liberty and Moses Harman's more avowedly pro-women's rights Lucifer. In "The Case of Women vs. Orthodoxy," Voltairine asserts that material conditions determine the social relations of men and women, suggesting that if economic conditions change, women's inequality would disappear. Though she, like her compatriots in both the communist and individualist camps, deplored the wretched living conditions of the working classes in the big cities and had a negative view of the capitalism of that time, Voltairine blessed capitalists for making women's economic independence possible. As unpleasant as the jobs might be, at least they were jobs actually available to women, a rarity in that time.

The relevance of Voltairine de Cleyre's views on marriage today

In today's more socially enlightened times, Voltairine's opposition to marriage and even living together may seem anachronistic and unnecessary. We need not, however, espouse living alone to see that her stance raises important questions about the extent to which individual autonomy is possible in a relationship that involves not only living together but the inevitable compromises of family life. Is it possible to maintain individuality within the confines of family obligations? Are family obligations distributed equitably or is it the wife or mother who must inevitably bear the major burden of responsibility for childcare and household work and the husband or father the major economic burden? Is the division-making power distributed equitably or is the one who is most economically independent the one who has the most say? Can autonomy be maintained if either the woman or the man is economically dependent? In a conflict, how can a woman maintain her autonomy without sacrificing either others in the family or herself? That issues are still a problem in many modern households is clear from studies such as sociologist Arlie Hochschild's The Second Shift, which shows that women still do most of the domestic cleaning and childcare even when they have jobs outside the home.

Though such questions have been explored by contemporary feminists, the issues raised are far from settled. This is not merely a matter of such superficial questions as "can a woman have it all?" that surface frequently in popular women's magazines. It is a fundamental question about the nature of the family structure as we know it. Though the issue of autonomy is a much discussed theme within feminist writings, the questions raised by Voltairine's analysis are far from being resolved in actual practice within the family.

Nor do such questions deal with another fundamental and related issue raised by the anarchist feminists: should the State be involved in the institution of marriage? A few feminists have commented on the legal and often unknown and unwanted baggage that comes with the State license but most have not confronted the question of why the State has the right to set the terms of what is essentially a private relationship and whether this interference results in more harm than good.

Living her beliefs

Though Voltairine was a founding member of Matilda Joslyn Gage's Women's National Liberal League in 1890 and, in 1893, a principal organizer of the Philadelphia Ladies Liberal League, she admonished women not to invest their hopes in organized movements. Like Emma Goldman, she believed that independence for women was best achieved by individual acts of rebellion. We must act "by making rebels wherever we can," by living our beliefs. Nor can we expect anything from men, she warned. The precious freedom of individual autonomy is not easily gained. "The freedom to control her own person" has to be wrested from men, she says in another of her feminist essays, "The Gateway to Freedom." "I never expect men to give us liberty. No, women, we are not worth it, until we take it."

This ability to put into practice what she preached was an important contribution of Voltairine's. "She also lived in conformity with her feminist principles" writes Marsh " which forced those who came into contact with her to confront her philosophy in concrete not just abstract." Though anarchist men accepted in theory the idea of economic independence combined with sexual liberation, Voltairine points out in "Sex Slavery," that even some of those who repudiate the State still cling to idea that they are the heads of families, that women's place is in the home. Many, such as Victor Yarros, a frequent contributor to Liberty, still expected the traditional division of labor within the home. Voltairine herself had personal experiences with this unwillingness on the part of some men to apply libertarian principles to home life, struggling with lovers in her life who were unwilling to treat her as an equal and ultimately rejecting them.

The discrepancy between theory and practice, between alleged advocacy of equalitarianism and actually more conventional behavior is a battle that is still being fought today, not just in conventional society, not just in the homes of mainstream feminists, but in the personal and even political lives of anarchists and libertarians. Mainstream and libertarian women alike still struggle with the issue of division of responsibility for childcare and housework, issues of autonomy and dependence, while many of the men deny, ignore or fail to come to grips with such issues. While few libertarians or anarchists today are so boldly retrogressive as to take the position openly, the notion of inherently determined gender roles is not totally dead nor is the anarchist family necessarily egalitarian. Such issues are even still being debated, for example, on individualist libertarian Internet discussion groups. Meanwhile, many libertarian magazines still subtly neglect issues that are associated with women, i.e., social welfare, reproductive rights, and worldwide oppression of women while at the same time claiming they are in favor of women's rights. Though the communist anarchist feminists have explored the application of the political to the personal in considerably greater depth than the individualists, they too complain about the gap between theory and practice in their camp. Voltairine's willingness to live out her principles can therefore serve both as a model and a challenge to today's feminists, whether mainstream or anarchist, liberal or libertarian.

Questioning traditional sex roles

Radical as her other feminist essays were, "Sex Slavery" is, in important ways, the most radical of all. It is an essay that is both striking in its modernity — expounding on the "constructed crime" of pornography, marital rape, sex role socialization, and the double standard — and breathtaking in its still radical rejection of both Church and State.

The impetus for this essay was the arrest of Moses Harman, the editor and publisher of Lucifer: the Lightbearer, the leading freelove/anarchist/feminist journal of the time. Running afoul of the stridently prudish, pro-censorship Comstock Act, which provided stiff prison terms for anyone who knowingly mailed or received "obscene, lewd, or lascivious" printed material through the mail, Harman had been arrested for printing a letter in 1886 in which the word "penis" was used. In this letter, a Tennessee anarchist named Markland, reporting a letter he had received, decried a case of marital rape in which the wife, still recovering from post-childbirth vaginal surgery, nearly hemorrhaged to death because her husband forced himself on her. For this "crime," Harman eventually spent two years in Leavenworth Federal Penitentiary.

As with many other anarchists of the time, Voltairine was vehemently opposed to the lack of rights that women suffered within institutional marriage. Though she was not active in the so-called Free Love movement (whose membership greatly overlapped the anarchist movement), she advocated similar positions of freedom for both women and men to choose whomever they wanted for sex partners and the right of women to seek sexual satisfaction for themselves. Carrying the anarchist rejection of coercion into the realm of the personal, she agreed with Harman that when a man forces himself on a woman, even if they are married, it is still rape.

In this essay, Voltairine also attacks the idea that sex roles are inherent in human nature, seeing them as the result of socialization. In a comment that reminds us that we haven't come as far as we sometimes think, she notes that little girls are taught not to be tomboys and boys aren't allowed to have dolls. "Women can't rough it like men," she queries. "Train any animal, or any plant as you train your girls, and it won't be able to rough it either." Many enlightened parents today may talk about nonsexist child rearing but Barbie Dolls and GI Joes still crowd the shelves of toy stores everywhere, suggesting that the struggle against culturally imposed sex roles that Voltairine decried is a battle yet to be won.

Nor is the idea that gender roles are the result of socialization practices rather than genetics a battle that has been won. Voltairine observed in "The Case of Women vs. Orthodoxy" that men of the "scientific 'cloth'" can be obstacles to women's freedom. If women are ever to have rights, she declares, they must not only pitch out the teachings of the priests but also those of the men "who hunt scientific justifications for keeping up the orthodox standard." Though most feminists would agree with Voltairine that these roles spring from training rather than biology, the idea that "anatomy is destiny" keeps resurfacing in other quarters in newer, more sophisticated, and seemingly scientific guises.

Voltairine's astute observation of a century ago is no less relevant today. The use of "science" to justify traditional gender roles has remained constant since her time, only the particulars have changed. Where once scientists claimed that males are smarter than females because males have larger brains or that males are more rational because they have larger parietal or frontal lobes, now it is claimed that males are more dominant than females because of differences in sex hormones and brain structure. Where once Freud claimed that women are morally inferior to men and inherently masochistic, now the psychiatric establishment subtly perpetuates the idea that women are more maladjusted and irrational than men through the use of questionable diagnostic categories such as Masochistic Personality Disorder and Premenstrual Dysphoric Disorder in the DSM (the Diagnostic and Statistical Manual, the "bible" of the psychotherapy community). *Plus ça change, plus c'est la même chose* (the more things change, the more they stay the same). Her observation not only reminds us that science has been used against women in the past, it reminds us to be alert for its misuse in the present.

Voltairine de Cleyre's Political Legacy

In "Sex Slavery," we find Voltairine's most radical position of all, a position that not only differentiated her from most of the mainstream feminists of her day but today as well — Voltairine's denunciation of the twin roles of the Church and the State in oppressing women. Declaring that "We are tired of promises, God is deaf, and his church is our worst enemy," she pointed out how it colludes with the State to keep women in bondage.

The Church teaches the inferiority of women while the State-constructed crime of "obscenity" keeps people like Moses Harman from telling the truth about the slavery of marriage. The State, she also believed, keeps women and men from having economic independence through its protection of monopoly capitalism and the subsequent detrimental effect on the ability to earn a living.

Though Voltairine was not alone in her denunciation of the pernicious role of religion in oppressing women, most of the criticisms were not welcomed by more conventional feminists. Elizabeth Cady Stanton's Women's Bible, issued in 1895–1898 and Matilda Joslyn Gages' Women, Church and State were both indictments of Christianity as destructive of women's rights. Neither book, however, was well-received within the mainstream women's movement of the time. The freethought movement, while abounding with women who criticized religion and its detrimental roles on both women and society, was also outside the mainstream.

Though there are feminists today such as Mary Daly, who criticize the Catholic Church, or Sonia Johnson, who criticize the Mormon Church, relatively few are willing to denounce the idea of religion per se or discuss its role in oppressing women. A few feminist writers such as Katha Pollitt and Barbara Ehrenreich have been willing to declare that they are atheists but it has mostly been left for women outside the feminist mainstream to strike modern blows against religion and the Bible as harmful to women in books such as the Freedom From Religion Foundation's Woe to the Women and journals such as the secular humanist Free Inquiry.

Left inadequately explored within the mainstream of feminism today are the many questions that Voltairine's analysis suggests. What is the role of religion in keeping women "in their place?" Are conventional religions inherently sexist? How can the misogynist content of the Bible be reconciled with feminist ideals? Are palliatives such as allowing women to be ministers enough? Voltairine's pointed analysis reminds us that this important area of social belief merits continued serious attention.

Most radical of all in a feminist context is Voltairine's anarchism itself. Few feminists today, even the most radical, are willing to explore the role of the State in oppressing women. Then as now, anarchists differ as to exactly what that oppression consists of, but modern anarchist feminists of all philosophical persuasions agree that the State is women's enemy. The communist and social anarchist feminists believe that the State protects capitalism, which in turn exploits women. The individualist anarchist feminists believe that the State has fostered economic oppression and institutionalized gender role stereotypes through laws that restrict women's choices, for example, protective labor legislation (which perpetuates the idea that women are weak) and protect men's interests at the expense of women.

What the anarchist feminists are calling for is a radical restructuring of society, both in its public and private institutions, a step the mainstream is not yet willing to take. Marsh put the essentially conservative nature of mainstream feminist political ideology this way: "Although late 20th century feminists recognize that political and legal rights wrested from the state have not resulted in fundamental equality," she writes, "they emphasize ERA and anti-discrimination statures because this can be accommodated without fundamental changes in the structure of society."

Contemporary anarchist feminists contend that mainstream feminists are unwilling or unable to recognize the authoritarian nature of the modern state as just another form of patriarchy. Mainstream feminists, say the anarchist feminists, would have to give up too much if they acknowledged that the power of the State is no different in form than the power of patriarchy. "To anarchist feminists" writes Howard Ehrlich, "the state and patriarchy are twin aberrations." Nor have modern feminists come to grips with the role of the State in perpetuating not only legal inequality but traditional sex roles and power relationships as well. Instead mainstream feminists merely confine themselves to asking for more and more government intervention, more and more laws. Directing their criticisms mainly against conservative Republicans, these feminists insist that if they can just change the administration, they can use the power of the State to remake things in a way that would be better for women. Anarchists see it very differently. In "Government is Women's Enemy," the authors write "If we pass laws that force our values on others, we are no better than men who have forced their values on us through legislation." Power is power and coercion is coercion, whether wielded by an individual man against his family or by a government against its people, say the anarchists. And for the anarchists, coercion is always a moral wrong.

Voltairine de Cleyre's feminist writings are a rich source of thoughtful analysis which raises provocative questions that need to be seriously considered by contemporary feminists. Voltairine and the 19th century anarchist feminists, unlike most feminists today, never failed to understand that the State is inherently hierarchical and authoritarian. The recognition that the State is the enemy of women is the political legacy of Voltairine de Cleyre and the questioning of the authority relationship in traditional marriage and the insistence on individual autonomy of women is her social and psychological legacy. It is a legacy that deserves to be both read and seriously explored.

References

Avrich, Paul. *An American Anarchist: The Life of Voltairine de Cleyre,* Princeton, NJ: Princeton University Press, 1978

Brown, Susan L., *The Politics of Individualism: Liberalism, Liberal Feminism and Anarchism* (Montreal: Black Rose Books, 1973).

Ehrlich, Howard J. "Toward A General Theory of Anarchafeminism," *Social Anarchism,* no. 19, 1994

Gage, Matilda Joslyn, *Women, Church and State* (Watertown, NY: Persephone Press, 1980; reprint of 1893 edition)

Gaylor, Annie Laurie (ed.), *Women Without Superstition* (Madison, WI: Freedom From Religion Foundation, 1997)

Gilman, Charlotte Perkins, in Carl Degler (ed.) *Women and Economics* (New York: Harper & Row, 1966

Kornegger, Peggy, "Anarchism: the Feminist Connection" and Marion Leighton, "Anarcho-feminism" in *Reinventing Anarchy* eds. Howard Ehrlich, Carol Ehrlich, David DeLeon, & Glenda Morris (London: Routledge & Kegan Paul, 1979.

Marsh, Margaret, *Anarchist Women 1870–1920* (Philadelphia: Temple University Press, 1981

Presley, Sharon, "Feminism in *Liberty*" in Michael Coughlin, Charles Hamilton & Mark Sullivan (eds.), *Benjamin R. Tucker and the Champions of* Liberty (St. Paul and New York: Michael Coughlin & Mark Sullivan Publishers, 1987),

Presley, Sharon and Kinsky, Lynn, "Government is Women's Enemy," and Joan Kennedy Taylor, "Protective Labor Legislation" in Wendy McElroy (ed.), *Freedom, Feminism and the State* (Washington, DC: Cato Institute, 1982.

Reichert, William O., *Partisans of Freedom: A Study in American Anarchism* (Bowling Green, OH: Bowling Green University Popular Press, 1976)

Sears, Hal, *The Sex Radicals: Free Love in High Victorian America* (Lawrence, KS: The Regents Press of Kansas, 1977

Stanton, Elizabeth Cady, *The Original Feminist Attack on the Bible (The Woman's Bible)* (New York: Arno Press, 1974)

Taylor, Joan Kennedy, *Reclaiming the Mainstream: Individualist Feminism Rediscovered* (Buffalo, NY: Prometheus Books, 1992).

Notes

"Those Who Marry Do Ill" was published in *Mother Earth*, January, 1908.

"The Woman Question," based on a lecture Voltairine de Cleyre gave in Scotland, was published in *The Herald of Revolt*, September 1913.

"The Case of Woman vs. Orthodoxy" was published in *The Boston Investigator*, September 19, 1896.

"Sex Slavery" is reprinted in *The Selected Works of Voltairine de Cleyre*, New York, Mother Earth, 1914

The early American anarchism of such figures as Lysander Spooner, Josiah Warren, and Benjamin Tucker is usually associated with a strong individualist proclivity. Hiskes here offers an overview of Benjamin Tucker, publisher of the journal *Liberty,* and argues that Tucker's vehement defense of individual autonomy is dependent upon an understanding of liberty which takes into account both the liberty of others and the relationship between the individual and community that is necessary to make it possible at all.

Originally published in issue 1.2.

Community in the Anarcho-Individualist Society
The Legacy of Benjamin Tucker
Richard P. Hiskes

I t is often remarked that American society and its politics were founded on ideas which for the most part were articulated and developed elsewhere. This is held to be particularly true in the fields of political theory and economy which it is frequently maintained that America has produced few political thinkers who do not owe a large intellectual debt to continental theorists such as Locke, Rousseau, or Marx. This short-changing of American political thought is somewhat accurate, but *only* if one assumes that the entire American political tradition can be summed up under the title of "liberalism," with a few periodic outbreaks of Marxism, socialism, or other imports.

There is another side to American political thought, however, one which presents a political viewpoint which is both unique and uniquely American. It is this side of the American political tradition which will be examined in thesis essay. It is a distinctly radical side, one which matured in the late nineteenth century, and was articulated by individuals who have in large part been either ignored or forgotten. Its representatives include the first American anarchist Josiah Warren, Steven Pearl Andrews, Lysander Spooner, and the cataloguer and publisher of them all, Benjamin R. Tucker (1854–1939). These men referred to themselves occasionally as anarchists, but more frequently simply as "individualists," and with their somewhat less radical colleagues espoused two fundamental principles: the absolute necessity for maximum personal freedom, and the concomitant demand for the gradual disappearance of the state. They expressed what they considered to be the values and principles upon which this nation had supposedly been founded but which had been quickly forgotten or replaced. They were, in Tucker's words, simply "unterrified Jeffersonian Democrats" (1893, p. 14)

In many ways Tucker was the single most important thinker in this school of individualist anarchism, and in his time was certainly considered its foremost representative. This is true for two reasons. First, none succeeded in expressing the tenets of individualism with more vigor and coherence than did Tucker. His trenchant criticism of the state and frequent vitriol aimed at fellow radicals and non-radicals alike were accompanied by a logic and reasonableness which were difficult to dismiss or ignore. Second, throughout his life Tucker did more to disseminate the ideas of anarchism that any of his contemporaries. As a publisher he translated and printed some of the "great books" of anarchy, including works by Proudhon and Leo Tolstoy. He also published many of the works of his contemporaries such as Warren, Andrews, and Spooner.

By far his most significant accomplishment, however, was Tucker's founding of the journal of radical thought named *Liberty*, which appeared regularly for twenty-seven years and which became a popular forum for the radical ideas of his time. *Liberty* was also the means by which Tucker propounded his own unique version of anarchism. Anarchism for Tucker was not primarily a doctrine of confrontation, but a practical program of cooperation and order. As a pacifist— a title he frequently rejected but a fundamental motivation he could not shake — Tucker viewed anarchy as the "mother of cooperation" (1893, p. 365), just as liberty — the synonym for anarchy — (1893, p. 63) was in Proudhon's words, "not the daughter, but the mother of order." Tucker's brand of anarchism in fact owed much to Proudhon, as his use of Proudhon's famous aphorism for *Liberty's* masthead would indicate. Yet anarchist principles as enunciated by Tucker were uniquely his own.

In the pages of *Liberty,* Tucker succeeded in articulating a theory of anarchy which was both a synthesis of other such theories and yet like none which had gone before. Into this amalgamation of ideas went the mutualism of Proudhon, the doctrine of equal liberty as expressed by Herbert Spencer, and the extreme individualism of his mentor Josiah Warren. It was Tucker's single-minded defense of the individual that distinguished his thought from that of other anarchist theoreticians, and perhaps stamped it as expressly American. All anarchists are individualists, of course, for all insist to some degree upon, in Warren's terminology, the "sovereignty of the individual." Yet because of this, he is a perfect example to use in arguing the two substantive points of this essay. The first point is an attempt to refute what is essentially the fundamental criticism of all individualist theories from Locke to Nozick: that because of its emphasis upon individual freedom and the liberty to pursue individual self-interest, individualism cannot consistently maintain a strong sentiment of fraternity, or as it will be referred to here, community. Second, community-building will be presented as *the* practical implication of this unusual brand of anarchism, notwithstanding its powerful individualistic bias.

The single and most troubling statement of Tucker's, which portrays his intensely individualistic approach to political and social life is found in a curious summary of what anarchism means. Anarchy is synonymous with individual liberty for Tucker, but even more than this, is summed up by its insistence upon personal freedom. "Anarchism is for liberty," argues Tucker un-controversially, but adds "and neither for nor against anything else (1893, p. 365). Few if any other anarchists could consistently go along with the latter half of this characterization of anarchism. Clearly, such a statement comes close to sheer egoism as far as relations with others are concerned, and from the standpoint of community is bothersome indeed, for where in this quest for maximum personal liberty is there room for the concern and care for other's welfare that must exist if communitarian relations are to prevail in society?

In order to answer this question it is first necessary to understand what Tucker means by liberty when he declares in the strongest terms possible that he, like all anarchists, is "for liberty"/ This is made even more pertinent in light of what contemporary theorists such as Joel Feinberg defines this view as "license," or as a belief that "society and the state should grant to every citizen 'complete liberty to do whatever he [or she] wishes'" (1973, p. 72). Now this certainly sounds anarchistic (and not very communal), though virtually no anarchists — and especially not Tucker — would consider it as either possible to live with such a view of liberty or advisable to do so if it were.

Liberty does not mean "license" for Tucker, but in its purest form simply the absence of force or coercion against the individual. As it stands, this sounds like an overly "negative" view of liberty, as well as "anarchistic" in Feinberg's meaning, yet two points should be made. First, like all conception of freedom, Tucker's can be interpreted as having both a positive and a negative side in Feinberg's and Gerald MacCallum's "triadic formula" (1967, pp. 312–334). Freedom belongs to the individual as *agent*, exempts him or her *from* the coerciveness of others (particularly the state) without prior consent, in order *to do* what he or she wants. Second, doing "what he or she wants" does not include, as Feinberg fears from anarchy, the freedom "to inflict blows on John Doe, to hold noisy parties under his window every night, and to help himself to Doe's possessions." For Tucker, liberty means "equal liberty," and for the individual this means obeying equal liberty's law of "the largest amount of liberty compatible with equality and mutuality of respect of and for others" (1893, p. 65). Thus liberty in Tucker's view is not "anarchistic" in Feinberg's meaning, is a simple a elegant concept, and is not unlimited for each individual.

But why are anarchists, as Tucker insists, "for liberty," and why are they for it to the virtual exclusion of everything else? Tucker answers this question first by arguing that liberty is not so essential because of any attributes of individuals which make them especially worthy of it. Natural right is not an argument for liberty, in other words, because "no individual has a right to anything, except as he creates his right by contract with his neighbor" (1893, p. 146). Instead, liberty rests its case on the grounds of utility in Tucker's view because it is "the chief essential to human happiness" (1893, p. 65). Furthermore, the utility and essentiality of liberty is also verified by the fact that it is a social as well as an individual expedient, for the maximization of liberty is necessary if society and social order are to survive. That Tucker believes this to be true is clearly apparent from his acceptance of Proudhon's dictum that "liberty is the mother, not the daughter of order."

But why is liberty the mother of order? And if it is, why is the preservation of individual liberty a *social* expedient? Furthermore, even if it is true that society must protect the individual liberty of its members if *it* is to survive, what has this to do with the maintenance of personal happiness by those individual members? Is their happiness so entwined with society's survival that liberty only promotes personal felicity through its provision of social order? The answer to these questions lies for Tucker in the relationship between society as a whole and the individuals who constitute it. In his view, society is more than just an artificial contrivance or instrument created and used by individual persons; it is a "concrete organism," whose life "is inseparable from the lives of individuals" (1893, p. 35). The importance of the organic metaphor in Tucker's thought, especially as it relates to his views of community and the state will be explored in a moment. What is significant here is its connection to his conception of individual liberty as both an individual expedient to personal happiness and as the mother of order.

Philosophers who refer to society as an organism often do so as part of an argument for *restraining* individual liberty in order to maximize a greater good of the "whole". Indeed, some of them, such as Plato, Rousseau, and Hegel, have been accused of incipient totalitarian leanings because of this position. Such a position, scoffed at by contemporary individualists such as Robert Nozick, does seem to be at odds with the fundamental anarchist belief in liberty, especially in Tucker's case, for he employs the metaphor to underscore the necessity of order in society. But social order necessarily involves restraints on individuals; therefore how can Tucker's demand for liberty be reconciled with the prerequisites and limitations on personal freedom which a healthy social order requires? Such a reconciliation is provided by Tucker in his advocacy of what Spencer called "the law of equal liberty.

When Tucker proclaims that he is "for liberty," he is referring not only to his own, but to that of all individuals. This is a very significant aspect of Tucker's libertarian stance, and exonerates him from the charge of egoism which he at times embraces and to which all individualists have been subjected. More importantly, it resolves the problem of how Tucker can consistently defend the individual's claim for perfect liberty while at the same time maintaining that society, and therefor its system of constraints, is, like perfect liberty, necessary for human happiness. Liberty, says Tucker, "is the most important thing in the world, and I certainly want as much as I can get of it" (1893, p. 41). However, other people also want as much as they can get of liberty; and, resolves Tucker, they should have it. How much should they (and I) have? "The largest amount of liberty compatible with equality and mutuality of respect, on the part of individuals living in society, for their respective spheres of action" (1893, p. 65). This is equal liberty, says Tucker, and is to be defended by the anarchist because it is Anarchism itself."

It is by means of this conceptualization of liberty in terms of equal liberty, then, that Tucker verifies his statement that the life of society and the lives of its inhabitants are inseparable. Furthermore, he also uses this concept of liberty to resolve the conflict between the necessity of maximum personal freedom and the necessity of a peaceful social order which at times must constrain one's freedom. Every individual wants liberty in order to attain happiness, and all should have it, asserts Tucker. Also, every individual should have liberty because if some do not social peace and order are jeopardized. But social order and peace (or simply, society) are also requisites of human happiness. Therefore, because as any game theorist knows, the only way in which all can have liberty relative to each other is if all share equally, equal liberty becomes a prudential imperative both for society and each individual. No rights or moral sanctions are invoked in this proof of the advisability of equal liberty as it is provided by Tucker, only considerations of interest— the interest of society and of each of its constituents.

The law of equal liberty is central to all of Tucker's thought, embracing not only his fundamental utilitarian ethic, but also his view of the organic nature of society and the imperative of individual liberty. This idea is also the foundation of his anarchism, for it is in contrast to society that Tucker portrays the state, and vilifies it for its flaunting of this most fundamental law. The law of equal liberty casts society as a "concrete organism" in which the individual is related to it as the paw of the tiger is related to the entire animal (1893, pp. 35–36).

The state on the other hand, is not a concrete organism; but in a passage in which he breaks with other organic theorists of society including Herbert Spencer, Tucker declares that the state is merely "discrete" as an organic form. What this indicates about the state and its component members is that "if it should disappear tomorrow, individuals would still continue to exist" (1893,

p. 36). This is not the case, however, in Tucker's view, for concrete organic forms such as tigers, or society. Though the state is an organism, it is "imperfect" in that it is not in a condition of total, symbiotic unity, as is the case with concrete organisms. Furthermore, as a discrete and therefore imperfect united organism, the efficacy of the state is prima facie questionable. It is the life of society, not that of the state, which is inseparable from that of the individuals within it, and the imperfection of the state as an organic form signals both its eminent inferiority and hence dispensability as a method of social organization.

The proof of this inferior position occupied by the state is in its direct and inevitable violation of the law of equal liberty. Government, argues Tucker, is the very enemy of equal liberty, for in order to exist it must abridge personal freedom to a point necessary for the maintenance of a monopoly of power over its area of control. As a result, the state compromises equal liberty in two ways: first it reduces everyone's freedom of action to a considerable extent by the imposition or threat of force. Thought the consequence of this action by the state may theoretically be equal, it is not equal *liberty*, for "equal liberty does not mean equal slavery or equal invasion," asserts Tucker, "it means the *largest* amount of liberty" for each compatible with that of others (1893, p. 65).

Second, in actual practice government does not restrict liberty on an equal basis for all citizens, but rather discriminates through its system of political favors and its generally corrupt conduct against certain citizens while it aggrandizes others. Because government must violate the liberty of individuals if it is to sustain itself, Tucker concludes with Spencer that government is born in aggression, and exists solely as "invasion, nothing more or less" (1893, p. 21–61). Tucker fervently urges its abolition and replacement with a system of social organization designed to protect the equal liberty of all. This type of social arrangement is simply anarchy, which as stated before, is in Tucker's mind the very synonym of equal liberty.

The state's violation of equal liberty is not its only sin: There is also its inherent rejection of cooperation, and by extension, community. Cooperation is an essential feature of Tucker's plan for the anarchist society: It is for the sake of renewing true human cooperation that he advances anarchism in the first place. "Anarchy," he points out, "is the mother of cooperation," just as it is of order. Furthermore, it is in his description of cooperation in the anarchist society that Tucker not only fully rids himself of the stigma of egoism with which all individualist theory is said to be marked, but embraces an idea of community which takes a most attractive and pragmatic form.

The extent to which Tucker magnifies the need for cooperation in the anarchists society must be viewed, as must all his ideas, within the context of his criticism of the state. Like other anarchists and radical individualists, Tucker believes that government effectively forecloses the possibility of true (that is, voluntary) cooperation by its reliance upon force. By coercing individuals into cooperation with each other by means of, for example, non-voluntary taxation, government takes away the impetus for involvement in voluntary, personal cooperative ventures by those same individuals. In other words, by forcibly channeling the cooperative instincts of the individuals into government operated enterprises, the state breeds a mentality of dependence upon itself rather than on voluntary associations. Consequently, when concerted action is required, people are much less likely to form their own cooperative associations over which they might retain full control, and much more inclined to resign themselves to "let government do it" attitude. The result of such resignation is the strengthening of the state and the concomitant weakening of individual freedom and the cooperative spirit. In short, cooperation atrophies in the state; under anarchy it is rejuvenated both as a necessity of life and as the clearest manifestation of anarchist liberty.

Without the coercively provided cooperation found in the state, expediency dictates that in the anarchist society voluntary cooperative associations arise to take its place. The first of these will defend members of society against "individuals who undoubtedly will persist in violating the social law by invading their neighbors" (1893, p. 25). Tucker is no believer in a simplistic view of the "basic goodness" of human nature. He realizes that in the absence of the "long arm of the law," some arrangement must be made to preserve social order in the face of a threat by either an external force or from belligerent members of society. For protection against such aggressive individuals, it is not enough that each person rely upon his or her own strength or coercive power, for not only will such force often be insufficient to repel the invasion, but when exercised in such a solitary manner by everyone, it may lead to social chaos. Therefore, what is needed in lieu of the state is cooperation among several individuals in order to combine their strength to provide for the common defense. In other words, a defensive association is required to protect against and, if need be, repel by force any invasive attempts launched against the members of the anarchist society.

This defensive association which Tucker proposes to take the place of the state has many interesting features, no the least of which is its similarity to the "dominant protective association" described by Robert Nozick in part on of *Anarchy, State, and Utopia* (1974). To summarize very briefly the features of this association, Tucker insists that all such defensive associations must be purely voluntary and based upon the free contract of all participating members. Additionally, any such defensive association must preserve the right of any individual within it to secede from the cooperative venture at any time. There are only two types of cooperation — compulsory and voluntary — and whereas the state is founded upon the former, defensive associations in the anarchist society will rely solely on the freely offered contributions of subscribing individuals. A contract which does not allow for voluntary secession — such as the contract which gives rise to the state — "makes oneself a slave"; and "no man can make himself so much a slave as to forget the right to issue his own emancipation proclamation" (1893, p. 48). To ensure that the defensive association does not become coercive, Tucker urges that there be a considerable number of them in the anarchist society. If defensive associations proliferate, competition will be promoted and service improved thereby, and the potential of each association for authoritarian control over its members will be checked as well.

Besides the inability to bind its members for life, the defensive association as Tucker envisions it cannot exercise absolute dominion over a territory. It does not have the right to coerce a non-member living in its territory to join the association, it may not evict a resident non-member, "require him to pay for any incidental benefits that he might derive from the association, or restrict him in the exercise of any previously enjoyed right to prevent him from reaping those benefits" (1893, p. 44). Finally, the multitude of defensive associations which Tucker foresees do not form a hierarchical pattern of authority in the anarchist society as a whole, and therefore in this final sense are to be distinguished from the differentiable levels of authoritarian control in the state.

Thus Tucker acknowledges the need for cooperation in the anarchist society. But such cooperation does not really seem like community, for it is not all-embracing of the lives of individuals, and it is mainly based a rather mundane — thought important — special interest of each individual: the need for defense. Furthermore, such a narrow, self-interested realm of cooperation seems to miss the whole point of community: its fundamental reliance not upon the self-interest of each individual: the need for defense. Furthermore, such a narrow, self-interested realm of cooperation seems to miss the whole point of community: its fundamental reliance not upon the self-interest of each member, but upon his or her concern for others' welfare and the desire for togetherness and social harmony. Yet, Tucker extends his dream of free cooperation beyond the narrow requirements of personal protection. He insists that cooperation must permeate *all* facets of individual life; indeed, there

must be *social union*. In a lengthy passage he argues that in the place of the
state anarchists

> ...have something very tangible to offer — something very rational,
> practical, and easy of application. We offer cooperation. We offer
> non-compulsive organization. We offer associative combination.
> We offer every possible method of social union by which men and
> women may act together for the furtherance of well-being. In short,
> we offer voluntary scientific socialism in the place of the present
> compulsory scientific organization which characterizes the State and
> all of its ramifications (1893, p. 365).

The significance of this quotation from *Liberty* as an indication of the communal sentiments alive in Tucker's brand of individualist anarchism should
not be underestimated, for here Tucker is expressing a belief in the virtue of
social cooperation and togetherness which goes far beyond simply the need
for defense. The demise of the state does not signal the end of social harmony,
but brings about a new and vital form of it, one that fulfills the absolute human need for association while it resurrects the ideal of personal freedom.

As an anarchist, Tucker describes a type of social union which is considerably different from that existing in the state. For Tucker, communal unity is
to be achieved between individuals in piecemeal fashion as more and more
cooperative associations are established to meet the needs of individuals in
society. In other words, Tucker expects numerous associations like the original type developed for defense to grow up in the anarchist society, each with
its own special function and mandate. As individuals join these associations
in order to further their own interests, the sense of togetherness and unity
between them grows both because of their increasing number of interlocking
and overlapping commitments, and because the very spirit of cooperation
is strengthened. Community exists in the anarchist society as a mosaic of
communal groups and interlocking individual commitments which is non-
hierarchical except in the sense in which each individual freely orders his or
her own interests and hence the associations to which he or she belongs.

To the criticism often expressed by classical community theorists such
as Durkheim and Ferdinand Toennis that such associations are not really
communal because they are usually partial in the sense of not embracing the
"whole individual" and are thus also short-lived, Tucker responds brilliantly.
Though he admits that each particular association is indeed only partial in its
mandate, and possibly short-lived as well if it fails in its purpose and is beset by the secession of its members, the spirit of cooperation pervades every
facet of social life and ensures that the *system* of cooperative associations will
continue. In short, society as a whole is transformed, and regains its natural

composition, in contemporary anarchist Murray Bookchin's words, "not of disparate individuals but of associative units and the associations between them (1978, p. 15). It is this system of cooperation which constitutes community for Tucker. And the spirit of togetherness, or in Tucker's words, "the concepts of mutual confidence and good fellowship" found within that system are to be obtained, "not by preaching" or by force, but " only by unrestricted freedom" realized under the "law of equal liberty" (1926, p. 15).

In conclusion, it is clear that within this most extreme expression of individualist ideas and disparagement of the state there remains a strong sense of and sentiment for community. But why is it important to realize this and why has so much time and space been devoted to this discovery? This expression of the communal sentiments alive in individualist thought is significant for several reasons. First, from a purely scholarly perspective, it is worthwhile to study Tucker's thought for the understanding that here is a vital and increasingly relevant part of the tradition of American political thought which has significant things to say about political organization from a highly theoretical point of view. As representative of the broader school of individualist and anarchist concepts in American intellectual history, Tucker's ideas have much to recommend them for continued study as significant contributions to American political thought and to the eventual remaking of American society.

Second, the emphasis which Tucker places upon the achievement of community in the individualist society is somewhat startling; particularly so because individualist thought generally is accused of being unconcerned with anything other than individual freedom and the pursuit of self-interest. As an extreme example of this school of thought, then, Tucker's communualistic ideas serve as a backdrop against which to evaluate this general criticism, especially as it has been repeatedly levied against the most notable of his intellectual inheritors, Robert Nozick. Most reviews of Nozick's book stress its allegedly harsh and unfeeling individualism and lack of concern for the presumed values of fellowship, mutual aid, and the care of the sick, elderly, and the poor. But this analysis of Tucker's ideas, which are certainly more extreme than Nozick's in their insistence upon individual autonomy and freedom from coercion, indicates that the individualist in the minimal state must not necessarily ignore the needs of others in order to preserve his or her freedom. On the contrary, it is by means of the voluntary cooperation and communal concern for others that the promise of the anarchist society is to be fulfilled.

Finally, what Tucker has to say concerning freedom, community, and the evils of big government has special, practical significance today for the current political ferment in this country. At a time when citizens are clearly weary of big government and its grasping and seemingly insatiable demands, it is at least worth considering that there is a tradition in America which insists that such need not be the case, and that an alternative is available which values community and fellowship as well as freedom from the coercion of the state. The end of the welfare state need not mean the end of welfare, but only the demise of a particular, and increasingly unpopular, form of it. Individualism can embrace a communal concern for others, and because it can, it is time to stop expressing the same tired objections to its efficacy as a model for political organization. Community is indeed, as Dante Germino states, "*the* political problem of our time," but it is a problem precisely because its achievement must not come on the heels of "some new collectivist idolatry" (1959, pp. 81–82). The lesson that Tucker and his fellow individualists urge is that cooperation need not be accompanied by force, and community and the concern for others' welfare which it implies is possible not because of government, but in spit of it, and will only truly flourish in its absence.

John Zerzan's uncompromising critique of human civilization is one of the most controversial branches of contemporary anarchism. In this analysis, Young opens with understandable skepticism. Are we really to accept Zerzan's argument that "symbolic culture" — as manifest in human language and measured time—is responsible for our currently alienated state and loss of freedom? As incredible as such a claim appears, Young manages to make some reasonable sense of it, distilling Zerzan's critique into a hypothesis palatable enough to be worthy of discussion rather than pat dismissal.

Originally published in issue 37.

Against Everything That Is
John Zerzan and the Anarchist Critique of Symbolic Thought
Daniel Dylan Young

"Sometimes in history things are reversed in a moment when the physical world intrudes enough to knock us off balance…The dogs in Pavlov's laboratory had been conditioned for hundreds of hours. They were fully trained and domesticated. Then there was a flood in the basement. And you know what happened? They forgot all of their training in a blink of an eye. We should be able to do at least that well. I am staking my life on it, and it is toward this end that I devote my work."

— John Zerzan

I. An Anarchist Critique of Symbolic Thought

What if someone told you that language is not a tool for human communication and understanding, but an inherently imprecise system which obscures objective reality and furthers coercive ideologies? What if they also said that symbolic culture, with its mythic roles and figures, its ritual taboos and ceremonies, leads inevitably to a mutilated experience of reality and a hierarchical social dystopia? What if they also made it clear that a confused, mutilated existence mediated by language and symbolic culture is not inescapable, and made the claim that for most of our existence the human race maintained social cohesion, equality, and environmentally sustainable ways of life because their minds were not hindered by the subjective detachment and the contrived hierarchies of symbolic thought? And what if they concluded that this limitless pre-linguistic consciousness was not lost forever, but that it is always there under the surface of our domesticated minds, waiting for a moment of trauma when our hollow symbolic categories collapse and our perception is cleansed?

Such an analysis is very difficult to accept, or even to consider seriously. It seems to attack everything that human cultures consider sacred, and everything that social scientists consider natural. Yet these are the core ideas in the writings of John Zerzan, a contemporary American anarchist thinker. His work draws upon and/or bears similarity to that of other so-called anarcho-primitivist writers who have criticized scientific rationality and the ideal of technological progress as irreconcilable with autonomy and equality — writers like Fredy Perlman, Ted Kaczynski, John Moore, or David Watson. But Zerzan combines these insights with the poststructuralist understanding of language as a complex system of symbols that produces and constitutes the reality of those who use it. From Zerzan's synthesis of these disparate theories comes the hypothesis that language and symbolic thought are the primary sources of social hierarchy and inequality. He contends that symbolic thought inevitably leads to complete objectification of the natural and social world — which means the conceptual transformation of all plants, animals and people from unique, dynamic lifeforms into manipulable objects. He also posits that dependence on symbolic thought requires dependence on the conceptual process of reification, by which the symbolic use values of objectified lifeforms are elevated to primary conceptual importance. Via the intellectual processes of objectification and reification, general symbolic categories based upon use value take primary social and psychological importance, ahead of all unique characteristics or individual circumstances.

Zerzan posits that once objectification and reification become socially ascendant, human alienation begins and social harmony ends. Symbolic thought causes these problems because it places artificial obstacles between the individual consciousness and the outside world, thereby destroying any possibilities for an understanding of the world based on interconnection and mutual benefit. Zerzan considers language and time consciousness as both the immediate signs of this initial alienation, and important devices for the spread and refinement of reified thought. He also attempts to show how, once symbolic thought is adopted to any degree, humans become increasingly dependent upon it because symbolic thought processes slowly make alternative ways of thinking impossible or undesirable. Therefore Zerzan labels symbolic thought inherently coercive and inegalitarian. In Zerzan's model of human history myth, ritual, domestication, and shamanism are all early coercive devices developed for the purpose of maintaining symbolic thought. The widespread adoption of agriculture, written literature, art and other forms of symbolic culture allow relationships based on hierarchical control and dependence to become the rule, rather than the exception. In time these early, crude tools of alienation have become refined into scientific rationality and capitalism.

At first glance Zerzan's condemnation and rejection of symbolic thought might sound like a childish and nihilistic rejection of reality, or an absurdly pessimistic opposition to everything that is. But this would be a very superficial dismissal of someone whose works go a long way towards establishing, through the use of anthropological evidence about various so-called primitive societies, a direct link between increased reliance upon symbolic thought and the presence of social hierarchy and inequality. Anthropological evidence about pre-historic humanity also serves as the basis of Zerzan's hypothesis that throughout most of its history the human species did not utilize either language or symbolic thought. He argues that from an anti-authoritarian, anarchist viewpoint, pre-linguistic consciousness independent of symbolic thought would have been infinitely superior to current human consciousness because of its necessary basis in face-to-face interactions and the experience of the immediate moment. With firm roots in social sensitivity, emotional intelligence, heightened senses and possibly telepathic intuition, pre-linguistic thought would have been far less prone to the rigidification, coercion and inequality that plague human societies organized around the categories and hierarchies of symbolic culture. Prior to the ascendancy of symbolic thought, Zerzan believes that human life was materially prosperous, socially harmonious, and inconceivably fulfilling. Zerzan also feels that this Edenic grace can be regained. Significantly, his ideas are not pure conjecture, and are always at least partially grounded in interdisciplinary evidence from the academic fields of anthropology, history, psychology, sociology, philosophy, linguistics, and physics.

Yet there are deeply problematic and possibly flawed areas of Zerzan's writings. To begin with, there is the question of the validity of much of the historical and anthropological evidence that he presents as fact. Beyond the problem of questionable facts, there are also the questionable assumptions upon which his writings are based: that humanity could return to a pre-linguistic, non-symbolic consciousness, and that this would actually be conducive to egalitarian social harmony. Finally, even if one accepts the bulk of Zerzan's ideas, there is the question of how his understanding can be used to guide future efforts to oppose symbolic thought. Can we successfully create temporary autonomous zones, where we are momentarily freed from the traps of language or symbolic thought? Should we engage in certain forms of issue based activism because they are in conformity with the larger critique of civilization? How can a revolutionary pre-linguistic consciousness be advanced when the only tools that we have to work with are linguistic or symbolic? Can we make a conscious effort to escape symbolic thought, or can we overcome our 30,000 years of training only by accident? Zerzan often seems to support the latter view, and he boycotts most traditional anti-authoritarian activism while simultaneously making optimistic statements like: "Ten thousand years of captivity and darkness…will not withstand ten days of full out revolution" (Zerzan, "Transition"). But if humanity's liberation must come through some sudden catastrophe or spontaneous revolution, what does this say about our ability to keep a newly established non-linguistic society from falling back into the prison of symbolic thought?

Though there may be flaws in Zerzan's overall understanding of symbolic culture, his ideas merit serious attention because of the insights they offer into the nature of human thought and language, the extent of dependence and coercion in contemporary society, and the possibilities for future anarchist reform and revolution. My objective is to bring into better focus the basic ideas and logical steps at the center of Zerzan's complex cultural critique.

II. John Zerzan: The Man Himself

When an interviewer asked him what he wanted from his own work and life, John Zerzan replied: "a face to face community, an intimate existence, where relations are not based on power…I would like to see an intact natural world, and I would like to live as a fully human being. I would like that for the people around me" (Jensen, 1998). As Zerzan's own writings show, these seemingly humble aspirations are currently unattainable due to the intricate web of capitalist technology that shapes every aspect of modern life. For an individual to extricate themselves from this network, if it is possible at all, means choosing an isolationist lifestyle that leaves the rest of humanity to be destroyed and ravaged by culture and technology.

In the face of these obstacles, Zerzan does the best that he can. His world view has certainly changed since he matriculated at Stanford in the 1960s to study political science, with the goal of becoming a college professor. He now calls this move "a giant waste of time" (Noble, 1995). Upon finishing at Stanford, Zerzan moved to the Haight-Ashbury area of San Francisco. He experienced first hand the political and social upheaval of the youth and student movements underway in San Francisco and Berkeley in the late 1960s, and he reports that this experience gave him a sense of possibility and an optimism that has stayed with him "even though thirty years later things are frozen, and awful" (Jensen, 1998).

Zerzan went on to get a master's degree in history at San Francisco State. He also spent three years in a Ph.D. program at the University of Southern California, but he never received his degree. He continued living in the Bay Area throughout much of the 1970s. For a time he worked as a labor organizer with what he has referred to as a "sort of do-it-yourself union" in San Francisco that was set up to advance workers' rights while avoiding the corruption and bureaucracy rampant in most American organized labor. The group was organized along libertarian guidelines, and "our general tactic was to help everybody with all of their issues, all of their grievances, defend everything, dispute everything" (Jensen, 1998). The group's founding principle was a theory advanced in the 1960s called "The Long March Through the Institutions," which held that the system could only be toppled by working inside existing rules and structures. During this period Zerzan also began writing political articles for publication, many of which dealt with labor issues and were published in the Detroit-based anarchist newspaper *The Fifth Estate.*

Zerzan left the union and withdrew from political organizing in general when he decided that working to help people with their individual problems only because it fit into your larger political theories was ultimately manipulative and dishonest. He moved to Eugene, Oregon in 1981, fleeing from the skyrocketing cost of living in the Bay Area. In the calmer sphere of Oregonian life he found that he could focus on his intellectual work with fewer distractions. Since then he has turned out dozens of critical studies dealing with different aspects of contemporary Western society, civilization, and symbolic thought. His articles have been most often published in the *Fifth Estate* and the quarterly magazine *Anarchy: A Journal of Desire Armed* (to which he is a contributing editor). His works have also been occasionally featured in other libertarian, anti-authoritarian and leftist publications. In 1988 he published his first book, a collection of essays entitled *Elements of Refusal* (newly available from C.A.L. Press). His second book, *Future Primitive,* was published in 1994 by Autonomedia. He has also edited two volumes: *Questioning Technology: A Critical Anthology* (with Alice Carnes, London: Freedom Press, 1998, also Philadelphia: New Society Press, 1991) and *Against Civilization: Readings and Reflections* (Eugene: Uncivilized Books, 1999). Since most of his work is published by non-profit collectives, Zerzan's cultural critique has no financial motivation or pay off. He has testified that since moving to Eugene, "in terms of income I do mostly child care and yard work to survive; I don't get any money from books, and I probably won't ever get any money from the books" (Noble, 1995).

For many years this way of life has brought Zerzan little recognition outside extreme leftist, Luddite and anarchist circles. It took the intrigue of terrorism for his ideas to gain mainstream media attention. In 1995, when the Unabomber case was still unsolved and a financially solvent investment for the capitalist press, *The New York Times* considered Zerzan worthy of a medium size article. Describing him as "an unpretentious and faintly melancholic man" and "a guru of sorts for anti-technology leftists," the article dealt briefly with the similarities between Zerzan and the bomber's views. It also pointed out how the Unabomber's terrorist activities had given anti-technology ideas wider exposure (Noble, 1995).

In the last half of 1999, the efforts of the mainstream media have made John Zerzan possibly the most well known anarchist in America (the only other contender would be with Noam Chomsky). This process began when the June 18th Reclaim The Streets demonstration in Eugene was spiced up with tactical property destruction against banks and corporate storefronts, followed by brutal attacks by rampaging riot police. These so-called "riots" had several notable results: intensified police repression against anarchists and others in Eugene; the mobilization of the entire state of Oregon's legal resource to scapegoat one Latino anarchist protester from out of town for the "riots" (Rob Thaxton AKA Rob Los Ricos is currently serving a 7 and a half year prison sentence for daring to defend himself against a rampaging riot cop); and a spate of media coverage in major west coast newspapers about the "new anarchists." On the whole these articles painted a ludicrous picture of John Zerzan as some kind of cult leader of a group of violent anarchist youths in training in the isolated college town of Eugene. But this mainstream media coverage was only the prelude to what followed the November 30th demonstrations in Seattle, where anarchists and others took a largely symbolic protest against the WTO to a new level by successfully creating a temporary autonomous zone in downtown Seattle where they smashed in the storefronts of corporations, occupied downtown Seattle streets, and built barricades out of dumpsters and newspaper boxes in order to temporarily repel the Seattle police. Much of the media coverage immediately following the events rabidly and ridiculously attempted to blame all property destruction that took place on "anarchists from Eugene," for whom John Zerzan was represented as either a real or a philosophical leader. This fabrication was repeated so often that some participants in the property destruction on November 30th found it necessary to state in their explanative communique about the action that: "While some of us may appreciate [Zerzan's] writings and analyses, he is in no sense our leader, directly, indirectly, philosophically or otherwise" (Acme Collective, 1999) The less frenetic follow-up coverage in the weeks following November 30th also tried to play up the spurious idea that most or all radical anarchists who attended the November 30th protest hailed from or were somehow connected with John Zerzan and the Eugene anarchist community (not to mention that all anarchists were portrayed as "anti-technology"). The December 13th issue of *Newsweek* magazine featured an article about the "New Radicals," which contained a sidebar on the "New Anarchism" with a collage including a picture of Zerzan and a short identification of him (it also included Noam Chomsky, Emma Goldman and the lead singer from the highly political but extraordinarily commercialized rock group *Rage Against the Machine*). More notably, on Tuesday, December 14th the CBS news program "60 Minutes II" also had an entire segment about the "Eugene anarchists" which included long interview segments with John Zerzan along with other members of the Eugene anarchist community.

Though he may be scapegoated for fomenting violence, Zerzan is not routinely involved in any form of property destruction, violence or armed revolutionary struggle. Talking about the largely intellectual role that he has taken in the revolutionary movement, Zerzan once remarked: "I've thought a lot about how I can best serve — and I realize that at least part of this answer is based on class privilege, on a wider set of options being open to me than to many others." This wider set of options means that as an educated first-worlder, it is not strategic or necessary that Zerzan immediately take up arms in order to bring about humanity's liberation. The system of divided labor has shaped things so that, "For me, words are a better weapon to bring down the system than a gun would be. This is to say nothing of anybody else's choice of weapons, only my own…. But my words are nothing but a weapon" (Jensen, 1998).

III. Anthropological Background: Primitive Affluence

As anarchist cultural critique, John Zerzan's writings are partly concerned with finding and analyzing models of human society that have workably approximated egalitarian anarchy. Like many contemporary anarchists, he finds affirmation of libertarian ideals in the historical examples of primitive foraging societies. In the last few decades serious anthropological research has brought to light the fact that a collectivist, state-less, non-coercive and relatively egalitarian social structure was the rule among primitive foraging societies. Dozens of anthropological studies have established egalitarian food-sharing as a dominant characteristic of both modern and pre-historic foragers, while division of labor or unequal distribution of resources are almost completely unknown among them (Barclay, 1996). At the same time, anthropologists have documented that active, extreme anti-authoritarian attitudes are an essential component of many extant hunter-gatherer societies (Zerzan, 1994; p. 35)

Often foraging societies encourage equality by actively discouraging sex and age discrimination (Barclay, 1996, p. 49). Division of labor based upon gender differences seems to be at a minimum among extant foragers, and Zerzan points out that women maintain autonomy and equal social status in primitive society partly because they engage regularly in the central economic activity of hunting for needed dietary protein. Other signs pointing to minimal patriarchy and sexism among primitive hunter-gatherers include attitudes about sexual intercourse, marriage and menstruation (Zerzan, 1994; p. 40-1) The mass of anthropological data seems to show that foraging societies in general are set up to afford women greater autonomy and higher social status than any other model of social organization.

All of these discoveries about the social structures of primitive foragers have come into acceptance alongside new ideas about their general material condition. The anthropological theory of "primitive affluence," increasingly accepted since the 1960s, supports the conclusion that primitive foragers labor much less in order to live much healthier lives than the average resident of an early agricultural society, or possibly even a modern industrial one. The lives of primitive foraging peoples, though they may be shorter on the average compared to our own (and this is still a point of contention), are not nasty or brutish, and their hand-to-mouth existence is not particularly stressful or labor intensive.

This all begs the question: if primitive societies require less labor in order to maintain affluent, healthy societies with greater equality and autonomy than our own, what are the positive attributes of modern industrial society that provide compensation for what we have given up? One plausible benefit would be the accomplishments of modern science in improving the quality of human life — specifically the modifications of the food supply made possible through widespread factory farming, and Western medicine's constant advances at prolonging human life. Zerzan addresses this issue several times in different writings. Dealing with the modern versus primitive food supply, he feels that the primitives win hands down. Compared to the average modern resident of a first world country, the diets of contemporary foragers (many of whom, like the San bushmen of the Kalahari, have been forced into arid and infertile foraging grounds) are far more diverse and they consume far fewer foods likely to lead to diseases or disorder (Zerzan, 1994; p. 32). Also the diets of foraging people are certainly better in every way than those of third world peoples impoverished through their slavery to first world economic powers. As to the issue of quantity of food, famine is much more a problem in early agricultural societies than in foraging ones, for reasons that will become clear.

In regards to the gifts of modern medicine, most primitives just don't seem to need them. Barring accidental injuries — which are extremely rare when you don't have automobiles, firearms, explosives, plains, trains, or large-scale warfare — foragers seem to have very few health problems. Among the few extant foraging societies, anthropologists have documented extraordinarily low rates of degenerative and mental diseases, not to mention cases of immunity to malaria, childbirth without pain, or skin so elastic that it doesn't wrinkle with age (Zerzan, 1994; p. 32–3). These findings fit in with some anthropologists' conclusions that the move from nomadic foraging to agriculture created most infectious diseases and led to a general decline in the quality of human health and the length of human life spans (Zerzan, 1994; p. 28) It also fits in with Zerzan's own assertion that "nearly all diseases are diseases either of civilization, alienation, or gross habitat destruction" (Jensen, 1998).

Besides a material technology whose only positive effect seems to be putting band-aids on the cancers that it has created, the other seemingly positive contribution of civilization would have to be symbolic culture: the stockpile of recorded knowledge that includes art, literature, science, mathematics, mythology and religion. In addressing this issue, Zerzan's writings make a break from other anarcho-primitivists. Many of these other theorists deal with the idea that scientific rationality and technology are far from neutral tools, and that hierarchy and coercion cannot be escaped if our current systems of technology are retained. But much of Zerzan's work is based upon the assumption that symbolic culture is also non-neutral — he attempts to show that symbolic thought is just as inherently coercive as technology, and just as antithetical to harmonious anarchist society.

IV. The Reification of Reality

Zerzan's definition of the process of "reification" is central to his argument that symbolic thought unavoidably encourages domination and coercion. Reification is the process of conceptually elevating an abstract mental construct so that it is considered just as important and just as objectively real as actual living beings or material elements of the world. In Zerzan's model, the process of reification works hand in hand with objectification to produce symbolic culture. Together these processes facilitate the manipulation of material elements as objects, but only at the loss of a more interactive and dynamic understanding of the objective world. Zerzan shows that once objectification and reification have become strong habits embedded in an individual or a society's consciousness, these processes are applied to more than just inanimate objects, so that eventually plants, animals and even people are dealt with as reified symbols. In the case of other humans, reification has the frightening effect of allowing symbolic categories such as race, gender, or occupation to take primary importance in our social interactions, completely subordinating unique individual traits. But, as he shows, this de-humanizing effect is not an accident: it is a central aim of symbolic thought, and the basis of civilization.

Zerzan argues that any amount of dependence on reified symbols will ultimately preclude conceiving of the world in non-reified terms. Eventually all interactions with other objects or organisms are modelled on control and coercion, rather than any kind of mutually beneficial, interactive relationship. This causes the exchange of a pure perception of reality for a conception in which the world around us is immediately categorized in terms of symbols representing different categories of manipulable objects. Or, to put it more simply, "symbols at first mediated reality and then replaced it" (Zerzan, 1997). As one's objectified view is narrowed by symbolic categories, one even loses awareness of the different possible ways to manipulate objects. One's way of life becomes centered around certain objects and certain uses for these objects that have been placed at central importance by one's symbolic conception. Other objects become useless, and other uses become unimaginable.

For example, even taking for granted a subject-object viewpoint of the food chain, where some things eat and others are eaten (ignoring the massive webs of cyclical energy sharing involved), a hungry modern American cannot immediately satisfy his or her hunger with whatever is immediately edible in his or her environment. For such an individual food is a very distinct category of cultivated, prepared, and often pre-packaged products. Food does not conceptually include anything that could be immediately foraged in the natural environment, and most human environments have been artificially modified so that very little that is edible grows or lives in them anyway. Even inside this strictly limited reified category of "food" there are other symbolic concepts that interfere with the ability to eat freely. Food must be obtained by shopping at a supermarket with money. The ritualistic activity of shopping, the controlled space of the supermarket, and the symbolic economic concept of money are all highly reified and rigid social constructs to which people must pay obeisance prior to being able to even eat. Then there are the origins of most modern food in factory farms, whose existence rests upon the reified justifications that individual humans can be used specialized tools in a system of divided labor, and that other plants and animals are only objects for human consumption.

Zerzan contends that human society was not always so totally immersed in reification. He holds that there are two forms of reification that have been crucial to the overall spread and advancement of symbolic thought: language and time. Not only were language and time the earliest by-products of humanity's alienation, they have also been highly effective tools for its propagation.

Language And Reification

Zerzan's opinions on language are partially based on studies of humans lacking the ability to speak due to physical problems or brain damage. These studies show that language is not necessary or inherent in advanced, complex human thought (Zerzan, 1997). Zerzan also hypothesizes from anthropological evidence that the tool-making skills utilized by primitive humans to maintain material prosperity were best taught by example (Zerzan, 1988; p. 28). Therefore he feels that the symbolic language upon which civilized humans are completely dependent is not necessary for a society living in harmonious anarchy or primitive affluence. From here he develops an argument that language is not only unnecessary for social harmony and equality, but that it is actually an impediment to maintaining a society predicated on egalitarian, face-to-face relations and concerned with immediate physical/material reality rather than inaccurate, mystifying symbols.

At several points Zerzan hypothesizes that the use of language initiated a conception of the individual subject whose interests were separate from the social collective or from nature. Speech, he suggests, is directly tied in with the distinct subject-object differentiation that is part of objectification. It also creates the possibility of communicating wholly without actual physical contact, which he conceives as a direct threat to a society predicated upon intimate, face-to-face interactions (Zerzan, 1997).

Zerzan concludes that any advantages that language affords are gained only at the loss of an unfragmented, collective understanding of the world and our place in it. As language facilitates an objectified viewpoint, it also closes off to us an understanding of the world as a connected whole. Language has this effect partly because of its symbolic bias. Zerzan points out that "even in the most primitive languages, words rarely bear a recognizable similarity to what they denote: they are purely conventional" (Zerzan, 1988; p. 25). This is because representing a visual, tactile, or even cognitive sensation using spoken sounds can never be anything but crudely correlational, and under most circumstances is based only upon social convention. Since language is symbolic, it must be reified in order to gain acceptance as the most central form of human understanding. What this reification means is that language, like all symbolism, allows you to gain access to reality only through certain imprecise conceptual pathways. The word for a certain object *may* suggest the object in its entirety and its larger relationship to the world, but it almost never does all of these things at once. And a word's strict dictionary denotation and usage conventions always limit it to defining only a tiny aspect of a culture's larger understanding of what the word signifies. Even this cultural understanding of the object is a severely limited concept restricted by the culture's own usage values. In this way Zerzan shows how words can never actually convey objective reality. Instead they use linguistic signifiers in attempts to convey symbolic representations, which are themselves only objectified perspectives on reality.

Because language is predicated upon symbolism, it is virtually impossible for a language to exist without having some kind of particular ideological assumptions guiding it. Zerzan characterizes ideology as "alienation's armored way of seeing," (Zerzan, 1988; p. 23) which limits our perception to particular reified lines of thought. Ideology and language work hand in hand to persuade the dominating and the dominated that their social roles are natural. They do this by creating "false separations and objectification.... This falsification is made possible by concealing, and ultimately vitiating, the participation of the subject in the physical world" (Zerzan, 1997).

Zerzan's characterization of ideologies also seems an apt description of the symbolic manner in which language itself functions. This is because Zerzan contends that language has its own ideology, steeped in the alienating values of objectification and reification that required and facilitated the original invention of language. Since any ideology ultimately functions in order to stomp out dissent through intellectual coercion and domination, he concludes that language cannot avoid serving the purposes of reified symbolic thought. Through the imposition of false limitations on our consciousness, language trains us to conceive of the world only in terms of separate, detached subjects manipulating rigidly categorized objects. As this viewpoint stomps out all opposition, the inevitable result is a conception of the world in terms of "reduced, rigidified subjects and an equally objectified field of experience" (Zerzan, 1998, "That *Thing*," p. 55).

A look at the structure of actual languages can show us how the ideology of reification has shaped them. If objectification begins with the practice of naming things, then perhaps reification first arrives with the invention of the pronoun, the linguistic device that allows unique individuals to become abstract entities denoted by their species or gender (Zerzan, 1998; p. 56). Some anthropologists have also concluded that early grammar and syntax were modeled upon the convention-based, reified social activities of religious ritual (Zerzan, 1997). Comparing different languages also yields insights. Zerzan argues that Sanskrit may be a less objectifying language in some respects because of the way in which it describes human consciousness. In modern English the totality of human consciousness is described either as an immobile "mind," which is active only through the dominating control of "minding" oneself or others, or in terms of the anatomically detached "brain." The term used in Sanskrit roughly translates as "working within" (Zerzan, 1988; p. 24). This implies a consciousness that is dynamic rather than static, and cooperative with the whole human being, rather than anatomically separated or hierarchically dominating. The language of the Navajo Native American tribes could also be seen as less alienated from material reality than modern European languages because most of its vocabulary centered around physical sensations and actions, rather than abstract concepts (Zerzan, 1988; p. 24).

As a language contains fewer words referring to actions and direct perceptions, and more referring to abstract concepts and rigid categorizations, it more completely reflects the ideology of symbolic thought. This is why abstract concepts and metaphors lend themselves to a loss of their original meaning, and to a reinterpretation based upon their use value to powerful social minorities. Language causes objective reality to be lost in a sea of words and reified symbols, and the history of change in language seems to suggest to Zerzan that we have been left "in an existence without vibrancy or meaning, [where] nothing is left but language" (Zerzan, 1998; p. 56). However, he feels that ultimately any attempts to address this problem through linguistic routes alone (he doesn't even consider possibilities, but one can imagine attempts to create a language utilizing minimal metaphor and abstraction) will be doomed to failure. This is because all languages have their roots in the alienating processes of objectification and reification. Even if a few tribal societies here and there have managed to hold out in anarchic equality while simultaneously developing language and symbolic thought, the fact remains that humanity in general has used these abstract tools to create a hellish world of hierarchy and domination. Therefore Zerzan finds that language's symbolic origins make it by nature an impediment to autonomy, equality and understanding.

Time And Reification

Zerzan contends that the civilized concept of time, like the tool of language, is an individual instance of reification that is also essential to the maintenance and proliferation of symbolic thought. He contends that time, as "an abstract continuing 'thread' that unravels in an endless progression that links all events together while remaining independent of them," (Jensen, 1998) is purely a product of human perception. Measured linear time, unlike material elements, is produced by its own measurement, which gains widespread acceptance only through coercive social elites who promote its importance (Zerzan, Winter 1994). Zerzan points out that even in the realm of science and physics irreversible time is understood to be not an absolute fact, but partially a product of human cognition — which Zerzan presents as skewed by alienation from objective reality (Zerzan, Winter 1994). Despite its minute and obsessive measurement, time remains an artificial and relative human concept. This reality, however, is directly contrary to the concept of time. Time is supposed to flow only with respect to itself and be utterly universal and independent of all individual perception.

To better understand this contradiction, it is necessary to look at the social purposes for which different concepts of time have been used. In 1944 the anarchist scholar and historian George Woodcock pointed out that in modern Western capitalist society, "The clock turns time from a process of nature into a commodity that can be measured and bought and sold like soap or sultanas" (Woodcock, 1998). In Zerzan's critique, the act of reifying time in order to maintain social control is charted back to the beginnings of symbolic thought.

Zerzan conceives of the period prior to divided labor and symbolic culture as an essentially timeless state. Pre-historic humans were primarily conscious of the possibilities of the immediate moment, and they adjusted to the sequences and rhythms of the natural world at an intuitive level, rather than struggling to consciously manipulate or control them. Zerzan imagines that after the loss of non-reified perception to symbolic concepts, early religious rituals arose as an attempt to regain a consciousness of the immediate moment, unburdened by an obsession with the passing of time (Zerzan, Winter 1994). But ritual fails in this respect because rituals themselves are abstractions that try to preserve events symbolically, thereby taking the participant further away from experiencing the immediate moment. Instead of allowing people access to the real immediate moment, rituals only allow them to live in a seemingly "timeless" space, which is detached from their actual surroundings in a distorted, reified manner. Zerzan points out that the detached "timelessness" of ritual is similar to the detached nature of measured time, where individual circumstances in a period of time are subordinated to the rules of rational universal measurement.

Zerzan believes that "the rise of agriculture magnified the importance of time, and especially reified cyclical time" (Jensen, 1998). As domestication made the exact counting of plants, land, and animals of utmost importance, the minute tracking of time also took primary social importance. Such measurements were needed in order to schedule the intense divided labor of sowing and reaping needed to produce the highest possible yield. Zerzan points out that in these early agricultural societies social elites used time as a source of power: in early civilizations such as the Babylonians or the Mayans, priests ran the calendars, and the surplus of the harvest went to them (Jensen, 1998).

In an agricultural society where the material surplus needed to feed religious elites was produced only through fastidious time-keeping by those same elites, centralized power and coercion were first justified as being necessary for the maintenance of an artificial religious order (Zerzan, Winter 1994). These early agricultural societies' conceptions of time were reified in that symbolic representations of different aspects of the planting and harvesting cycle became elevated to primary social and cultural significance. However, early agriculture was not completely alienated because it "still maintained at least a bow toward the natural world with its connection to the rhythms of the days and seasons" (Jensen, 1998).

With the innovations of the clock and the concept of "historical time," human alienation from nature went into overdrive. Historical time is the basis of culture; it is the idea of life not as a series of cycles, but as a distinct line of events. Certain events become reified into holidays or festivals, and take on an importance that outweighs both natural cycles and the experience of the immediate moment. People lead their lives constantly aware that what is happening now will never be as important as the events of some past time period, such as the birth and resurrection of Christ. Such events slowly replace natural pointers like solstices or equinoxes as the centers of perceived cyclical change. More important, the awareness of one's location in a specific spot on a strand of linear time facilitates the construction of a massive canon of symbolical cultural records and practices, which in turn ask that the individual to forget their own circumstances in order to conceive of their actions and perceptions through pre-existing symbolic hierarchies. Historical time's devaluation of the present moment also psychologically aids the deferment of pleasure and fulfillment. This mortgaging of the moment is at the core of every civilized religion that requires the sacrificing of pleasure in this life for rewards in the next. It also lies behind the modern notion of delaying immediate gratification in order to focus one's energy into labor that will increase individual wealth and further "progress"—thereby helping to create a better world for people living at some distant point in the future. Thus Zerzan asserts that historic time is also the "most elemental aspect of culture" and posits that "Time awareness is what empowers us to deal with our environment symbolically" (Zerzan, Winter 1994).

As to clock time, Zerzan holds that "mathematically divisible time is necessary for the conquest of nature, and for even the rudiments of modern technology" (Zerzan, Winter 1994). The perfection of calendars and clocks is therefore synonymous with the escalation of coercion. Mechanical time seems to demand individual or coerced renunciation of pleasure for the purposes of greater precision. In this way it sacrifices an understanding of people and the world as dynamic, spontaneous and unpredictable. Obsession with time is always at dissonance with biological rhythms. Clock time also adds to the cultural burden of historical time the permutation that: "Even when nothing was happening, time did not cease to flow. Events…are put into this homogeneous, objectively measured, moving envelope" (Zerzan, Winter 1994). While historical time turned a cohesive experience of temporal life into jagged, separate symbolic moments, clock time seeks to put these moments back together again, but in a way that flattens them out so that all experience is conceived as identical seconds ticking off on a chronograph. While historical time aids in the conceptual elevation of symbols over reality which is necessary for reification, clock time is explicitly a tool for facilitating the control of the detached subject over the objective world.

V. Zerzan's Model of Human History: The Degradation of Civilization

Zerzan's efforts to expose the alienating effects of symbolic thought are neither abstract nor ahistorical. As anarchist critique, Zerzan's works have the very real objective of exposing and opposing human social arrangements based upon coercion and inequality. To this effect all of Zerzan's writings attempt to show how his concepts of reification and alienation are based upon and clearly reflected in human history.

Zerzan never establishes the exact place or time when humans fell from grace and began to think symbolically. He posits that this process began somewhere hundreds of thousands of years ago, and slowly gathered steam until a virtual explosion in the manufacturing of symbolic culture took place around 30,000 years ago (Zerzan, 1988; p. 54). Prior to this time various human species had roamed the earth for several million years, creating complex tools and sailing between the islands of Micronesia without producing any material evidence of symbolic culture (Jensen, 1998). Zerzan contends that substantial differences in brain make-up were not behind the appearance of widespread symbolic culture, and bases this belief on archaeological evidence that humans 1.7 million years ago were able to produce tools that would require the same level of intelligence as modern humans. These early humans, who Zerzan believes were just as intelligent as modern people, were interconnected with each other and the natural world in a harmonious web of life that made fractured symbolic routes of understanding superfluous. This simple life of foraging continued unchanged for hundreds of millennia precisely because it could maintain harmonious inter-relation.

Such harmony could be maintained because prehistoric people didn't conceive of them selves as separate consciousness, detached from the objective world. Zerzan believes that primitive people's imminent awareness of interconnection allowed them to develop an understanding that made full use of the senses of touch, taste, smell, and hearing, which civilized humans almost completely subordinate to the detached experiences of sight and abstract intellectual understanding. In several of his works, Zerzan posits that civilized human social structures rely on a "hierarchy of the senses" (Zerzan, 1988; p. 54). Our alienated consciousness has constructed this hierarchy so that the physically detached and sensually uninvolved senses of vision and abstract intellectual understanding are of constant, crucial importance. They are ranked as slightly more important than hearing, which still allows a high level of detachment but can be sensed physically and can stimulate physical movement at an almost unconscious level. Hearing is, in turn, considered more important than taste and smell because they require physical proximity or contact. Finally, the intimate face-to-face contact of tactile sensation is given only minimal social importance in particular ritualized contexts, while being ignored or even demonized in all other non-controlled circumstances. Though Zerzan posits that this hierarchy is established due to a pre-existing state of detachment from the objective world, over time it is also a very important tool for maintaining and propagating this alienation.

Pre-historic humans may also have possessed some form of powerful intuitive communication, which a modern view might liken to telepathy or a sixth sense. Zerzan also proposes that the consciousness of unalienated pre-historic people could perpetuate harmony because of their different understanding of the dimension of time, which was rooted in the central importance of the immediate moment and the natural rhythms of organic life. This allowed for much more tolerant, open-minded, and spontaneous behavior than the civilized concepts of historic and linear time.

Yet at some point, through some kind of mistake or accident, certain humans became disconnected from this holistic understanding and interconnection with the rest of the natural world. Sometimes Zerzan posits that this may have come about through the invention of language, though at other times his understanding of the causal relationship between alienation and language is unclear. What *is* clear is that once the first humans broke their harmonious interconnection with the world as a whole, ripples of alienation spread out through the population. Feeling disconnected from the natural world, people began to conceive of themselves as distinctly separate entities with different interests from the larger social collective and natural world. They began to behave in a new way, objectifying material elements and even other life forms according to particular use values. This attitude eventually spread into their relations with other people.

Particular attitudes, concepts, and social institutions were crucial to the development of objectification as a social value. As I have already shown, language and time were essential intellectual tools in the increased prevalence of a symbolic understanding. Dependence upon language and time eventually produced the human institutions of mythology and ritual. Both are attempts to understand reality, but Zerzan contends that they are doomed to failure because of their own basis in inaccurate reified categories (Zerzan, Winter 1994). Sometimes myth and ritual attempt to justify aspects of a society which has lost its natural harmony due to its use of coercive, objectified ways of thinking. At other times myth and ritual function as safety valves, allowing respite from alienated life through a semblance of timeless communion or interconnection. But whether they apologize for or offer temporary respite from alienation, the ultimate objective of ritual and myth is always to allow people to continue living lives that are largely alienated.

Myth and ritual became necessary as a sense of material instability led to inequality and coercion in alienated human society. Objectifying individuals found themselves living in a natural world whose larger structures and cycles mystified them, and served their individual purposes only erratically. A feeling of instability developed due to these individuals' inability to deal with situations spontaneously based on their various senses or their telepathic intuition. In response they created simple religions that attempted to explain the natural world, in the hope that this would give them a feeling of control over it. To facilitate this control they also began to systematically compile knowledge about the material world into abstract categories based upon increasingly rigid conceptions of use value. At first this way of thinking was only applied to plants and animals for the purpose of increasing the efficiency of foraging activities. But eventually the same strategy was applied to human beings. Gender differences became more exaggerated, leading to inequalities in social status based on gender, which needed to be justified in terms of myth and ritual. The same process was also applied to age difference, and age-based inequality and gerontocracy became entrenched, replacing previous social structures in which all members of the society were evaluated equally. All of these changes necessitated the initiation of myth and ritual in order to maintain social cohesion.

A crucial step in the process of alienation in pre-historic tribal societies came with the establishment of the first division of labor in the form of shamans. Though the attempts of tribal groups to re-connect harmoniously through ritual and myth may have been only a hollow imitation of pre-linguistic consciousness, they still maintained the idea that such a collective escape from alienation was possible. With the ascendancy of shamans, this consciousness and the level of communication and power which it imbues became the possession of a limited group. Not only did the majority of humankind lose an understanding of the universe and their own lives as whole, they also became hostage to spiritual specialists (Zerzan, 1994; p. 26–7). The first seizures of power by shamans also meant the beginning of a system of divided labor, where particular tasks became the core of individuals' identities, rather than aspects like age, gender, or even unique individual attributes. At the same time shamans were also the first distinct social caste with the potential to maintain an elevated social status through a monopoly on a particular resource, in this case a monopoly over spiritual understanding and mystical power. It is debatable whether this power dynamic was in all cases intentionally established by the shamans themselves, and whether they immediately took advantage of the opportunities it offered to advance their individual interests over those of the collective. In fact, the potential for corruption in their positions of power may have gone largely unchallenged by the rest of the tribe precisely because the changes came on slowly, and at the time seemed only reasonable rather than threatening and malicious. Unfortunately, Zerzan contends, history has proven that the divided labor and specialized power of shamans and all their ilk was a terrible blow to human society, and one from which it has not yet recovered. Elevating an individual to central social importance is the beginning of power, and all power corrupts.

With myth, ritual and shamanistic power firmly entrenched, objectification and reification were eventually applied to all areas of human society. Zerzan maintains that the process continued at a very slow pace, but reached a critical mass about 30,000 years ago. It was at this point that symbolic culture and domestication of nature began to become widespread, and Zerzan holds that these developments are intrinsically linked.

The domestication of plants and animals requires an extremely objectified view of other life forms. Domestication is based on the notion that it is acceptable to make another species completely dependent upon you ostensibly for the purposes of improving one's own material conditions. However, current anthropological knowledge points to the fact that pre-agricultural foraging societies actually had a higher quality food supply than early agricultural ones. The food supply of foragers is also more stable than that of agricultural societies, since a diet based upon a wide variety of non-cultivated food sources is far less likely to be effected by the droughts, pestilence, or blights that cause crop failure and starvation in societies dependent on the cultivation of a select spectrum of plants. Dependence on agriculture also tends to destroy alternative food sources through material and conceptual routes: not only do the members of agricultural societies become conceptually blinded to the possibility of a varied, non-cultivated diet, but they also make irrevocable alterations to their environment that destroy non-cultivated food sources. This not only makes them more dependent on their own agricultural endeavors, but also on trade with other agricultural groups.

All of these facts lead Zerzan to conclude that the adoption of widespread domestication of animals and plants required the coercion of shamans or another elite minority in order to force it on the majority, for the reasons of maintaining religious power structures (Zerzan, 1988; p. 33). From historical and anthropological texts Zerzan uncovers evidence that animals (and possibly plants) were originally domesticated for purely ritual religious purposes. He supports this claim not only with direct evidence from ancient religious and other art and literature, but also from the simple fact that many long domesticated animals possessed in their original wild state few of the characteristics which now make them useful to humans for domestication: "Before they were domesticated sheep had no wool suitable for textile purposes . . . Wild cattle were fierce and dangerous; neither the docility of oxen nor the modified meat texture of such castrates could have been foreseen" (Zerzan, 1988; p. 70).

The advocacy of agriculture by higher social castes for non-ritualistic purposes was probably based upon the realization that the autonomy afforded by a traditional life of nomadic foraging by small tribes made it more difficult for them to consolidate and enlarge their own power. This may not even have been an opportunistic move, but simply another misguided attempt to restore social harmony. Zerzan holds that such failures, which ultimately have taken humanity further and further from the experience of life as whole and harmonious, have guided culture and civilization from the beginning. In this case intensified domestication of plants and animals would bring a tribe's livelihood in line with inegalitarian social structures based upon obedience and dependence. This is due to the fact that domestication of plants and animals doesn't just take away the autonomy and independence of the domesticated life forms. Just as abolitionists criticized American slavery for degrading slavemasters as well as slaves, Zerzan shows how humans who relied upon domestication of animal life were simultaneously indoctrinated into dependence and domestication themselves.

This early domestication of humanity at the behest of its early elites may have been accomplished through several different routes. Agriculture requires a large group of people coordinating their productive activities according to strict schedules. It also requires much more intensive physical activity and a greater time commitment than foraging. Therefore it is likely that the only way elites could compel the larger tribe into such an undertaking would be through the manipulation of deeply entrenched ideas of symbolic power manifested in gods or abstract ideals of community. General acceptance of the division of labor (accomplished through millennia of escalating reification) also made people susceptible to the advice of social elites who had cultivated specialized spiritual, social or intellectual skills only at the sacrifice of these abilities among the general population. The acceptance of limited domestication of plants and animals for ritual purposes in tribal societies also played an important role in their acceptance of intensive agriculture: it made them much more likely to believe the lie that the dependent relationships of domestication are healthy and inevitable, rather than destructive and parasitic.

While Zerzan's critique tries to show us just how far back the roots of coercion, bondage, and inequality in human society reach, he is still an anarchist who believes that uprooting them is always an imminent possibility. He holds that nearly everyone is aware of the hollowness of civilization at some level, and that the domestication of humanity itself is neither total nor complete (at least not yet). He also holds that people were just as imminently aware of this fact 30,000 years ago, when the parasitic nightmare of manipulating the natural world through intensified agriculture was fresh and new. Zerzan contends that the ascendancy of agriculture as a social form prompted a widespread dissonance between the memory of a life of natural harmony and an understanding of the coercive, painfully artificial world that was being created.

Unfortunately for humanity, this growing dissatisfaction was co-opted into the channels of symbolic culture. Using art and religion (which have been inextricable for almost their entire history) humanity made yet another misguided attempt at realizing harmony, doomed from the start due to its reliance on symbolic thought. This attempt was guided mainly by elites of differing levels who wanted to better control the lower ranks of specialized laborers. Yet it also had contributors and supporters from all areas and levels of society, who understood only that they were looking for a way to make their lives whole. Thus the archaeological record from this period reveals a massive escalation in the production of artifacts of symbolic culture — both an increase in pre-existing forms like simple religious iconography, and the appearance of new forms of symbolic culture such as complex architecture and written literature.

With the establishment of agriculture, humanity had reached a new level of dependence upon symbolic thought, which is still being refined today. The ascendancy in the last few centuries of a holy trinity of capitalism, technology, and scientific rationality simply represent a new development in this alienated process. Zerzan agrees with the playwright Max Frisch that technology is "the knack of so arranging the world that we need not experience it" (Zerzan, 1998; p. 54). Seen in this way the ideal of technological progress is simply an accelerated version of the millennia-old objectified viewpoint, in which the world is seen in terms of detached conceptions of manipulable objects, compiled into abstract categories. The obsession with control that this detached viewpoint fosters has finally brought humanity to dream and hope for a totally artificial world in which the coercion of nature has been perfected through scientific rationality. At the same time capitalism works over-time to simultaneously destroy older religious or aristocratic hierarchies of value, while reducing all aspects of life to its own mythic field of monetary evaluation. The fact that some aspects of capitalism and scientific rationality seem in conflict is less important to Zerzan because both of them are totally incompatible with a face-to-face existence free from symbolic representation. But at the same time he does not contend that the individual permutations of different systems of coercion should be ignored — in fact they must be carefully studied and understood in order to be effectively opposed.

In the last few decades of humanity's alienated history there are two new developments that Zerzan considers significant. The first is a type of alienation that he feels may have revolutionary potential. This is manifested in high levels of popular first world cynicism and disenchantment with everything from electoral politics to high culture to everyday life. It can also be observed through constantly escalating levels of crime, chronic mental and physical illness, and other social problems that resist scientific efforts to coerce them out of existence. Zerzan believes that the desperation behind these new developments could mean that humanity is finally ready to accept the truth that has been there all along: that culture and society predicated on symbolic thought cannot escape coercion and alienation, and that time, language and all other symbolic tools must be abandoned in order to attain social and natural harmony.

Unfortunately, the other significant contemporary development that Zerzan notes is the co-opting of this widespread disenchantment into philosophies that pose no actual resistance to consumer capitalist society. This is especially true of poststructuralist and postmodernist thinkers, who show how symbolic language is inherently incapable of providing coherent, non-ideological understanding, yet refuse to imagine any alternative. Though he draws upon their perceptive critiques, Zerzan condemns many of these thinkers for their own denial that any absolute, unmediated understanding of reality can exist free from the inaccurate representation of symbolic thought. I will cover this dispute in greater detail below.

Zerzan contends that technological, capitalist culture's disenchantment with its own representation of the world is not due to the failure of its particular system of symbols. Capitalism's brash and lewd monetary symbolism, or science's honest but failed attempts at representing reality, have only made it undeniably clear that symbolic culture not only fails to deliver the fulfillment it promises, but that its claims are merely distractions intended to keep individuals in line with larger cultural structures of hierarchy and coercion. These problems cannot be repaired through a new and more equitable distribution of wealth and resources, or even by replacing hierarchical power structures with collective ones. Humanity can never regain full autonomy and social harmony until it has jettisoned all its objectifying practices, from the domestication of animals to the reliance upon symbolic thought and language. Any attempts at partial revolution will be doomed from the start.

VI. Structuralism, Poststructuralism, Postmodernism & John Zerzan: Strong Similarities & Severe Differences

Zerzan maintains that the mounting alienation of humanity is clearly manifested in the direction of philosophical thought in the twentieth century. His own ideas, of course, must be included in this. Even if his most often quoted and referenced thinkers are Freud, Nietzsche and Levi-Strauss, Zerzan's theories about language and symbolic culture are clearly indebted to the entire body of twentieth century structuralist, poststructuralist and postmodernist thought. Zerzan acknowledges this, but, as I have indicated, he is extremely critical of certain elements in the works of these other contemporary thinkers.

Zerzan's analysis of language is explicitly based upon the work of structuralist Levi-Strauss, who established that humanity's use of language consists of carving up the world based upon symbolic categories (Eagleton, 1996, p. 108). There are also clear parallels between structuralism's understanding of human society as recurring instances of mythical roles and sequences of events, and Zerzan's idea that alienated society relies upon individuals' subordinating unique and spontaneous impulses to reified conceptual identities. But an essential breaking point can be identified in structuralism's refusal to claim any ability to make value judgments, not even the judgment of which subjects' are more worthy of close scrutiny and analysis (Eagleton, 1996, p. 122).

Zerzan also attacks structuralism as amoral and apathetic for its flight from history and its complete denial of individual agency — instead it contends that mythological roles or the spirits of individual texts manifest themselves through the people who live or write them (Eagleton, 1996, p. 112). Lastly, Zerzan chastises structuralism for asserting that consciousness is completely prescribed by language, an idea that is also a convenient means of denying the validity of conflicting ideologies or dissatisfaction with a society's dominant ideology (Zerzan, 1994; p. 104–5).

Many poststructuralist thinkers criticized structuralism along similar lines. Derrida proposed that both spoken and written language functioned through a process of differentiating and dividing, with the objective of establishing ideological hierarchies of meaning and value based upon polar opposites. He also showed how literature is not based upon set archetypes, because language is an unstable element that can never transmit or hold absolute meaning. Therefore any understanding, communication, or even identity predicated upon language can never be absolute, pure or permanent. Since he also sought to show how all human consciousness could be perceived as a language-based "text," Derrida was forced to conclude that absolute reality and unmediated existence were impossible dreams.

While many of Zerzan's ideas are distinctly similar and probably indebted to Derrida, he also questions central aspects of Derrida's critique. Zerzan's main criticisms of Derrida focus on his refusal to question humanity's reliance on language for communication and understanding, and his refusal to consider the origins of language. Zerzan condemns this as an intellectual act of cowardice because "the essence of language, the primacy of the symbolic, are not really tackled, but are shown to be as inescapable as they are inadequate to fulfillment" (Zerzan, 1994; p. 116). He is also critical of Derrida's seemingly abstract and ahistorical preoccupation with linguistics, which fails to acknowledge the material corollaries of the linguistic hierarchies that Derrida's system of deconstruction was meant to overturn.

Zerzan's criticism of other poststructuralist and postmodernist thinkers follows a similar pattern. While he acknowledges the validity of their ideas within a certain intellectual sphere, he identifies a major failing in their refusal to form any cohesive theory or larger historical and social analysis that would put their particular area of expertise into context. This often noted problem with poststructuralism/postmodernism can be understood if we view these largely French strands of thought as responses to a particular historical situation: the failure of the 1968 Paris uprisings, following their co-optation by adherents of hierarchical Communist ideology (Eagleton, 1996, p. 142). In the disillusioned backlash to this turn of events, all complicated, well-articulated social and political theories became suspect as coercive or authoritarian. Social criticism became minutely focused on individual fields or problems, and large scale social analysis was neglected.

The events of 1968 may also have produced a cynicism in French thought, which is manifested in the poststructuralist/postmodernist tendency to downplay human agency, including both the agency of those elite groups who have primary responsibility in maintaining ideologies and social hierarchies, and the agency of those who seek to oppose it. Zerzan identifies this as a major problem and sometimes a major contradiction. In the case of Michel Foucault, Zerzan criticizes his vision of individuals as agency-less "subjects," unable to objectively understand that their own actions are guided by relativistic values determined by the particular historical era or "episteme" in which they live. Zerzan argues that this vision of the individual subject would make Foucault's own ostensibly ahistorical analysis impossible (Zerzan, 1994; p. 122). Zerzan also attacks the postmodernist belief that humans can never conceive of a natural world that exists separate from our own objectifying intentions. Zerzan finds that their refusal to look beyond what currently exists ultimately serves as an apology for coercion and hierarchy, and a means for perpetuating it. Zerzan points out that while older thinkers like Freud understood that humanity had made a clear choice between civilized or primitive ways of living and understanding (though Freud, unlike Zerzan, clearly valued the civilized over the primitive), in postmodern thought the alienating envelope of symbolic culture has become so refined and opaque that even well-read philosophers are unable to imagine a world without it. Zerzan concludes that these defeatist poststructuralism/postmodernism attitudes do not constitute a radical critique of society — in fact they are closer to an ostensibly "neutral" analysis that tacitly supports the coercive degradation of civilization through its detachment. All of this leads Zerzan to surmise that: "Postmodernism is apparently what we are left with when the modernization process is complete and nature is gone for good" (Zerzan, 1994; p. 119).

The postmodernist and poststructuralist thinkers that Zerzan criticizes would probably label Zerzan's own ideas as the daydreams of a misguided and rebellious child. Since poststructuralists largely ignore the question of origins, the majority of their works are predicated upon the idea that what currently exists always has existed. This makes the conception of a society free of symbolic thought or coercion impossible. If the nature of our reality is dictated by the nature of our discourse, then we cannot build a reality free from symbolic thought when we have only the tools of language and reified conceptions to work with. However, Zerzan says almost the same thing at many places in his writings, and by surveying his writings it becomes clear that he is not depending on a systematic effort to bring about the end of symbolic thought. Rather, he is expecting a massive, spontaneous shock to the system of alienated life that will awaken people to their currently degraded and debilitated state.

VII. Problematic Areas: Facts, Assumptions, Tactics

Even if one can conclude that the anthropological, psychological and sociological evidence upon which Zerzan's ideas are based is all correct, there is still a major problem with his assumptions about prelinguistic human consciousness and prehistoric society. Under close scrutiny, seemingly endless questions arise. Was the seemingly stable harmony of ancient human society (that is the absence of organized violence and the extraordinarily slow rate of social change revealed by archaeological records) really due to a non-symbolic consciousness, in which the conceptual processes of objectification and reification did not arise? Did ancient humans really conceive of the world always in terms of an interconnected harmonious whole? Was objectification ever necessary? Was reification ever necessary? Zerzan rails more against the latter than the former, but it is difficult to tell whether his idealized prehistoric humans might have occasionally relied on either process. His argument that objectification and reification must inherently lead to alienation seems to testify against the possibility, yet it is hard to conceive of any human society that would not recognize the value of some amount of shared knowledge compiled into use-based categories. How else would people be able to pass on knowledge about efficient foraging techniques, predators and other natural threats, or simple herbal medicinal cures for those rare occasions when they were mildly ill? Or are we to believe that they had access to all of these things through a body of accumulated knowledge maintained telepathically rather than through spoken or written means? Can humanity really have a culture — that is a non-genetically transmitted body of knowledge — without using any symbolic tools of communicative understanding?

Though Zerzan might tell us that these questions only plague us because we have lost the ability to understand and conceive of the world as would a non-linguistic human, such an assertion seems problematically evasive in and of itself. As one dissenting contributor to *Anarchy: A Journal of Desire Armed* pointed out: "The purpose of analysis is, in every tradition I've encountered other than that of the Western intellectualism Zerzan decries (but in which he is hopelessly mired), to understand the natural order rather than to abstract it into something it isn't, but which we wish it were, or think we can make it" (Jaimes, 1993). This critic perceived Zerzan's writings to have the central argument that what humanity really needs to do in order to create a utopia is to immediately renounce all symbolic categories of thought and give up control of the objective world completely. Characterized in this way, Zerzan's contentions seem just as ridiculous as the guiding principle of scientific rationality: that what humanity really needs to do in order to create a utopia is to symbolically categorize every aspect of the world in order to absolutely control it. As Derrida might point out, Zerzan's ideas are based upon polar oppositions, and are therefore nothing but manipulative ideology.

Or are they? Zerzan is an anarchist who is relatively uninvolved in traditional activist circles, nor does he hold any apparent social power besides his unavoidable status as a white, male first-worlder. He has argued that writing is a less coercive form of communicating his political ideals than social activism, because nobody *has* to read his books. On the other hand, an anarchist who is actively involved in helping people with individual problems could conceivably use their positive influence to create support for anarchism which is based on misguided sentiment rather than real understanding and support for equality, autonomy, and collectivity. Yet this question of tactics seems to pose a dilemma, because Zerzan's ideal, unalienated humans are characterized as active and emotional, rather than detached and rational. How are contemporary anarchists to avoid symbolic, emotional ideology without becoming imminently rational, and thereby losing the warmth and spontaneity necessary for the future revolution which Zerzan characterizes as a collective celebration?

This brings us directly into the question of what kind of anarchist tactics (revolutionary or otherwise) are supported by Zerzan's critique of symbolic thought. Zerzan states that: "Tactics arise organically in large part from your starting position" (Jensen, 1998). But if your starting position is a wholesale rejection of symbolic thought and language as inherently coercive, and you live in a world wholly predicated upon these conceptual devices, where does that leave you? It would seem to leave you paralyzed over the question of how much you can compromise without being co-opted and eventually losing sight of what you were initially fighting for. An attack on symbolic culture rooted in written literature alone seems doomed to failure. But when asked once about the possibility of developing new, anarchist ways of life right now, inside of hierarchical society, Zerzan replied: "While some living arrangements or experiments are more pleasant than others, none escapes the defining hold of a world never more alienated than today's. There is no place to hide, no way to pretend that life can coexist with the global contagion in health or fulfillment. To argue otherwise is to argue in favor of the system that degrades and destroys" (Zerzan, 1993). Again we see an intense reliance on polar opposites, which almost seems to create a paradox in Zerzan's ideas. Real fulfillment and egalitarian society can only be experienced in the immediate moment — but it cannot be experienced in *this* immediate moment. Therefore Zerzan's idea of anarchy has the potential to remain nothing but a concept of gratification endlessly deferred into the future, just like the religious ideals of heaven or the capitalist dreams of material security that he attacks.

Zerzan might plausibly argue that *my interpretation* of *his idea* of anarchy is so hopelessly mired in symbolic linguistics that it can only appear problematic and self-contradicting. If it did not seem that way it would be one of those symbols masquerading as natural that Barthes identified as the basis of authoritarian ideologies (Eagleton, 1996, p. 135). Ultimately Zerzan's anarchy is not an abstract political concept embodied in the dead texts of nineteenth-century political thinkers, but a vibrant way of life that lives and breathes through the caring and cooperative interactions of humans living separately and/or opposed to hierarchical civilization. But doesn't this mean that we are promoting harmonious anarchy any time that we alter our way of life in order to promote autonomy and equality without sacrificing mutually beneficial relationships and a sense of collectivity? Is this kind of compromise to the constraints of existing hierarchy comparable to using symbolic language in order to expose the coercion of symbolic thought? And are not both tactics attempts to "escape the defining hold of a world never more alienated," without actually entirely destroying that world first?

Other anti-civilization anarchists have conceived of the problem in vastly different terms than Zerzan. Many of them reject the rational scientific viewpoint for an unselective embrace of spiritual systems of understanding. This tactic has its own problems: it rejects one way of thinking as inherently coercive, but embraces another general body of thought without thorough examination of the different types of relationships it encourages. There is no reason why a society based on a spiritual understanding of reality cannot be just as coercive as one based in scientific rationality. Zerzan tells us that this comes from the fact that all systems of understanding are coercive because they rely upon symbolic thought, and that we must reject them in order to embrace a more intuitive, emotional and sensual understanding.

The late Fredy Perlman, possibly the first and certainly one of the most outspoken anarcho-primitivists, had a different view on the possibilities of symbolic thought and culture. In his interpretive history of the world, *Against His-story, Against Leviathan* (Detroit: Black and Red, 1983), Perlman contended that opposition to the hierarchy and inequality of civilization can be accomplished through an explicitly anti-authoritarian symbolic culture. One example that he uses is that of Native American tribes whose symbolic mythology encouraged individual autonomy rather than dependent social relationships (Perlman, 1983, p. 240–52). If he had known about them Perlman probably also might have brought up Zerzan's own oft-touted example of the Mbuti pygmies of Zaire, an extant group of forager-hunters whose tribal custom encourages such anarchist ideals as gender equality and consensus-based decision making (Barclay, 1996, p. 47–9).

In response to Perlman, Zerzan might argue that autonomy predicated on symbolic culture never lasts. Symbolic thought is always trying to increase coercion and hierarchy, and only an impossible level of diligent human effort can even stall its progress. Zerzan observes that any level of reliance on symbolic thought creates a level of objectification and alienation that eventually corrupts all areas of human life, whether it is through religious dogma or capitalist economics. Yet the existence of any group which has simultaneously maintained harmonious anarchy and utilized symbolic thought casts a shadow of doubt over Zerzan's wholesale rejection of all symbolic culture.

Perlman's views, though no less based in polar opposites than Zerzan's, also have the advantage of emphasizing the positive possibility that liberation is a constantly imminent possibility for all humanity. In Perlman's perception, it might be possible for people to make use of the pre-existing tools of language, mythology, art, and literature in order to bring about revolution and anarchist society. Though Zerzan agrees that immediate revolution is possible, he feels that none of the devices which have historically maintained hierarchy and coercion can be drawn on in order to accomplish liberation. At base the difference between Zerzan and Perlman seems to be where they draw the line between coercive and non-coercive societies. While Perlman's analysis at least leaves some known societies that can serve as examples for future efforts, Zerzan's vision has no basis in any social situations that humanity has previously known — or at least in anything that we can *remember*, unless we accept Zerzan's assertions that the biblical tale of Eden and other myths of a past Golden Age are alienated humanity's only remaining memorials of pre-symbolic society.

VIII. Possibilities

What I hope to convey in this survey of John Zerzan's ideas is an optimistic feeling of increased possibilities. At first this may seem contradictory to the content of his writings, which attempt to prove that the last 30,000 years of history have seen the continual coercion and domestication of the natural world and the human race. At times he even argues that our past mistakes have altered our way of thinking and our natural environment in order to make any return to innocence immensely difficult. Yet we must conclude that Zerzan would not still be writing (or breathing) unless he believed that such a return was still possible. Just the fact that we are able to read Zerzan's writings about the failure of symbolic culture means either that symbolic thought is not entirely dominating, or that its attempts to limit our perception have not yet been totally successful. Either way, there seems to be hope. If we can be conscious of the nature of our own discourse, then we can formulate a coherent understanding of our situation. And if we can consciously criticize our own language, then it would seem possible to actively reject certain aspects of it. Though Zerzan's writings may not prove beyond a reasonable doubt that all language is coercive, they do show in great detail how our current language and symbolic culture uphold the idea that objectification and hierarchy are normal and desirable. Therefore rejecting or altering aspects of our current language and culture are necessary in order to increase equality or social harmony. If we can consciously effect change in our language, then we can consciously effect change in our way of thinking as well.

With this in mind, the possibilities for experimentation in our social and intellectual lives become endless, rather than being fixed and set by coercive institutions of cultural power like the Church or the State. The bottom line must always be whether new arrangements of thought or society encourage healthy, mutually beneficial interaction, rather than parasitic dominance or dependence. This is because these are the goals of the anti-authoritarian anarchist mindset that makes an open field of human experimentation possible. What this non-coercive, collective anarchy also means is that no way of seeing, thinking, or being can ever become fully accepted unless it is actually acknowledged as equally valuable and fulfilling by all people. If such agreement is possible, and the conceptual arrangement of non-linguistic consciousness is universally agreed upon, then Zerzan's specific vision of future anarchy may be realized. In the short term, his critique remains of crucial importance not because it leads us directly to a new absolute truth, but because it leads us to question institutions that have previously been taken as natural, unquestionable and unalterable: symbolic thought, symbolic culture, language, objectification, reification, and domestication. It is this questioning of seemingly sacred and natural institutions that has always been the defining characteristic of anarchist critique. Zerzan has pushed the limits that much further, with beneficial results for all who take the time to read his works, and hopefully even for those who do not.

IX. Works Cited

Acme Collective. "Black Block Communique." 14 Dec. 1999. <http://www.infoshop.org/octo/wto_blackbloc.html> (27 Dec. 1999)

Barclay, Harold. *People Without Government: An Anthropology of Anarchy.* London: Kahn & Averill, 1996.

Elliott, Michael. "The New Radicals." *Newsweek.* 13 Dec. 1999. p. 38.

Jaimes, M. Annette. "Letters." *Anarchy: A Journal of Desire Armed.* (Summer 1993.) 1999. <http://www.spunk.org/texts/pubs/ajoda/37/sp000798.txt> (14 Mar. 1999)

Jensen, D. "Enemy of the State: An Interview with John Zerzan." Oct. 1998. <http://www.wave.net/tsn/djensen/zerzan.htm> (14 Mar. 1999)

Noble, Kenneth. "Prominent Anarchist Finds Unsought Ally in Serial Bomber." *New York Times.* 30 April 1995.

Woodcock, George. "The Tyranny of the Clock." 1999. <http://www.extext.org/Politics/Spunk/library/writers/woodcock/sp001734> (14 Dec. 1998)

Zerzan, John. *Elements of Refusal.* Seattle: Left Bank Books, 1988

Zerzan, John. *Future Primitive And Other Essays.* New York: Autonomedia, 1994.

Zerzan, John. "Letters." *Anarchy: A Journal of Desire Armed.* (Summer 1993.) 1999. <http://www.spunk.org/texts/pubs/ajoda/37/sp000796.txt> (14 Mar. 1999)

Zerzan, John. "On The Transition." April 1999. <http://elaine.teleport.com/~jaheriot/futurep.htm> (10 Dec. 1998)

Zerzan, John. "Running On Emptiness: The Failure of Symbolic Thought." *Anarchy: A Journal of Desire Armed.* (Spring/Summer 1997.) <http://deoxy.org/failure.htm> (14 Mar. 1999)

Zerzan, John. "That *Thing* We Do." *Anarchy: A Journal of Desire Armed.* 16.1 (Spring/Summer 1998).

Zerzan, John. "Time And Its Discontents." *Anarchy: A Journal of Desire Armed.* (Winter 1994.) 1999. <http://www.eskimo.com/~recall/zertime.html> (25 Nov. 1998)

X. Additional Sources

Rudinskas, Kristina. "Cultural Forum To Host Anarchist." *Oregon Daily Emerald.* 26 Jan. 1998.

Zerzan, John. "Age of Grief." April 1999. <http://elaine.teleport.com/~jaheriot/agegrief.htm> (10 Dec. 1998)

Zerzan, John. "New York, New York: 20 Years since the '77 Blackout." *Anarchy: A Journal of Desire Armed* 15.2 (Fall-Winter 1997–98.)

Written as an introduction to the anthology *Chomsky on Anarchism,* this brief glimpse into the relationship between Chomsky and the anarchist tradition portrays the famous linguist as a "fellow traveller," but hardly a major contributor to the anarchist canon. Graham divorces Chomsky's linguistic ideas from any relevance to political ideology, and argues that Chomsky's depiction (with Edward Hermann) of the manipulation and manufacture of consent by political elites—itself not an explicitly anarchist critique—may nonetheless be his most significant contribution to anarchism.

Originally published in issue 39.

Chomsky's Contributions to Anarchism
Robert Graham

I
n the interview with Peter Jay included in this volume [*Chomsky on Anarchism*] as "The Relevance of Anarcho-Syndicalism," Noam Chomsky describes himself not as an "anarchist thinker," but as "a derivative fellow-traveller" (page 135). I think this is a fair assessment. While Chomsky has often expressed his sympathies with socialist currents in anarchist thought, for the most part he has avoided making any direct contributions to anarchist theory. On many occasions he has expressed his doubts that anarchism can or should even be considered a "philosophy," a term he is uncomfortable with, regarding those anarchist ideas he finds worthwhile simply as common sense (page 181).

On those rare occasions when he has written about the possible connections between his theory of language and human freedom (as in "Language and Freedom," also included in this volume), Chomsky's statements are very modest, tentative and exploratory. When I interviewed him in the early 1980s for the anarchist news journal *Open Road*, he cautioned me that he did not argue that his linguistic theories have revolutionary implications; rather his point was that "they are merely suggestive as to the form that a libertarian social theory might assume" (*Language and Politics,* page 394).

More recently Chomsky has written:

> "I feel that far too little is understood to be able to say very much with any confidence. We can try to formulate our long-term visions, our goals, our ideals; and we can (and should) dedicate ourselves to working on issues of human significance. But the gap between the two is often considerable, and I rarely see any way to bridge it except at a very vague and general level" (Tom Lane interview, *ZNet*, December 23, 1996).

Consistent with his general libertarian approach, when people ask Chomsky that perennial question, "what is to be done," Chomsky, unlike Lenin and scores of others, tells them this is something they must decide for themselves. Many people are disappointed by this kind of response, expecting Chomsky to show some leadership here, but he does offer his own opinions and sug-gestions on general strategies for social change, including his controversial proposal that anarchists should work to strengthen democratic state power as a way to combat and constrain the private tyranny of capitalism, without losing sight of their long term vision of a free, stateless society (page 193).

When discussing anarchism, Chomsky often refers to Rudolf Rocker's claim that modern anarchism represents "the confluence of…two great cur-rents…Socialism and Liberalism," such that "anarchism may be regarded as the libertarian wing of socialism" (page 123). Chomsky identifies most closely with anarcho-syndicalist currents in anarchist thought, regarding the decentralized, communitarian anarchism of people like Kropotkin as "pre-industrial," whereas the anarcho-syndicalist approach is seen by him as a "rational mode of organization for a highly advanced industrial society" (page 136). Chomsky is also very sympathetic to left-wing Marxism, such as council communism, which he argues is closely inter-related with anarcho-syndicalism (page 136).

But where Chomsky most directly draws from anarchist ideas is in his crit-icisms of the role of intellectuals in modern societies. Unlike most academic commentators, Chomsky isn't afraid to acknowledge Bakunin as one of the first and most perceptive critics of the "new class" of intellectuals who seek to create, in Bakunin's words, "the reign of scientific intelligence, the most aristocratic, despotic, arrogant and elitist of all regimes" (page 151). Chomsky himself has been relentless in exposing the role of intellectuals in seeking to maintain and expand authoritarian and hierarchical modes of social organi-zation, and in "manufacturing" or "engineering" the consent of the populace to existing inequalities of wealth and power, particularly in capitalist democ-racies, where resort to more overt and repressive forms of social control is more difficult (pages 167–171).

I think Chomsky's most lasting contribution to radical ideas will likely be this critique of the role of intellectuals and the media in controlling, diverting and suppressing dissent and discontent in ostensibly democratic countries. The "propaganda model" of the media that he developed with Ed Herman, most notably in Manufacturing Consent, is one of his few ideas outside of language theory to have received any appreciable notice in academic circles, buttressed with impressive empirical evidence.

His contributions to specifically anarchist ideas is much more modest, and by his own admission not particularly original. The conception of anarchism as the confluence of classical liberalism and anti-authoritarian socialism goes back well before Rudolf Rocker, to such 19th century writers as Charlotte Wil-son, who helped with Kropotkin to found the English anarchist paper, Freedom (see her article, "Anarchism," reprinted in my anthology, Anarchism: A Documentary History of Libertarian Ideas, Volume 1: From Anarchy to Anarchism (300CE–1939)).

When put in proper context, his argument that anarchists should help strengthen democratic state power to restrain the worst excesses of capitalism is not as strange as it sounds, or that much different from what other some other anarchists have advocated and practiced, such as the anarchists who fought for the eight hour day.

But when one looks more closely at some of Chomsky's examples, it is difficult to see how the actions he favours can truly be said to strengthen democratic state power. In one interview, he refers to a lengthy strike that ultimately forced the authorities to begin enforcing their own health and safety laws (ZNet Tom Lane interview). To me, this is more an example of the working class power of direct action being used to call the state authorities to account, rather than the strengthening of state power. As Rudolf Rocker put it in a passage from Anarcho-syndicalism that is not quoted by Chomsky in his "Notes on Anarchism," legal rights "do not originate in parliaments, they are rather, forced upon parliaments from without... The peoples owe all the political rights and privileges which we enjoy today...not to the good will of their governments, but to their own strength." I don't think Chomsky would disagree — in fact, he has said much the same thing, for example: "Protection against tyranny comes from struggle, and it doesn't matter what kind of tyranny it is" ("Creation and Culture," audiotape, Alternative Radio, Nov. 25 1992).

Chomsky's most significant contribution to anarchism is that he has been able to communicate anarchist ideas and achievements to a much wider public than probably any other contemporary anarchist writer. His 1969 essay, "On Objectivity and Liberal Scholarship," also reproduced in this volume, was for many of us, including myself, our first introduction to the constructive achievements of the anarchists in the Spanish Revolution, something that had been suppressed and distorted by both liberal and Marxist historians.

His "Notes on Anarchism," which originally appeared in the New York Review of Books in 1970, then as the introduction to Daniel Guérin's Anarchism, and then reprinted many times thereafter, presented an eloquent and persuasive case for the continuing relevance of anarchist ideas, even if he appeared to agree with Guérin that the main purpose for rehabilitating anarchism was to revitalize Marxism (page 128 — I say "appeared to agree" because Chomsky has also said that the "concept 'Marxism' belongs to the history of organized religion" — Language and Politics, page 395). It was ironic that George Woodcock, whose earlier book, *Anarchism: A History of Libertarian Ideas and Movements,* portrayed anarchism as one of history's great lost causes, should then criticize Chomsky for his narrow, neo-Marxist conception of anarchism, when it was Chomsky and Guérin who were portraying anarchism as part of a living tradition of liberatory theory and practice rather than as an historical relic.

Chomsky's more recent works do not contain as many references to anarchists and anarchist ideas, perhaps because, as he put it, "virtually no one shared my interest in anarchism (and Spanish anarchism)…and the deepening of my own understanding of the (left) libertarian tradition back to the Enlightenment and before was completely isolated from anyone I knew or know of" (quoted in Robert F. Barsky, *Noam Chomsky: A Life of Dissent*).

Perhaps the publication of *Chomsky on Anarchism* will help introduce anarchist ideas to another generation. On the other hand, if Chomsky's current audience is not much interested in anarchist ideas, then they aren't likely to read this book. It may be that Chomsky has too successfully compartmentalized his "anarchism" from his activism. Let's hope not.

Contemporary
Voices

In the course of reviewing this anthology of poetry, Schleuning analyzes the characteristics that distinguish political poetry from "art for art's sake" poetry. In so doing, she offers a preliminary sketch of an aesthetics of political poetry that broadens our appreciation of these linguistic memories of our collective identity.

Originally published in issue 23.

Poetry Like Bread:
Poets of the Political Imagination (Martín Espada, editor)
Neala Schleuning

May I risk some reflections on a lovely little collection of contemporary Latin American political poetry? The cultural workers who are included in Poetry Like Bread are welcome additions to the long illustrious tradition of great revolutionary poets like Garcia Lorca, Pablo Neruda, Ann Akhmatova, Serge Esenin, William Wordsworth.

Political poetry, some would argue, is an oxymoron. Great art cannot be political the critics say; it is above politics, and thus political art cannot be "good" art, precisely because it is political. The inclusion of politics as subject matter spoils the purity of the art, the aesthetics of the practical and the everyday squelches the Muse. Politics is realism, art lies in the realm of the ideal.

In other cultures and other times, however, political art is recognized and celebrated for what it is: the vibrant testimony to the human spirit. There are special qualities which distinguish political poetry from art-for-art's-sake poetry. The differences are readily apparent in the themes and the content of the poems; the voices with which the poets speak; the role of the poet; and the aesthetics of political poetry.

The content of political poetry. "The People" are always present in political poetry. They are the subject and the object, the audience, the voice, the bearers of collective memory. They are the inspiration for the entire genre. The "people" are portrayed in their collective, heroic role as participants in the great struggle and the great conversation about human freedom. The events described in political poems are political events, or they are the politicization of everyday events. Events are recalled to awaken, to remind, to honor martyrs, to raise awareness of the shared experiences of oppression, to inspire people to resistance.

The common, everyday life of people is often celebrated and honored. The words of political poetry are often tied to community, to a particular struggle, to a vision, or often to work. While there are too few poems in this collection about work and its place in revolutionary change, in "Carrying My Tools,"

Luis J. Rodríguez (U.S.) reminds us of the relationship between self-esteem, work and social change. The "tools" he describes might just as easily be the tools of change. The poem begins with the litany of tools the average skilled worker might carry and the pride of the worker in tools which were "cherished like a fine car / a bottle of rare wine,/ or a moment of truth." "Without tools, what kind of person could I be?" he asks at one point. He concludes with a metaphor of the poet as worker and maker of social change: "So there may not be any work today,/ but when there is, I'll be ready./ I got my tools."

The voice of political poetry. The task of the political poet is to awaken, to rouse the people to take action, especially political action with other people. Most often the political poet speaks with a collective voice: his country, her tribe, their race, gender, sexual orientation. Where the self is expressed, it is a self set in community. The poet is self-conscious about his or her role in the greater community. This role is beautifully described in Claribel Alegría's poem "Carmen Bomba: Poet," where she describes the worker who sings his poems to his neighbors every day.

There are three primary voices the political poet uses: the voices of the prophet, the mourner, and the rebel.

The Voice of the Prophet. In "A Lesson," (from A Call for the Destruction of Nixon and Praise for The Chilean Revolution) the great Chilean revolutionary poet Pablo Neruda wrote, "To judge unceasing crimes ordered by an infamous scoundrel/ is the duty of a wandering poet." Many political poems are a ringing challenge by a prophet speaking for and to the people, warning them of their oppressors, inspiring them to hope and action. This role as prophet calls for a certain self-consciousness and a sense of responsibility on the part of the poet to effect social change. The political poet also serves in the role of the Muse of Change. The poet as prophet must be filled with hope for the future, writes guerrilla fighter-poet Otto René Castillo (Guatemala): the poet speaks always with a sense of destiny: "for a thousand years I carry our name/ like a tiny future heart,/ whose wings begin to open tomorrow." Margaret Randall writes in the poem, "Immigration Law," "Give me a handful of future / to rub against my lips." The task of the political poet is to carry the vision of freedom and joy, while at the same time rousing the people to struggle against their oppressors and work to achieve that vision. The political poet must warn, awake, arouse, inspire.

The Voice of Suffering. It is fashionable in the U.S. today to criticize those who would focus on any kind of victimization ("Don't be so negative."). As part of a concerted effort at massive cultural denial of the level of violence in our culture, for example, a backlash has developed which is aimed primarily at silencing the many testimonies of women's abuse and victimization, and hence the women's movement as a political movement. These attacks on the women's movement also cast a cloud of uncertainty over all political stories of pain, sorrow and tragedy shared by other oppressed people. The awareness of anguish and death and suffering is a staple of political poetry, precisely because an awareness of suffering and of one's oppression can be instrumental in inspiring political rebellion and change. The voice of suffering in political poetry is never self-defeating or pitying, but rather is joined with a righteous anger that moves the reader to action against the cause of that suffering. As poet Leo Connellan (U.S.) writes, out of suffering comes life: "You lived through days you / never thought you'd see / the end of and yet/ tomorrow was no relief."

Suffering is also not a private experience only. In political poetry it is a shared event, a public event. Honduran poet Roberto Sosa writes in "The Common Grief" about the Disappeared who were victims of political violence and the women who waited for them: "We wait with heads unbowed / fused stitch by stitch like a scab to the sutures of a wound / No one can sever or divide our common grief. / Amen." Out of shared grief, the poet tells us, we can also find the courage to rebel.

The Voice of Rebellion and Resistance. No matter how oppressed people are, Jack Hirschman (U.S.) writes in the poem "Haiti," they will eventually rebel and rise up against their oppressors. The task of the political poet is to keep that vision and that hope bright:

> *And the backs,*
> *those backs with everything written on them,*
> *which have bent like nails hammered into the wooden cross*
> *of the land for ages,*
> *will plunge their arms into the ground*
> *and pull out the weapons they've planted.*

In Martín Espada's (U.S.) poignant and powerful poem, "Federico's Ghost," a young migrant boy working in the fields picking tomatoes is purposely poisoned by an airplane pilot spraying the fields with insecticide. He becomes a martyr for the other workers, who begin a silent campaign of sabotage to honor his rebellious spirit: "Still tomatoes were picked and squashed / in the dark, / and the old women in camp / said it was Federico." Ernesto Cardenal puts it even more simply in his poem, "The Peasant Women from Cuá"— their dreams are subversive."

Claribel Alegría's (Nicaragua) poem "From the Bridge" is a powerful metaphor about one person's transition to revolutionary resistance. She challenges the reader to understand and respond to the pain and suffering and death of oppressed people by contrasting those who would continue to bind up the wounds of the oppressed and those who would change the situation that creates the pain in the first place. In the poem she moves herself, and the reader, from victim to action through the transformation from observer to the fierce revolutionary poet who is able "to peer out / through these pitiless / scrutinizing eyes / to have my claws and this sharp beak."

The aesthetic of political poetry. There is "good" political poetry and "bad" political poetry, and it is here that the critic on the Left walks through a minefield, for to challenge the poetry of a revolution or a revolutionary, might, in some eyes, be viewed as challenging the ideas and ideals of the revolution or the movement itself. Sometimes poetry is mediocre as poetry but great as politics. It is not enough to simply list wrongs and injustices and call for change. To be poetry the poet must metamorphose this message, must transform it, energize it, distill it, make it an arrow into the heart of the mind of the reader. Fortunately, the poets in this collection are skilled at their craft, and wise in their politics. One test, of course, is whether the poem "works," even if you don't know anything about the political content. Do the voices convey the story of the political experience? The denouement to closure, the inspiration to action?

A few of the poets in this collection speak with the voice of self-identity rather than collective identity. I notice this problem particularly with North American poets. In a powerful, bold and stark poem, Sara Menefee (U.S.) points a finger in accusation at these poets of privilege and indifference: "you northamerican poets / masters of ennui-in-the-face-of-armageddon / welcome to the South African township of New Brighton," and concludes with the lines: "now tell the people here about your stalled aesthetics / your government grant your shattered linguistics / in the glare of Soweto and Sharpeville." This self-absorption can be problematic in assessing how truly "political" the poetry is. The preoccupation with finding the personal, individualistic self often obscures the large political agenda of revolution and change. Our own personal awareness and empathy is important, but it is only the beginning of change. Some of the best poems in the collection speak to the search for political and cultural identity and the restructuring of reality that search demands. The poems of Cheryl Savageau (U.S.) fall into this category of a search for self-in-community. In the poem "Looking for Indians," she writes "I ask my father / what kind of Indian are we, anyway." and concludes

Each night my father
came home from the factory
   to plant and gather,
to cast the line out
over the dark evening pond,
   with me, walking behind him,
looking for Indians.

There are other voices in political poetry. The Voice of Beauty in political poetry is characterized by a quality of simplicity and clarity. A good example is Jack Hirschman's lovely little poem, "This Neruda Earth," that weaves together in one microcosm the beauty of community, of earth, of political change. There is a place for humor, too, in the great drama of social change. We can almost see the gentle smile of Sandinista Minister of Culture Ernesto Cardenal (Nicaragua) when he writes, "The armadillos are very happy with this government."

The voice of joy in resistance is celebrated in Clemente Sota Véléz's (Puerto Rico) poem entitled "#35 from The Promised Land", when he writes: "with the hands / of the peon / that / are / rainshowers of uncommon poetry / with a fresh breeze of frenzy / perfect / like the violent confusion of spirit / that / opens / its doors wide / to the most / insubordinate sunrises." Political poetry resounds with a purity of passion, an aesthetic of power: the power of the idea, the power of lived experience, the power of passionate resistance. It is ultimately about change and transformation, about stripping away the old life, whether it is the former personal life, the former collective life: as when Julia de Burgos writes, "In all my poems I undress my heart." At the heart of political poetry, however, is the hard core of the aesthetics of action: Nicaraguan Sandinista Daisy Zamora says it best in the poem "Precisely."

Precisely because I do not have
the beautiful words I need
I call upon my acts
to speak to you.

Poetry Like Bread: Poets of the Political Imagination edited by Martín Espada. Willimantic, CT: Curbstone Press, 1994. Pb $12.95.

Reviewing the essays of *Minding Nature,* which proposes to "move toward both democracy and ecology," Biehl ultimately determines the book to have failed in its stated mission. Either the selected philosophers are focused on ecology, and not democracy, or democracy, with little to say about ecology. Biehl decries the mysticism of their arguments that has gone unquestioned by the essayists. A large segment of the article is devoted to the writings of Murray Bookchin, the single thinker whom Biehl deems to have met the criteria of the book's mission, but whose reviewers she found to be overly critical and myopic in their Marxist interpretation of his writings.

Originally published in issue 25.

Minding Nature: The Philosophers of Ecology
(David Macauley, editor)
Janet Biehl

Minding Nature sets out to trace ideas of democracy and nature in the thought of a variety of philosophers and social theorists who, according to editor David Macauley, "have enabled us to rethink the possibility of creating a more democratic *and* ecological society." The book, which is part of Guilford's ecosocialist series "Democracy and Ecology," consists of thirteen essays, many of which originally appeared in the ecosocialist journal *Capitalism Nature Socialism*. Each essay highlights a single thinker whose work will in some way help us "move toward both democracy and ecology."

Given this goal, the choice of thinkers who are subjects of the essays is, however, sometimes peculiar. Politically they range over a wide spectrum: some (like Herbert Marcuse and Jürgen Habermas) are critical theorists, one is an orthodox Marxist (Ernst Bloch), one is a quasi-Marxist social democrat (Barry Commoner), and one is a fascist (Martin Heidegger). They are joined by a theorist of the public sphere (Hannah Arendt), a regionalist (Lewis Mumford), an anarcho-communist and social ecologist (Murray Bookchin), and a philosopher whose political orientation is undefined (Hans Jonas). An arcane philosopher (the phenomenologist Maurice Merleau-Ponty), jostles against popular writers on concrete environmental topics (Rachel Carson and Paul Ehrlich). Most of the thinkers discussed did their work during the twentieth century, but two are entirely preindustrial (Thomas Hobbes and Charles Fourier). Conspicuously missing are the anarchists Reclus and Kropotkin, which suggests that one purpose of the book is to explore the possibilities for an ecosocialist tradition that could parallel the better-defined ecoanarchist tradition.

As might be expected with such diverse thinkers, the essay's discussions stray far afield from democracy and ecology, to a broad array of topics including religion, language technology, science, ethics, political power, and capitalism; many interesting ideas are raised that deserve consideration. But I will limit my own social-ecology reading of this book to asking how well it succeeds in helping us "move toward both democracy and ecology."

The writings of Thomas Hobbes, of course, express no such goal but rather some of the obstacles it faces: as essayist Frank Coleman argues (although somewhat overstating the case), Hobbes's vision is "a principal reason that the domain of nature is presently at risk." As an authoritarian, Hobbes typically expressed the bourgeois-capitalist's conception that nonhuman nature is a realm of scarcity. Modernism, Coleman shows, posited a "defect of nature" — that is, a limitation of natural resources or scarcity. Capitalism "generates the perception" of natural scarcity, then tries to "extricate" us from it "through the biblically derived project of dominion over the earth." These passages of Coleman's essay are a fine statement of the presumption of scarce resources that provided a rationale for capitalist exploitation, not to speak of nation-state domination.

Charles Fourier, in turn, properly belongs to the various traditions that have attempted to avert these social developments. Still, essayist Joan Roelofs's characterization of Fourier as "red-green" is grating, since the absence of coercive institutions in Harmonian society ("passionate attractions" among individual members were to be its ordering principle) places Fourier at least as squarely in the black-green tradition. As a preindustrial thinker, however, his phalansteries were almost entirely agricultural, indeed even horticultural, in nature; cities and machines remained in the dim background. As such, his "ecology," too, is one that minimizes cities and machines and emphasizes agriculture and rural living. Roelofs finds these features of Harmonian society appealing, including its "labor intensive" nature, since "human capital is most important for productivity"; but Harmonian work will be not only tolerable but pleasurable. As a theorist of democracy, however, Fourier is of scant interest: Roelofs herself admits that his phalansteries offered no processes for democratic decision-making.

Since Fourier's time, the most militant sectors of the various socialist and anarchist traditions have shared at least one thing in common: an aversion to religion, which (apart from Christian socialists and the like) was most often seen as a source of oppression. Anarchists and socialists alike favored taking a secular, rational look at both nature and society, the better to comprehend those realities. This atheism was always salutary, and today some parts of the fragmented left, including but not limited to social ecology, have refused to change with the political weather by adapting themselves to today's prevailing religiosity. One might expect that this book, as a project of ecosocialists, would treat the topic of nonhuman nature in similarly secular terms. But if anything, when the topic arises, the essays tend toward spiritualistic sensibilities and in some cases mysticism.

Accordingly, several authors in this book seem to identify the historical causes of the ecological crisis less as social than as idealistic in nature, pinning its deepest roots in erroneous ideas, especially religious beliefs. Essayist Michael Zimmerman avers that "dualism between humanity and nature leads to serious ecological (and social) problems." For essayist David Abram, "The ecological crisis may be the result of a recent and collective perceptual disorder in our species." If the ecological crisis is caused by ideas, in this line of thought, then ideas are what can provide a solution — especially religious or spiritual ideas. By his understanding of the human subject as "embodied," says Abram, Merleau-Ponty offers us a new "ecological thinking," a "renewed awareness of our responsibility to the Earth." But Abram takes this thinking to a mystical level when he associates Merleau-Ponty's statement that "the flesh of the world…is sensible…it is absolutely not an object" with the "Gaia hypothesis," the mystical notion (based on an extrapolation of some scientific facts about the Earth's temperature) that "the Earth's biosphere acts as a vast, living physiology." Such mysticism (like Zimmerman's urging that "we need to step back from our incessant action" in favor of "meditative 'thinking'") is in accordance with nature romanticism but not with a socially active movement that tries to build a democratic, ecological society.

In some cases the essayists must contort their subject to make him or her relevant to ecological thought. Apologizing for the fact that Merleau-Ponty was a "committed humanist," even a "recalcitrant" one — as if humanism and ecology were incompatible — Abram takes the notion of "embodiedness" into antihumanism, rejecting the notion that "language [is] that power which humans possess and other species do not." So "embodied" is language, in his reading, that it nears dissolution into carnality, while "the real Logos," he tells us, "…is Eco-logos." In this avowedly "creative reading" of Merleau-Ponty, the phenomenologist becomes "the voice of the earth." Abram "creatively" inserts nonhuman creatures, especially cats and birds and whales, into his subject's thought: their absence from Merleau-Ponty's actual writings, he assures us, "is not crucial." Abram even speculates about a parallel between animal abuse and Stalin's purges: knowledge of animal abuses by science and agribusiness, he thinks, might have been "as crucial for [Merleau-Ponty's] rethinking of philosophy, as were the revelations concerning Stalin's purges when these were disclosed in Europe." Such formulations only serve to trivialize human suffering and have no place in a socialist or leftist outlook.

That Martin Heidegger also has a place in this book is equally bizarre and equally symptomatic of its spiritualistic tilt. Michael Zimmerman has long sought to convince deep ecologists of the relevance of Heidegger's thought to their ideas. In his essay here he continues this effort — albeit recently in somewhat modified form, some very damning facts about Heidegger's relationship with National Socialism having come to light several years ago. Zimmerman now advises that Heidegger's "relationship with National Socialism" was "complex" (although party membership — the man remained a member of the Nazi party until 1945 — is a rather unambiguous fact). In any case, his article is explicitly addressed not to ecosocialists but to deep ecologists, warning them rather mildly of Heidegger's "political drawbacks" and "reactionary political views."

One has to credit Zimmerman for persistence, however: he still maintains that "radical ecologists can learn from Heidegger's philosophy." (His project, incidentally, is contradicted by his fellow essayist Lawrence Vogel, who warns that "Heidegger's existentialism gives us no good reason to care about future generations or the long-term fate of planet Earth.") But what exactly can ecologists learn from this fascist? "Heidegger is right that certain kinds of naturalism are dangerous," Zimmerman advises — but if Heidegger ever issued such a warning, he does not mention it. Warnings against National Socialism's "dangers" seem hardly to have been what Heidegger had in mind — the movement he supported was the one that made those dangers into genocidal realities. Least of all can we say that Heidegger has much to contribute to a philosophy of democracy.

Other thinkers discussed in this book are far more relevant to democratic thought but are not in any sense nature philosophers or philosophers of ecology. Hannah Arendt's writings, most notably, are highly significant for her ideas on democratic political communities and active political citizenship, as well as civic virtue and engagement; her implied commitment to face-to-face decision-making certainly makes her relevant for philosophies of direct democracy, including social ecology's libertarian municipalism. As essayist David Macauley rightly points out, Arendt "identifies herself with or praises the revolutionary tradition, direct political action and direct democracy (rather than representation), decentralization, forms of organization such as the council system (rather than political parties), and *potestas in populo*."

But her relevance to ecological thought is far from clear. Her writings on democracy in *The Human Condition* suggest, if anything, that the achievement of democracy depends upon the transcendence of nonhuman nature. Essayist Macauley, aware of this problem, admits that "Arendt follows Locke and Marx in characterizing nature as the 'realm of necessity' which must be overcome…in order to reach the 'realm of freedom'.… Arendt's concept of nature is therefore as 'blind' as Marx's." Yet he also tries to suggest an "ecological" Arendt by taking up her rather trite discussion of the earth as seen from outer space and inflating it, suggesting that she is afflicted by "earth alienation." "Themes of homelessness and rootlessness are at the center of Arendt's political concerns," we are told: Arendt "feels that we must recover the earth as our home." None of this is convincing as ecological philosophy, least of all by comparison with her general ideas on nonhuman nature. As if Macauley also realizes that Arendt cannot be reconstructed into a nature philosopher, he acknowledges in the end that she was an "urban" and "cosmopolitan" thinker.

In a similar vein, Joel Whitebook's "The Problem of Nature in Habermas," written in the late 1970s and reprinted here with a retrospective introduction, took up the "challenge" of "thinking both democracy *and* ecology" in the thought of the Frankfurt School theorist Jürgen Habermas. Habermas, Whitebook showed, objected to linking the two in a political sense. A defender of the Enlightenment, he attempted to advance "the completion of modernity's unfinished project of democratization"; yet his position in relation to ecology was "troubling" for ecologists, since it "appeared to relegate nature to the status of a meaningless object of instrumental control." Using a framework that was largely social ecological in nature (as social ecology was understood in the late 1970s), Whitebook attempted to resolve this dilemma, seeking "the transformation of our relation to the natural world," in such a way as to address the ecological crisis, while still preserving the "indisputable achievements of modernity," including its "advances in democratization." He admits, however, that "the results" of his own article "were anything but conclusive," since "Habermas's transcendentalism necessarily precludes any reconciliation with nature." Once again, democracy remains unreconciled with an ecological approach.

Far more of the thinkers discussed in this book suffer from the opposite problem: their ideas are pertinent to a discussion of nature and ecology but have little to do with democracy. In his discussion of Rachel Carson's *Silent Spring*, essayist Yaakov Garb compares this celebrated work with Bookchin's *Our Synthetic Environment*, which treated similar themes and many others and was published six months before Carson's book's 1962 publication, to much less notice. Garb points out that "Bookchin's account of the dangers of pesticides was part of a comprehensive and politically forthright chronicle of the many assaults on the environment and human well-being that he claimed were inevitable in an industrial capitalist society." By comparison, Carson limited her concerns to the strictly environmental and "remained safely within the bounds of the American mainstream," ignoring the social concerns that Bookchin expressed. Least of all was Carson a theorist of democracy (nor, to be fair, was Bookchin in 1962): her "call for democratic control and public accountability of scientists and the chemical industry" was "partial and often indirectly phrased."

As for the regionalist Lewis Mumford, essayist Ramachandra Guha pulls together many of his ideas from a wide variety of sources to remedy a lacuna in American environmental history: recognition of Mumford's significance. Unfortunately, in his eagerness to assemble Mumford's thoughts on nonhuman nature, Guha's essay creates the illusion that Mumford wrote systematically on ecology and espoused a thought-out ecological philosophy. But as Guha himself also admits, Mumford did not present his ecological ideas systematically at all; instead they are "scattered through his writings"; some of the quotations Guha assembles are culled from relatively ephemeral writings. One could make the same point about Mumford as a writer on democracy: his references to it, while they exist, are also scattered, and usually they are references to representative democracy, not face-to-face or direct democracy. Mumford's writings have significance for social ecology, especially on the aesthetic dimension of green cities, but they leave this reader wishing that he had theorized more coherently about both ecology and democracy.

The most complete nature philosopher discussed in *Minding Nature* is Hans Jonas, whose *The Phenomenon of Life* also influenced the development of social ecology. Essayist Lawrence Vogel does a fine job of synopsizing Jonas's ideas on purposiveness, metabolism, emergent mind, and evolution. He rightly shows that, despite his attributions of value as an "objective reality" to nonhuman nature, Jonas would have rejected biotic egalitarianism: "although Jonas believes that nature carried value independent of us because Being is 'for itself' from the inception of life," he writes, "the moral worth of life only comes into being with the phenomenon of obligation, and obligation requires the evolution of a being capable of moral responsibility" — that is, a human capability. Here Jonas is fully in accord with social ecology. (His nature philosophy, it should be noted, diverges from social ecology in that it culminates in an "imperative of responsibility" rather than social ecology's "potentiality for freedom"; where Bookchin seeks an ontological foundation for a principle of social freedom, Jonas sought "an ontological foundation for a principle of responsibility for the future."

Moreover, Jonas, whose ideas were explicitly anti-utopian, "grounds an ethics in the depths of Being" (rather than in Becoming, as social ecology does), which leaves his ethics more static than developmental. Still, as a humanist, Jonas would agree that, as Vogel puts it, "we not only must, but should — out of respect for what nature has achieved in us — appreciate the ecosystem from the perspective of its suitability for our [human] well-being." (Disappointingly, essayist Vogel himself takes a dim view of metaphysics like that of his own subject, arguing instead for an ethics that builds on "feelings" rather than reason and that is "more concrete and generally persuasive." He even criticizes Jonas for omitting the existence of "a conscious perspective outside our own *for* whom our destiny matters" — which can only mean something divine. His conclusion to his otherwise useful essay, which expresses this viewpoint, represents not only a contribution to the dumbing-down of philosophical thought but yet another depressing defection from the secularism of the socialist tradition.)

Mysticism surfaces yet again in Henry T. Blanke's article on Marcuse — both in Marcuse's thought and in the essayist's own approval of it. Marcuse, it should be noted, was not much concerned with the ecological crisis, at least not until the early 1970s. Contrary to Blanke, the "domination of nature" as such was not "central" to Marcuse, who was patently concerned with people, not with nonhuman organisms. In *Eros and Civilization* he wrote about the "domination of nature" out of his general concern for domination, as a member of the Frankfurt School. In the 1950s and 1960s he tried to link the "domination of external nature" — i.e., nonhuman nature — with Freudian ideas of repression, and by extension he posited a strong connection between the "domination of internal and external nature." His aim in doing so was not to conserve ecosystems, but to articulate the psychoanalytic underpinnings for a civilization that would be free of sexual repression.

In general, in the 1950s and 1960s, Marcuse sought to shift the balance of civilization's concerns away from the reality principle and toward the pleasure principle. If he advocated shorter working hours and reduced consumption, it was in order to free the pleasure principle — not to avert the destruction of the biosphere. Indeed, where Bookchin advocates social arrangements that would shorten working hours in order that people could manage their own affairs as citizens in a democracy, Marcuse wanted shorter working hours in order to foster erotic liberation.

It is my own belief that the presumed connection between "the domination of internal and external nature" is highly misleading. In the first place, "external nature" can't be dominated; "the domination of nature" is an anthropomorphic phrase whose meaning vanishes on closer examination. Some forces of nature can be controlled by human beings, who are certainly polluting the biosphere, mineralizing organic life, and simplifying the complex development of natural evolution. But nature as a whole cannot be "dominated," least of all by people who are a part of that "nature."

Second, the existence of a "homology between human nature an external nature (both animated by erotic energy)" is not at all self-evident. One would certainly like an ecological society to be a sexually liberated one as well, but the idea that sexual repression has much directly to do with the damage inflicted on the biosphere seems rather far-fetched. Capitalism has much more to do with it. Once upon a time, certainly, the Calvinist work ethic provided a psychological supplement to the economic and social forces that generated the rise of capitalism. But today's sex-drenched popular culture suggests that erotic repression is hardly necessary for the continued success of capitalism.

One point that Blanke does ably demonstrate, however, is that Marcuse's thinking in *Eros and Civilization* is "unabashedly mystical." But again, far from condemning him for it, he actually praises him, even arguing that Marcuse's mystical consciousness "points to the radical nature of his thinking." He approvingly says that "Marcuse anticipates a leitmotif of those ecological theorists" — perhaps Blanke means deep ecologists? — "who call for a radically new relationship with the environment grounded in a mystical consciousness." Anticipating the objections of critics of mysticism, he invokes the failure of social revolution in Europe: "Western Marxists," he says, employed "consciousness, subjectivity, and depth psychology" to explain this failure.

The assumption that a reversion to mysticism is warranted because traditional socialism, a failure, rejected it, is highly questionable. If socialist and anarchist thought had made an appeal to religion and spirituality, certainly they might have been more successful — but they would have done so at the price of their radicalism. They would also have been more successful if they had accepted capitalism — but does that mean that socialists and anarchists should now accept capitalism?

Irrationalistic mindsets, when introduced into politics, are most likely to produce quietism on the part of the powerless and manipulation on the part of the powerful. Yes, earlier generations of radicals, like seventeenth-century Protestant sects, were mystical, but they were mystical in a framework that was exclusively religious to start with. Introduced into what remains of the Left today, religiosity does little more than teach people to accept existing conditions. The fact is that our best means of apprehending reality tell us that religion, including mysticism, is a lie: there is no God, not even "a conscious perspective outside our own *for* whom our destiny matters"; there is no "oneness" or "greater self" of which we are a part, except for nature itself. To adopt the belief, or make outward professions of belief, that any supernatural or intranatural being or spirit exists is a moral and intellectual abdication.

Nor is mysticism capable of contributing to a democratic outlook or fostering civic virtues in citizens — the virtues about which Hannah Arendt, for example, to Macauley's approval, wrote. Direct democracy, and the processes of decision-making endemic to it, depends on the ability to rationally debate alternatives based on facts and ideas that are accessible to all. Mystical thinking is, by definition, not publicly available; it is intrinsically a private experience, one that can seldom, if ever, be shared; nor can its "insights" even be expressed but remain ineffable. As such it is hardly a mindset that fosters citizenship: one cannot persuade one's fellow citizens of the rightness of one's own views on rational grounds if one's views are based on ineffable, incommunicable insights.

By assessing these thinkers in terms of their ideas on democracy and ecology, I am aware that I am placing many of them on a Procrustean rack. Many of them had no intention of focusing on either of those issues, and as thinkers they should be judged by their intentions. The problem is that in seeking essays on subjects who addressed both democracy and ecology, editor Macauley had a difficult task on his hands: few of them exist in recent social theory and philosophy.

Among all the thinkers discussed in this book, only one — Murray Bookchin — offers ideas that are both ecological and democratic and thereby fulfills the book's agenda. His political ideas on ecology — social ecology — are among the earliest to have been formulated and have not been surpassed in quality, depth, and breadth. As for his ideas of democracy — a direct democracy, embodying community self-management — he has developed them in several books and articles since the early 1970s. Bookchin's ecological views are secular rather than mystical, which is one reason that, unlike his fellow essay subjects, his thinking is both democratic and ecological. He underpins both his democratic and his ecological ideas with a philosophical system called dialectical naturalism, conjoining them into a unified whole. Ironically, the thinker who is best able to fill the ecosocialists' bill is a social anarchist.

Given his unique distinction among these thinkers, the treatment he receives is quite disproportionate (if not exactly surprising, considering the ideological contradiction between ecosocialism and ecoanarchism). Suddenly it no longer suffices to be a philosopher of both ecology and democracy. Indeed, Bookchin comes in for a degree of criticism far more intense than the other thinkers receive — even those whose ideas are sorely lacking in either a democratic or an ecological dimension. In order to provide a social-ecological response to their criticisms, which also suggests the nature of the debate between ecosocialists and ecoanarchists, I will necessarily address Alan Rudy and Andrew Light's essay on Bookchin at greater length than the others.

The primary criticism that Rudy and Light make against Bookchin concerns the issue of labor. "Our central critique," they write, "is that Bookchin powerfully underplays the importance of labor as a mediating force within and between the social relations of humans, and within and between humans and the nonhuman natural world." Bookchin, they argue, "neglects…labor as a category of analysis" and "social labor as a defining characteristic of capitalism and its contradictions." Rudy and Light themselves, it should be noted, prefer "analysis informed by Marxist investigation of economic, political, and environmental crises."

By calling for a "transclass" constituency for a social revolution, the essayists argue, Bookchin omits the notion of class from his analysis and program. Certainly Bookchin long ago rejected Marxism's image of the industrial proletariat as the hegemonic revolutionary agent, but Rudy and Light exaggerate this rejection to absurd proportions, accusing him even of "skepticism about the existence of the working class in any meaningful form." This would be a remarkable error indeed, but it is not one that Bookchin commits. His issue was never the existence of the working class but its revolutionary potential in the industrial workplace.

Rudy and Light further object that by subsuming exploitation under the category of domination, Bookchin fails to perceive that "capitalist exploitation" arises "as the central moment of a qualitatively different mode of production." He fails, they say, to recognize "the qualitative transformation of the social forces and relations of production and reproduction" in order to "understand *why*, as well as *how*, economic, political, and ecological crises occur under capitalism."

Bookchin has explained on numerous occasions that he did not intend for the terminology of "hierarchy" to replace "class," nor that of "domination" to replace "exploitation." In 1970, when he faced his Marxist critics after writing "Listen, Marxist!" he wrote: "Exploitation, class rule, and happiness, are the *particular* within the more *generalized* concepts of domination, hierarchy and pleasure."[1] As he has often said, he feels that Marx covered the subject of exploitation very thoroughly already, and he had no improvements to offer on it.

Nor is his work on domination in contradiction with Marx's work on exploitation. Continuing: "Is it conceivable that I could have used terms like 'capitalist' and 'bourgeois' without working with a 'class-based analysis'?" What was actually frustrating his Marxist critics, he pointed out, was that his class analysis was not "a *Marxist* 'class analysis'" — one "in which the industrial proletariat is driven to revolution by destitution and immiseration." But "a 'class analysis' does not necessarily begin and end with Marx's nineteenth-century version," and the class struggle "does not begin and end at the point of production."[2]

Bookchin also wrote in 1970 that he had made "no claim that a social revolution is possible without the participation of the industrial proletariat." Rather, he tried to show "how the proletariat can be won to the revolutionary movement by stressing issues that concern the quality of life and work."[3] Here and in later writings, Bookchin tried, not to ignore class struggle, but to take it out of its erstwhile confinement to the factory and bring it into the neighborhoods; he addressed working people not as workers in their workplace but as members of a community or neighborhood, and as subject to a variety of other oppressions in addition to class exploitation.

This contribution to left-radical social theory is highly original and is based not on academic speculation but on revolutionary history itself: "Every class culture," he wrote in 1986,

> was always a community culture, indeed a civic culture....While the factory and mill formed the first line of the class struggle in the last century,...its lines of supply reached back into the neighborhoods and towns where workers lived and often mingled with middle-class people, farmers, and intellectuals. Wage earners had human faces, not merely mystified "proletarian" faces, and functioned no less as human beings than as class beings....This communal dimension of the industrial era is of tremendous importance in understanding how class conflicts often spilled over beyond economic issues into broadly social, even utopian, concerns.[4]

Historically, revolutionary class struggles have been based in municipalities even more notably than in factories. Red Petrograd in 1917 and Barcelona in 1936–37 both had strong neighborhood and civic cultures and were crucial arenas for their respective revolutions. Even earlier, the uprisings in Paris in 1848 and in 1870–71, with the Paris Commune, were largely neighborhood affairs, where people fought behind barricades located in their own neighborhoods. Working people defended not just their workplaces but the communities of which they were a part — and gained solidarity through their neighborhood civic cultures, which existed in cafes, squares, streets, and parks; local branches of clubs and societies; as well as local National Guard battalions and defense committees.

What alternative to Bookchin's approach do Rudy and Light offer? Their attacks on him for rejecting the proletariat might lead one to think that they stand for standard Marxist class struggle in the industrial workplace; and they do seem to confine ecological struggles, for example, to the factory alone when they write that "with cost-cutting, worker health declines, unemployment rises, resources are depleted, and pollution increases."

But for all their talk of wage labor and production and exploitation, Rudy and Light's "social labor" concept is actually by no means limited to the labor of the industrial proletariat within the factory: "within the socially organized labor of each mode of (re)production," they write, in their definition of "social labor," "is included the (re)production of ethics, culture, gender, politics, economy, art, and geographical and ecological space." Although the idea is expressed in somewhat different terminology — omitting urban space and civic culture — Rudy and Light, as much as Bookchin, are dispensing with the industrial-proletariat-within-factory in favor of a broader concept of community whose members are afflicted not only with class but other oppressions as well, facing a common ecological threat.

The difference, in their case, is that their Marxist language obscures their expansion of the concept, while Bookchin is quite clear about what he is doing. No more than Bookchin do our eco-Marxists really want to confine ecological struggles to the workplace: they find arenas of struggle not in the factory alone but in "the destruction of the conditions for capital's own (re)production: human beings and their reproductive health; global, regional, and local ecosystems; and the organization of *communities and social spaces in and through which people interact with their ecosystems*" (emphasis added). What are the issues in these spaces if not the "issues that concern the quality of life and work" that Bookchin frequently discusses — issues that pertain not to the factory alone but the broader community? These authors appear to have created a straw Bookchin, then appropriated his actual position for themselves.

Astonishingly, Rudy and Light then take it upon themselves to lecture Bookchin about the fact that *capitalism has limits*. "Capitalism must grow in order to survive, much less prosper, but it cannot grow indefinitely." This is a remarkable statement to make to the man who, more than anyone else, has popularized the Marxian concept of capitalism as a "grow or die" economy in the ecology movement. The idea that capitalism is on a collision course with the biosphere, a favorite among the ecosocialists, is certainly not news to Bookchin. He wrote in 1968 that "the contradiction between the exploitative organization of society and the natural environment is beyond co-optation: the atmosphere, the waterways, the soil and the ecology required for human survival are not redeemable by reforms, concessions, or modifications of strategic policy." (A footnote added: "The economic contradictions of capitalism have not disappeared," although they are without "the explosive characteristics they had in the past").[5]

In March 1974, to take another instance, he wrote that "capitalism... turns the plunder of nature into society's law of life.... A society based on production for the sake of production is inherently anti-ecological and its consequences are a devoured natural world." The prospect that "the biosphere will become so fragile that it will eventually collapse from the standpoint of human survival needs" will eventuate "from a society based on production for the sake of production" is "merely a matter of time."[6] Some of the ideas circulating around *Capitalism Nature Socialism* — like the "second contradiction of capitalism" — are essentially restatements of this idea, albeit in Marxist dress.

On the subject of the nature of capitalism, Rudy and Light make Bookchin's analysis seem ridiculous when they quote him as saying that "'*the* grand secret from which [the market] draws its power' is 'the power of anonymity'" (emphasis added). "In fact," they scold, "the key to capitalism after mercantilism is not anonymity in the marketplace, but the wage labor that is at the root of production." But the reader who refers to Bookchin's original passage, from which the "grand secret" quotation is taken, will find no such definitive declaration: anonymity, Bookchin wrote there, is "*a* grand secret" of the market — not "*the* grand secret" — hardly the same thing.[7] Rudy and Light would do well to quote their subjects more accurately if they wish to carry on a fruitful debate. Nor is it true that "Bookchin treats capitalist economics as 'the buyer-seller relationship,'" or at least not exclusively. In fact, the central points of Bookchin's critique of capitalism are its commodification (of which anonymity is a feature) and its growth imperatives.

Another flaw in Rudy and Light's presentation is that they appear to have stopped reading Bookchin after about 1986, and thus their description of his views on technology is not only wrong but wholly unrecognizable. In 1986, they observe, Bookchin wrote that he would "'temper the importance [he gave] to the technological "preconditions" for freedom.'" But our eco-Marxists leap from this quotation to assert categorically that Bookchin "no longer believes modern technology to have the potential to eliminate scarcity" and to announce that "Bookchin's views on technology have changed," consigning to the past his "idea of retaining certain forms of technology that had emerged under capitalism."

These supposed renunciations of postscarcity, they go on to judge, are the "greatest problems" of Bookchin's utopian philosophy. But actually, the "tempering" in Bookchin's quote had nothing to do with abjuring the idea of postscarcity; he was speculating that in precapitalist times it might have been possible to achieve communism even without a postscarcity technology, because needs (and not only fetishized needs) were fewer. Rudy and Light to the contrary, postscarcity remains very much in Bookchin's present thinking, as any number of his technophobic disputants among anarchists will testify, and as Rudy and Light would know had they consulted *Remaking Society, Social Anarchism or Lifestyle Anarchism?,* and especially *Re-enchanting Humanity.* (The latter contains an entire chapter on technology, including a sharp criticism of technophobia.)

Rudy and Light go on to object to the absence of an internationalist framework in Bookchin: for him, they say, the "transclass constituencies necessary for truly liberatory social movements are situated almost exclusively in the North." It is true that Bookchin is most interested in revolutions whose most prominent aims have been universal social and political liberation; since the Third World was historically an arena of colonization for Western capitalist nations, their subsequent movements for liberation have understandably been far more nationalistic than universalistic in content; and as movements to achieve independence from imperialist oppressors, their orientation has understandably been more materialistic, seeking to develop domestic production.

But Bookchin has long adduced another reason, one Rudy and Light do not mention, for advising Euro-American radicals to concentrate on revolutions at home rather than in the Third World. As he explained to his Marxist interlocutor in 1970, an excessive focus on Third World movements on the part of American radicals had led "to a bypassing of the social tasks in the First World....[Our] real job is to overthrow domestic capitalism by dealing with the real possibilities of an American revolution."[8] The same problem prevails today: somehow it is much easier to express solidarity with uprisings overseas than to try to organize one in the heart of the empire. Yet it is precisely the job of Euro-American radicals, Bookchin has long argued, to generate social revolution at home, especially in countries that have historically been and continue to be the sources of oppression for the Third World, whether colonial or "postcolonial." If Bookchin's focus, in his writings on revolutionary practice, is largely on revolutionary protagonists, it is not in order to "lay the blame for the failure of these struggles" on them but so that present-day radicals may learn and absorb their lessons, in order to avoid repeating them.

Finally, Rudy and Light fault Bookchin for offering a political program that is "unreasonable." Presumably they mean libertarian municipalism — although it is far from being the "gradualist movement in which communities guard themselves with militias against 'the ever-encroaching power of the state'" described by Rudy and Light. On the contrary, libertarian municipalism is a concrete program for forming a revolutionary movement, building a dual or counterpower, carrying out a social revolution, and constructing an ecological anarcho-communist society. How this can be construed as "gradualist" and defensive escapes me, especially coming from those who later accuse Bookchin (once again, wrongly) of advocating "a move from international capitalism directly to ecocommunism." The process of forming a dual power, such as libertarian municipalism offers, is neither gradualist nor immediatist but a viable, empowering program for a revolutionary transition.

Equally fallacious is their accusation that Bookchin's "political program... suggests localism in the face of an increasingly powerful, internationally coordinated capitalist world system"; Bookchin, far from being a localist, is a critic of localism and a fervent advocate of confederalism and internationalism.

At the same time they accuse Bookchin of demanding of revolutionaries "impossible measures of success." What measures? Bookchin belongs to the libertarian socialist tradition that has long sought to eliminate the state and capitalism. Eliminating them would be the "measure of success"; if Rudy and Light believe that that is an "impossible" standard to meet, then it's unclear why they claim in any sense to wear the mantle of Marxian socialism, which at least sought to eliminate capitalism if not the state.

Marxists that they are, it is certainly to be expected that they would hold a favorable view of the state, as "serv[ing] the interests of the public as well as those of political and economic elites"; and it's not surprising that they would find some things to be "worth saving" about "hierarchy and domination." But what is surprising is that they themselves offer no program beyond a vague assertion of "myriad cultures and individual acts of resistance within the capitalist workplace," "acts" whose nature remains undefined, in contrast to Bookchin's clearly spelled-out program.

Rudy and Light do, however, call militantly for analysis of capitalism's contradictions — which surely exist. But are we to wait for those contradictions to generate the conditions for a social revolution? Shouldn't we be developing a program and building a revolutionary movement now, in preparation for coming crises? There is no substitute for either activism or analysis, for theory or practice. (Given the importance Rudy and Light attribute to analysis, incidentally, one wonders why they do not criticize their spiritual and mystical colleagues for obscuring such analysis.)

Insofar as this book sets out to delineate an ecosocialist intellectual tradition, in sum, it must be considered a failure. Too often, by the admission of many of the essayists themselves, a thinker who is strong on democracy is weak on ecology, and vice versa. The only exception is the anarchist, who is scolded for rejecting Marxist categories. If this book represents the best the ecosocialists can do along these lines, then their prospects for developing a intellectual tradition are not at all auspicious.

Notes

1. Murray Bookchin, "A Discussion on 'Listen, Marxist!'" *Post-Scarcity Anarchism* (San Francisco: Ramparts Books, 1971), p. 265.

2. Ibid., pp. 248, 249.

3. Ibid., p. 250.

4. Murray Bookchin, *The Rise of Urbanization and the Decline of Citizenship* (San Francisco: Sierra Club Books, 1986), p. 214.

5. Murray Bookchin, "Post-Scarcity Anarchism" (written 1968), in *Post-Scarcity Anarchism* (Berkeley: Ramparts Press, 1971), p. 38.

6. Murray Bookchin, "Toward an Ecological Society," *Win* (Mar. 28, 1974); republished in *Toward an Ecological Society* (Montreal: Black Rose Books, 1980), pp. 66–67.

7. Rudy and Light's quote appears on page 33 of *Minding Nature.* The original quotation is in "Market Economy or Moral Economy?" in *The Modern Crisis,* 2nd revised ed. (Montreal: Black Rose Books, 1987), p. 84.

8. "Discussion," pp. 256, 257.

Attempting to answer the question, among others, "when does a revolutionary period begin?", Cohen draws on the example of scientific paradigm shifts in the understanding of species' change. He then extends outward to question leftist movements' use of theory and ideology to foster, or more usually, get in the way of, the change they hope to create in the world. Cohen leaves the reader with the question "how is self organization possible?" as well as with an urgent understanding of its necessity.

Originally published in issue 25.

Dear Social Anarchism...
Mitchel Cohen

Thomas Martin opens a complex discussion on integrating Chaos and Dynamic Systems theory into political analysis ("Steps Toward a Post-Western Anarchism," #23). Combined with insights from radical ecology movements, these new areas of scientific study have already begun to transcend the limits of their own disciplines to influence the emergence of new philosophies, social movements, and our understanding of consciousness itself.

What value do these new revelations hold for radicals? Well, for one, they bring to the fore questions that we have been barely able to formulate, and hold out the possibility of dramatic leaps in consciousness that will enable us to answer them.

In recent years, and in line with the dominant ideology of Western science, it has been standard leftist fare to reduce, or "linearize," the dialectical interaction of what we see as isolated variables. (Sure, we give lip-service to their "interpenetration," but in reality we hardly have any idea what that means, other than a very vague understanding that "things impact on each other.") Thus, leftists have historically cited the limitations inherent in "the objective conditions" as the culprit whenever revolutionary movements don't succeed in seizing state power (assuming that that's even a desirable goal), or "the subjective factors" whenever the various social democratic parties sell us out —"the masses aren't ready," "it's not a revolutionary period," etc. But what exactly do we mean when we speak of "revolutionary periods," "objective conditions," or "subjective factors"? Those categories have been taken for granted by the Left for so long that they have become stale catchwords used to dismiss or rationalize complex or dynamic processes. They need to be re-examined.

When, for instance, does a revolutionary period begin? How much change does a particular period in capitalism have to undergo before it becomes a recognizably new period, requiring new strategies for change? What are its components? Does it exist "objectively," independent of activists' perception, let alone influence? If so, is our activity necessary to bring it about? What do we do in non-revolutionary periods that would be different, as strategies and tactics, than what we'd do in revolutionary ones and how do we organize ourselves accordingly to achieve those different goals?

These questions are hardly limited to problems in understanding the transformation from non-revolutionary to revolutionary periods, but extend to evolution as well, the transformation of anything into something else. Take Darwin's great leap: the transformation of populations of a particular kind of animal or plant into a new species. Darwin explained this transformation brilliantly, in a new way: the "invisible hand" of natural selection (as in Adam Smith's "invisible hand" of the emerging capitalist market) gives the appearance of someone or some force "selecting for certain characteristics" over a wide quantity of chance variations in a population, eventuating in qualitatively new species, but (according to Darwin) in actuality it is just the population propagating itself. Those having more surviving offspring eventually expand the numbers in the population having their characteristics. Thus, should environment, disease, natural enemy or any other situation serve to limit organisms with one characteristic more than others, nature could be seen as privileging — or "selecting for"—organisms with the characteristics that eventually emerge — an analysis that, in its time, blew apart the dominant Christian paradigm of pre-determined species made by God.

But was this as definitive a refutation of Christianity as it once seemed, let alone of Lamarck's construct of the transmission of acquired characteristics in individuals? "In the wild, in breeding, and in artificial life, we see the emergence of variation," as Darwin discussed; "but we also clearly see the limits of variation narrowly bounded, and often bounded within species. No one has yet witnessed, in the fossil record, real life, or computer life, the exact transitional moments when the system of evolution pumps its complexity up to the next level. There is a suspicious barrier in the vicinity of species that either holds change back or removes it from our sight. As the French evolutionist Pierre Grasse said, 'Variation is one thing, evolution quite another; this cannot be emphasized strongly enough… Mutations provide change, but not progress.'"(Kevin Kelly, "Deep Evolution: The Emergence of Postdarwinism," Whole Earth Review, Fall 1992.) Exactly when and how do new species emerge, new qualities, from the plethora of quantifiable variations?

Chaos and dynamic systems theory is giving rise to new interpretations of this 150-year-old debate, not by reasserting Christianity's dogmatic claim for the making of species or Lamarck's for individual heredity, but by re-examining the questions those frameworks were grappling with through new eyes. Both Darwin and Lamarck, let me point out, devised mechanisms that worked (correctly or not) over qualitatively different layers of complexity — Darwin, on populations (and not the individuals making it up — horizontal array); Lamarck, on individuals inheriting acquired traits (vertical array). Darwin's mechanism worked, in a way, like insurance statistics today: You could tell a great deal about populations — how many people will die of heart attacks during the month of July in Lower Manhattan, for example, and even refine it further to sex, race, age group, etc. But if a particular individual asks: "Will I get a heart attack in Lower Manhattan during the month of July?" the mechanism has nothing to say. Because both Darwin's and Lamarck's mechanisms found expression in the characteristics of the population — that is, as new qualities (new species)—the collision of their paradigms, so long as constructed within the same level of complexity, was inevitable. But is there nothing more to be learned than "one was right and the other was wrong"?

Utilizing the new sciences, we can now look at relationships between different levels of complexity — molecular, cellular, organismic, class, ecosystemic and planetary, each qualitatively different and discretely organized — and begin to understand how what occurs in one level is sometimes "sealed off" from, and sometimes impacts on and is co-determined by what happens on other levels. In general, we incorrectly apply ways of seeing pertinent to events on one level to other levels and the movement between them, assuming a uniformitarianism — the general validity and application of the same "laws" over time and dimensionality — to, for example, attempts to account for the direction of a particular electron in a given place and time. From our macro perspective it does seem "logical" that we be able to do so; but as it turns out, nature does not work that way.

Over time, we've learned that events in levels that we really didn't know about previously (such as that of the genes) are not determining entities, as believed by, for instance, Hawkins in his popular book The Selfish Gene, but depend upon and interact with the surrounding macro environment — in this case, the chemistry of the cell — in ways that do to Darwin what his paradigm did to Lamarck! Note, for example, the Mississippi alligator: eggs that develop in the temperature range 26–30% C hatch females; take the same eggs, with nothing else changed, raise the temperature to between 34–36% C, and they will hatch only males. Eggs that develop between 31–33% C produce alligators of either sex, with the probabilities changing from female to male as the temperature rises. (Temperature itself changes for each egg based on, among other variables, the egg's location within the nest.) The sex of the individual alligator, as well as the sexual dispersal over the population, is determined in each egg by the intersection of variables from different levels: temperature, genes, location of the egg in the nest, and environment within the eggs.

The new sciences of chaos and dynamic systems theory are making headway in understanding multi-level interaction, holding revelatory implications not only for the particular framework but for the way we think and the political work we do. They can help us ascertain the boundaries (or limits) of levels, the processes by which chaos organizes itself into recognizable patterns (new qualities) which self-develop, the relationships that exist among qualities within particular levels as they negate and supercede, and the process by which measurable qualities generate new qualities, which themselves become quantities in a higher-level process — to use the old phrase, the way they "dialectically leap" dimensions — the missing territory in understanding process and motion. We are inventing a new calculus of natural and, hopefully, political transformation.

These concerns are not necessarily new. Dialectical philosophy has long discussed the transformation of slave societies into feudalism, feudalism into capitalism and, eventually capitalism into socialism. All of these temporarily stable (yet increasingly dynamic) forms, each with their own contradictions, characterized whole social and economic epochs within the history of class society in general. The debates over how such transformations took place, what order they took place in, did they indeed succeed each other sequentially at all (or does it only seem that way after the fact?), why did class society itself emerge and how, and what is the role of understanding — consciousness — of historic macro processes in future transformations, are all still being debated today. It seems unavoidable that we begin questioning similar processes within capitalism as well, questions concerning the transformation of one period within capitalism to another. Yet, until now, no one has done that. The questions are similar as before: How do we recognize a new period, revolutionary or otherwise? What criteria are valid? All, as before, are subsets of more general philosophical considerations: When and how does anything become anything else? How do we know when it does? And, how do we frame this question without falling into the pounding of Kant's "categorical imperative"?

Most leftists assume that a certain amount of quantity piling up produces (either on its own or with our help), new objective qualities — another way of saying that the whole is greater than the sum of its parts. What exactly does that mean? Is it indeed the case? How, exactly, does one quality differ from another quality? What is the role of quantity in that? How do changes at the micro-level impact the macro, and vice-versa?

We know that there is a relationship between the objective conditions of our lives and the ways we think and feel; but, when it comes to political and social action, the objective and subjective are often worlds apart. What is objective, what is subjective, is the separation of the two legitimate, and what is the history of that separation? How can one avoid the Enlightenment's baneful legacy of conceptualizing the world in terms of such false dualities? (For more on this question, see The Re-Enchantment of the World, by Morris Berman; Gender/Body/Knowledge: Feminist Reconstructions of Being and Knowing, by Alison Jaggar and Susan Bordo; The Dialectical Biologist, by Richard Levins and Richard Lewontin; Beyond Bookchin: Preface for a Future Social Ecology by David Watson; and "Deep Evolution: The Emergence of Postdarwinism" by Kevin Kelly.) What kinds of different strategies for social revolution would emerge as we learn to think non-dualistically? Is that even possible? Would we even still be thinking in terms of "strategies" at all?

We also know that our situation constrains even the questions we think to ask — including the ways we perceive that very situation. Yet, leftists have yet to see the importance of transforming our situation so that we would be in a position to ask the kind of questions we need to ask, let alone be able to answer them. As a result, we always end up racing to catch up with changes that have already occurred, forever chasing the bus down the avenue of luck. ("I just chased the bus all the way home and saved $1.50," my roommate once beamed, proudly. To which I responded: "Schmuck! Why didn't you run home behind a taxi-cab and save $9?!") Why are we always playing "catch-up"? Because we have no general, systematic set of criteria for understanding movement, especially the motion of capitalism at transitional junctures as it begins to leave one period and enter another, and what that new period is based on. Our problem is not finding ways to move faster and faster. It's to leap out of that paradigm altogether. We need to begin thinking about such creatures as "revolutionary periods," "objective conditions," and "subjective factors" in new and more holistic, non-reductionist ways. These cannot be found in the approaches of Western science, anarchism, or post-Marx Marxism (what Engels calls "scientific" socialism) as understood and practiced thus far. The problem, philosophically, is one of "motion": the transformation of something into something else: an appreciation of qualities, how they arise and how we know them when they do.

Instead, we too often fall back — without realizing it, usually — into a form of positivism known as "stage theory," and into relying upon labels, assumed categories, "common sense" frameworks based on false dualities, and clichés. Consequently, using the old "rationalized" ways of thinking in which we are trapped, the Left has been unable to keep pace with, on the one hand, the rapid globalization of capital (spatially) and, on the other, its real domination, suddenly (across dimensional complexity), over ever-greater facets of daily life including the privatization and exploitation of the genetic code itself. The genetic determinist paradigm which dominates capitalist science is the primary means through which this happens, these days, a form of reductionist materialism in which particular molecular configurations are said to determine all sorts of events, characteristics and behavior of the greater organism, including people. And so we have the claim that genes, 1) determine most features of an individual's physiognomy (including the brain); and 2) thereby determine their consciousness and behavior. The federally funded Violence Initiative Project, for example, is searching for "the gene that causes criminal behavior."

Many, including some gay groups, are touting the idea that homosexuality is "genetically based." (It's not.) From such a reductionist model (which is a ruling framework of our society) there is no basis for understanding where social behavior, let alone consciousness — undoubtedly irreducible to its cellular parts and neuron networks — comes from. Or, is consciousness simply an electric current, with an exaggerated sense of its own importance?

Things were not always this way. The view of nature which predominated in the West down to the eve of the Scientific Revolution, writes Morris Berman in The Re-Enchantment of the World, was totally different than the framework through which we see things today.

"[It] was that of an enchanted world. Rocks, trees, rivers and clouds were all seen as wondrous, alive, and human beings felt at home in this environment. The cosmos, in short, was a place of belonging. A member of this cosmos was not an alienated observer of it but a direct participant in its drama. His [sic] personal destiny was bound up with its destiny, and this relationship gave meaning to his life. This type of consciousness — what I shall refer to in this book as "participating consciousness" — involves merger, or identification, with one's surroundings, and bespeaks a psychic wholeness that has long since passed from the scene. Alchemy, as it turns out, was the last great coherent expression of participating consciousness in the West.

"…[Science, as the dominant mode of thinking in the current epoch] can best be described as disenchantment, non-participation, for it insists on a rigid distinction between observer and observed. Scientific consciousness is alienated consciousness; there is no ecstatic merger with nature, but rather total separation from it. Subject and object are always seen in opposition to each other. I am not my experiences, and thus not really a part of the world around me. The logical end point of this world view is a feeling of total reification: everything is an object, alien, not-me; and I am ultimately an object too, an alienated "thing" in a world of other, equally meaningless things. This world is not of my own making; the cosmos cares nothing for me, and I do not really feel a sense of belonging to it. What I feel, in fact, is a sickness in the soul." (Morris Berman, The Re-Enchantment of the World, Bantam Books, 1984.)

To our detriment, however, radicals have not been particularly perceptive in observing what has been lost as capitalism came to dominate the world, which is seen by many as a progressive historical stage despite "abuses" (such as genocide, slavery, colonization, etc.) without which "the next stage" — anarchism, or communism — would be impossible. Analytical thought, essential to capitalism's reduction of everything to the realm of quantifiability, assumes and upholds an "objective" detached stance from which to view the world, further separating subject from object and losing whatever traces of participatory non-neurotic ways of being that once flourished. The Neurotic — which is, after all, almost everyone in this culture — fetishizes that separation and, consequently, the source of his or her own neurosis. The duality is not only maintained "logically"; it reproduces itself in us emotionally; we actually fear transcending it, rejecting what participatory consciousness would mean and failing to appreciate the beauty of what has been lost. In so doing, we perpetually undermine the revolutionary movements we participate in and, sadly, our ability to transform the world.

Perhaps we are about to come out of the long national nightmare of philosophical stagnation. New conceptualizations and methodological approaches do appear promising: "Fractals," for instance, are self-referential mathematical maps in which each part contains and reproduces the whole within it, no matter how small it is sliced. (These are discussed in *Chaos: Making a New Science*, by James Gleick.) Self-referential (or "recursive") operations and philosophies are also discussed — brilliantly, in my opinion — in *Gödel, Escher and Bach: An Eternal Golden Braid*, by Douglas Hofstadter, and are precursors to the emergence of a full- fledged, truly dialectical philosophy. And, in his award-winning book, *How the Leopard Changed Its Spots: The Evolution of Complexity*, Brian Goodwin offers the first readable account of the spontaneous self-organization of living (and even non-living) biological fields, in which what counts "is not the nature of the molecules and other components involved, such as cells, but the way these interact with one another in time (their kinetics) and in space (their relational order— how the state of one region depends on the states of neighboring regions). ...This is the emphasis on self-organization, the capacity of these fields to generate patterns spontaneously, without any specific instructions telling them what to do, as in a genetic program. These systems produce something out of nothing, no plan, no blueprint, no instructions about the pattern that emerges." (p. 51) These patterns "cannot be predicted from a knowledge of the properties of the component parts in isolation. To understand these complex nonlinear dynamic systems it is necessary to study both the whole and its parts, and to be prepared for surprises due to the emergence of unexpected behavior," (77–78) as enumerated elegantly in the writings of Stephen Jay Gould.

From such arcane beginnings we can usefully plumb these new developments to understand the tension between the ever-expanding value-creating abilities of workers and their negation and the reappropriation in the production process (via capitalism's private accumulation of value) which goes on constantly in every work day, in every part of every work day and, contrary to Engels and aft (in whose expositions the division between necessary and surplus labor is walled-off into discrete categories or "stages" — antecedent of the historical theory of "stages," or Stalinism), in every fragment of every fragment of every moment, simultaneously creating and negating, producing and consuming, objectifying and subjectivizing, freeing and determining, and particularizing and universalizing.

How can these contradictory processes go on at the same time in the same place with the same material? How is self organization possible?

Even in discussing the relationship of consciousness and subjectivity to politics — all to rare, as it is — we objectify that relationship to begin with; we look at subjectivity "objectively": What are the conditions in which people become conscious of their own role in history, etc. In so doing we reproduce that duality even as we strive to transcend it, therein undermining the possibility of radically transforming our conditions despite whatever new information we gain.

"Because disenchantment is intrinsic to the scientific world view," writes Berman, "the modern epoch contained, from its inception, an inherent instability that severely limited its ability to sustain itself for more than a few centuries. For more than 99 percent of human history, the world was enchanted and man saw himself as an integral part of it. The complete reversal of this perception in a mere four hundred years or so has destroyed the continuity of the human experience and the integrity of the human psyche. It has very nearly wrecked the planet as well. The only hope, or so it seems to me, lies in a reenchantment of the world."

And that reenchantment begins, I think, in the self-organization of dynamic systems, of which our consciousness and our actions (conscious or not) are a part. Tom Martin points us in the right direction. As I have very little in the way of mental and social tools to understand how, from chaos, self-organization can (and often does) emerge. Opening the question, as Tom has done, is excellent. As in anything, however, the devil is in the details. And we haven't much time.

"My object all sublime
I shall achieve in time
To let the punishment fit the crime —
The punishment fit the crime."

Originally published in issue 40.

Burn Bibles not Flags!
Sam Sloss

The Senate vote on Flag desecration was close last June and you can be assured it will come up for just before July 4th every year — especially if it is an election year. Should the Senate ever pass this Amendment, protesters of government policies (right, left, and middle of the road) will need a new symbol to get media and citizenry attention. I recommend protesters turn to Bible burning as the new alternative.

Why Bibles? Because burning Bibles is the perfect way to draw attention to your cause. In fact, it may draw more attention and ire than Flag burning ever did. In addition to TV, newspapers, and blogs, your protest will be covered by virtually every Church during weekend services.

Bible burning can be used by all political persuasions. Those opposing fundamentalist religious policies like gay bashing can burn King James versions. Fundamentalists might burn a New Revised Standard Version or a New American Standard Bible. Die-hard Republicans might consider burning The Jefferson Bible.

Those favoring building walls along our Southern and Northern boarders to keep out immigrants might burn Spanish and French versions of the Bible. And there are always gender neutral Bibles like Today's New International Version that should appeal to Promise Keepers and other groups that insist on the man as head of the family.

Supporters of hierarchy might burn Gnostic Bibles. They say history repeats itself. Unlike burning oil, we won't run out of Bibles. As the best-selling book for hundreds of years, Bibles are found in every hotel/motel room and in nearly every home. Even I, a skeptic, have several. And should Bible burning really catch on, it could be a boom for the publishing industry which has experienced some rough times.

Bible burning is the perfect sequel to a Constitutional Amendment endorsing idolatry. What better way to demonstrate our Flag's Godlike status? With greater protection for Flags than Bibles, we can finally end our denominational squabbling united in the one true religion of nationalism.

The next two essays, which form the basis of a series on urban and historical crises that remains unfinished, chronicle the aftermath of two critical moments in recent American history. Using the events following the Rodney King beating in Los Angeles in 1992, and the Oklahoma City bombing in 1995, Dr. Ehrlich offers a succinct analysis of the lessons to be learned from each. From the de-politicization of the Los Angeles riots to the initial assumption of Arab involvement in Oklahoma City, Ehrlich demonstrates how much, and sometimes how little, our situation has changed.

Originally published in issue 21.

Los Angeles, 1992 — The Lessons Revisited
Howard J. Ehrlich

The social explosion that occurred in the south central neighborhoods of Los Angeles from April 29 through May 2, 1992 was devastating. As many as 52 people died, 8,000 injuries were reported, over 12,000 people were arrested and jailed, hundreds were deported and almost all had their lives disrupted. Over 1,000 buildings were burned with more than half that number totally destroyed, and the estimated financial costs from arson, damage and theft were placed at 750-800 million dollars. This was neither the first nor will it be the last of such upheavals. Our question is: *What have we learned from this?*

Lesson one. Civil disorders are complex events. The motives for involvement are mixed. This was neither a commodity riot nor a political insurrection. It was both, and much more. There were petty thieves and organized thieves, and there were people who stole food and people who stole luxuries. There were young adults and older ones who engaged in recreational violence, and others in racial violence. It is important to understand that not only were the motives of participants and bystanders mixed, but also that people don't behave out of a single motive. Then, too, motives change over time and in retrospect.

There was manifest in these events a strong antiauthoritarian impulse, a rage against authority. I think this is what frightened so many observers. I don't think, however, that we should confuse this with a genuine anarchist impulse. These were actions against those in authority, no actions against the nature of authority.

Lesson two. Cities have changed. The 1965 insurrection in the Watts area of Los Angeles had been highly politicized (which is why I think the term "insurrection" is appropriate). It was confined primarily to the Watts area and almost all of the participants were Black. The 1992 events were substantially less politicized. While it spread beyond a single neighborhood, the disruptions that occurred reflected the new ethnic mix of our cities. Unlike past urban disorders, this was not a Black-White conflict. In Los Angeles we observed an interethnic melee involving Blacks, Anglos, Latinos, Koreans and other Asian Pacific ethnics. This is the future of ethnoviolence in America.

Lesson three. The police. American police have precipitated almost nine out of ten race-related urban disorders since the turn of the twentieth century. The Los Angeles police, which had been lauded as a model of a disciplined, militarily-oriented, high-technology department, have been depicted also as undisciplined, trigger-happy, and likely to use excessive force.

The character of a city's police department is determined by its political elites. In Los Angeles the elites had clearly decided to use the police as agents for containing its burgeoning population of people of color. For example, the city paid out 8.7 million dollars to settle police brutality suits in 1990. That year, the LAPD had the second highest rate, among major city police departments, of fatal shootings of civilians. It had been the leading police department in the number of persons killed annually since 1985. In the calculus of elite cost-benefit ratios, the political elites were apparently willing to pay those costs — and to sacrifice those lives — to contain and control its ghettoized population. (The Los Angeles Sheriffs Department is also no slouch as gunslingers, having fatally shot an average of 42 people a year since 1986.)

Lesson four. The political elites. Racial and ethnic group relations are not on the agenda of the political elites. Following the insurrectionary explosion in Watts in 1965, the McCone and Koerner Commissions (investigative bodies appointed respectively by the governor of California and the president of the United States) issued reports which pointed to many of the conditions underlying that disorder. The listing of conditions, which could be the chapter headings for a social problems textbook, included poverty, housing segregation, inadequate housing, employment discrimination, poor educational facilities, inadequate financial and consumer services in the community, and police abuse. In the years that followed, little had been accomplished, if not attempted, to resolve those problems in Watts, in South Central Los Angeles, in the city as a whole. If anything, the economic situation in the city had become worse. Just one example: between June 1990 and February 1992, the Los Angeles area lost 300,000 jobs.

The California Assembly Special Committee on the Los Angeles Crisis concluded, in its report of September 1992, "that the causes of the 1992 unrest were the same as the causes of the unrest of the 1960s, aggravated by a highly visible increasing concentration of wealth at the top of the income scale and a decreasing Federal and State commitment to urban programs serving those at the bottom of the income scale."

Lesson five. The courts. Too many people think that the courts are the place to achieve justice. It is especially important for those at the bottom of the socioeconomic hierarchy to believe that there can be a measure of justice in society. And so, even though most Americans felt that the video of the Rodney King beating was sufficient evidence of the guilt of his police assailants, there was a respectful waiting period during which people waited for justice to be done. The explosion that ensued reaffirmed a solid principle of sociological theory: when people no longer feel that there is justice in society, they will rebel.

Lesson six. Repression. The combined response of the political elites and the police apparatus was repressive; that is, it went beyond the bounds of "normal" police work. Furthermore, this repression entailed the collaboration of the federal government.

- A curfew was declared, April 30, which allowed the police to arrest anyone out after dark. The curfew was not widely announced, nor (according to the ACLU) was it published in Spanish-language media. Many people arrested and jailed were unaware that they were violating a curfew. Further, homeless people arrested for curfew violations were, in effect, being jailed for being homeless.
- Bails were often excessive; arraignments sometimes took as long as seven days; jails were grossly overcrowded; some people were imprisoned for long periods on buses; people were intimidated into pleading guilty in order to avoid (threatened) lengthy detention and potentially severe sentences.
- For weeks after the initial disorders, many permits for public protests, demonstrations, and rallies were refused and many peaceful demonstrators were arrested. The decision to grant a permit or make arrests was often related to the political content of the demonstrations.
- The regional American Civil Liberties Union office estimated that 12,545 people had been arrested.
- Within two days of the start of events, an estimated 1,000 federal agents descended on the area: marshals, Drug Enforcement Administration (DEA), Bureau of Alcohol, Tobacco, and Firearms as well as the FBI and the Immigration and Naturalization Service (INS). While the FBI and DEA worked with local police and sheriffs targeting gangs, the LAPD and the Sheriffs Department turned over approximately 1500

people, almost all of whom had been illegally detained, to the INS. Many of them were undocumented immigrants, but they had not been involved in looting, curfew violations, or other violations relating to the disorders. Hundreds of people were deported with many signing voluntary deportation orders after being threatened with heavy bail and long prison sentences.

Lesson seven. It could have been me. Every person of color, every person who speaks with a non-English accent, every person who has experienced or witnessed aggressive or violent police actions, knows that if the police could publicly, viciously beat Mr. King and get away with it, if they could so publicly repress those who protested their actions, then none of us are safe.

Lesson eight. You can't effectively organize inside a crisis. Community organizing takes time, and you can't organize to respond to a possible crisis (the aftermath of the verdict in this case) unless there is already an infrastructure of community associations and coalitions. True, there were small groups who were organized and made plans, but the residents of South Central Los Angeles were mainly so alienated and organizations so isolated that they could not act in coalition. This is doubtless true of city neighborhoods, especially poorer neighborhoods, all over the country.

Lesson nine. "Denial" is the major American response to ethnoviolence. The events of April 29th to May 2nd should have communicated three messages. First, that there are communities across America where racism, poverty, and a deliberate policy of political abandonment has created a volatile brew. The first in Los Angeles have already spread across the country. I read accounts of political protests in 41 American cities, including the major disorder in Las Vegas. It is likely to recur nationwide over the next several years. Second, American society is far more violent today than it was at the time of the urban insurrections of the 1960s. The disorders of this decade will be on a larger scale going beyond local neighborhoods, be more physically violent, and be more spectacular so as to fit into the programming of local TV. Third, that regardless of the attempt of the news media and the political elites to deny it, there are some genuine political grievances and social inequalities that need to be redressed. The critical point in the recent history of American urban insurrections is how the political demands are met. If we gauge the present response to the political manifesto of the Los Angeles gangs, the Bloods and the Crips, demands bolstered by their continuing truce and the reduction of local violence, then we would have to conclude that no one is listening. (The manifesto, a serious political statement, though surprisingly reformist and nonradical in most of its proposals, called for changes in the physical environment, and funding for reforms in education, law enforcement, economic development and welfare. Among the alternative media, it was described in *The Nation* and reprinted in *Z Magazine*. It did not appear in the mainstream national press.)

Lesson ten. The news media reinforces the elite agenda. The establishment news media is intolerant of complexity. Moreover, it tells only those stories which fit the prevailing agenda. Without the connectives or typical embellishments, this was the story they told about the events in Los Angeles:

Things were bad in South Central Los Angeles. The police who brutalized Rodney King were wrong. Rodney King was wrong. The jury acquittal of the police charged in the beating was wrong. The riot was wrong. This was a Black riot. The four Black men who were televised beating the white truck driver were as wrong as the four cops who were televised beating King. The motive for the riot was really looting. The political rage expressed was all rhetoric. This is what you expect from central city Black kids.

There were some good, Christian, law-abiding people in the area. What we need to do is get rid of the bad cops; keep the gangs under control, weed out the violent gang members, the drug dealers, and illegal immigrants; and seed the area with some new buildings, new jobs, and more small businesses owned by local residents.

See? The System works.

Lesson eleven. Most people of wealth and power believe that the system does work. There is no commitment to fundamental social change in the country. Don't expect it in South Central Los Angeles. The socioeconomic conditions of that area were produced by a confluence of capitalism, authoritarianism, and racism. It is unlikely that these dominant ideologies are going to change. That being the case, it is unlikely that much about the area will change.

Here are some of the questions we need to ask about the elite proposals for rebuilding Los Angeles:

- Will the prejudice and institutional forms of discrimination that led to the segregation of this population end?
- Will the level of ethnoviolence that has intimidated the population be dissipated?
- Will the new jobs that may come be congruent with the needs of the community and the educational and skill levels of the residents?

- Will the new businesses be worker owned and managed or will ownership be from the outside and management along a standard, bureaucratic, authoritarian model?
- Will the real estate belong to the community in land trusts or other cooperative forms or will the land remain as a basis for speculations and profit?
- Will most of the money generated by residents remain in the community or will it continue to be drained by nonresident landowners, banks, and other profiteers?
- Will the police be subject to community control and review or will they remain as an outside army?
- Will the residents be able to effect significant political control over the community?

If the goal of reconstructive efforts is primarily to build new buildings, provide a modicum of new jobs, and finance more minority businesses, then it won't work. Our goal has to be to build a new, nonauthoritarian, nonviolent society in the shell of South Central Los Angeles. Anything short of that will only recapitulate the conditions that will generate another social upheaval.

Some Observations on the Oklahoma City Bombing
Howard J. Ehrlich

Ordinary people can do terrible things. We all know this, and some of us are scared by the thought. You may remember several years ago when the respected filmmaker Costa-Gavras produced Betrayed, a film about the American right-wing. It was panned by reviewers and moviegoers. The over-riding critique was that it was "unrealistic." Why? Because it treated the right wing extremists as ordinary, everyday folk. They were kind to their mothers and loved their children. In the American national character, people who do terrible things are either demonized or declared crazy, and so not capable of decent human behavior.

To be sure, some perpetrators of terrible things are evil and some are crazy, but most are not. If we can acknowledge this as our first lesson, we can move on to examine the social implications of this tragedy.

The ethnocentrism of the media. It was 9:02 Wednesday morning, April 19, 1995, that a rental truck carrying an estimated 4,000 pounds of explosive detonated outside of the Alfred P. Murrah Federal Building. The blast was felt as far as 30 miles away. When the rubble was cleared and the final count grimly recorded, 166 people were dead, including 19 children who had been in the second floor day care center. Approximately 400 people were injured.

The news media responded to the event with electronic speed. Even before any investigation could be initiated newspeople across the country had iden-tified Middle East terrorists as the perpetrators. They found support from their conclusions from a handful of "counterterrorism experts." The CNN terrorism consultant, like many of them a former CIA officer, said: "It's clear, I think, that there must have, almost certainly, to have been a foreign origin to this, and probably one in the Middle East, although, of course, I have no facts to confirm this yet." As one critic commented "Seldom have so many been so wrong — so quickly." The ethnocentrism of the news media was clear in two ways: First, in the stereotypic of Arabs and other Middle Easterners; and second, in the denial that ordinary Americans could be engaged in Terrorist activities.

The ethnocentrism of the news media should be no more surprising to use that was our first lesson. Unfortunately, the media response to this and other recent exposes of its biases makes it clear that there are no self-correcting mechanisms within the news industry, nor is there any motivation for serious change. The reader/viewer is left with the responsibility for identifying those biases and reinterpreting the daily news accordingly.

Meet the everyday racist. When it became clear that no foreign cabal had invaded Oklahoma, and as it looked more and more likely that only a few ordinary men were involved, Americans remembered a lesson from their past. That lesson? There is a small, organized, frightening, violent, paranoid, radical right wing in the U.S. For a moment the country did a collective double-take at the specter and spectacle of the militia, the survivalists, the Klan, the neo-nazis and the like. Fortunately for the American psyche, they were a spectacle so they didn't have to be taken too seriously. Look at what they were saying: The United Nations and Jewish bankers are undermining the national sovereignty of the United States. UN helicopters are already spying on Americans. Road signs have been coded with secret messages to help direct invading troops. Plans are underway to monitor civilians by branding them with bar codes and even implanting microchips in people's bodies. While all of this is going on, the federal government is attempting to disarm the population through gun controls, and even by force as the Waco and Ruby Ridge incidents demonstrated.

The focus on the extremists was misguided, but not accidental. It was simply another way of saying that ordinary people don't do this. The focus, to reiterate, should have been on the everyday right-winger, that ordinary person who, politically alienated and economically threatened, has received social support from a circle of people similarly searching for answers and security. It is this right wing which has adopted an American nationalism, a sense of White, Christian separatism (if not superiority), and a belief in patriarchy and the reestablishment of a traditional family ideology. It is the everyday bigot who is the bulwark of discrimination and ethnoviolence. The mainstream political leadership focuses on the right-wing extremists because they are a threat to the status quo. The everyday racist is the status quo. It is this sector of society that we need to focus on.

The response to random violence is random repression. The peace movements around the world discovered a long time ago that the means to peace had to be nonviolent. On a philosophical level, movement activists argue that means and ends have to be consistent, and that if "peace" (meaning a nonviolent state of affairs) is your goal then it needs to understood that it cannot be achieved by violent means. On a practical level, the peace movement recognized that violence always brought about an increase in the repressive activities of the state, and that was inimical to the well-being of all. The right wing, which sees people and society as inescapably violent, views violence as a necessary and consistent means to their ends. Violence, whatever its source, activates an agenda of repression. Within a few days after the Oklahoma City bombing, President Clinton and members of Congress activated their agendas.

The official title was the "Omnibus Counterterrorism Act of 1995." Its details are still fluid and it will not be passed in '95, but its current provisions would likely do more damage than the bomb that inspired it. Its meaning, capsulized by Gregory Nojeim, the legislative counsel of the American Civil Liberties Union, is: "(1) Individuals and institutions will be subject to harassment and intimidation; (2) any alien can be labeled a supporter of terrorism and deported without proper evidence or appeal; (3) legitimate charitable organizations can be intimidated or even shut down at the whim of government officials; and (4) peaceful political activities by Americans will become subject to a legislative chill." While many of the provisions of this bill would probably be found unconstitutional after years of litigation, in the meantime great harm would be done to many people — not to mention to our fundamental rights of free speech, free association, and due process.

It isn't that we really need more laws. There is no question of the illegality and immorality of the act of bombing that occurred. Moreover, no one seriously argues that this bill, if law, could have prevented the Oklahoma City bombing. What we need to be conscious of is that violent acts such as this invariably come to be used by people in power to further expand the scope of their control.

Write your own history — and other agendas. There were other agenda items as well, and while they may have come from different political actors they seemed all of a piece. There we some, Mr. Clinton among them, who thought this an opportune time to attack "hate radio." Others, mainly media pundits, revived the 1950s catch phrase, "extremists of the left and right." Although no one implicated left-wing activists in the bombing (or, for that matter, hate radio), the idea of left wing extremism was invoked as a neutralizing agent. For example, Suzanne Fields, the nationally syndicated Washington Times columnist, was disturbed that the bombing was associated with ultraconservative politics and declared that "leftist radicals planted more than 100 bombs on college campuses" during 1968 and 1969 (April 27). Months later, after the counterterrorism bill had been stalled in Congress, an unidentified "senior administration official" cited in the New York Times attributed the lack of legislative speed to a coalition of far right and far left members of Congress.

There is an underlying theme in these commentaries which link left and right. One is that people are no damn good — a theme which has as its counterpoint the idea that we need to be able to defend ourselves against others. Thus, any attempt at gun control would leave us defenseless. The other theme is that our real enemy is the left, and that we shouldn't let ourselves be distracted by right wing excesses. Finally, there was the "control agenda," which seems to appeal to people's insecurity. The appeal is that such incidents as Oklahoma City are beyond the control of people and that the only way to deal with them is to increase the power of the police and other law enforcement agents.

Perspective. One of the consequences of such a massive tragedy is that is distracts us from looking beyond the immediate spectacle. When the trial of those accused of the bombing begins, people will once again be captured by the grief of survivors who lost their children, friends, and lovers. We will be fascinated by the psychology of the presumed perpetrators, and engrossed by the trial if it is televised. These are natural reactions, but we must not let ourselves become absorbed in this. We need self-consciously to wrench ourselves from the spectacle and reaffirm with others, and to ourselves, what the truly significant lessons of Oklahoma City are. We cannot prevent random acts of violence by random individuals. We can educate ourselves and others so that not only in there no support for such acts, but there is no support for the everyday acts of prejudice and ethnoviolence.

Practice

This article is a comprehensive look at community organizing from an anarchist perspective. Since the 1960s, anarchist organizers have been looking for a way to present a non-elitist perspective on community organizing. Knoche offers a detailed set of points to strengthen the organizers' work in local communities, arguing for retaining anarchist principles within their work.

Originally published in issue 18.

Organizing Communities
Tom Knoche

Many anarchists probably cringe at the notion of any person or group being "organized" and believe that the very idea is manipulative. They can point to countless community organization leaders who ended up on government payrolls. They can't see how winning traffic lights and playgrounds does any more than help the system appear pluralistic and effective.

Such skepticism makes sense. Community organizing has always been practiced in many different ways to accomplish many different things. In reviewing the history of neighborhood organizing, Robert Fisher summed it up this way:

> While neighborhood organizing is a political act, it is neither inherently reactionary, conservative, liberal or radical, nor is it inherently democratic and inclusive or authoritarian and parochial. It is above all a political method, an approach used by various segments of the population to achieve specific goals, serve certain interests, and advance clear or ill-defined political perspectives. (Fisher, 1984; p. 158).

If we just look at some of the progressive strains of community organizing thought, we still face a lot of confusion about what it is and how it is used. Saul Alinsky, a key figure in the development of community organizing as we know it today, wrote:

> We are concerned about how to create mass organizations to seize power and give it to the people; to realize the democratic dream of equality, justice, peace, cooperation, equal and full opportunities for education, full and useful employment, health and the creation of those circumstances in which man can have the chance to live by the values that give meaning to life. We are talking about a mass power organization that will change the world (Alinsky, 1971, p. 3).

The Midwest Academy, a training institute for community organizers founded by some ex-civil rights and SDS leaders, asserts that:

> More and more people are finding that what is needed is a permanent, professionally staffed community membership organization which can not only win real improvements for its members, but which can actually alter the relations of power at the city and state level. These groups [citizen groups] are keeping government open to the people and are keeping our democratic rights intact (Max, 1977; p. 2).

A senior member of ACORN (Association of Communities Organized for Reform Now), a national association of mostly urban community organizations, describes the goal of organizing as strengthening people's collective capacities to bring about social change (Stables, 1984; p. 1). ACORN organized local communities, then employed its constituency at the national level, attempting to move the Democratic Party to the left.

Finally, a participant in a workshop on community organizing I conducted a number of years ago characterized community organizing as "manipulating people to do trivial things."

In this article, I will focus on how community organizing can be useful in advancing an anarchist vision of social change. Community organizations that build on an anarchist vision of social change are different from other community organizations because of the purposes they have, the criteria they have for success, the issues they work on, the ways they operate and the tactics they use.

My experience with community organizing spans a 16-year period including four years in Baltimore, Maryland and twelve in Camden, New Jersey. I have primarily worked with very low income people on a wide range of issues. I will draw heavily on my personal experience in this article. I use the term "community organizing" to refer to social change efforts which are based in local geographically defined areas where people live. This is the key distinction between community organizing and other forms of organizing for social change which may be based in workplaces or universities, involving people where they work or study instead of where they live. Some issue-oriented organizations are considered community organizations if their constituency is local.

Goals of Anarchist Organizing

Anarchist community organizing must be dedicated to changing what we can today and undoing the socialization process that has depoliticized so many of us. We can use it to build the infrastructure that can respond and make greater advances when our political and economic systems are in crisis and are vulnerable to change.

The following purposes illustrate this concept.

1. Helping people experiment with decentralized, collective and cooperative forms of organization.

We have to build our American model of social change out of our own experience; we can't borrow revolutionary theory in total from that developed in another historical and/or cultural context. Community organizations can help people log that experience and analyze it. Because of our culture's grounding in defense of personal liberty and democracy, social change engineered by a vanguard or administered by a strong central state will not work here.

David Bouchier is on the right track when he says, "for citizen radicals evolution is better than revolution because evolution works" (Bouchier, 1987; p. 139). We must learn new values and practice cooperation rather than competition. Community organizations can provide a vehicle for this "retooling." "This means that a cultural revolution, a revolution of ideas and values and understanding, is the essential prelude to any radical change in the power arrangement of modern society. The purpose of radical citizenship is to take the initiative in this process" (Bouchier, p. 148).

Any kind of alternative institution (see Ehrlich, et al., Reinventing Anarchy, p. 346), including cooperatives, worker managed businesses, etc., that offers a chance to learn and practice community control and worker self-management, is important. We must experience together how institutions can be different and better. These alternative institutions should be nonprofit, controlled and staffed by residents of the community they serve, and supported by the people who benefit from them. Most charities and social service agencies do not qualify as alternative institutions because they are staffed and controlled by people who usually are not part of the community they serve; they therefore foster dependence.

The recent proliferation of community land trusts in this country is an exciting example of community-based, cooperative and decentralized organizations. Through these organizations, people are taking land and housing off the private market and putting them in their collective control.

I have been a board member of North Camden Land Trust in Camden, New Jersey since its inception in 1984. The land trust now controls about thirty properties. A group of thirty low income homeowners who previously were tenants without much hope of home ownership now collectively make decisions concerning this property. The development of the land trust embodies many of the elements that describe community organizing grounded in a social anarchist vision for society.

2. Increasing the control that people have over actions that affect them, and increasing local self-reliance.

This involves taking some measure of control away from large institutions like government, corporations and social service conglomerates and giving it to the people most affected by their actions. David Bouchier describes this function as attaining "positive freedoms." Positive freedoms are rights of self-government that are not dependent on or limited by higher powers (Bouchier, p. 9).

In the neighborhood where I live and work, residents are starting to demand control over land use decisions. They stopped the state and local governments' plan to build a second state prison on the waterfront in their neighborhood. Instead of stopping there, the residents, through a series of block meetings and a neighborhood coalition, have developed a "Peoples' Plan" for that waterfront site. Control of land use has traditionally rested with local government (and state and federal government to a much more limited extent), guided by professional planners and consultants. Neighborhood residents believe they should control land use in their neighborhood, since they are the ones most directly affected by it.

The concept of self-reliant communities described by David Morris (1987) also helps us understand the shift in power we are talking about. Self-reliant communities organize to assert authority over capital investment, hiring, bank lending, etc. — all areas where decision making traditionally has been in the hands of government or private enterprise.

3. Building a counterculture that uses all forms of communication to resist illegitimate authority, racism, sexism, and capitalism. In low-income neighborhoods, it is also important that this counterculture become an alternative to the dominant culture which has resulted from welfare and drugs.

The Populist movement can teach us a lot about building a counterculture. That movement used the press, person-to-person contact via roving rallies and educational lectures, an extensive network of farm cooperatives and an alternative vision of agricultural economics to do this (Goodwyn, 1976; 1981).

Every movement organization has to use the media to advance its ideas and values. Educational events, film, community-based newspapers, etc., are all important. The local community advocacy organization in North Camden has done a good job of combining fundraising with the development of counterculture. They have sponsored alternative theater which has explored the issues of battered women, homelessness, and sexism. After each play, the theater group conducted an open discussion with the audience about these issues. These were powerful experiences for those who attended.

The question of confronting the dominant culture in very low-income neighborhoods is one of the greatest challenges facing community organizations. Many families have now experienced welfare dependence for four generations, a phenomenon which has radically altered many peoples' value systems in a negative way. People must worry about survival constantly, and believe that anything they can get to survive they are entitled to, regardless of the effect on others. It has not fostered a cooperative spirit. The response of low-income people to long-term welfare dependency is not irrational, but it is a serious obstacle to functioning in a system of decentralized, cooperative work and services.

One experience in this regard is relevant. A soup kitchen called Leavenhouse has operated in Camden for 10 years, during nine of which it was open to anyone that came. A year ago, the soup kitchen changed into a feeding cooperative on weekdays. Guests now have to either work a few hours in the kitchen or purchase a ticket for five dollars which is good for the entire month. Daily average attendance has dropped from 200 to about 20. The idea of co-operating to provide some of the resources necessary to sustain the service is outside the value system of many people who previously used the kitchen. Leavenhouse realizes now that it must address the reasons why people have not responded to the co-op, and is planning a community outreach campaign designed to build some understanding, trust and acceptance of the idea of a cooperative feeding.

The 20 people who have joined the co-op have responded favorably. They appreciate the more tranquil eating environment and feel good about their role in it. The co-op members now make decisions about the operation of their co-op. Friendships and information sharing (primarily about jobs) have been facilitated. Fewer people are being served, but meaningful political objectives are now being realized.

4. Strengthening the "social fabric" of neighborhood units — that network of informal associations, support services, and contacts that enables people to survive and hold on to their sanity in spite of rather than because of the influence of government and social service bureaucracies in their lives.

John McKnight (1987) has done a good job of exposing the failure of traditional social service agencies and government in meeting people's needs for a support structure. They operate to control people. Informal associations ("community of associations"), on the other hand, operate on the basis of consent. They allow for creative solutions, quick response, interpersonal caring, and foster a broad base of participation.

A good example of fulfilling this purpose is the bartering network that some community organizations have developed. The organization simply prints a listing of people and services they need along with a parallel list of people and services they are willing to offer. This strengthens intra-neighborhood communication. In poor neighborhoods, this is especially effective because it allows people to get things done without money, and to get a return on their work that is not taxable.

Concerned Citizens of North Camden (CCNC) has supported the development of a Camden "Center for Independent Living" — an organization that brings handicapped and disabled people in the city together to collectively solve the problems they face. Twelve-step groups are another example of informal, nonprofessional associations that work for people.

Criteria For Success

Many community organizations measure success by "winning." The tangible result is all that matters. In fact, many organizations evaluate the issues they take on by whether or not they are "winnable." The real significance of what is won and how it is won are of less concern.

For organizations that embrace an anarchist vision, the process and the intangible results are at least as important as any tangible results. Increasing any one organization's size and influence is not a concern. The success of community organizing can be measured by the extent to which the following mandates are realized.

1. *People learn skills needed to analyze issues and confront those who exert control over their lives;*
2. *People learn to interact, make decisions and get things done collectively — rotating tasks, sharing skills, confronting racism, sexism and hierarchy.*
3. *Community residents realize some direct benefit or some resolution of problems they personally face through the organizing work.*
4. *Existing institutions change their priorities or way of doing things so that the authority of government, corporations and large institutions is replaced by extensions of decentralized, grassroots authority; and*
5. *Community residents feel stronger and better about themselves because of their participation in the collective effort.*

Picking Issues

Much of the literature about community organizing suggests that issues should be selected which are: 1) winnable; 2) involve advocacy, not service; and 3) build the organization's constituency, power and resources. "Good issue campaigns should have the twin goals of winning a victory and producing organizational mileage while doing so" (Staples, 1984; p. 53).

These guidelines have always bothered me, and my experience suggests that they are off the mark. Issues should be picked primarily because the organization's members believe they are important and because they are consistent with one or more of the purposes listed above. Let me offer a few guidelines which are a bit different.

1. Service and advocacy work must go hand in hand, especially in very needy communities.

People get involved with groups because they present an opportunity for them to gain something they want. It may be tangible or intangible, but the motivation to get involved comes with an expectation of relatively short-term gratification. The job of community organizations is to facilitate a process where groups of people with similar needs or problems work together for the benefit of all. Through this process, people learn to work cooperatively and learn that their informal association can usually solve problems more effectively and quickly than established organizations.

I will offer an example to illustrate this point. When Concerned Citizens of North Camden (CCNC) organized a squatter campaign in 1981, the folks who squatted and took all of the risks did so because they wanted a house, and because they believed squatting was the best way to get one. Each one of the original 13 squatter families benefitted because they got title to their house. The advocacy purpose was served because a program resulted that allowed 150 other families to get a house and some funds to fix it up over the subsequent five years. Because CCNC has stayed involved with each family and facilitated a support network with them (up to the present), 142 of the houses are still occupied by low-income families.

The government bureaucracy tried to undermine this program on numerous occasions, but without success. Participants willingly rallied in each crisis because they benefitted in a way they valued deeply. The squatter movement allowed them to win something that they knew they would never realistically be able to win through any traditional home ownership programs. The squatters were poor, most had no credit histories and most were Hispanic. Official discredit, for whatever reasons, was meaningless because people knew the effort had worked for them.

In my experience, I have never been part of a more exciting and politically meaningful effort than the CCNC squatting effort in 1981. The initial squatting with 13 families was followed by five years of taking over abandoned houses which the City reluctantly sanctioned because of the strength and persistence of the movement.

2. Issues that pit one segment of the community against another — for example, issues that favor homeowners over renters, Blacks over Puerto Ricans, etc. — should be avoided.

Most issues can be addressed in ways that unify neighborhood residents rather than divide them.

3. An informal involvement in broad political issues should be maintained on a consistent basis.

While I believe the kind of decentralized associations which form the basis for any anarchist vision of social change are most easily formed and nurtured at the local level (neighborhood or citywide), people must also connect in some way with broader social change issues. Social change cannot just happen in isolated places; we must build a large and diverse movement.

We need to integrate actions against militarism, imperialism, nuclear power, apartheid, etc., with action on local issues. They often can and should be tied together. This requires getting people to regional and national political events from time to time, and supporting local activities which help people to connect with these broader issues.

4. Avoid the pitfalls of electoral politics.

This is a very controversial area of concern for community organizations. The organizations I have worked with in Camden have vacillated in their stance vis-à-vis electoral politics.

The danger of cooptation through involvement in this arena is severe. Whenever a group of people start getting things done and build a credible reputation in the community, politicians will try to use the organization or its members to their advantage.

I have yet to witness any candidate for public office who maintained any kind of issue integrity. Once in the limelight, people bend toward the local interests that have the resources necessary to finance political campaigns. They want to win more than they want to advance any particular platform on the issues. We delude ourselves if we believe any politicians will support the progressive agenda of a minority constituency when their political future depends on them abandoning it.

I have participated in organizing campaigns where politicians were exploited because of vulnerability and where one politician was successfully played off against another. It is much easier for a community organization to use politicians to advance a cause if neither the organization or its members are loyal to any officeholder. My experience says that any organized and militant community-based organization can successfully confront elected officials — regardless whether they are friends or enemies.

Operation

For organizations committed to the long-term process of radical social change, the way they operate is more important than any short-term victories that might be realized. The discipline, habits and values that are developed and nurtured through an organization's day-to-day life are an important part of the revolutionary process. Some guidelines for operation follow.

1. Have a political analysis and provide political education.

Lower-class and working-class neighborhood organizing must develop long-range goals which address imbalances in a class society, an alternative vision of what people are fighting for, and a context for all activity, whether pressuring for a stop sign or an eviction blockage. Otherwise, as has repeatedly happened, victories that win services or rewards will undermine the organization by "proving" that the existing system is responsive to poor and working people and therefore, in no need of fundamental change (Fisher, 1984; p. 162).

Any organization which is serious about social change and committed to democratic control of neighborhoods and workplaces must devote considerable energy to self-development — building individual skills and self-confidence and providing basic political education. The role of the state in maintaining inequality and destroying self-worth most be exposed.

This is particularly necessary in low income and minority neighborhoods where people have been most consistently socialized to believe that they are inferior, that the problems they face are individual ones rather than systemic ones, and where poor education has left people without the basic skills necessary to understand what goes on around them. Self-esteem is low, yet social change work requires people who are self-confident and assertive.

This dilemma is another of the major challenges in community organizing. The socialization process that strips people of their self-esteem is not easily or quickly reversed. This problem mandates that all tasks be performed in groups (for support and skill-sharing), and that training and preparations for all activities be thorough.

2. Be collectively and flexibly organized; decentralize as much as possible.

Radical organizations must always try to set and example of how organizations can be better than the institutions we criticize. All meetings and financial records should be open and leadership responsibilities rotated. Active men and women must work in all aspects of the organization — office work, fundraising, decision making, financial management, outreach, housekeeping, etc.

Teams of people should work on different projects, with coordination provided by an elected council. Pyramidal hierarchy with committees subordinated to and constrained by a strong central board should be avoided. The organization must remain flexible so that it can respond quickly to needs as they arise.

3. Maintain independence.

This is extremely important and difficult. No organization committed to radical social change can allow itself to become financially dependent on the government or corporations. This does not mean that we can't use funds from government or private institutions for needed projects, but we can't get ourselves in a position where we owe any allegiance to the funders.

In 1983, the Farm Labor Organizing Committee was involved in a march from Toledo, Ohio to the Campbell's Soup headquarters in Camden, New Jersey. They were demanding three-party collective bargaining between Campbell's, the farmers it buys from, and the farm laborers who pick for the farmers. A coalition of groups in Camden worked to coordinate the final leg of the march through Camden. Many community-based organizations in Camden, however, refused to participate because they were dependent on donations of food or money from Campbell's Soup.

The bankruptcy of such behavior was driven home last year when Campbell's closed their Camden plant and laid off 1,000 workers. They made no special effort to soften the impact on the workers or the community.

All resources come at a price — even donations. We simply cannot accept funds from individuals or groups who condition their use in ways that constrain our work, or we must ignore the conditions and remain prepared to deal with the consequences later.

Alternative funding sources are providing a badly needed service in this regard. In Philadelphia, the Bread and Roses Community Fund raises money for distribution to social change organizations. In 1983, it spun off the Delaware Valley Community Reinvestment Fund, an alternative lending institution which provides credit for community-based housing and community development projects. Social change organizations in the Philadelphia/Camden area are extremely indebted to these two support organizations. They play a vital role in helping organizations to maintain their independence.

4. Reach out to avoid isolation, but keep the focus local.

Community-based organizations must maintain loose ties with other grassroots groups. Progressive groups should be able to easily coalesce when that makes sense. We can always benefit from ideas and constructive criticism from supportive people who are not wrapped up in the day to day activity of our own organization.

This is another way in which left-wing fundraising/grantmaking groups like the Bread and Roses Community Fund in the Philadelphia area play an important role. They identify and bring together those groups in the region with a similar political agenda. Through Bread and Roses, the community advocacy organization in North Camden (CCNC) has maintained a very loose but productive relationship with the Kensington Joint Action Council (KJAC) in Philadelphia. KJAC squatted first, and helped CCNC plan its squatter campaign. CCNC spun off a land trust first and assisted KJAC in the development of their own land trust, Manos Unidas. Some ideas they developed for their land trust in terms of building camaraderie among members are now being considered by North Camden Land Trust.

Statewide and national organizations try very hard to pull in active local organizations and get leaders involved in issues at the state level. Be wary of the drain this can place on the local work. Cloward and Piven, in their Poor Peoples' Movements, do a wonderful job of illustrating this danger in their discussion of welfare rights organizing. Successes are won via direct action, not via formal organization.

5. Do not foster cross-class ties.

This applies especially to community organizing in low income areas where the local resources are extremely scarce. Many well-to-do "do-gooder" organizations like to have a ghetto project. It makes them feel good. Community organizations do not exist to alleviate ruling class guilt. Dependency on upper-class skills and money is a problem. Poor and working people must wage their own struggle.

An illustration of this is provided by the soup kitchen in North Camden. Suburban church folks, once they heard about Leavenhouse, were more than willing to send in volunteers each day to prepare and serve the meal. Leavenhouse told them not to bother, except perhaps occasionally with two or three people at a time. This allows the soup kitchen to develop local ownership, and for neighborhood residents to feel good about taking care of each other. It avoids the traditional social service model where one group comes into the city and delivers a service to another group of people who lives there and takes it.

Leavenhouse does accept money and goods donations from outside the neighborhood, but its basic operating costs are covered with the rent of the community members who actually live at Leavenhouse. The outside income is extra; without it Leavenhouse will not shut down.

6. Have a cultural and social dimension.

Cultural and social events not only help to build a counterculture, but they help people feel good about who they are and where they come from. This is an important dynamic in overcoming powerlessness. Political music and film are especially effective in building class unity and strength, and in providing basic political education.

7. Staff the organization, to the greatest extent possible, with local workers and volunteers.

This seems to be obvious, but many community organizations draw on outsiders to perform the bulk of their work.

In Camden, nonprofit community organizations which provide affordable housing do it in three different ways. One organization matches suburban church groups with vacant houses. The church groups then purchase materials and provide volunteer labor to do the rehabilitation work. Another group relies on contractors to perform the work, few of which are based in Camden. A third group has hired and trained neighborhood residents to do all rehabilitation work. The workers are paid a decent wage for what they do. The latter approach develops skills in the neighborhood, allows neighborhood residents to feel good about improving their community, and fosters cooperative work habits which the construction grew members will carry into other organizations in the community.

Since the crew employed by the third organization is paid a decent wage, the first organization mentioned above rehabilitates more houses for less money. Again, when the commitment is to social change, the short-term tangible results are not the most important measures of success.

Tactics

A considerable body of literature has been written about tactics in organizing and political work. I do not want to rehash all of that here, so I'll offer just a few guidelines about tactics that have consistently proven themselves. The discussion here is relevant to advocacy campaigns designed to take some measure of authority from government or private interest and put it in community control, or to force a reallocation of resources (public or private) in the interest of the community.

1. Be disruptive

The tendency today is for community organizations to be less militant and confrontational, working through established community and political leaders to "engineer" the changes they want. No tendency could be more dangerous to the future of community organizing. The historical record and my experience say the opposite. We must be disruptive. No guideline is more important in the consideration of tactics. We can't move the system by testifying at hearings, negotiating at meetings and lobbying elected officials.

We must defy the rules of the system that fails to meet our needs. We must use guerrilla tactics that harass, confront, embarrass and expose that system and its functionaries.

2. Clear, precise and measurable demands are the cornerstone of any organizing campaign.

A group must know exactly what they want before they begin to confront the opposition.

3. Gradually escalate the militancy of your tactics.

The tactics in a campaign should gradually escalate in militancy, so that people new to political struggle are not intimidated. Let the militancy of the tactics increase at about the same pace as the intensity of their anger.

4. Address different targets simultaneously.

The tactics should be simultaneously directed at different parts of the system that are responsible for the injustice or grievance that needs to be resolved.

In the campaign to stop construction of a second state prison in their neighborhood, North Camden residents directed tactics at the Commissioner of Corrections, the private landowner who was willing to sell the waterfront to the state for the prison, local politicians, the governor and the two gubernatorial candidates.

5. Avoid legal tactics.

Legal challenges are difficult. They take a lot of energy and money, people who aren't trained in the law have a very difficult time understanding the process, and they are easy to lose. I have never experienced success with a legal challenge.

When North Camden residents opposed construction of the first state prison in their neighborhood, they sued the state on environmental and land use grounds because the state planned to use valuable waterfront land for the prison. After a year of preparations, the case was heard before an Administrative Law judge. He threw the case out on a technicality. Understand that he was appointed by a governor who made a public commitment to construct 4,000 more prison beds during his term in office.

Our legal system is set up to protect the interests of private property. Using it to dismantle the institutions that thrive on private property is obviously problematic.

6. Use direct action.

Direct actions are those that take the shortest route toward the realization of the ends desired, without depending on intermediaries. A simple example might help to clarify. If a group of tenants is having a problem with a landlord refusing to make needed repairs, they can respond in several ways. They could take the landlord to court. They could get the housing and health inspectors to issue violations and pressure the landlord to make repairs. Or they could withhold rent from the landlord themselves, and use the money withheld to pay for the repairs. Along the same vein, they might picket the landlord's nice suburban home and leaflet all of his neighbors with information about how he treats people. The first two options put responsibility for getting something done in the hands of a government agency or law enforcement official. The latter course of actions keeps the tenants in control of what happens.

At a major state-funded construction project in Camden, residents wanted to make sure that city residents and minorities got construction jobs. Following the lead of some militant construction workers in New York City, they organized people who were ready to work, and blocked the gate to the job site at starting time. Their position was simple: they would move when local people were hired. The group got talked into negotiating and supporting an affirmative action program that would force the contractor to hire local people whenever the union hall couldn't provide a minority or city resident to fill an opening. The enforcement of that program was so mired in red tape that only a handful of local workers got hired. The group would have fared much better if they had stuck with their original tactic — the most direct one.

7. Have fun.

The tactics used should be fun for the participants. This isn't always possible, but often is. Street theater can often be used to change a routine action into a fun one. Let me provide a few examples.

When Concerned Citizens of North Camden (CCNC) ran its homeowner program (the program which resulted from the squatting in 1981), the City tried various mechanisms to discredit it. On one occasion when they threatened to cut some of the public fund involved in it, CCNC conducted a funeral march with about 100 people and carried a coffin from North Camden to City Hall where a hearing was being held on the Community Development Block Grant funds. Right in the middle of the hearing, a squatter came out from inside the coffin and told the crowd how the people's movement could not be silenced and made a mockery of the whole hearing. The effect was spectacular, as was the press coverage the next day.

When trying to stop the second prison, residents circulated a special issue of the community newspaper that made fun of the land owner, the mayor and the Commissioner of Corrections. The front page of the paper included photos of the three, captioned with the names of the Three Stooges (the resemblance was striking). The text on the front page made fun of each person's role in the project. We circulated the paper at a big public meeting which all three of these individuals attended. It helped give people courage and set the atmosphere for people to freely speak their minds. When people talk about the prison campaign, they laugh and remember "the three stooges."

Finally, when the homeless problem started to escalate in Camden (1983), we learned that people were being turned away from available shelters because there was not enough space. Leavenhouse, the local soup kitchen, then started to serve its meals on the steps of City Hall one day each week. This created a party atmosphere; a couple hundred people would gather to eat and hang out every Wednesday at noon. As the weather got colder it became less fun, but the persistence was important. Three months after we started, in December, the City agreed to make a public building available as a shelter and agreed to adopt a policy that no homeless person would be denied shelter in Camden. The good aspect of this action was that homeless people were able to participate and help make it happen. It was a concrete way that they could have fun and feel good about helping to improve their own situation.

Concluding Comments

The kind of community organizing described here is not easy or straight-forward. It can be extremely frustrating, with many pitfalls, temptations and diversions pushing if off the track and allowing it to assume a more liberal posture. This article described some of the main challenges: overcoming the welfare/drugs culture; maintaining independence; and working with people with few skills and low self-esteem. One other deserves mention — mobility.

In our society, mobility is expected. People are supposed to move to take a better job, to find a better house, etc. It is acceptable to displace people to build new expressways and universities. The average American moves once every five years. This mobility affects the stability of community organiza-tions. Leaders and workers may get trained, get involved and then leave be-fore they have been able to give much back to the organization. The drug traffic in many low-income neighborhoods exacerbates the stability problem; families face crises on a regular basis which take priority over community involvement.

The revolutionary work of community organizations would be enhanced with more populations stability. Why aren't jobs created for people where they are? Why aren't a mix of housing types and sized available within all communities? Why isn't displacement avoided at all cost? We need to address these questions if our communities are going to be more fertile areas for com-munity organizing.

Community organizing from an anarchist perspective acknowledges that no revolution will be meaningful unless many Americans develop new values and behavior. This will require a history of work in cooperative, decentral-ized, revolutionary organizations in communities, workplaces and schools. The task before us is to build and nurture these organizations wherever we can. There are no shortcuts.

Works Cited

Alinsky, Saul D. *Rules for Radicals*. New York: Random House, 1971.

Baldelli, Giovanni. *Social Anarchism*. New York: Aldine-Atherton, 1971.

Bouchier, David. *Radical Citizenship*. New York: Schocken Books, 1987.

Boyte, Harry. *Community is Possible*. New York: Harper & Row, 1984.

Cawley, Kaye, Mayo and Thompson (eds.). *Community or Class Struggle?* London: Stage 1, 1977.

Ehrlich, Ehrlich, DeLeon and Morris (eds.). *Reinventing Anarchy*. Boston: Routledge & Kegan Paul, 1979.

Fisher, Robert. *Let the People Decide: Neighborhood Organizing in America*. Boston: Twayne Publishers, 1984.

Fisher, Robert and Romanofsky, Peter (eds.). *Community Organization for Urban Social Change*. Westport: Greenwood Press, 1981.

Foner, Phillip S. (ed.). *The Life and Writings of Frederick Douglass*. New York: International Publishers, 1975.

Goodwyn, Lawrence. *Democratic Promise: The Populist Moment in America*. New York: Oxford University Press, 1976.

Piven, Frances Fox and Cloward, Richard A. *Poor People's Movements*. New York: Vintage Books, 1979.

Kahn, Si. *Organizing*. New York: McGraw-Hill, 1982.

Lamb, Curt. *Political Power in Poor Neighborhoods*. New York: John Wiley and Sons, 1975.

Max, Steve. "Why Organize?" Chicago: Steve Max and the Midwest Academy, 1977.

McKnight, John. "Regenerating Community" in *Social Policy*, Winter 1987, pp. 54–58.

Morris, David. "A Globe of Villages: Self-Reliant Community Development," in *Building Economic Alternatives*, Winter, 1987, pp. 7–14.

Robinson, Chris. *Plotting Directions: An Activist's Guide*. Philadelphia: Recon Publications, 1982.

Roussopoulos, Dimitrios (ed.). *The City and Radical Social Change*. Montreal: Black Rose Books, 1982.

Schecter, Stephen. *The Politics of Urban Liberation*. Montreal: Black Rose Books, 1978.

Speeter, Greg. *Power: A Repossession Manual*. Amherst: University of Massachusetts, Citizens Involvement Training Project, 1978.

Staples, Lee. *Roots to Power*. New York: Praeger, 1984.

Ward, Colin. *Anarchy in Action*. New York: Harper & Row, 1973.

What begins as a discussion about the utility of taxes ends up as an indictment of bureaucracy. In detailing a life that spans from clerical work to prison internment, Meyerding offers first-hand accounts of how routine procedures — a hallmark of productive efficiency — are a dehumanizing force that allows individuals to absolve themselves of a sense of responsibility for the collective consequences of their actions.

Originally published in issue 13.

"Paying Taxes: It's Just Routine"
Jane Meyerding

The group of eight white, middle-class Americans had gathered to talk about war-tax resistance.[1] "I don't mind paying taxes," said one man. "In fact, I want to help pay for government services — for things like the highways and the national parks. But I don't want to pay for the arms race."

Going on around the circle, several other people gave their agreement to the first speaker's words, each adding an item or two to the list of government services they supported and wouldn't want to do without — subsidized railroads, environmental protection activities, food and drug safety regulations, the constitutional guarantees safeguarded by the Supreme Court, welfare, and son on. What a bleak and dangerous world it would be without the federal government!

Sitting there, listening to these good and thoughtful people, I began to feel like I'd been infected with a case of terminal cynicism. Every governmental beneficence mentioned by the group immediately turned over in my mind to reveal its negative side. "Highways" reminded me of the government's overinvestment in private transportation at the expense of public, mass transit. "National parks" produced a graphic mental image of animals and birds dying slow, painful deaths after exposure to government supported poisons spread to kill coyotes. (Not to mention the government supported policy of "denning" — burning baby animals alive in their dens.)

"Environmental protection" — the dismantling of the EPA and the raising of "acceptable" pollution levels (at the request of the polluting industries). "Food and drug safety" — DES (diethyl-stilbestrol), "acceptable" carcinogens, "dumping" of dangerous drugs in Third World countries. Even "welfare" produced no rosy glow in my mind. Although I was (and am) as safely white and middle-class as anyone in the group, I had known too many women and children forced to rely on this uncertain, oppressive, self-serving government bureaucracy.

Under what circumstances, I wondered, would I, too, want to pay non-war taxes?

The answer to that question, I suspect, is "never." As I see it, the government is a massive series of offices designed to establish and perpetuate routines. The purpose of these routines is to maintain the status quo — keep the poor poor and the rich rich, the powerful strong and the disempowered weak — while disguising the facts of responsibility. Reality — the bloody, personal reality of individual lives — is filtered through these offices and comes out as clean, dry, harmless, and impersonal statistics. If the established routing dictates that a certain number of individuals must freeze to death every winter because the are poor, or that certain amount of torture and murder must be supported (and supplied the wherewithal) because of US economic interests...well, that's just the way it works out. Nothing personal. These byproducts of government routing are seen as unfortunate but inevitable facts of life, rather than as symptoms of a very basic, systemic pathology.

Although incredibly resistant to change, the mass of governmental routine can spread itself very quickly to cover new situations. The Cuban "boat people" — the thousands of refugees who left Cuba for the US in 1980 — are a case in point. According to a newspaper report, 354 of these Cubans were incarcerated in the McNeil Island federal prison while the Immigration and Naturalization (INS) routine was applied to them; all 354 were men, and all had been accused and/or convicted of committing a crime in Cuba. Knowing nothing of this, I happened to answer a newspaper ad that winter for part-time transcription typists and wound up transcribing tape recordings of their INS hearings. The job paid $7 an hour — more than I've ever made, before or since.

As I sat there, wired to the tape player hour after hour, the INS routine through which these men were being processed gradually became clear to me. Certain INS forms and documents came up again and again in (and as) evidence: I-589, "the State Department letter," the Refugee Act of 1980.... Moreover, there began to grow in my mind a graphic understanding of how the hurriedly established routine presented a very different fact to its creators and administrators than to the Cubans who were its victims. A major reason for creating the routine, in fact, was to enable the individual human beings employed by the INS to "process" several thousand other human beings — the refugees — without the moral implication of the situation and their role in it.

I was amazed at how quickly a newly established routine can come to take precedence over the chaotic reality of human lives. In every case, the INS court upheld the artifacts produced by the routine as more valid than the living, breathing, remembering, spoken testimony of the Cubans themselves.

For example: several of the defense lawyers objected to the admission as evidence of the I-589 forms. An I-589 is a "request for asylum" and, in these cases, the I-589s were filled out by INS agents who were communicating with the Cubans through interpreters (many of whom were not fluent in modern Cuban Spanish) in a large barracks room filled with dozens of other agents interviewing other refugees through other interpreters while typists sitting at the same small tables with the agents, refugees and interpreters transcribed the agents' handwritten notes onto the forms. These interviews followed a period of intense stress and confusion — imprisonment in Cuba, sudden release, and virtual expulsion in many instances, after a televised invitation from the president of the United States saying the US would welcome them "with open arms." Then there was the crowded and dangerous boat trip to the near-mythical "land of the free" — where they were immediately imprisoned. The refugees had received mixed messages from all sides — for example, being told "sign here or you won't be released" and then being targeted for deportation on the basis of the "statement" they "voluntarily" signed. When I realized that the "applicant's statement" on the I-589 was actually the INS agent's version of what he thought the refugee meant to say to the interpreter, and that the hearing judge and even the refugees' own lawyers, despite their best efforts and the slow, relatively calm setting of the courtroom, were unable to understand many of the refugees' references to peculiarly Cuban institutions, customs, and cultural assumptions...

Well, it seemed patently obvious to me and to the refugees' lawyers that the I-589 forms were not worth diddlyshit as evidence. But listen to the judge: "I will overrule the objections. I admit this document as a statement made by the applicant. I admit it both for substantive and impeaching purposes. And I admit it as being a government document that was prepared in routine course" of INS procedures [emphasis added]. The document — born of routine — was considered a more trustworthy expression of the applicant's reality than his own words spoken there in the courtroom. And whenever there was a discrepancy between the routine-blessed document and the words of the human being, the judge invariably chose to believe the piece of paper.

We are governed by routines, not by men. Most men — and women — would not be willing to perform the "necessary" work of government if it were not disguised and morally neutered by its transformation into routine. Only because they are protected by routine are most people willing and able to "do very bad things before they are yet, individually, very bad" people.[2] Unfortunately, routine does not always protect its functionaries from eventually becoming the very bad people they would never have set out to be.

For example, consider the people who work in jails and prisons — not the prisoners, but the government employees. It is a tremendous moral responsibility to incarcerate people, a responsibility so deep, and so deeply moral, that most people could not stand it without the protection of established routine.

In this country, not only do jails and prisons remove individuals from their families, friends, and all the associations and activities which make up their daily, individual lives, they also subject prisoners to various intense forms of abuse. The primary form of abuse is the degrading assumption that the prisoners have consciously and deliberately chosen to behave immorally (as defined by the system) and thus have forfeited the right to basic respect for their lives and identities. Additionally, and in consequence, prisoners are abused by being deprived of adequate health care and/or subjected to medical maltreatment; by being denied humane living conditions as they are defined in this culture; and by the direct physical abuse of beatings and forcible drugging, All the abuses of the US injustice system stem, however, from the first abuse: the denial of the prisoner's humanity, the humanity they hold in common with those who imprison them. And this quintessential abuse — this denial — is made possible, and inevitable, by routine.

I remember when, during the first weeks of my imprisonment in a state penitentiary, I was among a group of newly arrived cons being given a tour of the prison. Well, certain parts of the prison, anyway. Our first view of the place — after the obligatory stripping and confiscation of personal effects, body cavity search, and delousing — had been limited to the isolation cell block. There we saw, in addition to our own small cell for 23 hours a day, only the one corridor where we were allowed to sit on the floor three times a day and smoke a cigarette. For company, we had the muffled screams and hoarse, distant hollers coming up through the floor from the hole — the punishment cells — in the basement.

One thing we did catch a glimpse of on our tour was the prison's main clerical office. I remember thinking, as we were led quickly through the emptied room, how familiar it looked: a largish room filled with old desks positioned so as to give each secretary the best illusion possible of a little privacy, a little place of her own, a little control over her own life. Since I was 16, I've worked mostly as a clerk/typist or a secretary, and I could have sat down at any one of those desks and felt right at home. Everything in the desk would have been exactly where I expected it to be: the stationery, the paperclips, the tea bags and stale sugar cubes. Like any office I've ever worked in, each desk carried a few personal items, too — virtually identical to those I'd seen a hundred times before: the picture of the kids, the perennially drooping plant that never blooms, the half-used box of cut-rate tissues. And yet...

The women who sat at these desks were no longer my co-workers, no longer the ones I routinely shared complaints and coffee breaks with. The work they did — their routine — was making it possible for the state of Connecticut to saturate my hair and scalp with DDT and forbid me to wash it off for 12 hours. The forms they typed and filed were what made it routine and acceptable for the man who called himself a doctor to force his hands into my vagina. Of course it was of much greater significance that the work of these secretaries was a part of what made it possible for the state to lock up hundreds of women, some of them sick, most them mothers of small children, for long periods of time in subhuman conditions. But somehow it was the details that caught at my mind as I was marched through that office. The personal details. Would the woman who worked every day at that desk be able to look in my eyes without anger, without shame, as these things were done to me?

I hope not. On the basis of my later experiences, however, I would guess that her acceptance of these mundane horrors would depend on how long she had work there. The routineness of such work provides a necessary psychological distance to those who do it and automatically functions as its own justification. The system of offices — the bureaucracy, and the hierarchy within that bureaucracy — ensures that the workings of any subsystem (for example, the injustice system of cops, courts, and cares) are so fragmented as to obscure the assigning of responsibility. And then the routine, should any questions arise, simply and effectively restores the status quo by means of the inarguable fact that "it's routine." "You're not responsible, it's just routine." "We always do it that way; it's routine."

I have heard judges publicly state that they have no responsibility for what happens to the people they sent to jail. To these functionaries in the judicial routine, there is simply no connection between their action (sending a person to jail) and the result of their action (the physical and mental damage done to that person by the violent guards and lousy conditions in the jail). You can lay it all out for them, say "this is what it's like in the jail; here is what happens to people you send there." But their routine must go on — because it is the routine — and other routines, though interdependent, are not their responsibility.

If judges, safe on their high and respected benches, can deny responsibility for their actions, how can we expect any more from those — the prison's clerical workers, for example — who are equally caught up in the established routine, though less highly placed, less distanced from their victims, less well respected, and far less well paid, The routine carries us all along, and the longer we depend on its comfortable reassurance ("don't worry, it's not your responsibility, not your problem"), the less we feel it when the routine requires us to cause pain to others.

It's happened to me that way. As a secretary working for a medical school M.D., (that is, a professor, researcher, and writer as well as a regular doctor), I've regularly had to answer phone calls from people in pain, worried about their symptoms, fearful of upcoming surgery, or angry at the quality of their treatment by the doctors other clinic personnel. It was the most rewarding part of the job, at first: dealing with people instead of tapes, papers, and machines; feeling I had an opportunity to help someone in need; and being more in touch with the clinical aspect of the work I was doing. Before long, however, I discovered that the established routines of the medical school/hospital/clinic complex made it virtually impossible for me to interact with these patients honestly, to give them the help they wanted, or to make this aspect of my job more meaningful to me than was the mechanical transcription of tape-recorded lectures and letters. I had no responsibility to the patients, only to the routine; my only responsibility was to carry out the routine prescribed for dealing with patient phone calls. I was to listen only long enough to assign each call to one of a few given categories and then route it according to the routine established for that category.

Most significant to me was the way this established routine managed to convert me from a rebellious individualist to a convinced and grateful user of the system. Here's how it happened: gradually, it became clear to me that my personal efforts to help each individual caller were not doing any good. No matter what special arrangements I tried to make for the patient's aid and comfort, as soon as the patient and I hung up our phones the established routine took over, ignored my efforts to make a special case out of the patient's problems, and continued to deal with the patient according to the same old laborious, bureaucratic, impersonal procedure as always. It didn't take long for me to get very frustrated by seeing my careful, time-consuming, and personal attention to individual patients get steamrollered each and every time. And like most people in such situations, I increasingly found myself taking out my frustration on the people on whose behalf I had originally wanted to do battle with the routine and all its supporters. I was still polite, of course; I'd be fired if I wasn't polite on the phone. But I put less and less of myself into it; it didn't do any good to take extra trouble, so why bother? The more fully I realized how little room there was in the routine for personal attention or personal responsibility, the more unreasonable patients seemed to me when they expected to be dealt with as individuals instead of categories. Phone calls from patients made me feel frustrated and angry, and eventually the transference was made: "Patients just cause trouble [that is, make me feel bad] calling up here, wasting my time, when there's nothing I can do for them. They ought to know better; they are tiresome fools." Blame the victim.

The ostensible reason for routines, of course, is efficiency, Without a routine, how can we possibly accomplish all that needs to be done, or deal with all the people who must be dealt with? The hidden reason for routines is that they obliterate personal responsibility for the results of one's actions, and therefore we don't have to care. We don't have to care about the people whose lives are controlled or impaired by or through the work we do, because our work is not personal. It's just routine.

Well, I think there are some things we should care about. Some things should not be handled by routine procedures, because then they begin to be seen as "routine" themselves. When imprisonment, for example, becomes a routine procedure (handled according to a series of established routines). The personal, individual horrors that result from incarceration also become routine, become acceptable, become perhaps even inevitable and — finally — necessary. And because they are part of the routine, no one is responsible for them. If some unusual circumstance (such as rebellion) makes it necessary to "deal with" these horrors — you guessed it: a new routine is developed (or an old one is adapted) to handle the problems caused by the original, unchanged routine. Examples of these secondary routines include the Nuclear Regulatory Commission; the "task forces" at all levels of government which intermittently study prison conditions, police brutality, racial and sexual discrimination, and so on; the "Animal Care Committee" at your local university's biological research facility; etc.

The basic fallacy, I think, is an increasing overestimation of our own abilities. We tend to believe we can easily handle not only prisoners, immigrants, and patients, but the whole world, if only we set up more offices to funnel the information through and more complex information management technology to process it into the familiar, dead statistics. But those statistics can give us only a distorted, misleading picture of reality, because the living reality of hundreds of millions of diverse, complex human beings is far beyond our capacity to understand, much less "handle." As far as I can tell from my own experience and my own slowly acquired knowledge of the world, each person is actually capable of handling no more than her own self — and sometimes not even that. It takes years of acculturation (the informal but rigorous equivalent of schooling) for a person to learn the skills of parenting in order to successfully "handle" — be responsible for — even one other person.

Nevertheless, we think we have the capacity, as a nation, to extend our self-interested manipulations worldwide through improved technology, and especially through our grasp of military technology. We think we are capable of handling the world by controlling the threat of nuclear mass destruction. Why do we think this? Picture in your mind the thousands of offices, thousands of rooms where individuals go every day to sit at their desks and handle the innumerable details of this routine by which we believe we control the world. Each person, like all of us, has a stake in her or his work, in her desk with its illusion of privacy and self-control, in his status as a person whose work is meaningful and respected, in the money each needs and is paid for performing fragmented pieces of the huge routine. Naturally, they have a stake in the routine: it's a vital part of their lives. And most of them are well able to handle the demands of their particular job. But they cannot handle — cannot be expected to handle — the responsibility for the destruction of the world and all of its inhabitants, even though their work is an integral part of the routine leading to that destruction.

Again, because of an established routine, the people whose actions cause or contribute to horrors and disasters are relieved of responsibility. Because we approach "mutual assured destruction" through an established routine, we are able to fool ourselves into believing that we are in control of the situation. It is precisely when — because an established routine is in operation — no one is finally, personally responsible, however, that the power of routine is most complete and most free from human control.

Although I am uncomfortable with the tendency of many new wave antiwar (for example, "nuclear freeze") people to overuse the metaphor of the holocaust, I can see a clear parallel here between the role of routine in that situation and in the situation we face today. How did the holocaust happen, after all? It happened according to a set of established routines:

> North of Munich was collection of old stone huts at a place called Dachau. Here Himmler built the first concentration camp: a prison in which communists and social democrats were incarcerated. Every aspect of the organization of this camp was controlled with bureaucratic efficiency. Forms appeared in triplicate, statistics were carefully maintained, and the ruthless machinery of the police state began to emerge.[3]

And later:

> At the Nuremberg trials each of the SS defendants justified his behavior during the war with great tenacity....They were only too ready to agree that "the war entailed much suffering," but by phrasing it in this passive *they*, they implied that they could not be regarded as active instruments in this process. They were victims of the war as assuredly as were those who had been killed. Their real enemy was Heinrich Himmler, the boss, who had no real understanding of administration, of how to run the business.[4]

Even when the routine has been smashed, the people who worked within the routine are unwilling, perhaps unable, to see that the responsibility was theirs all along. It was just routine, after all: just a matter of one little routine details after another.

Government routines are very powerful, they can be deadly, and I can't think of any circumstances under which I would want to pay for their support. Far better, for me and for the world, that I should use that same money — the money the government would otherwise take from me — to support and encourage those who are oppressed by governmental routines and those whose resistance exposes these routines as the deadly nonsense they really are.

Resources

The National War Tax Resistance Coordinating Committee (NWTRCC) is a coalition of local, regional, and national groups working on war tax issues. NWTRCC, P.O. Box 85810, Seattle, WA 98145. (206) 522–4377.

Endnotes

1   War tax resistance: the theory and practice of resisting payment of federal income taxes on grounds of conscience. War tax resisters often refuse to pay the percentage of their taxes that corresponds with the percentage of the federal budget spent on the military.

2   The quotation is from C. S. Lewis's *That Hideous Strength*, taken out of context.

3   Quotations from G. S. Graber's *History of the S.S.*, New York: David McKay, 1978.

4   Quotations from G. S. Graber's *History of the S.S.*, New York: David McKay, 1978.

This history of microwave (pirate) radio in the United States is devoted to the founding and expansion of a small radio station in Springfield, Illinois. WTRA began as a low-budget outlet in a housing project community, but the FCC's attempts to shut it down strengthened its resolve and helped politicize the movement.

Originally published in issue 17.

Anarchy on the Airwaves:
A Brief History of the Micro-Radio Movement in the USA
Ron Sakolsky

I n the United States, in response to the government carrot of licensing status and the stick of antipiracy crackdowns, many once-adventurous community radio stations have toned down their oppositional elements and have consciously or reflexively become engaged in a process of self-censorship. One signpost pointing to a road leading in a different direction is the micro-radio movement, originating not on a college campus or in a university-based community like many of the National Federation of Community Broadcasters (NFCB) stations, but in the heart of the black ghetto. The origins and evolution of this movement is an ongoing story that is consistent with an anarchist model of networking. The first five years of this history is recounted here with reference to WTRA/Zoom Black Magic Liberation Radio in Springfield, Illinois.

The story unfolds at the John Hay Homes, a sprawling, low-income public housing project located in Springfield's east side community. It is a housing project that is almost exclusively African-American. Located just a short distance from the enshrined home of Abraham Lincoln, it's a part of Springfield that isn't on the tourist map. During the mid-eighties, the John Hay Tenants Rights Association (TRA) was formed to do issue-based, neighborhood organizing.

Focusing first on expressway opposition and related school traffic safety issues, it then moved to the issue of the inadequate representation of the Eastside community under the archaic commission form of government. The TRA called instead for community control, opposed school busing, and even challenged the legitimacy of the local black bourgeoisie who claimed to represent them in an historic voting rights lawsuit then pending and which eventually replaced Springfield's commission form of government with an aldermanic one. They then opposed an ordinance sponsored by their newly elected black alderman which involved the purchase of scab coal from a Shell-owned mine, which violated the boycott on Shell in response to its South African holdings, and they politically skewered the alderman's plan for a weak-kneed civilian review board for the police, proposing instead a much stronger one modeled on that of Berkeley, California.

Angered and dismayed by media coverage of these actions and organizing campaigns, the TRA, in 1986, hit upon the idea of a community-based radio station to represent its point of view directly to its constituency and to communicate more effectively with a community which has an oral tradition and a high rate of functional illiteracy.

The idea was not unusual in itself. Nationally, ACORN (the Association of Community Organizers for Reform Now) had started to think about community radio as an organizing tool around the same time. However, the ACORN vision was more centralized in focus, more closely tied to coordinating national ACORN organizing goals among the local chapters, promoted relatively high wattage for maximum outreach, featured a professionalized model of radio programming, and was strictly legal.

In contrast, WTRA (as the station came to be called) was based on a decentralized model, had a symbiotic relationship to its community with no official membership base and no national ties, was low watt, disdained professional trappings, and was not only illegal in the eyes of the Federal Communications Commission (FCC), but defiantly so. Yet, because of Springfield's apartheid housing patterns, it was clear that even a station of less than a watt with a radius of between one and two miles could cover 70% of the African-American community, the prime audience which the station desired to reach. Since it was not to be a clandestine signal, it would, by its very openness, challenge the power of the federal government.

Given the TRA's non-compliance with FCC rules and regulations, though it continued to be involved in more mainstream community organizing activities, its primary funding agent, the Campaign for Human Development, canceled its grant. Fortunately, before that cancellation, $600 in grant money had already been spent to purchase the equipment necessary to set up the radio station. All that remained was to find an empty spot on the dial and start broadcasting.

The FCC model for radio broadcasters is based on scarcity. Asserting that the electromagnetic spectrum is finite, in the public interest, the FCC benignly agrees to act as the impartial gatekeeper for access to the airwaves, even though, as is typically the case with community radio, the signal is kept within state boundaries and involves no interstate communication. However, another explanation of federal radio communications policy might start with a question recently posed by M'banna Kantako, founder of the TRA and "deprogramming" director of the radio station since it has been on the air, "Why is it that in this country you cannot buy a radio transmitter fully assembled, but you can buy an AK-47?"

The persona of M'Banna Kantako has been intrinsically linked to the evolution of the radio station from its inception as WTRA, into Zoom Black Magic Liberation Radio, and, most recently, into Black Liberation Radio. It is from his apartment at the John Hay Homes that the station emanates, and his living room is a gathering place for political activists, neighbors and friends to discuss the issues of the day. It is a focal point for community animation in which grievances are aired and aspirations articulated around the radio transmitter.

His name wasn't always Kantako. At first, he used his given name, DeWayne Readus, but later discarded it as a slave name, choosing for himself the name M'banna Kantako, symbolizing refusal, resistance, rebellion, and a connection with Africa. According to Kantako, "We were on the air 3 years before the FCC bust. It was just a party thing, and we partied because we didn't know that we were being wiped out. Once we got hip to it and started to identify those things that are used to wipe us out, like the police, then we became a threat to the government, and then, of course, they used another apparatus, the FCC, to declare us illegal."

Just before the cease and desist order was issued, Kantako, who was himself blinded as a young man in a beating he took at the hands of the police, had broadcast a series of shows which involved community people calling in and giving personal testimony about police brutality, or as Kantako calls it, "official government-sponsored terrorism." Springfield Police Chief Mike Walton (later fired in a sordid sexual misconduct scandal) quickly complained about the illegality of the station to the FCC, and in April of 1989, the feds knocked on Kantako's door, demanding that he stop broadcasting or face a fine of $750 (that's $150 more than the cost of the station's equipment) pursuant to Section 301 of the Communications Act of 1934 for being an unlicensed station. Upon shutting down the station for a little less than 2 weeks to reflect on the situation, Kantako recalled from history that during slavery there had been laws against the slaves communicating with one another.

Bringing that history up to date, as Kantako told Rich Sherekis of the Illinois Times back in January of 1990, "We weren't sitting around when they made those laws about licensing... We were sitting in the back of the bus somewhere. So why should we be responsible to obey laws that oppress us?" Furthermore, as he pointed out later that month at a conference on radio censorship held in Chicago, those laws are selectively enforced. "If you are saying, 'Don't give a damn about nobody. Get you a house. Get you a dog. Get you a swimming pool, and the hell with everybody else,' then they will not only leave you on the air, they'll give you a bigger transmitter! But if you start talking about people coming together to fight against the system that's oppressing all of humanity, all across the planet, then they will find you. There is nowhere you can hide."

So, he decided to go back on the air as an open act of civil disobedience, risking having his equipment taken, with fines that could go as high as $10,000 and criminal penalties as much as $100,000 and one year in prison. By this act, WTRA was not simply resuming operations, but consciously challenging the exclusion of low income people, particularly African-Americans, from the airwaves and offering an affordable alternative. Since 1978, for the FCC to license a station, it requires a minimum of 100 watts (replacing the old minimum standard of 10 watts). Start up costs for such a station are around $50,000 (including equipment costs, engineering surveys, legal fees and proving to the FCC that you're solvent.) These requirements effectively silence many potential radio voices due to excessive costs.

As Kantako has put it, "It's kind of like those black tie dinners at $25,000 a plate. You can come, if you've got $25,000. For anything you need to survive, they put a price tag on it, and if you don't have it, you don't survive. They call our broadcasting controversial. We call it survival material." In relation to the police, such survival material today includes broadcasting local police communications live from the police scanner he has set up in his apartment to monitor the police, to (in a more humorous vein) making a recording at a Central Illinois barnyard of oinking and squealing pigs to be aired later for a full 90 minutes as a "secretly-recorded meeting at the Springfield police station."

While he likes a good joke at the expense of the police, when he flipped the switch to go back on the air, Kantako was very serious about his historical mission. In his words to the press that day, "Somebody tell the children how WTRA served as an advocate for the people when the police wouldn't police themselves…Somebody tell the people how we fought police brutality by broadcasting the personal testimonies of African-American victims." While he was not arrested, the FCC made clear to him that he was in violation of the code.

In spite of the fact that the station was well under 10, much less 100, watts, the only exemption to the FCC's licensing requirement seems to be fore extremely low power operations — 250 microvolts per meter — that can be heard no more than 25 yards away. So, unless it upped its wattage 100 fold, the station would not qualify for an FCC license. However, as Kantako has noted in expressing his contempt for the FCC licensing process, "Anything the government gives you, they can take away." He calls the FCC the "thought patrol." As he explains, "It's not legal in this country for people to do anything to empower themselves, and in particular the black community. Don't no government give you freedom of speech. Don't no government own the air."

Just who are the "thought patrollers?" According to John. T. Arthur in The Ace (The Association of Clandestine Radio Enthusiasts), the FCC's 1990 budget was $100 million, employing 1,899 people with a payroll of $72 million alone, 13 monitoring sites, and a myriad of signal offices. As he puts it, "These bureaucrats have the strange idea that they can suck in your tax dollars while they harass and intimidate you — the taxpayers — and all the while operate outside, or at the very edge of, American law." If you think this is far-fetched, consider that the FCC is presently trying to get official law enforcement status for Field Operations employees, permitting them to carry guns and make arrests. Yet the objectives of the FCC Commissioners, as listed in the 1990 Budget, call for the FCC "To Eliminate Government Actions That Infringe Upon The Freedom of Speech and The Press."

Kantako is calling their bluff by demanding that the government pay more than just lip service to the First Amendment's guarantee of free speech and the 14th Amendment, which provides equal protection under the law. In terms of the latter, while blacks compose 12% of the nation's populations, they only own 2% of its radio stations for an exclusion rate of 600%, which is even more dramatically high if class and gender are brought into the picture. Providing equal protection by waiving license requirements or by setting up a separate category for amateur or personal, low power community broadcasting licenses are political choices which the FCC seems unwilling to offer to the citizenry at the present time. Yet the 1934 Federal Communications Act calls for "fair, efficient and equitable" distribution of radio services. (Low power, community licenses has been recently suggested by Tom Kneitel of Popular Communications in a March 1991 editorial.)

The types of voices heard on WTRA when it started, and those heard on Black Liberation Radio today have changed over the years. This change represents a situation in which equitable access to radio for young people decreased as a direct result of the government clampdown on the station. While so far the FCC has not invaded Kantako's apartment or stolen his equipment, the local constabulary has upped the ante with a constant barrage of police harassment directed at anyone who has something to do with the station. This has particularly affected the youth who were once the mainstay of the station and who, like the station, were unlicensed, being essentially teenagers learning radio skills and doing live hip hop mixes on the air, laying down the black liberation soundtrack of the Nineties.

As the start there were as many as 16 young people regularly on the air. All 16 have now been expelled from school by the school authorities and their police patrols for, as Kantako puts it, "anything from reading books by Malcolm X to not wanting to eat red meat." In spite of the harassment, there are still youth involved with the station, but they come and go. Moreover, in addition to radio, many youth continue to be involved in TRA's Marcus Garvey Freedom Summer School and/or the Malcolm X Library.

It is because of such police retaliation that many stations choose to be clandestine, but the fact that the FCC and the Springfield police have not more directly attempted to shut the station down is probably related to its very visibility. Not only does it have a high profile nationally, with favorable articles appearing in a range of publications from the progressive press to underground 'zines, news stories on NPR and MTV, a potential constitutional court case ("Black Liberation Radio vs. the FCC") presently being researched by the National Lawyers Guild, but also it has support internationally from the World Association of Community Broadcasters (AMARC), along with articles appearing in the Italian and German press on the struggle.

Yet all of this publicity would not protect the station were it not for the strength of its grassroots community support. Kantako is not some outside agitator, but a lifelong resident of the community in which the station is situated. As he said recently, "I love to brag about the community I live in. This is a group of people that society has no need for and instead of laying down and dying, they've said 'let's arm ourselves with the necessary knowledge and we'll make a place for ourselves.' If those in charge of the money won't include us, then we'll include ourselves." Going full circle, it is just this kind of spirited resistance that in turn has generated the national/international support in the first place and continues to do so. In this regard, an attempt to evict the station from its local base in the John Hay Homes in July of 1990 was beaten back by a national letter writing campaign.

Nationally speaking, for a period of about a year, WTRA became involved with Zoom Black Magic Radio. Upon attending a Chicago conference on "Censorship On The Radio" which was put together by Lee Ballinger, associate editor of *Rock and Roll Confidential*, Kantako found himself on a panel with Walter Dunn, Jr., better known as the "Black Rose." The Rose, also an African-American, operates Zoom Black Magic Radio in Fresno, CA, a 125 watt unlicensed station with a 24 mile radius that has been busted twice by the FCC for being unlicensed. As the Rose put it in Chicago, "I don't have a radio license. Why should I waive a right for a privilege?" As a result of the conference, Kantako and Dunn, recognizing their complimentary struggles, symbolically linked their stations as parts of the Zoom Black Magic Radio family. Kantako even dropped the call letters WTRA as a further attempt to disassociate himself from official government labeling devices.

Today the link is merely one of informal solidarity. After hearing a sample tape of Zoom Black Magic programming, Kantako realized that his station was more oppositional in its stance than was the case for the Rose, and so the station added the word Liberation to its name (Zoom Black Magic Liberation Radio). According to Jim Hougan, who visited the Fresno station in 1990, "Dunn is a gadfly, not a revolutionary. His attacks on the black 'booooj-wah-zee' may be culturally subversive in the San Joaquin Valley, but he's not out to overthrow the government." Like Dunn, Kantako is critical of what he has called in one of his rap tunes, the "black rednecks," but his more radical inclinations eventually caused him to fully disassociate himself from the Zoom Black Magic name in 1991, when the station came to be called Black Liberation Radio.

Just as the choice of a name for the station has had important symbolic implications, so too the station grappled with choosing a phrase that would accurately describe its identity. Rejected immediately as a descriptor was the term "pirate radio." This was done for several reasons. Firstly, the term "pirate" conjures up piracy on the high seas and the connection between that piracy and the slave trade made it an unacceptable name. Secondly, the name has been associate with radio hobbyists, vanity broadcasting and radio hijinx, and Kantako was a serious programmer with a political message. Thirdly, the name "pirate" emphasizes illegality (what it isn't, rather than what it is), leaving out the chance to define itself positively. Finally, pirates are typically clandestine. So in spite of the term pirate's romantic outlaw image and the history of clandestine political broadcasting, a new term was chosen. It is the term micro-radio that Kantako uses to describe the movement of which he is a part and Black Liberation Radio is used to identify the station itself.

All of the above usages of the term pirate are, of course, a far cry from the original radio pirates of the Twenties that came on the air and usurped the frequencies and call letters of licensed stations in order pass themselves off as those stations whose credentials they hijacked. In fact, in recent times, this kind of trickery is more frequently done by the government than by privately operated pirate stations. For example, during the Gulf War, Clandestine Confidential (Feb. '91) reported a CIA pirate that probably used the studio of Radio Cairo to wage psychological warfare against the Iraqi troops and to provide disinformation to the Iraqi population by masquerading as Radio Baghdad, complete with the same introductory theme, bridge music and a hired actor impersonating Saddam Hussein. In a similar vein, the Voice of Free Iraq was almost certainly a British operation.

As to its political stance, a distinguishing feature of liberation radio is that it is counter-hegemonic. If it defines itself as a liberation radio station, the programming is expected to be openly oppositional. During the recent war in the Middle East, Black Liberation Radio was the only station in Springfield that offered a position that was vigorously critical of the US government with both the commercial stations and the university-based NPR station (WSSU) busily involved in collaborating with the process of manufacturing consent. As Kantako has said, "If anything, what people should have got out of the Persian Gulf Massacre is how tightly the media is controlled by the military industrial complex. …Your station will get community support if you start telling the people the truth because all over the planet folks are dying to hear the truth and one way this multinational conglomerate has stayed in charge is by purposely making the people ignorant."

In addition to news and commentary, Black Liberation Radio has a music policy that offers a "yard-to-yard" mix of hip hop, reggae and African music with a political flavor that consciously eschews racist, sexist or materialistic (my Mercedes is bigger than yours) music. As Kantako says, "Our music format is designed to resurrect the mind, not keep the mind asleep." He also plays "talking books" on black history, culture and liberation struggles that he receives from the audio service for the blind.

In addition to content, another way that the micro-radio movement intrinsically challenges cultural hegemony is on the networking level. It is a model of organization concerned more with spreading information that with hierarchical control. In this regard, Kantako has even produced a 20 minute video on how to set up your own micro radio station which he has distributed widely around the country to those wanting to get started. I recently asked Kantako what his vision was for the micro-radio movement, since it is a term he coined himself. He replied, "I would like to see lots of little stations come on the air all over the country so you could drive out of one signal right into another. If you have a gap. You could run a tape until the next one came into range. I'm not interested in big megawatt stations. When you get too big, you get what you got now in America which is basically a homogenized mix of nothing, a bunch of mindless garbage which keeps the people operating in a mindless state. We think that the more community-based these things become, the more the community can put demands on the operators of these stations to serve the needs of that community."

So, anarchist that I am, I envision myself behind the wheel of my van, cruising the USA of the future with a map of micro radio stations lighting my way from coast to coast, reflecting the wide array of cultural diversity that exists beneath the surface gloss — a vision that is the antithesis of the lockstep national unity of the new world order.

I smile broadly as I recall a recent radio interview with Kantako in which he was asked what he would do if the FCC came and took his equipment. "We're prepared," he said, "to be a mobile station until we get some equipment again. We can run our station off of a 10-speed bike if necessary." Then, when asked, "How can our listeners support you in your struggle? Should we write the FCC?" M'Banna's reply was immediate, "Go on the air! Just go on the air!"

"I am a woman living in an egalitarian and intentional community." In this first- person case study, Syd describes her motives for participating in this village-like communal living situation—a society where she can live out anarchist theory in practice. This comprehensive glimpse of life at Twin Oaks offers insight into direct-democratic decision-making, flexible work options, shared income, and communal property.

Originally published in issue 17.

Living in Community
A Look at Twin Oaks in the Context of the Contemporary Communities Movement
SYD

I am a woman living in an egalitarian and intentional community. We call ourselves "egalitarian" primarily because we are income-sharing, but also because in theory and in practice (in work, games, decision making and child-rearing) we advocate equal rights for all human beings. There are no bosses here. We have managers who oversee budgets of labor and money, and who take responsibility for recruitment and general operations oversight in their areas, but they receive no extra privilege or wealth because of it. The communal setting is intentional because we are much more explicitly and implicitly involved with one another than people in a non-intentional community (i.e. most neighborhoods). There are hundreds of intentional communities existing in the US alone.

The particular community to which I belong is called Twin Oaks, which was established in 1967. We have about 70 adult members and 11 children here currently, a number that has been fairly stable over the past fifteen years. Twin Oaks is a member of the Federation of Egalitarian Communities (FEC), a network of closely aligned communal groups formed in 1976.

The FEC's goal is to help people discover the advantages of a communal-living alternative through outreach, to provide services to member communities that the groups alone could not afford (by sharing skills and resources), and to promote the growth of a more sustainable and egalitarian world. We cooperate on publications, conferences, and recruitment efforts, and provide mutual support and information to one another, including labor exchange between member communities. Each of the Federation communities:

- holds its land, labor and other resources in common;
- assumes responsibility for the needs of its members, receiving the products of their labor and distributing these and all other goods equally, or according to need;
- practices non-violence;
- uses a form of decision making in which members have an equal opportunity to participate, either through consensus, direct vote or right to appeal or overrule;

- works to establish the equality of all people and does not permit discrimination on the basis of race, class, creed, ethnic origin, age, gender, or sexual orientation;
- acts to conserve natural resources for present and future generations while striving to continually improve ecological awareness and practice;
- creates processes for group communication and participation and provides and environment which supports people's development (from "Sharing the Dream," a Federation brochure).

The FEC is also associated with the Fellowship of Intentional Communities (FIC), a loose network of other intentional but quite disparate communities and the FEC is a member of the National Communal Studies Association, the International Communal Studies Association, and the North American Students of Cooperative Organizations.

Why I Chose Intentional Community

Twin Oaks offered me some exciting prospects: clear streams, clean air and beautiful rural woodlands; organic gardening; a place to learn and share skills; a place where gender stereotypes are challenged and experimentation with lifestyle accepted; a socially conscious group of self-motivated individuals.

In as many ways as possible, I wanted to quit using energy and materials, including my own human energy, for the purpose of profits placed before human needs. I wanted to stop relying upon and contributing to boring systems not aimed at supporting human development.

I made the decision to live outside of mainstream society so that I would not have to drive a carbon monoxide-spewing car every day down concrete and asphalt during the same hours that everyone else is also trying to get someplace to punch a clock; so that I wouldn't have to buy $200+ outfits in order to "look presentable" to a boss, and to use chemicals on these suits to have them dry-cleaned after every third wearing. I moved to intentional community so that I could devote at least half of my work efforts to something that made the world a better place; not dirtier, or fancier for the rich who can afford to buy it, or more entertaining to distract us from the real problems in this world.

Community is one place where I could put my feminist utopian anarchist theories to the test. I do not have to appear as a doll or a shell with no brain of my own in order to be pleasing to men. I am not required to put efforts into keeping my body within a range of desirability for fucking: to have make-up on my face, to shave my legs, to wear nylons, to take much time and consideration in choosing and matching my wardrobe, or to wear high heels or other clothes or accessories that would interfere with my ability to move freely and comfortably. I realize that women can and do realize at least some of these physical liberations in places other than intentional communities, but in addition I really appreciate being free of obnoxious billboards, and blatant sexist remarks. We still have our share of racist, sexist, and classist baggage to deal with, but the overt maliciousness is greatly reduced here. I also like not having strangers for neighbors.

Also important for the liberation and growth of women is the issue of safety. At no time of day or night do I feel physically endangered at Twin Oaks. Even when I feel that someone is very angry at me here, I trust that our commitment to refrain from physical violence would deter most members, even if only for fear of expulsion. Also, I feel that my housemates are close at hand and would provide support if necessary. I know of no physical assault against a woman to have occurred here. We have over 400 acres of land which I can roam freely and feel insulated by. I can be alone, or with others, and not fear harassment or injury. I think that this kind of freedom from threat of harm is difficult to find elsewhere, and the influence of such an omnipresent threat takes its toll on women physically, mentally, and emotionally. To say that there is no coercion, deceit or vengeance here would be untrue — there are mental and emotional kinds of violence that we must stay alert to, and people obviously experience these in varying degrees.

No one comes here practiced for Utopia. I found that we all bring our socialized selves with us, each with a different level of commitment and idea of what the ideal community is. We have plenty of disagreement and changes to make, but each new problem brings us a broader horizon and more experience to draw upon.

Twin Oaks: A Village-Like Society in Itself

At Twin Oaks we support ourselves by growing a lot of our own food and having cottage industries on the farm that earn us income to buy the things we cannot provide for ourselves. We design and build our own buildings and maintain them almost entirely by ourselves. We even have our own sewage treatment plant. We live in group residences, not nuclear family homes, own all the property (land, vehicles, buildings) together, and use input from all members to make decisions affecting the community. The community provides all the basic necessities of living: food, shelter, utilities, clothes, health care, and toiletries. Members and children each receive an allowance for the extras we like to buy. Twin Oaks functions as a small cooperative society thriving in central Virginia, trading or buying goods and services from the "outside" society only when necessary.

The people living in Twin Oaks have agreed to uphold the fundamental values of cooperation, non-violence and sharing. We strive to be a model of a society that is fair and equal. At Twin Oaks, we practice income-sharing. We decide together how we will spend the money that we have made each year with the community's industries. Except for $45 a month for each member (the current personal allowance), all of our income goes into maintaining and/or expanding our community: buildings, materials, or amenities that are for members' use.

We have a community agreement that we will keep a balanced gender ratio in the membership. With a few exceptions we routinely work, eat and recreate in mixed gender groups. We have one floor of a resident reserved for women's rooms only, with a library that is "Women's Space" after 6:00 in the evenings.

We are not a religious group, so we rely on our shared social and economic vision to provide some degree of cohesion. Twin Oaks embraces the idea of diversity, which can make group unity more difficult. In practice, we often are caught in a pattern of choosing uniformity. Our commitment to maintain the personal autonomy and comfort of members (often before meeting the needs of visitors) is a conflict in an all-inclusive egalitarianism.

Avenues to Empowerment

My personal lifestyle in community is empowering and self-affirming. Particularly because I am a woman, I feel it is important to share my story and offer the resources of the Intentional Communities Movement to other women. Because I see part of my privilege as being educated in academia, I want to include those in mainstream educational systems in my outreach. I owe my first exposure to the principles and theory of anarchism to a professor I had in a private college in Minnesota (thank you Wendell Bradley)! I have found it extremely fulfilling to begin living the ideals of a non-hierarchical political and economic system now, and relieving myself of the guilt of being merely an armchair intellectual, a radical theorist with a lack of radical change being manifested in my personal life.

The structures at Twin Oaks help to sustain the egalitarian ideals we have. The most obvious is our income sharing policy and property code. The monetary benefits we reap from the community are the same, regardless of gender or what work one does or how long one has been a member. The property code says that members cannot keep private property or assets that earn them income while living at Twin Oaks. (The option remains to manage property or have a community account that earns income for the community to share, while one is a member. The principal of the account would be returned to a leaving member.) We may bring personal possessions with us if we can keep them in our bedrooms. We do not own personal vehicles, and don't have room for lots of clothes or furniture. The community buys cars, trucks and vans that any member may use, and furnishings for all public and private spaces are provided by the community.

We value domestic labor (housekeeping, child care, cooking) at the same rate as income-producing work. This empowers members who have children to have choices about being with kids and not losing work credit, or not always doing child care, because there is cooperative care provided. We encourage skill-sharing and consciously open up non-tradition work opportunities for both men and women. Consequently, we have women who maintain our vehicles, drive tractors and do construction, and men who can competently care for children, do laundry and cook. All of these job assignments are still voluntary, of course.

Our labor system works by people claiming credit for work done. We trust that everyone records their work honestly. This and other practices such as not having locks on doors, having easy and equal access to the use of our vehicles, and the community checkbook being available to any member are policies based on trust that feel personally empowering to me.

Work Doesn't Have to be Painful

The labor system at Twin Oaks gives me a great deal of choice and flexibility. Each week I decide how much and what kinds of work I want to do. Except for washing dishes and cleaning bathrooms (which are rotated among everyone) all jobs are filled voluntarily by those who live here. As long as I complete my share of the work, no one complains about what kind of work I do. I can also choose when and how to work. If I would like to sleep until 10:00 some days, or every day, I can decide to do that without asking anyone's permission. I can schedule work with friends, or discuss business over a meal. Knowing when to stop working and limit myself to personal or recreational thoughts sometimes is a great challenge for me here without clear boundaries of my work spaces. It can be a great pleasure, however, to feel an affinity with my co-workers, knowing we have a greater goal in common than simply a menial and temporary task.

Work and play can be somewhat integrated here. I can choose some tasks that are solitary, and others where I can be in a social environment. We try to make all workplaces as enjoyable as possible.

A "work week" is currently 47 hours, but that number is not comparable to the standard 40-hour work week in mainstream society. At Twin Oaks, "work" includes such things as washing dishes, shopping, attending to children, doing personal laundry and maintaining one's residence. No one in our community has to go someplace else to work. We all get a minimum of two and half weeks of vacation a year, but by working "over quota" (more than the 47 hours/week) we can save up labor credits to take more time off. An average Twin Oaker takes about six weeks of vacation a year.

Each year we host a women's gathering with the theme of "Celebrating Our Diversity" which I have had the opportunity to help organize. This is an exciting way to meet and connect with women who live outside Twin Oaks and to build solidarity among the Twin Oaks sisters. This is a prime example of integrating work and fun!

Some Specific Work Areas

I choose to participate in several of our work areas. I can also change my schedule from week to week. Part of my work is with the Federation. I've also helped to manage the visitor program. One day of the week I am a driver and errand person. I have done gardening, child care, construction, and vehicle servicing. I have become comfortable working with big machines and power tools, and have learned how to drive standard transmission vehicles since I moved here.

I also make hammocks, which are our main source of income. Almost everyone at Twin Oaks makes hammocks some of the time, so the work is very spread out and flexible. We can weave any time of the day or night, indoors or out in the sun, alone or with a friend, or even at meetings. We also have an indexing business and a chair industry. We hope to begin a soyworks operation this year to produce tofu and other food products.

Quality of Life

Twin Oaks tries to make use of the many resources we have available on our land. We have a large library, a river to swim in, community-selected videos (art, popular, and documentaries), yoga, co-counseling classes, a large music collection, dances and parties, high quality amateur dramatic productions and talent shows, canoeing, woodland walks and stunning sunsets, but no network television. This allows and encourages us to create more of our own culture; to be active, creative participants in our environment rather than passively accepting what the media wants to feed us. I enter into artistic projects with people occasionally and constantly observe the skills and talents around me. My life feels like a thorough, well thought out, unfolding, developing, exciting, important political act. I get to feel, viscerally, how the personal is the political and vice versa. The two are intertwined. I am living, improving, developing a life based on sharing, cooperativeness and nonviolence.

I have access to current political information here that the community purchases, as well as petitions, newsletters, and chances to participate directly in movements, because I am surrounded by others here who also want to make a difference in the world. We have a community fund where I can get monetary support and/or labor credit for doing "outside" political work. We also donate thousands of dollars each year to organizations whose causes we support. Many people here participate in electoral or grassroots politics on some level.

A Political and Economic Statement

Just by living here, I reduce my reliance on the capitalist market/distribution system and the Almighty Dollar. I actually extract dollars from the profit-seekers, because we all buy fewer non-essential items here, and there are economies of scale that allow fewer trips to the store, fewer appliances, and therefore lower capital investment and energy use per capita. By not seeing mainstream magazines, billboards, or network television, we are not as prey to manufactured "needs." The food we do buy is in bulk (less packaging), and the entertainment I get is mostly shared (books, music, conversation, talent shows) and not purchased. We generate far less waste per person than in the average North American household. About half of our food comes from our organic gardens. Our excess food is composted, turned back into the earth to give the soil nutrients. I can relate more in harmony with plants, animals and people here than elsewhere. I get to pet a calf, say hello to a cat, and spend time with a young child, in the amounts I want to. I do not have to own them or be responsible for them all the time, which happens to suit me well.

We practice direct democracy here, with no political or spiritual leader. Since we are a secular community, the cohesion we have is based on the fundamental values we share and the friendship and respect we have for one another.

I work on the quality of my communication here and get support for that. I find more people at Twin Oaks than in most settings I'd lived in before who care about the way we talk, and devote time to getting clear understandings, being precise.

Without paying someone to listen to me, or to make a syllabus for me, I can engage others in a discussion on a topic of interest or a particular book. Beyond the material infrastructure we have build, we have a self-determined environment for learning: to think, to ponder, to read, to communicate, to give feedback and share with one another what's good, what could be better. We compare outlooks together on what's really going on in the world, share predictions for the future, ideas that we can work on together. Because of our intentioned connection which goes beyond any classroom or office, we seek to know how we might encourage each other more by support and affirmation than by competition.

I don't know if I'll be here for the rest of my life, but intentional community of some kind seems a spiritual and political challenge that I'm sure will play a part in my life for a long time to come.

Endnote

If you would like to order the Directory of Intentional Communities, a 310 pp. Reference about existing communal groups and cooperative resources, or books specifically on Wimmen's Land, write to: Community Bookshelf, Rt. 1. Box 155, Rutledge, MO 63563.

In another account of communal living, William Walker describes a scenario called the roundhouse co-op, in which small groups of people share space, property, child-rearing and even sexual partners on a rotating basis. As with many other valid organizational structures for a commune, the roundhouse format comes with its own issues and constraints, and maintaining an optimal size group can be a delicate task.

Originally published in issue 13.

The Roundhouse Co-op:
A possible alternative to the nuclear family, communal family, and "free association" formats
William F. Walker

T he nuclear family — with or without an attendant extended family organization — and the harem remain the dominant forms of family organization in nearly all present societies. Polygyny and various forms of communal or cooperative family organization are the rule in a few societies and are present as a minor counterculture component of many Westernized nations. In most Western societies, where the traditional extended family organization is often lacking or geographically fragmented, single adults with children, and loosely adherent extended families formed through serial polygamy (divorce and remarriage) or by two or more divorced same-sex adults and their children living together, have become important adjuncts to the nuclear family.

Anarchists traditionally have advocated "free associations" between the sexes with minimal contractual obligations. However, such issues as property, liability and income, rights and obligations, and parental responsibilities are often poorly delineated in such relationships. Also, many people would feel unduly insecure with such a tenuous hold on a partner. Some anarchists have instead opted for various forms of the communal family. Although anarchist communes often try to minimize the common problems experienced in more collectivist communes, in practice this is often difficult to achieve or creates its own problems.[1]

In some Western nations, greater acceptance of living together without a marriage contract and easy divorce have considerably reduced the contrast between how mainstream society actually operates and how anarchists think it should operate. In addition, less generally accepted options such as extramarital affairs, long-term mistresses, mate swapping, and spouses working in different cities or living in different apartments provide at least part of the familial variety of opportunity for auxiliary romances and feeling of partial independence that many adults desire within a traditional nuclear family structure.

Again, these options serve to partially remedy those limitations of the nuclear family that strike fear in the hearts of many anarchists. Given enough time, imagination and open-mindedness, is it possible that the nuclear family can and will be patched up with enough escape clauses to allow it to function as a reasonable facsimile of the anarchist's ideal? Perhaps for some. However, I propose that there is a better way for many people, for at least part of their life — perhaps better than "free associations" or communes, under the right circumstances. That way is what I call the roundhouse co-op and closely related forms. To my way of thinking, the roundhouse co-op has the potential to achieve most of the desirable features of the "naked" nuclear family, the extended nuclear family, "free associations" and communes, while minimizing most of their respective potential shortcomings.

The "naked" nuclear family is heir to the "extended" nuclear family, just as today's mobile individualistic societies grew out of largely stationary clannish societies. The "naked" version has lost some desirable as well as undesirable influence of the extended version. The latter often has served as a buffer against some of the internal and external vulnerabilities experienced by mates in "naked" families. On the other hand, an extended family may hinder individual expression and technological progress, especially when older members of a clan exert a domineering authority over younger adults. The roundhouse co-op, unlike some modern communal organizations, is designed to replace much of the lost buffering function of the extended family with a minimum of group interference in individual freedom. Of course, friends and family often partly serve this function in "naked" nuclear families and "free associations." However, additional intimates are likely to be the most effective for many buffering functions.

In general, it is expected that roundhouse co-ops will consist of four to eight people. More than eight is likely to be undesirably unstable in personnel composition, awkward to accommodate in the orthodox roundhouse living arrangement, may give the group the appearance of being too powerful, and may provide too dilute a commitment to and understanding of the individuals with whom one is intimate.[2] In the most orthodox version, equal numbers of each sex are included, in the case of purely heterosexual groups. If only four people are involved, a variant of the roundhouse living arrangement, the shuttlehouse co-op, may be a simpler design. In this arrangement, each person has his or her own section of the overall residence. A moveable partition between each two sections allows an individual to close off direct contact with either or both cospouses. In general, it is expected that one partition will be open most of the time and that the two partitions will alternate after an arbitrary time period. When the group is feeling especially cosy, the may want to open all partitions. This type of physical arrangement cannot be extended beyond four people without some compromises. It is possible to have a larger network shuttlehouse co-op, with overlapping shuttlehouse units. Also, a larger communal organization might consist largely of shuttlehouse or roundhouse units.

With more than four people, the co-op may want to go to the orthodox roundhouse type of living arrangement, which consists of an outer and inner set of apartments arranged in a circle. The inner set can rotate, whereas the outer set does not. This arrangement may involve the entire apartments or just an upper bedroom section. In both the shuttle and roundhouse living arrangements, the idea is to provide conditions that encourage each person to live temporarily as a pair with each cospouse, while having their home base close at hand. The rotation periods need not be even, as some pairs may be more compatible than others at a given time. Especially in the case of larger, relatively less cohesive co-ops, the short-term pair or nuclear family setting may provide individuals with the psychologically rewarding illusion of being more than isolated individuals within a group. Also, each potential pair within the co-op is "forced" to assume the identity of a pair (unless strong objections are voiced). I think this will help to discourage the development of factions and jealousies which could threaten the integrity of the co-op. It provides an obvious cue as to "who's whose" at a given moment in those co-ops where the temporary pair is given strong emphasis. (Of course, it is not expected that this cue is to be slavishly obeyed at all times!) Presumably, this will tend to reduce the time and hassles often involved in negotiating sex in a more unstructured group setting. Thus, I see adequate emphasis upon the rotational nuclear family within co-ops as a stabilizing influence for many co-ops, as well as being desirable psychologically for many people. Certainly, I expect the importance of these factors to vary from one co-op to the next, and through time within a given co-op.

The simpler arrangement, where the co-op members occupy a series of separate apartments or bedrooms within a dwelling may serve adequately or even better than the roundhouse arrangement for some. Especially, co-ops that tend to function as a tight-knit social group may "get by" without a special physical arrangement to pair the various combinations of spouses. However, I believe the long-term stability and personal satisfaction within most such groups would be significantly increased by the roundhouse or shuttlehouse design.

The individual in a "naked" nuclear family can be in a very vulnerable position with respect to his or her own spouse. If that spouse becomes temporarily incompatible, violent, permanently disabled, alcoholic, workaholic, unemployed, financially bankrupt, mentally ill, wants to move far away, dies, engages in criminal activities, etc., these can completely dominate one's life in a negative way. In addition, the nuclear family can (but need not) be a prison to those who either have or develop close physical or emotional relationships with others of the opposite sex. Some people commonly suffer "burnout" with one legitimate spouse, especially if the spouse is overly possessive. Friendships with either sex may be limited by their appeal to one's spouse. Easy divorce has reduced the potential magnitude of these negative influences, but still there is often a reluctance to leave when it appears one is leaving purely to escape the spouse's bad luck. Others are reluctant to leave because they feel they have no realistic alternative, or fear retaliatory bodily harm by their spouse.

With communal ownership of property and money in nuclear families, there is the opportunity for constant bickering over finances, gold digging, communal liability for debts and negligence, etc. The nuclear family tends to promote overpossessiveness[3] and competition between rival lovers and families. Children are also vulnerable to the weaknesses, abuse and ill luck of their parents. Nuclear families are, of course, generally more readily mobile than larger groups, an important factor in highly mobile societies. However, larger groups are not necessarily expected to be less stable in personnel composition than nuclear families if the group structure helps to stabilize satisfaction within the family.

Communal family arrangements serve as one alternative to those who are turned off by the real or imagined problems with the nuclear family format. Thus, vulnerability to the present or future quirks, abuses and weaknesses of one spouse or set of parents is much reduced. Presumably, overpossessiveness and envy are discouraged. Income and wealth is often put in a common pot. People may choose to have children or can be sterile while allowing otherwise very compatible mates to have children. Legitimate variety in sex or platonic romantic partners is often provided, eliminating the problem of burnout. Also, one is unlikely to find her- or himself alone as the head of a household of kids. Children can be reshuffled to allow the most compatible combinations to interact the most.

But as a good anarchist, maybe you don't want to completely surrender your individuality, privacy, wealth or your freedom to work outside of a communal framework. Maybe it's good to have a degree of possessiveness toward certain material goods and personal accomplishments outside the commune. Many people would not want to relinquish these freedoms or luxuries, once tasted. Also, some communes are ruled by an informal elite based on seniority or aggressiveness (see Whole Earth Review 51:78, and 53:139), even though equality is supposed to reign. The danger of rape or VD spread in large communal groups and the possible hassle of constantly having to negotiate

romance may discourage many from communal families.⁴ The fact is that
even in most long-lived communes in North America, the commune is only a
transient stage lasting perhaps a few years in the lives of most of its members.
Perhaps that is all some of them expected of it. Many others leave because of
disillusionment.⁵

The roundhouse co-op is designed to promote most of the buffering and
group comradeship functions of communes while minimizing most of their
too-frequent traits that many consider undesirable, if not intolerable. Thus,
even between the sexes there is no communal money or property (unless
such is agreed upon), although some income redistribution between the sexes
would probably be standard. It is important (for peace of mind) that members of a co-op not be liable for the debts and negligence of other adults in the
co-op. Such matters should be spelled out in detail in the marriage contract.
An important potential function of the co-op would be for wealthier members to provide low-cost working capital for poorer members to get started
in a business or career. The latter may otherwise lack a source of sufficient
starter capital at a reasonable cost. The members of the co-op can have work
lives independent of each other. Individuals can move to another area for an
extended period as a job or schooling dictates without placing excessive child
rearing burdens on the remaining members, and without the need of dragging along spouses who would rather stay where they are. As in the case with
most communes, there would be group responsibility for children.

Roundhouse co-ops may be more prone to certain problems than nuclear
families or free associations. Greater instability in personnel composition due
to a greater number of people is intrinsic. This instability seems a small price
to pay for the added security and variety of multiple mates. Hopefully, the
greater choice of possible partners in the co-op may be a stabilizing factor.
Jealousies may be more frequent, especially with extreme contrasts in wealth
and other measures of career success, popularity, etc. This is probably the
single most dangerous factor likely to threaten the success of roundhouse
co-ops. Possible conflicts in child rearing principles, dwelling design, etc.,
are more likely with more adults involved. More confusion and stress caused
by having to adjust to the idiosyncrasies of more people and parents would
bother some people; but others would thrive on the increased variety. In general, these problems are expected to increase in severity as the size of the
roundhouse increases.

In summary, the roundhouse and shuttlehouse co-ops are proposed as
plausible, workable approximations of the social anarchist's ideal of the family
as a "free association" of consenting adults. It is argued that for many people
they may promote "the greatest individual development with the greatest

communal unity." By insisting upon a high degree of individual autonomy and upon living arrangements designed to foster the experience of each person being part of several nuclear families in rotation, it is anticipated that these co-ops will be broadly applicable even in highly mobile, individualistic societies in which some form of the ideal nuclear family is preferred by most people for a least part of their adult lives. These co-ops are designed to provide most of the buffering functions of traditional extended nuclear families and communal groups with fewer attendant sacrifices in individual autonomy. By resisting the temptation to communalize wealth and property, the separation of members from the co-op is facilitated, bickering over finances and property use should be largely eliminated, and the danger of a "laissez-faire" approach to work developing within the co-op is reduced. These co-ops would seem most likely to succeed among small groups lacking extremes in individual wealth, fame or popularity; among people with a minimum of overpossessiveness and jealousy, and with a certain tolerance for sharing their private life with a group; and among people who have settled in one geographical area for an extended period. Co-ops lacking these characteristics may, like too many communes and nuclear families, serve only as a transient refuge or battleground for many of its members. In their most orthodox versions, these co-ops do require specially designed dwellings. The shuttlehouse and related network co-options do not require a radical departure from conventional housing, although more constraints in design details are involved. The roundhouse design will require some adjusting to odd-shaped rooms. Also, pipe and wiring systems would have to be specially designed for a rotating dwelling.

Summary

Small cooperative family units living in dwellings specially designed to encourage each adult to share, in rotation, a common sub-dwelling unit each potential mate are considered as a plausible alternative to nuclear families, communes and "free associations" or pairs. These co-ops, termed roundhouses or shuttlehouses, are designed to facilitate the attainment of an optimal balance of individual identity, nuclear family living and extended family buffering. Each adult member has an individual section of the group dwelling in which most of their personal possessions are kept, and each retains their autonomy with regard to wealth, legal liability and employment. As a group, they are responsible for any children, engage in some income distribution and provide emotional, financial, and other support for each other. The roundhouse and shuttlehouse arrangements are designed to help stabilize interpersonal relations within the co-op by: (1) providing an obvious cue as to who's whose at a given time, and (2) "forcing" each potential pair of adults to live as a unit periodically, thus creating the illusion of each person being part of several nuclear families in rotation.

Endnotes

1 For some recent firsthand discussions of bad experiences in anarchist and other communes, I suggest: Jim Campbell, "Anarchy Down on the Farm," Kick It Over 17:15; "Backscatter About the Farm," Whole Earth Review 51:78; C. L. "Cory" Koral, "A commune that doesn't really work," Whole Earth Review 53:139.

2 The international community in Auroville, India, has experimented with various group sizes in one dwelling, and concludes that eight to ten adults is the maximum desirable size (Auroville Review 6:13).

3 Here defined as possessiveness to the point of unduly interfering in the freedom of one's lover to lead an independent existence and to flirt or engage in more intimate behavior with other persons.

4 See David Talbot's discussion of this problem in "Unspeakable Pleasures: Erotic Adventures in the '80s," New Age Journal, Feb. 1986, p. 27.

Caroline Estes' article serves as a brief introduction to the use of consensus decision-making in organizations of varying sizes. With several decades of experience using consensus models on a regular basis (as a Quaker, and as a member of an intentional community), Estes offers concrete examples of its effectiveness as well as counter-examples of "strategic mistakes" that resulted from not using consensus. In the second half of the article, she outlines a number of practical tips for implementing consensus decision-making into a group.

Originally published in issue 10.

Consensus
Caroline Estes

Decision-making by consensus is a very old process about which there is much new interest. Primitive tribes and cultures have used it for thousands of years. Early Jesuits in the 17th century called it Communal Discernment. The Society of Friends (Quakers) have used it for over three hundred years, calling it "seeking unity" or "gathering the sense of the meeting." In the past decade or two, it has come into use in settings as diverse as businesses, intentional communities, and social action groups.

In simplest terms, consensus refers to agreement (on some decision) by *all* members of a group. The consensus *process* is the process the group goes through to reach this unity of agreement. Its assumptions, methods and results are different from Robert's *Rules of Order* or parliamentary process.

During the past 25 years, since I was first exposed to the use of consensus in Quaker meetings, I have been involved in some widely different situations in which consensus has been successfully used. In 1965, at the time of the Free Speech Movement in Berkeley, I watched this process being used in both the small council that was the governing body and the large mass meetings of up to 5,000 persons. The council was made up of such diverse representatives as Goldwater Republicans, Marxists, Maoists, Democrats, Republicans, Socialists, "Hippies" and simple activists. Mario Savio, leader of the movement, said that during the entire, tense, dramatic time, the group made only two strategic mistakes in carrying out the sit-ins, marches and confrontations, and these were the two times they came to a place where they weren't able to reach consensus, and so they voted. Both votes led them in the wrong direction. Similarly, in the large mass meetings, there was consistent agreement among those assembled, after much talking and discussion. There is no doubt it was a tense and exciting time — and that the unity in that group was very strong.

Since then I have worked with many groups that use this type of decision-making, whether in community gatherings, neighborhood meetings or family meetings. I have found that it works as more than just a decision-making technique, because the unity and understanding it fosters serve in many ways to advance the basic purposes of these groups.

The Basis

Consensus is based on the belief that each person has some part of the truth and no one has all of it, no matter how much we would like to believe so, and on a respect for all persons involved in the decision that is being considered.

In our present society, the governing idea is that we can trust no one, and therefore we must protect ourselves if we are to have any security in our decisions. The most we will be willing to do is compromise. This leads to a very interesting way of viewing the outcome of working together. It means we are willing to settle for less than the very best — and that we will always have a sense of dissatisfaction with any of our decisions unless we can somehow maneuver others involved in the process. This leads to a skewing of honesty and forthrightness in our relationships.

In the consensus process, we start from a different basis. The assumption is that we are all trustworthy (or at least can become so). The process allows each person complete power over the group. The central idea for the Quakers was the complete elimination of majorities and minorities. If there were differences of view at a Quaker meeting, as there were likely to be in such a body, the consideration of the question at issue would proceed, with long periods of solemn hush and meditation, until slowly the lines of thought drew together towards a point of unity. Then the clerk would frame a minute of conclusion, expressing the "sense of the meeting."

Built into the consensual process is the belief that all persons have some part of the truth, or what in spiritual terms might be called "some part of God" in them, and that we will reach a better decision by putting all of the pieces of the truth together before proceeding. There are indeed times when it appears that two pieces of the truth are in contradiction to one another, but with clear thinking and attention, a whole may be perceived which includes both pieces or many pieces. The "either/or" type of argument does not advance this process. Instead the process is a search for the very best solution to whatever is the problem. That does not mean that there is never room for error — but on the whole, in my experience, it is rare.

This process also makes a direct application of the idea that all persons are equal — an idea that we are not entirely comfortable with, since it seems on the surface that some people are more equal than others. But if we do indeed trust one another and do believe that we all have parts of the truth, then at any time one person may know more or have access to more information but at another time, others may know more of have more access or better understanding. Even when we have all the facts before us, it may be the spirit that is lacking and comes forth from another who sees the whole better than any of the persons who have some of the parts. All of these contributions are important.

Decisions which all have helped to shape, and in which all can feel united, make the eventual carrying-out of the necessary action go forward with more efficiency, power, and smoothness. This applies to persons, communities and nations. Given the enormous issues and problems before us, we need to use the ways that will best enable us to move forward together.

The Process

How does this process actually work? Consensus can be a powerful tool, yet like any tool, it needs to be used rightly. Its misuse can cause great frustration and disruption. To make the most of its possibilities we need to understand its parts and its process.

Consensus needs four ingredients — a group of people willing to work together, a problem or issue that requires a decision by the group, trust that there is a solution, and perseverance to find the truth.

It is important to come to meetings with a clear and unmade-up mind. That is not to say that prior thinking should not have been done, but simply that the thinking must remain open throughout the discussion — or else there is no way to come to the full truth. This means everyone, not just some of the group. Ideas and solutions must be sought from all assembled, and all must be listened to with respect and trust. It is the practice of oneness for those who are committed to the idea — or the search for the best possible solution, for those who are more pragmatic.

The problems to be considered come in all sizes, from "who does the dishes" to "how to reach accord on de-escalating the arms race." The consensus process begins with a statement of the problem — as clear as possible in language as simple as possible. It is important that the problem not be stated in such a way that an answer is built in, but that there be an openness to looking at all sides of the issue — whatever it may be. It is also necessary to state it in the positive: "We will wash the dishes with detergent and hot water," not "We will not wash the dishes in cold water." Or, "we need to wash the dishes so they are clean and sanitary," not, "The dishes are very dirty, and we are not washing them correctly." Stating the issues in the positive begins the process of looking for positive solutions and not a general discussion on everything that is bad, undesirable or awful.

The meeting needs a facilitator/clerk/convener, a role whose importance cannot be too strongly emphasized. It is this person whose responsibility it is to see that all are heard, that all ideas are incorporated if they seem to be part of the truth, and that the final decision is agreed upon by all assembled.

Traits that help the facilitator are patience, intuition, articulateness, ability to think on his/her feet and a sense of humor. It is important also for a facilitator to look within to see if there is something that is missing — a person who has been wanting to speak but has been too shy, an idea that was badly articulated but has the possibility to help with the solution, anything that seems of importance on the non-verbal level. This essence of intuition can often be of great service to the group by releasing some active but unseen deterrent to the continued development of a solution.

The facilitator must be able to constantly state and restate the position of the meeting and at the same time show that progress is being made. This helps the group to move ahead with some dispatch.

And last but by no means least — a sense of humor. There is nothing like a small turn of a phrase at a tense moment to lighten up the discussion and allow a little relaxation. Once you have found a good clerk or facilitator, don't let him/her go.

Often there are those who want to talk more than is necessary and others who don't speak enough. The facilitator needs to be able to keep the discussion from being dominated by a few and to encourage those who have not spoken to share their thoughts. There are a number of techniques for this. One is to suggest that no one speak more than once, until everyone has spoken; another is to have men and women speak alternately. This is particularly helpful for a short time if one gender seems to be dominating the discussion. However, it is not well to have any arbitrary technique used for too long. It is well to use these ways to bring a balance into the group, but these artificial guidelines should be abandoned as soon as possible. For instance, alternating of men and women might be used for one session — but then let whoever wants to speak in the next session. My experience is that a single two- or three-hour session with guidelines usually establishes a new pattern, and there is little need for the artificial guidelines to be continued.

No matter how well the discussion is carried forward, how good the facilitator, and how much integrity there is in a group, there sometimes comes a point when all are in agreement but for one or two. At that point there are three courses open. One is to see whether the individuals are willing to "step aside." This means that they do not agree with the decision but do not feel it is wrong and are willing to have it go forward, but do not want to be a party to carrying the action forward.

During the gathering of the sense of the meeting, if more than two or three persons start to step aside from a decision, then the facilitator should be alert to the fact that maybe the best decision has not yet been reached. This would depend on the size of the group, naturally. At Alpha, an intentional community, it is okay for one person to step aside, but as soon as another joins that one, the clerk begins to watch and to re-examine the decision. It might be that at that time, the facilitator would ask for a few minutes of silence to see if there was another decision or an amendment that should be considered that had been overlooked and would ease the situation.

Another possibility is to lay aside the issue for another time. This alternative always seems to raise serious questions. However, we need to have some perspective on what we are doing. It is likely that the world will continue to revolve around the sun for another day, week, or year, whether we come to a decision at this moment or at another; and the need to make a decision now is often not as important as the need to come to unity around whatever decision is made.

Personal experience has shown me that even the most crucial decisions, seemingly time-bound, can be laid aside for a while — and that the time, whether a few hours or days, is wisely allowed and when again assembled we come to a better decision than was possible in the beginning.

The third possibility is that one or two people may be able to stop the group or meeting from moving forward. At that time there are several key ingredients to be considered. On the part of the meeting, it is important that the meeting see the person who is holding the meeting as doing so out of that person's highest understanding and beliefs. The individual(s) who are holding the group from a making a decision must also have examined themselves well to know that they are not doing so out of self-interest, bias, vengeance or any other emotion or idea except the very strong feeling and belief that the decision is wrong — and that they would be doing the group a great disservice by allowing it to go forward.

This is always one of those times when feelings can run high, and it is important for the meeting, or group, not to use oppression on those who differ. It is hard enough to feel that you are stopping the group from going forward, without having additional pressure exerted to go against your examined reasons and deeply felt understandings.

In my personal experience of living with the consensus process full-time for 12 years, I need to say that I have seen the meeting held from going forward on only a handful of occasions, and in each case the person was correct — and the group would have made a mistake by moving forward.

There is another situation which does occur, though rarely, where one person is consistently at odds with everyone else. Depending on the type of group and its membership, it would be well to see if this person is in the right organization or group. If there is a consistent difference, the person cannot feel comfortable continuing, and the group needs to meet and work with that person.

One reason it is important that each decision be well seasoned is that the consensus is a very conservative process. Once a decision has been made, it takes a consensus to change the decision. This means that whatever has been arrived at needs to be able to be relied on for some time, and thus decisions should not be arrived at in haste. One way a decision can be tried, but not necessarily need to be changed, is to put a time limit on it. For instance, if you want to try a new way of handling the cleaning of the house, then you might say: "We will allot one hour a day to housekeeping for the next month. At the end of the month, either we will reconsider the decision or it will no longer be operable." At Alpha Farm we have done this on a number of occasions, usually trying a decision for a year and then either making a final decision or dropping it entirely. This necessitates keeping minutes, which is another aspect of consensus that needs to be heeded.

Minutes on decisions that have been made need to be stated by the clerk or facilitator or minute-taker at the time of the decision, so that all present know they have agreed to the same thing. It is not well for minutes to be taken and then read at the new meeting, unless there is to be a meeting very soon. The reason for this seems obvious: those who make the decision are the ones to carry it out — and if there is a month or more before they are stated, then the same people may not all be present, and the minutes may or may not be correct, but the time for correction is past. This is a particularly important but little-adhered to part of the process.

Recently, I was privileged to facilitate the first North American Bioregional Congress, held in Missouri. Over 200 persons arrived from all over the continent, and some from abroad, and worked together for five days, making all decisions by consensus. Some of those present had used the process before or were currently using it in the groups they worked with at home; but many had not, and there was a high degree of skepticism when we began as to whether such a widely diverse group of people could work in that degree of harmony and unity. On the final day of the Congress, there were a very large number of resolutions, position papers and policies put forward from committees that had been working all week long. All decisions that were made that day were made by consensus — and the level of love and trust among participants was tangible. Much to the surprise of nearly everyone, we came away with a sense of unity and forward motion that was near-miraculous, but believable.

Editor's note: this article was reprinted from *In Context* (a quarterly of humane sustainable culture).

Twenty years after Estes, Mark Lance revisited the concept and practice of consensus at a level both deeper in theory and practical description. Where Estes' provides an introduction, Lance offers a fuller analysis. His position in the Department of Philosophy at Georgetown University affords him a good philosophical background, and the department itself provides him with a working decision-making group. Lance draws an important distinction between procedures, which dictate the rules of decision-making, and practices, which are the methods by which issues are raised and proposed solutions are discussed. Ultimately, he argues that specific procedures—especially consensus vs. supermajority rule—are substantially less significant as long as the practice is open, inclusive, and respectful.

Originally published in issue 38.

Fetishizing Process
Mark Lance

I f one were forced to explain consensus process in five minutes, one might begin with a brief pitch about the kind of discussion that should precede the group taking a decision. Such a pitch would be fairly vague, and would deal with such things as listening, including all points of view, critical discussion and argument, and creativity in the formulation of possible compromises and syntheses. But one would quickly switch from the topic of discussion to the specific procedure that is used to take a formal decision. Here the account is not at all vague, as precise as any sort of voting procedure. One would explain how a position is proposed, how people have the choice of supporting, standing aside, or blocking, how a position can only be adopted by the group if no one blocks, etc. (It is likely, and relevant, that the majority of people who have been part of decision making under the banner of "consensus process" have little more than such a five minute understanding of what is involved.)

If one had much more than five minutes to explain consensus process, one would say little more about the formal procedure for taking decisions. This part really can be defined in a few minutes. One would, however, go into far more detail on the complex, less precise, more deeply contextual business that precedes actually taking a decision. That is, one would focus on the process of discussion, option formulation, argument, etc.

In what follows, let us call the complex process of discussion — a process about which much can be said, but the proper functioning of which is unlikely to be definable via a set of precise rules — "practice". The set of formal rules that define a method of taking a decision will be referred to as "procedure". This distinction, in itself, is nothing surprising or new, but I want to argue that it is of great import to the debate between majority voting and consensus. Such debates are central to anarchist theory as they concern the form and content of democratic inclusion. Indeed, if anything is essential to anarchism, it is the idea that social decisions are to be taken by everyone affected, and that this inclusion must involve substantive participation of each in deliberation and decision-making. Thus a dispute on the nature of such participation is a dispute about the very essence of anarchism.

But I argue that the debate between voting and consensus is deeply flawed. First, many advocates on each side run together procedure and practice in a pernicious way — criticizing procedures of the other side, while defending not their own procedure, but rather their conception of practice. Second, it turns out that the right answer to how we ought to structure ourselves — around a norm of consensus or a norm of majority rule — depends crucially on whether we are talking about procedure or practice. In short, and rather misleadingly, procedures should be closer to majority rule, but only in the service of a practice which is geared around a deep commitment to consensus. In arguing for this second point, I show that consensus procedure is actually deeply unsuited to radical organizations. But at the same time, I begin to make the case that a focus on procedure itself is ultimately the real problem, which brings us to the third and most important point. An anti-authoritarian democratic organization must not understand itself as defined by a set of formal procedures. Rules can be used, as tools of a virtuous community with a largely functional practice, but they should be no more than tools.

Understanding the goal of democratic community to involve a search for the right set of formal rules that we can then blindly follow with no further obligation to their proper and just implementation is no better than understanding it as a search for the best and most just king. Making a fetish of a process — worshiping a way of doing things — can be every bit as oppressive as making a fetish of personal authority.

More heat than light

One might expect discussions of decision-making process by anarchists to be among the most intellectually sophisticated, civil, and collaborative of debates in political philosophy. After all, the idea that people can, without authoritarian or hierarchical oversight, reach just decisions among themselves in a way that expresses and at the same time nurtures the autonomy of the individual is central to anarchism. So surely, at least in their internal discussions of how to achieve these goals in existing organizations, anarchists would strive to exhibit the sorts of collaborative process they advocate for society at large.

On the other hand, there is the real world.

Though there exist careful and respectful contributions to the anarchist debate on group process, one finds a great deal more by way of caricature, denouncement, and table-pounding. Advocates of consensus, for example, try to associate voting with coercion, unthinking mechanism, rigidity of thought, and an endorsement of liberal representationalism.

Consensus means making decisions by the united consent of all. It is noncoercive, as it avoids imposing anyone's will on others. ... Consensus is really more natural than majority vote....In consensus, the group encourages the sharing of all viewpoints held by those with interest in a topic. These viewpoints are then discussed in a spirit of respect and mutual accommodation. New ideas arise and viewpoints are synthesized, until a formula emerges that wins general approval. ...Consensus is "organic"—unlike mechanical voting."[1]

Consensus is a decision-making process that reflects commitment to the right of every person to influence decisions that affect them. ...Consensus is a creative process. It is a process for synthesizing the ideas and concerns of all group members. Unlike voting, it is not an adversary, win/lose method. With consensus, we do not have to choose between two alternatives. Instead we can create a third, a fourth or more as we see that problems may have many possible solutions. Those who hold views different from ours do not become opponents; instead, their views can be seen as giving us a fresh and valuable perspective. As we work to meet their concerns, our proposals may be strengthened. When we use consensus, we encourage each person's active participation, and we listen carefully to what each person says."[2]

Or finally: "Voting is a process in which people express their preferences — whether strongly heartfelt or weakly ephemeral. Voters are usually forced to choose between two proposals — ostensibly opposite, but often both unacceptable: "would you rather be poked in the eye with a stick or hit on the head with a rock?" The decision is reached by simplistically adding up these preferences. [Voting] often encourages cagey manipulation."[3]

"Those who hold views different from ours do not become opponents; instead, their views can be seen as giving us a fresh and valuable perspective,"... unless they advocate voting. If they advocate voting, it seems, there are few limits to the caricatures and red herrings we can utilize. Why, if we advocate voting, can we not be respectful of and learn from different views? Why must we consider only two proposals? Why must we coerce people, or ignore their right to influence decisions that affect them?

But those who oppose the current trend towards consensus in anarchist circles are, if anything, worse:

The only collective alternative to majority voting as a means of decision-making that is commonly presented is the practice of consensus. Indeed, consensus has even been mystified by avowed "anarcho-primitivists," who consider Ice Age and contemporary "primitive" or "primal" peoples to constitute the apogee of human social and psychic attainment. I do not deny that consensus may be an appropriate form of decision-making in small groups of people who are thoroughly familiar with one another. But to examine consensus in practical terms, my own experience has shown me that when larger groups try to make decisions by consensus, it usually obliges them to arrive at the lowest common intellectual denominator in their decision-making: the least controversial or even the most mediocre decision that a sizable assembly of people can attain is adopted — precisely because everyone must agree with it or else withdraw from voting on that issue. More disturbingly, I have found that it permits an insidious authoritarianism and gross manipulations — even when used in the name of autonomy or freedom.

I can personally attest to the fact that within the Clamshell Alliance, consensus was fostered by often cynical Quakers and by members of a dubiously "anarchic" commune that was located in Montague, Massachusetts. ...In order for that clique to create full consensus on a decision, minority dissenters were often subtly urged or psychologically coerced to decline to vote on a troubling issue, inasmuch as their dissent would essentially amount to a one-person veto. ...Having withdrawn, they ceased to be political beings — so that a "decision" could be made. ...On a more theoretical level, consensus silenced that most vital aspect of all dialogue, dissensus. The ongoing dissent, the passionate dialogue that still persists even after a minority accedes temporarily to a majority decision, was replaced in the Clamshell by dull monologues — and the uncontroverted and deadening tone of consensus. In majority decision-making, the defeated minority can resolve to overturn a decision on which they have been defeated — they are free to openly and persistently articulate reasoned and potentially persuasive disagreements. Consensus, for its part, honors no minorities, but mutes them in favor of the metaphysical "one" of the "consensus" group.

The creative role of dissent, valuable as an ongoing democratic phenomenon, tends to fade away in the gray uniformity required by consensus. Any libertarian body of ideas that seeks to dissolve hierarchy, classes, domination and exploitation by allowing even Marshall's "minority of one" to block decision-making by the majority of a community, indeed, of regional and nationwide confederations, would essentially mutate into a Rousseauean "general will" with a nightmare world of intellectual and psychic conformity. [4]

[Murray Bookchin]

(Don't we all feel empowered to dissent from Murray's position?)

Dissent must therefore be encouraged, not discouraged. Only through a principled discussion of what is at stake in an issue can the truth be clarified. It is liberals — those who accept the system — who water down and obscure truths to platitudes with which everyone can agree and who seek consensus in the form of "peace." In an age of accommodation like ours — as in all ages — it is liberals who would deny the importance of clarifying radical truths.

Majority rule is the democratic method of determining the will of the large group in decision-making. For majority rule protects the minority's right to dissent, and majority rule exempts them from the obligation to carry out a group decision with which they disagree. In order for diversity of opinion to be valued, therefore, majority rule in large groups must be viewed as an acceptable process.

[Janet Biehl]

It is indicative, I suppose, of the depth of feeling on this issue that these serious thinkers and activists could engage in such a breathtakingly irrational string of caricatures. For present purposes, I want to focus on one aspect of the caricature: that each side in this debate characterizes the other as defending a formal procedure, which is then held to a very high standard: essentially, to be foolproof. That is, if we can imagine, or cite actual instances of, behavior consistent with the procedure which violate core values or otherwise give rise to practices of deliberation we don't approve of, this is grounds for rejecting the procedure. On the other hand, each side defines itself, not in terms of the formal procedure, but rather the procedure together with a vaguely stated collection of good practices, just institutions, and virtuous agents.

Bookchin and Biehl, for example, define consensus as the procedure in which decisions are only adopted after universal assent (perhaps with stand-asides) and in which one person can block action. Then, Bookchin gives us an example of a group — the Clamshell Alliance — that abused this procedure by pressuring others into accepting the consensus.[5] (One hardly need speak here of his transparent guilt-by-association ploy of mentioning primitivists.) Biehl and Bookchin both conclude from examples like this that consensus in general denies the existence of minorities, bullies them into conforming, waters down radical truths, even leads to "a nightmare world of intellectual and psychic conformity!"[6]

Many advocates of consensus, similarly, define "majority rule" in terms of the procedure of voting on two pre-selected choices. They assume that people come to these choices and vote their antecedent inclinations ("whether strongly heartfelt or weakly ephemeral"), that such decisions are not "discussed in a spirit of respect and mutual accommodation," that no effort is made to reformulate options, or to come up with others, that those with differing views are treated as "opponents," and that manipulation is likely to be engaged in.

That is, in both cases what is criticized is the practice of concrete, far from ideal groups who utilize the procedure in dispute. Certainly there is no essential reason why dividing opposing votes into blocks and stand-asides must lead to a suppression of dissent. Indeed, as a simple matter of logic, consensus assigns greater, indeed dictatorial, power to minorities. The mere fact that we are going to vote is obviously no guarantee that some nefarious majority won't try to pressure minorities into accepting their position on the grounds that a unanimous vote shows strength, solidarity, etc. So it is really completely obvious that the Bookchin/Biehl worries have nothing to do with the choice of which procedure one employs.

Nor, however, is there any reason why a commitment to majority rule requires lack of discussion, limiting options to two, or treating people as opponents. A group can engage in any sort of fair-minded, inclusive, open-ended discussion it likes, reformulating positions, trying out options to see if there is unanimity, learning from dissent, etc., all ending up in a majority vote on the proposal that seems to have most support in the discussion. Thus the advocates of consensus quoted above are no more focusing on essential features of groups that use voting than are Bookchin and Biehl focusing on essential features of consensus groups.

If there is an intelligible claim being made in either argument, it can only be that the pernicious sort of behavior in question is more likely in fact to follow from the use of the procedure being attacked. But neither side — nor any other literature that I'm aware of — makes any serious attempt to argue that one procedure is more likely than the other to be abused in this way. Presumably, such an argument would require concrete statistical evidence, and I'm skeptical that any significant generalizations are forthcoming. In my own rather extensive experience with activist groups, I've seen both procedures used well, and both abused, with about equal frequency.

By contrast, note how each group discusses its own approach: "In consensus, the group encourages the sharing of all viewpoints held by those with interest in a topic. These viewpoints are then discussed in a spirit of respect and mutual accommodation. New ideas arise and viewpoints are synthesized, until a formula emerges that wins general approval." Or for a more expansive account:

> So what would an alternative revolutionary decision making process look like, you ask? To begin with, a fundamental shift from competition to cooperation. ...Cooperation is more than "live and let live." It is making an effort to understand another's point of view. It is incorporating another's perspective with your own so that a new perspective emerges. It is suspending disbelief, even if only temporarily, so you can see the gem of truth in ideas other than your own. It is a process of creativity, synthesis, and open-mindedness that leads to trust-building, better communication and understanding, and ultimately, a stronger, healthier, more successful group. ...The last and most visible step towards revolutionary change in group process is the manner in which members of the group interact with each other. Dominating attitudes and controlling behavior would not be tolerated. People would show respect and expect to be shown respect. Everyone would be doing their personal best to help the group reach decisions which are in the best interest of the group. There would be no posturing and taking sides. Conflicts would be seen as an opportunity for growth, expanding people's thinking, sharing new information, and developing new solutions which include everyone's perspectives. The group would create an environment where everyone was encouraged to participate, conflict was freely expressed, and resolutions were in the best interest of everyone involved.[7]
>
> [C.T. Lawrence Butler]

It is interesting that when allowed to speak for themselves, the advocates of voting espouse similar practices. Here is Bookchin again.

Even so knowledgeable a historian of anarchism as Peter Marshall observes that, for anarchists, "the majority has no more right to dictate to the minority, even a minority of one, than the minority to the majority."⁵ Scores of libertarians have echoed this idea time and again.

What is striking about assertions like Marshall's is their highly pejorative language. Majorities, it would seem, neither "decide" nor "debate": rather, they "rule," "dictate," "command," "coerce" and the like. In a free society that not only permitted, but fostered the fullest degree of dissent, whose podiums at assemblies and whose media were open to the fullest expression of all views, whose institutions were truly forums for discussion — one may reasonably ask whether such a society would actually "dictate" to anyone when it had to arrive at a decision that concerned the public welfare.

[IBID]

A purer case of talking (yelling) past one another could hardly be constructed. What emerges is that there are two fundamentally distinct dimensions of assessment going on, which we may call "procedural" and "practical." Procedural assessment looks to the formal rules that are explicitly adopted by the group as governing decision-making process. Practical assessment looks to the practices of the group, and the underlying habits, psychologies, traditions, and context that support the continuation of those practices. What is striking about the debate between consensus and majority rule, then, is that each side defines the other exclusively in terms of a procedure, while defining themselves first and foremost in terms of practice.

To engage in "direct democracy" as Bookchin defines the term requires that one vote only after a full discussion. Direct democracy is, by definition, a procedure employed by a "free society that not only permit[s], but foster[s] the fullest degree of dissent, whose podiums at assemblies and whose media [are] open to the fullest expression of all views, whose institutions [are] truly forums for discussion." That Bookchin intends this to be a definitional truth can be seen from the fact that he never so much as considers other uses of voting to be relevant to the system he is endorsing. Similarly, advocates of consensus process define consensus as a procedure that is used by a respectful community of serious dialogue, a group which functions as a forum for fair discussion. Ask any consensus advocate how they can endorse giving one difficult person the ability to veto every decision unless we adopt his view and she will tell you that such a thing is not consensus process at all.

Now in neither case are we simply asked to ignore the possibility of procedural abuse. Advocates of consensus typically describe in some detail the sorts of attitudes that are necessary in order for participants to function in the way they should, and in some cases, explain the kinds of discipline, training, facilitation, and practice that are needed for people to carry this off. Bookchin, similarly, has written about the kinds of institutions that a society needs, and the sorts of attitudes and work that people will need to bring to those institutions, in order for society to function well in genuinely democratic forums. But this merely highlights my point: the practice of the participants, their skills, habits, relations, and virtues — along with the broader societal structures and institutions that engender and support these — are where the action is.

Two case studies

In this section we look at two decision-making institutions. One is a self-identified radical organization devoted to an ideology of inclusiveness and diversity, with the goal of liberatory social change, and operating by consensus. The second is a mainstream institution — an academic department — with no commitment to a radical agenda, operating officially by a formal voting mechanism. My point will not be to suggest that voting leads to better behavior than does consensus, but rather to highlight some aspects of respectful practice, and to indicate just how little formal procedure has to do with the quality of human interaction that goes on.

The first case involved the Mobilization for Global Justice (MGJ), the largest coalition of the Global Justice Movement to arise out of the uprising in Seattle in 1999.[8] In Summer and Fall 2001, MGJ was planning for a convergence and demonstration around the annual meetings of the IMF and WB in Washington DC. A wide range of education, legal protest, and civil disobedience had been planned, generally in accord with the way these things had been going on for the past couple years. MGJ in DC was a large, diverse, and vibrant group, albeit one which in retrospect had two significantly different sorts of members. On the one hand, a wide range of grassroots protest, activist, or direct action groups were a part of MGJ. On the other, a number of formal NGOs with paid staff took part.

The attacks against civilians in New York and Washington, DC on Sept. 11, 2001 caused something of a crisis throughout the progressive community. Clearly this was an event that had deeply affected the American public and nearly everyone realized that it changed the political context in ways that called for a re-thinking of strategies and tactics. Going into a crucial meeting following the attacks, nearly every member group in MGJ would have supported scaling back the level of confrontation with police, many supported eliminating civil disobedience altogether actions, and a handful of NGOs favored completely canceling the protests.

Representatives of this latter group arranged to be in the position of facilitator on the day in question. After a bit of unfocussed discussion, a proposal was put on the board. "The MGJ will go ahead with its plans for protests during the meetings of the financial institutions" (or something very much like that). Immediately, representatives of the group in favor of canceling the event announced that they were blocking this proposal. Objections, arguments, discussion, etc. were met with stony rejection. The proposal was blocked, and the events were cancelled. It was estimated by those present that roughly 80% of the people in attendance opposed canceling things. But they had no real say. There was no real discussion or response to the arguments the majority made, merely condescending lectures on being responsible protestors, and stony refusal to consider the block.[9]

Let us contrast with this case, the general practice of a quite different organization, one that is not in any way explicitly radical, but rather an academic department: the department of philosophy at Georgetown University. For the last 15 years or so, this department, in its internal deliberations, has been a veritable model of civility, rationality, and respect. It is a large department, as such things go, with around 24 members. It is ideologically, philosophically, and methodologically highly diverse including analytic and continental philosophers, conservatives, liberals, socialists, capitalist libertarians, and (one) anarchist, committed Catholics, and atheists.[10] Nonetheless, in almost every case, members of the department genuinely respect one another and, in the few counter-instances, nonetheless recognize the importance of treating their colleagues with respect and civility. Discussions are always open, intellectually sophisticated, and creative. Everyone in the department participates in discussions. Graduate student representatives to department meetings, and really any other graduate student with strong views on the matter, participate fully and openly. New members quickly learn that one does not try to score points, put down colleagues, ignore the arguments people are making, or, for that matter, blindly endorse anyone else's opinion. That just isn't the way things are done in our department.

Procedurally the Georgetown philosophy department works by a version of majority rule, officially following Roberts' Rules in discussion, majority vote when there are two options, and a complicated variant of majority rule when there are more options. In reality, no one in the department knows much about Roberts' Rules, and voting is usually a rather pointless afterthought. In the first decade of my participation, only a handful of votes ended other than unanimously, for the simple reason that discussion almost always led to a position that struck everyone as the rational one. And of the few cases in which there has been a vote, most have been overwhelmingly in one direction, with those who disagreed fully accepting the majority decision.

It is clear enough that the problem with what went on at MGJ wasn't primarily due to the use of consensus procedure. Had majority vote been the procedure, the NGOs could, for example, have engaged in a mass mobilization of members. (Part of the problem that day was that things were rushed, and these groups by way of their paid staff and better communication networks were able to prepare for the meeting much more quickly.) If they had done so, and turned out 51% of the people at the meeting, they could still have controlled the outcome, in roughly the same manner. Indeed, for all Bookchin's (correct) insistence that majority rule need not involve a tyranny of the majority, dictates or commands, it is perfectly clear that it can involve such things. There is certainly nothing in the procedural rules of voting that prevents this. (Think how many states are now passing patently heterosexist laws. Though these are usually the result of legislators rather than popular votes, there is little doubt that popular votes would turn out the same way in most cases. Such majority support hardly renders these laws less repellent, or the arguments behind them less vapid.)

Thus, whatever virtues the GU philosophy department instantiates are also independent of its commitment to voting procedures. At least as far back as Plato's Republic, it has been noted that when the procedure is majority vote, it is possible to mobilize the mob through graft, rhetoric, fear, or other irrational means, so as to force decisions on the minority that are neither wise nor just. Clearly, as Plato is at pains to emphasize, there is no essential connection between what the majority believes and what is right and just. (Of course there is also no such connection between what everyone believes and what is right and just. If we all agree, perhaps it is simply because we share our ignorance, prejudice, or bigotry.)

Why consensus procedure is inherently conservative.

Defenders of consensus procedure often suggest that the MGJ case arose because of a violation of that procedure. Some suggest that consensus procedure properly includes a rule against re-opening questions unless there is a consensus to do so. Others suggest that there was a problem in the formulation of the proposal, or the structure of the debate. This is all fair, but I think it misses the main point. I want to claim that any formal procedure can be abused. But in this section, I focus on consensus procedure, and offer a quite general abstract argument against it.[11]

While consensus decision-making is typically put forward as a radical alternative to voting, or at least as more suited to radical or revolutionary projects, it turns out that consensus rules are deeply conservative in their very structure. Recall that, according to consensus procedure, a proposal is formulated, and then it must receive unanimous support — ignoring stand-asides — to be adopted by the group. That is, if one person opposes it, the group cannot adopt it. The first problem with this procedure is that it doesn't prescribe a procedure based on the content or meaning of a proposal, but rather based on arbitrary features of its formulation. Suppose, for example, that a group is faced with a situation in which they would normally engage in some sort of protest action. Perhaps they are an anti-war group, and the US has just launched an invasion. Say for purposes of argument that all but one of the people thinks that a protest should be held, but one strongly opposes this for whatever reason. Here are two ways to formulate the disagreement.

Formulation 1:
Group A endorses protesting the invasion.
Group B (one person) opposes protesting the invasion.

Formulation 2:
Group B (one person) endorses remaining quiet about the invasion (doing nothing)
Group A opposes remaining quiet about the invasion.

The difference between these formulations comes to nothing under a majority voting procedure, but is absolutely crucial under consensus. If the proposal is "Let us hold a protest" then the one person opposing can block and nothing happens. But if the proposal is to do nothing, then any one of the many who support protesting can block, thereby forcing a protest.

Now in a case like this, it is probably natural to think that formulation 1 is the right one. What we need consensus for is to do things, and if we cannot reach consensus on what to do, the group will do nothing. But even if this distinction between action and inaction makes sense in all cases, it is not one that radical groups should be happy assigning such significance to. Isn't it a staple of our analysis that inaction is a form of action? When one goes about one's life and ignores political, economic, cultural disputes, don't we consistently argue that one is thereby supporting the status quo, playing a concrete role in keeping the system functioning? Sitting on one's ass may be the right thing to do in a given situation, but we radicals always insist that it is nonetheless doing something, something that calls just as much for justification as anything else.

How strange, then, to endorse a decision-making process that essentially privileges doing nothing over doing something, for that is exactly what consensus procedure is, on the current understanding. If we insist that the formulation of a proposal must be in the positive — a proposal to do something rather than to remain inactive — then we are legislating that one strongly held opinion can prevent action, while all-but-one's equally strongly held opinion is still insufficient to force action. Thus, if the earlier argument about the role of inaction in an institutionalized setting is correct, consensus process is deeply conservative, privileging acquiescence with the status quo far more than does voting.

It should be obvious that most forms of so-called "modified consensus" aren't any better motivated. Requiring ¾ or 2/3 for a positive decision to be taken still privileges complacency over action. Unless one goes all the way to a principle like "attempt to find consensus, and if that fails, vote" one is stuck with a procedure that is asymmetrical between action and inaction. And I can see no way that one should embrace such asymmetry.

I should emphasize that I'm not here criticizing the distinction within consensus procedure between blocks and stand-asides. This is certainly a useful distinction. (Though one could go further. Obviously our opposition to various proposals does not always fall neatly into one of two categories. There is a range, even a multi-dimensional space, of attitudes towards a given proposal that one could adopt. Support/stand-aside/ block is more nuanced than support/oppose, but only by a factor of 3–2.) What I object to is any procedure that isn't symmetrical between support and opposition to the proposal in question.

Suppose a Palestinian solidarity group is considering making a statement affirming the Right of Return. Say some people feel deeply opposed to such a statement, while supporting the goals and practices of the group in other ways, while others feel deeply committed to the essentiality of such a statement, feeling that silence on that issue is an insult to the majority of Palestinians who live as refugees. Why should either commitment be made more important than the other, by the very rules of argument? In each case, one could have a deeply held moral opposition/support, which one thought to be essential to the well being of the group. However we settle this, choosing between

Formulation 1: We will affirm our support for the Right of Return, and

Formulation 2: We will take no stand on the Right of Return

and thereby choosing to give one or the other group veto power over the other, is clearly not a rational way to settle things.

How such a deep dispute will go — extended debate, creative compromise, even the group breaking up — should not be settled in the abstract, much less by some legislated structure of group procedure. There is simply no way that a procedure that privileges one deep conviction over another is going to help. We have to argue. And if argument fails, one group is going to have to give up on a deeply held conviction. Aside from specific arguments about the Right of Return, its political importance, the tactical issues of affirming it or remaining silent, etc., how could one possibly think to find a wise settlement. But that is exactly what Consensus rules purport to do — settle such disputes formally, prior to substantive consideration of the issues.

Virtuous practice and the need for procedure

I can well imagine a defender of consensus objecting to the previous argument. "Certainly," they might agree, "there is something inherently conservative in allowing one person veto power over actions. But that is not a fair way to characterize consensus process. Consensus requires that we don't think of the ability to block as a veto power available to us whenever we disagree with the way the group is heading. Consensus procedure cannot be divorced from consensus practice and evaluated separately, and when we look to them together we see that blocks are only used when one has a deep objection to the action under consideration, an objection that one sees as important enough to warrant preventing the group from acting."

Such a response, however, misses the point for two reasons. First, there is still no justification for the procedural asymmetry between action and inaction. Why not also give everyone an "inaction block". Why, if I feel that failing to respond to, say, a congressional declaration denouncing the Right of Return, is deeply morally impermissible, indeed incompatible with the very point of our solidarity organization, should I not be able to block our doing nothing? To say that I cannot do this in principle, while others can, in principle, block doing anything about this racist bill, is to embrace a procedural conservatism, no matter what else is packed into the account of practice.

The second problem is that appeal to good practice as a defense of a given procedure misses the whole point of procedure. I noted earlier that the accounts of practice given by sophisticated defenders of consensus and voting are remarkably similar. All focus on the need to include the positions of everyone, to inculcate careful and critical rationality, to be open to new ideas, to allow for creativity in the formulation of alternatives, to appreciate the importance of reaching agreement, etc. In short, there is an emphasis in these discussions on the kinds of virtues that democratic citizens must possess, and the kinds of institutional habits and structures that are conducive to training new citizens to embody such virtues and to maintain them in the ongoing group decision making.

Though, in this article I have nothing substantive to add to the discussion of democratic practice,[12] my point is surely not to criticize this emphasis. Indeed, however virtuous practice is to be spelled out — and, again, for present purposes I want to take some such idea for granted — my main point is to argue that the understanding, implementation, and maintenance of virtuous practice is central to democratic society. But at the moment, I ask the narrow question of what role there is for procedure when people and groups fully embody rational, moral, and political virtues. We have already argued that when people are sufficiently lacking in virtue, neither voting nor consensus procedure will help. If a sizable percentage of the group is determined to abuse procedure, then whatever procedure you choose will be abused.

But what if we have the opposite situation: everyone is virtuous — respectful of others yet committed to arguing for the truth as they see it, listening carefully and critically, well informed and sharing of information, interested in what is best for the group, its members, and society as a whole, etc? Well, in a situation like this, just about any procedure will do. It could be the "let Lelia decide" procedure, because Lelia, being virtuous, won't decide without going through the whole open and inclusive discussion with her comrades. She will take part in the discussion — not as a duty of fairness, but out of a desire to find the truth — and at the end of the discussion, when the best position — as far as we are able to determine in this context, with this information, given our level of intellectual skill — emerges, she will choose that position, as would anyone else in our perfect community. And exactly the same choice would result from voting, consensus, etc.

So if procedure is completely beside the point for fully virtuous groups, and helpless in the face of highly vicious groups, when is it useful? Well clearly for those groups that are somewhere in between. We rightly fall back on procedure precisely when a group that is generally respectful and non-manipulative is running into local restricted difficulties. Perhaps one or another person is feeling a bit intimidated and is not participating. Perhaps there is a disagreement that we are not resolving by argument. Perhaps someone is not bothering to do their homework before entering into discussion.

In a case like these, there is a point to engaging in some sort of reasonably well defined procedure to attempt to deal with the problem — go around the room and ask everyone to speak before others do, accept that moving forward is important and agree to vote, make up a list of the things that people are responsible for studying before the meeting. Two points are clear, however. First, while reasoned debate, respectful discussion, and other aspects of practice are intrinsically valuable to this process, the point of procedures is purely instrumental. We adopt procedures as a pragmatic tool for getting around a concrete problem in the course of our discussions.

Not only must we see procedure as instrumentally pragmatic, but we must also recognize a second point: that the usefulness of any procedure will vary widely with context. Since there exists an enormous range of ways that things can go wrong in a group, we have no reason to find one all-purpose procedure to fall back on — "well we try to discuss, but if that fails, we vote", but why? Maybe what is called for is a go-around in which everyone tries to come up with a possible resolution never before mentioned, or we go home and cool off, or we bring in a facilitator, or we read a relevant book, or some of us stand aside, or we divide into two groups, or merge with a larger one, etc. Each of these could be a perfectly reasonable procedural response to a particular sort of problem.

Thus, what we need is not a procedure, much less an identification of good process with such a procedure, but a well stocked tool kit of ways to deal with the sorts of difficulties that come up within generally well-functioning, but fallible groups. And even more, we need well skilled craftsman to use those tools. Just as some are skilled in perceiving psychological symptoms, others at constructing experimental designs, and still others at developing complex political strategies, there are those who have honed a serious skill at mobilizing procedural tools to deal with the sorts of breakdowns that beset discursive communities. These are the people we call facilitators, mediators, or trainers. And we should make use of them. Of course this is not to say that we defer to facilitators — mindlessly follow their guidance regarding process — anymore than we should defer to a formal procedure. But if it seems to the group that someone is a useful facilitator — that is, that they can help us by guiding us in the implementation of a range of contextually useful procedures — we should take advantage of that.

Practical endorsement of contextual procedures

When the group comes to the view that the most important thing is a decision, even though discussion is not moving towards consensus on any particular decision, one fall-back is to reach consensus on the appropriateness of voting. Such a decision should always be seen as a recognition of some sort of failure. Assuming that the choice is substantive, then one decision is, in reality, the better one. So the fact that we cannot find perceptions, considerations, arguments, data and the like that supports one or the other is a sign that we are arguing badly, are missing something, are not in possession of adequate data, or that some of us are not being reasonable. But still, such kinds of things happen in the crush of real-world circumstances, and when they do, we sometimes decide quite fairly, to vote.

If we do so decide, then the argument of section 2 means that our procedure should be symmetrical. Thus, while it need not be as simple as majority vote, the procedure will be closer, in such a circumstance, to voting than to consensus procedure. But I want to urge that it is misleading, nonetheless, to think of this as an endorsement of voting over consensus.

By way of illustration, let me recall a particular decision taken by the Georgetown philosophy department. On the day in question we had a highly disputed decision before us for which there was no possible compromise. That is, this was the sort of decision for which there were exactly two options. And the department came into the meeting strongly divided. Group A felt that accepting the proposal before us was right and important for the future of the department. Group B felt that rejecting the same decision was equally important. And so, we discussed the matter. We argued, back and forth, brought up new considerations, laid out ways of thinking about the issue, creatively tried to relate the decision to other ones we had made, to contextualize the issue within the broader goals of the department, etc. …for several hours. And very few minds were changed. Sensing that we were making little progress, the chair finally called for a vote. And the motion passed, something like 16 — 8, whereupon we prepared to leave, assuming the chair would pass this decision on to the dean.

Before we could do so, the leading voice in Group A — the winning group — stopped us. "Wait," she said.[13] "I've never seen us adopt an important decision with such a split vote. It may not be our rule, but it is our practice to discuss things until we arrive at a view we all respect. And we always take account of everyone's concerns. I worry that the minority are going to feel bullied here, and so think we should discuss this more." Though not thrilled to have to stay longer, everyone immediately heeded the call and resumed their chairs.

Whereupon the leading voice of the losing group said "Absolutely not. We made our arguments, gave our reasons. As always, everyone listened, took us seriously, and we failed to convince you. So I will not hear of re-opening the issue. We have a case where we disagree and a strong majority of the department thinks one way. The only reasonable thing for any of us to support in such a case is that vote as we find it."

What went on here: majority voting, or consensus? It is obviously misleading to characterize things either way. We found no consensus on the issue at hand, but we equally did not simply vote. Rather, we reached a consensus in favor of going with the majority position. We recognized that our collective rationality, our group virtue, was insufficient to reach a consensus on the issue at hand, and therefore made use of a formal voting procedure. But our local failure sparked an expression of a deeper structural kind of virtue — both virtue on the part of each participant, and a collective virtue embedded in the habits of discourse among them. And it was precisely this kind of virtue which was missing in the Mobilization for Global Justice. Rather than carry on respectful and careful discussion until we found consensus, if not on what to do, at least on what procedure to employ, a small minority forced the mechanical application of one particular procedure down the throats of the majority on the grounds that it had been adopted earlier. In the context of such social vice, it was no consolation whatsoever that the procedure had a happy name like "consensus".

Contentious concluding remarks

So where are we? Though I've hardly argued in detail for such grand claims, I urge that a number of conclusions are made plausible by the foregoing discussion.

- A key goal of any anarchist strategy must be the development of discursive, social, and rational virtue in each other.
- Any viable anarchist society must institutionalize things like schools, discussion forums, and critical process discussions, which will allow us to form and maintain such virtues in ourselves.
- The only fully democratic way to reach a decision is to have a discussion the end of which is a consensus on what is the right decision.
- If our local lack of virtue prevents a fully democratic decision-making practice in a particular case, there are any number of procedural rules, and people skilled at applying such rules, to which we might turn in attempting to deal with the problem.
- If we find that we need to make a decision, but cannot reach consensus on what the right decision is, we should by all means give symmetrical authority to both action and inaction. There is no grounds for privileging one over the other in the abstract. (Of course we might agree that in this case either caution or action is to be privileged due to particular factors.)

- If we cannot come to consensus on a given issue, then the issue becomes how to make a decision, and consensus is demanded on this. Though we will likely vote, such a procedure can only be just on the basis of a rationally and morally arrived at consensus on the appropriateness of voting in this case. Voting is often the right procedure to turn to, and far more likely to be procedurally correct than is consensus procedure, but whatever authority voting procedure has will derive from consensus practice.

This all seems to point to a particular practical recommendation for anyone aiming to form an anarchist organization: do not write down any procedure as part of the defining structure of the group! Any procedure you try to legislate is as likely to be abused, as likely to give people a crutch to lean on, or an excuse to avoid careful thinking, discussion, and inclusive labor. No procedure guarantees wise decision making, and a wide variety of procedures can be useful in arriving at wise decisions. So do not privilege one over another in the abstract. If you must have a constitution, say "our group will attempt to take each other seriously, to look at issues rationally, to engage in careful, respectful, critical, rigorous analysis and argument, and to arrive at the wisest and most just decisions on all issues before us." If you need to say more than this, then say much more. Say that among the tools we will use in trying to arrive at such just and wise decisions are ... and then initiate and ever-growing list of useful techniques.

Above all, remember that constitutions, like the rules they record, are no better than the people who implement them. So the task is just as much to make better versions of ourselves as it is to make better versions of society.

Endnotes

1 "Coming to Consensus: Tips for Cooperation and Collaboration in Decision Making, or How to Run Meetings So Everyone Wins" By Mark Shepard [http://www.markshep.com/nonviolence/Consensus.html

2 NONVIOLENT ACTION HANDBOOK Group Process, by Sanderson Beck [http://www.san.beck.org/NAH1-Nonviolence.html]

3 "Notes on Consensus Decision Making," Randy Schutt [http://www.vernalproject.org/RPapers.shtml#CoopDecMaking]

4 What is Communalism? The Democratic Dimension of Anarchism, Murray Bookchin — from The Anarchy Archive [http://dwardmac.pitzer.edu/anarchist_archives/bookchin/CMMNL2.MCW.html]

5 I have not researched this example, so I am simply taking Bookchin's word about it for purposes of argument. Nothing of import here hangs on the actual case.

6 Lions and Tigers and Bears, oh my!

7   "A Revolutionary Decision-Making Process " [See http://www.consensus.net/
     revolutionary.html]

8   The account that follows is from personal experience. I was centrally involved in
     the MGJ planning process for this convergence. Though my work was primarily
     with the educational series associated with the protests — the People's Summit — I
     also attended general MGJ meetings. There are many others who have confirmed
     my memory of the events, though it is only fair to say that there are also those
     who dispute this account of what went on. For purposes of the general argument
     I am making here, nothing much hangs on this. You could just as well treat this as
     a hypothetical example of a way that consensus procedure could be abused. But I
     believe it is important for us to appreciate the real harm done, in the very contexts
     in which we work, by such abuse. And it is also important for us to develop habits of
     confronting efforts to so abuse our practice. I take the inclusion of a real case, rather
     than a hypothetical one, to be a small step along the way toward such habits.

9   And the effects of this shameful manipulation were significant. The vacuum created
     by the pullout of MGJ was filled predictably by ANSWER [IAC, WWP], a significant
     event in the (now, apparently and thankfully, temporary) rise to prominence of this
     authoritarian organization. So deep were the feelings of hurt and betrayal by the
     actions on this day and subsequent "defenses" of them — defenses that often involved
     character assassination and verbal abuse — that MGJ in its previous form effectively
     disbanded. Nearly all the grassroots activists pulled out and joined other coalitions,
     generally with far fewer resources. Most NGOs stayed, but their subsequent protest
     actions and educational events were a shadow of their previous strength. It is
     noteworthy that one leader of the putsch in Sept. consistently defended the choice
     to cancel events — I heard this defense four times at different forums over the next
     two years — by saying that there had been consensus support for canceling, a use of
     language that can only be called Orwellian.

10 It is worth saying explicitly that I am not suggesting anything about academia at large.
     Few are the academic departments which function the way this one does. Many are
     irrational, spiteful, dogmatic, and oppressive institutions.

11 Though the objection of this section is really quite obvious, so far as I know, it has not
     been discussed elsewhere. Given the nature of the point, I would not be surprised to
     learn, however, that it has been pointed out by someone I'm unaware of.

12 I have a good deal to add, both in terms of the underlying philosophical ideas and
     specific practices, in Awakening Reason.

13 Roughly. This is not an exact quote, but closely captures what was said.

Martin approaches the age-old question of governance in an anarchist setting with this three-part article on democracy. The first part offers a critique of the traditional electoral process; the second part covers a variety of common alternatives (referendum, consensus, federations); and the third part discusses a little-known process called demarchy, whereby individuals are selected at random to fulfill roles necessary to the maintenance of social organizations.

Originally published in issue 21.

Democracy without Elections
Brian Martin

For many a jaded radical, the greens are the most exciting political development for ages. The green movements claim to bring together members of the most dynamic social movements, including the peace, environmental and feminist movements, combining their insights and numbers. This is something that many activists have long sought.

Beyond this, the rapidly achieved electoral success of green parties has really captured the imagination. The German Greens have been the center of attention for over a decade precisely because of their election to parliaments. A number of other green parties have also been electorally successful.

But wait a moment. Before getting too carried away, isn't it worth asking whether elections are an appropriate way forward? After all, electoral politics is the standard, traditional approach, which has led to those traditional parties that have so frustrated many a radical. Isn't there a danger that participation in the electoral process remains a trap, a bottomless pit for political energy which will pacify activists and masses alike?

My aim here is to take a critical look at elections and their alternatives. I start in Part One with a summary of the case against elections. Much of this will be familiar to anarchists, but it may be useful in bringing together the arguments and perhaps raising one or two unfamiliar ones.

If elections have limitations, then what are the alternatives? This is a harder question. In Part Two I look at some of the methods favored by those supporting "participatory democracy," namely, actual rule by the people rather than through elected representatives. These participatory methods, naturally enough, have both strengths and weaknesses. One of their key weaknesses is that it is hard for them to deal with decision making involving large numbers of people without succumbing to some of the same problems as representative systems.

Finally, in Part Three I present the idea of demarchy, a participatory system based on random selection. This is, I believe, a most promising alternative. It is little known, but in recent years there have been important theoretical developments and practical experiences.

One: the case against elections

The idea of elections as the ultimate democratic device is a deep-seated one in the West. It is hard to escape it. Children are taught all about elections in school, and may vote for student councils or club officers. Then all around us, especially through the mass media, attention is given to politicians and, periodically, to the elections which put them in power. Indeed, the main connection which most people have with their rulers is the ballot box. It is no wonder that electoral politics is sanctified. If a country has no elections, or only sham elections, this is taken as a sign of failure.

Elections in practice have served well to maintain dominant power structures such as private property, the military, male domination and economic inequality. No one of these has been seriously threatened through voting. It is from the point of view of radical critics that elections are most limiting.

The theory of representative democracy and popular sovereignty is based on some hidden, convenient fictions. Here I'll concentrate on the practical shortcomings of electoral systems, though it would be possible to relate these to theoretical assumptions.

Voting doesn't work. At the simplest level, voting simply doesn't work very well to promote serious challenges to prevailing power systems. The basic problem is quite simple. An elected representative is not tied in any substantial way to particular policies, whatever the preference of the electorate. Influence on the politician is greatest at the time of election. Once elected, the representative is released from popular control (recall is virtually impossible before the next election) but continues to be exposed to powerful pressure groups, especially corporations, state bureaucracies and political party power brokers.

We all know examples of politicians who have "sold out," relinquishing their claimed ideals and breaking their solemn promises. Ironically, this is just as true for right-wingers as for left-wingers. The radical right was very disillusioned by Ronald Reagan.

Usually the sell-outs are attributed to failures of personality, but this is both unfair and misleading. Politicians are morally little different from anyone else. The expectations and pressures on them are much greater. Positions of great power attract both the most ambitious and ruthless people and bring out the worst features of those who obtain them.

It is not the individuals who should be blamed, but the system in which they operate.

In principle, elections should work all right for moderately small electorates and political systems, where accountability can be maintained through regular contact. Elections can be much better justified in New England town meetings than in national parliaments making decisions affecting millions of people. In these large systems a whole new set of reinforcing mechanisms has developed: political party machines, mass advertising, government manipulation of news, pork barreling (government projects in local areas), and bipartisan politics. The party machines choose the candidates, canvass voters and impose platforms. Mass advertising treats candidates like soap powders, emphasizing personality over policies. Government manipulation of the news includes a variety of techniques by which the mass media become dependent on government suppliers and shapers of information. Government largess in select regions is a standard technique to attract (or threaten) voters. Finally, bipartisan politics, namely, the adoption of identical or near-identical policies by allegedly competing parties, reduces the range of issues which are subject to political debate. In essence, voters are given the choice between Tweedledee and Tweedledum, and then bombarded with a variety of techniques to sway them toward one or the other.

This is a depressing picture, but hope springs eternal from the voter's pen. Some maintain the faith that a mainstream party may be reformed or radicalized. Others look toward new parties. When a new party such as the greens shows principles and growth, it is hard to be completely cynical.

Nevertheless, all the historical evidence suggests that parties are more a drag than an impetus to radical change. One obvious problem is that parties can be voted out. All the policy changes they brought in can simply be reversed later.

More important, though, is the pacifying influence of the radical party itself. On a number of occasions, radical parties have been elected to power as a result of popular upsurges. Time after time, the "radical" parties have become chains to hold back the process of radical change. Ralph Miliband gives several examples where labor or socialist parties, elected in periods of social turbulence, acted to reassure the dominant capitalist class and subdue popular action. The Popular Front, elected in France in 1936, mad its first task the ending of strikes and occupations and generally dampening a popular militancy, which was the Front's strongest ally in bringing about change. The Labor government elected in Britain in 1945 mad as few reforms as possible, leaving basic social structures untouched. By contrast, the US New Deal Democratic administration which took office in 1933 did undertake structural changes- in order to restore and strengthen capitalism. Miliband in these examples writes form the Marxist perspective in which the state is the servant of capitalism. His insights about the reluctance of "reforming" political leadership of the state to challenge the economic foundation of society applies even more strongly to the unwillingness of this leadership to challenge state power itself.

The experiences of Eurosocialist parties elected to power in France, Greece and Spain in the 1980s have followed the same pattern. In all major areas — the economy, the structure of state power, and foreign policy — the Eurosocialist governments have retreated from their initial goals and become much more like traditional ruling parties.

Voting disempowers the grassroots. If voting simply didn't work to bring about changes at the top, that would not be a conclusive argument. After all, change in society doesn't just come about through laws and policies. As feminists and other say, "the personal is political," and that means just about everything. There are plenty of opportunities for action outside the electoral system.

It is here that voting makes a more serious inroad into radical social action: it is a diversion from grassroots action. The aim of electoral politics is to elect someone who then can take action. This means that instead of taking direct action against injustice, the action becomes indirect: get the politicians to do something.

On more than one occasion, I've seen a solid grassroots campaign undermined by an election. One example is the 1977 Australian federal election in the midst of a powerful campaign against uranium mining. Another is the 1983 Australian federal election at a crucial point in the campaign against the flooding of the Franklin River in Tasmania.

At the simplest level, energy put into electioneering is energy not put into direct action. Some activists feel resentful that their campaign is hijacked by election priorities. This can be compensated, to some extent, by the heightened interest in the issues during an election campaign. The more serious problem is the loss of energy that usually occurs after the election.

In the December 1977 election, the pro-uranium Liberal Party was reelected. This was very demoralizing for the anti-uranium movement which had hoped for a victory by the Australian Labor Party with its new anti-uranium platform. Yet, in retrospect, the movement was having considerable success even under the Liberals. A stepped-up campaign should have been called for. But this was hard to achieve. Many anti-uranium activists, notably those who were Labor Party members, had participated in 1977 because of the upcoming election. After Labor's defeat many of them dropped out of the movement, leaving those remaining feeling less than encouraged. The election campaign was a diversion from long-term strategy against uranium. It raised activity temporarily, to be followed by a more persistent decline.

Another problem is the centralization of power in social movements which is encouraged by the desire to influence politicians. The campaign against the flooding of the Franklin River in Tasmania illustrates this. A long well-orchestrated campaign by a variety of means culminated in December 1982 in a "blockade" against construction work on the dam, using classic nonviolent action techniques. During the blockade, a national election was called for March 1983. The leaders of the Tasmanian Wilderness Society and the Australian Conservation Foundation negotiated with the leaders for the Australian Labor Party, and made the deal. The conservationists would support Labor for the House of Representatives; Labor, if elected, would act to stop the dam.

My main point here is the undemocratic fashion in which deals are made in the political system. It is also interesting to note the aftermath of these negotiations. The blockade was downgraded; Labor, with the support of the mainstream environmental organizations, won a close election. The new Labor government did not use its financial power directly against the dam, but rather just supported a legal action in the High Court to use federal power (in relation to a World Heritage listing) to stop a state project. This case won by one vote in the High Court. During all this time, the environmentalists were disempowered, waiting for powerful politicians and judges to decide the fate of the river. The aftermath was a powerful backlash in Tasmania, using the rhetoric of the state's rights, against environmentalists.

Incidentally, the 1983 Labor government decided to renege on several remaining planks of its anti-uranium platform. The anti-uranium movement reemerged on Labor's election, and sank again after this "betrayal."

It should be a truism that elections empower the politicians and not the voters. Yet many social movements continually are drawn into electoral politics. There are several reasons for this. One is the involvement of party members in social movements. Another is the aspirations for power and influence by leaders in movements. Having the ear of a government minister is a heady sensation for many; getting elected to parliament oneself is even more of an ego boost. What is forgotten in all this "politics of influence" is the effect on ordinary activist.

The disempowering effect of elections works not only on activists but also on others. The ways in which elections serve the interests of state power have been admirably explained by Benjamin Ginsberg. Ginsberg's basic thesis is that elections historically have enlarged the number of people who participate in "Politics," but by turning this involvement into a routine activity (voting), elections have reduced the risk of more radical direct action.

The expansion of suffrage is typically presented as a triumph of downtrodden groups against privilege. Workers gained the vote in the face of opposition by the propertied class; women gained it in the face of male-dominated governments and electorates. Ginsberg challenges this picture. He argues that the suffrage in many countries was expanded in times when there was little social pressure for it.

Why should this be? Basically, voting serves to legitimate government. To bolster its legitimacy, if required, suffrage can be expanded. This is important when mass support is crucial, for example during wartime. It can be seen in other areas as well. Worker representatives on corporate boards of management serve to co-opt dissent; so do student representatives on university councils.

Ginsberg shows that elections operate to bring mass political activity into a manageable form: election campaigns and voting. People learn that they can participate — they are not totally excluded. They also learn the limits of participation. Voting occurs only occasionally, at times fixed by governments. Voting serves only to select leaders, not to directly decide policy. Finally, voting doesn't take passion into account; the vote of the indifferent or ill-informed voter counts just the same as that of the concerned and knowledgeable voter. Voting thus serves to tame political participation, making it a routine process that prevents mass uprisings. The expansion of suffrage helps to reduce the chance that a revolt by an oppressed or excluded group will be seen as justified; with the vote, it is easy for others to claim that they should have used "orthodox channels."

Voting reinforces state power. Ginsberg's most important point is that elections give citizens the impression that the government does (or can) serve the people. The founding of the modern state a few centuries ago was met with great resistance: people would refuse to pay taxes, to be conscripted or to obey laws passed by national governments. The introduction of voting and the expanded suffrage have greatly aided the expansion of state power. Rather than seeing the system as one of ruler and ruled, people see at least the possibility of using state power to serve themselves. As electoral participation has increased, the degree of resistance to taxation, military service, and the immense variety of laws regulating behavior, has been greatly attenuated.

The irony in all this, as pointed out by Ginsberg, is that the expansion of state power, legitimated by voting, has now outgrown any control by the participation which made it possible. States are now so large and complex that any expectation of popular control seems remote. Yet, as he comments, the "idea that electoral participation means popular control of government is so deeply implanted in the psyches of most Americans that even the most overtly skeptical cannot fully free themselves from it." Needless to say, this statement applies to many countries besides the United States.

Using Ginsberg's perspective, the initial government-sponsored introduction of some competition into elections in the Soviet Union and Eastern Europe takes on a new meaning. If the economic restructuring seen as necessary by Communist Party leaders was to have any chance of success, then there had to be greater support for the government. What better way than by introducing some choice into voting? Increased government legitimacy, and hence increased real power for the government, was the aim.

Change in Eastern Europe has gone far past that planned by governments, of course. Still, it is revealing that a key demand of reformers has been to introduce multiparty elections. What is sought is a change in the running of government, not in the basic mechanisms of governance.

Although expanding the franchise does help legitimate government, it certainly does not close off political struggle. The introduction of voting and the expansion of suffrage may institutionalize political activity, but they do after all allow the activity. Elections may reduce the chance of radical challenges to the status quo, but that chance does exist. Electoral politics legitimate government to the extent that governments are to some extent dependent on the will of the people — however routinized and institutionalized the expression for the people's will may be. Because elections provide a channel for radical change, even though a very constrained channel, the hope of radicals is maintained and their reliance on elections is encouraged.

Ginsberg's analysis leads to the third major limitation of electoral politics: it relies on the state and reinforces state power. Of course this is simply another facet of the two previous objections, namely that elections don't work to bring about radical change (because the state machinery is designed for other interests) and that elections disempower the grassroots (because energy is channeled into the state). The basis of an anarchist critique of voting is that voting participates in the legitimation of the state. If the state is part of the problem — namely, being a prime factor in war, genocide, repression, economic inequality, male domination and environmental destruction — then it is foolish to expect that the problems can be overcome by electing a few new nominal leaders of the state.

It is possible to paint a more sophisticated picture of the state, in which there are continual struggles inside and outside the state apparatuses to shape policies and to serve and empower different groups of people. In this picture, it is worth struggling within the state, for example for welfare measures for the poor or against aggressive military policies. There are few who would object to this. But even with this more sophisticated picture, the fundamental critique of the state can still apply.

The basic point concerns whether the organizational structure of the state is neutral or not. If the structure of the state is assumed to be neutral, then the exercise of state power can be seen as the playing out of various power struggles, such as capitalist power versus workers' power or male power versus female power. If the structure of the state is neutral, then that state can be seen as a site for class struggle, gender struggle, etc. This is a typical perspective adopted by Marxists, some feminists and most liberals. It is quite an improvement from the picture of the state as a complete tool of the capitalist class. But it does not question the basic assumption of the neutrality of the state structure, which as a consequence can be captured one way or another, either by the simplistic image of taking state power or by the more sophisticated image of working in and against the state.

The basic anarchist insight is that the structure of the state, as a centralized administrative apparatus, is inherently flawed form the point of view of human freedom and equality. Even thought the state can be used occasionally for valuable ends, as a means the state is flawed and impossible to reform. The non-reformable aspects of the state include, centrally, its monopoly over 'legitimate' violence and its consequent power to coerce for the purpose of war, internal control, taxation, and the protection of property and bureaucratic privilege.

The problem with voting is that the basic premises of the state are never considered open for debate, much less challenge. The state's monopoly over the use of violence for war is never at issue. Neither is the stat's use of violence against revolt from within. The state's right to extract economic resources from the population is never questioned. Neither is the state's guarantee of either private property (under capitalism) or bureaucratic prerogative (under state socialism) — or both.

Voting can lead to changes in policies. That is fine and good. But the policies are developed and executed within the state framework, which is a basic constraint. Voting legitimates the state framework.

One response to the limitations of electoral politics is to campaign against voting and elections. This is useful in raising awareness of the limitations of electing one's rulers. But such a critique needs to be supplemented by the promotion of alternatives to the state. That is a harder task. After all, there's no use in criticizing electoral methods if there isn't anything better.

Two: Alternatives to Elections

What participatory alternatives are there to the state and electoral politics? This is a topic on which there is a large literature, especially by anarchists. So I can do no more than highlight some of the relevant answers and experiences. I will emphasize some of the limitations of the standard responses to this problem, since it is essential to be as critical of alternatives as of the existing system.

Referendums. One set of alternatives is based on direct mass involvement in policy-making through voting, using mechanisms including petition, recall, initiative and referendum. In short, instead of electing politicians who then make policy decisions, these decisions are made directly by the public.

Referendums have been used widely in the United States, often to the dismay of powerful groups. The fluoridation of public water supplies as a measure to reduce tooth decay has resulted in hundreds of referendums, for example. The more frequent result has been against fluoridation, much to the consternation of proponents, who as a result have counseled against referendums and tried for implementation directly by governments.

In practice, referendums have been only supplements to a policy process based on elected representatives. But it is possible to conceive of a vast expansion of the use of referendums, especially by use of computer technology. Some exponents propose a future in which each household television system is hooked up with equipment for direct electronic voting. The case for and against a referendum proposal would be broadcast, followed by a mass vote. What could be more democratic?

Unfortunately, there are some serious flaws in such proposals. These go deeper than the problems of media manipulation, involvement by big-spending vested interests, and the worries by experts and elites that the public will be irresponsible in direct voting.

A major problem is the setting of the agenda for the referendum. Who decides the questions? Who decides what material is broadcast for and against a particular question? Who decides the wider context of voting?

The fundamental issue concerning setting of the agenda is not simply bias. It is a question of participation. Participation in decision making means not just voting on predesigned questions, but participation in the formulation of which questions are put to a vote. This is something that is not easy to organize when a million people are involved, even with the latest electronics. It is a basic limitation of referendums.

The key to this limitation of referendums is the presentation of a single choice to a large number of voters. Even when some citizens are involved in developing the question, as in the case of referendums based on the process of citizen initiative, most people have no chance to be involved in more than a yes-no capacity. The opportunity to recast the question in the light of discussion is not available.

Another problem with referendums is a very old one, fundamental to voting itself. Simply put, rule by the majority often means oppression of the minority. This problem is more clear-cut in direct voting systems, but also appears in representative systems.

Historically, the referendum approach assumes the existence of a bureaucratic apparatus for implementing the decision made. Referendums don't implement themselves, certainly. Who does? The state. Referendums, in practice, are a way of increasing participation within the parameters of centralized administration. This latter problem is not intrinsic to the referendum as a method. The challenge is to recast the referendum as part of a more participatory political process.

Consensus. Consensus decision-making has become widely used in a number of social movements in the past couple of decades, especially in parts of the antinuclear power movement. In general parlance, "consensus" means gaining general agreement, but within social movements it has been given a more precise, operational meaning.

The basic aim is for a group of generally like-minded people to reach a common decision without greatly alienating anyone. This might be a collective working on a newspaper or a group planning a direct action against a military facility. Voting is avoided for several reasons. Those who lose a close or bitterly contested vote often fail to support the majority position, and sometimes even end up leaving the group. Lots of energy is wasted in lobbying and building factions for the purposes of winning votes rather than developing the best campaign. Finally, innovative proposals are often ignored because they seem to stand no chance in a vote.

The basic procedure in consensus decision making is that various options are canvassed and discussed. If everyone seems to be agreeing, then a test is made for consensus. If no one disagrees, consensus has been reached. If anyone disagrees, they are encouraged to spell out their objections. Consensus is blocked if there is strong disagreement by even one person (or, in modified consensus, by a specified small fraction).

If consensus is blocked, then the group seeks ways to reach agreement. The arguments can be reexamined; new proposals can be raised and discussed; the decision can be postponed until a later time. For example, the group may break itself into a number of small groups which readdress the issue, seeking a resolution.

In many cases, the procedure works remarkably well. Those with divergent views generally see that they are taken seriously, and this builds the cohesion of the group. Sometimes a minority view eventually becomes the consensus view: there is no quick vote to overwhelm it. Most encouraging of all, sometimes brilliant new solutions are developed in the efforts to reach consensus.

That consensus methods often work well should come as no surprise, since they have long been used in an unacknowledged manner in all sorts of situations. For many organizations, official votes are ritualistic only. A vote is seldom taken unless it is obvious beforehand that everyone agrees, or at least that no one strongly disagrees.

The practice of consensus decision-making formalizes the process. This is most important as the group gets larger. For large groups there are various methods involving subgroups and delegates which ensure that the basic consensus approach is followed.

An important difference between consensus and normal "meeting procedure" is the role of leadership. The conventional method has a formal leader (the chair) and a set of formal rules for setting the agenda, speaking, making motions, voting, etc. — the familiar Roberts rules of order. The consensus approach has no formal leader, but has instead "facilitators" who are supposed to help the group do what it wants to. The facilitators are crucial to the success of consensus. They are supposed to test for consensus, encourage less articulate group members to participate, offer suggestions for procedure, summarize views expressed, etc. The ideal is when every group member helps in facilitation, so there is no obvious leader at all.

Consensus, then, is a method of decision-making without voting that aims for participation, group cohesion, and openness to new ideas. Combined with other group skills for social analysis, examining group dynamics, developing strategies and evaluation, consensus can be powerful indeed.

Yet anyone who has participated in consensus decision-making should be aware that the practice is often far short of the theory. Sometimes powerful personalities dominate the process; less confident people are afraid to express their views. Because objections normally have to be voiced face-to-face, the protection of anonymity in the secret ballot is lost. Meetings can be interminable, and those who cannot devote the required time to them are effectively disenfranchised. The biggest problem for consensus, though is irreconcilable conflict of interest.

The best treatment of this problem is *Beyond Adversary Democracy* by Jane Mansbridge. Mansbridge distinguishes between two types of democracy. What she calls adversary democracy is the familiar electoral approach. It is based on the assumption of conflicting interests, majority rule, secret ballot and equal protection of interests. What she calls unitary democracy is like friendship. It is based on a high degree of common interest, consensus-like methods, face-to-face decision-making,, and a rough equality of mutual respect.

Mansbridge closely analyses two cases in detail: a New England town meeting which formally uses voting but in practice often seeks consensus, and a work collective which uses formal consensus methods.

Mansbridge points out that the standard approach is to assume conflicting interests and to use adversarial methods, but that unitary interests are much more common than generally realized. Hence, seeking unity, rather than assuming conflict, is often preferable. Her most important point, though, for my purposes here, is that consensus has a complementary weakness: it can't handle deep-seated conflict.

Much of such conflict is derived from an inequality of power. To imagine employers and workers in a typical enterprise trying to reach consensus is difficult. They don't have common interests or, very often, equality of respect. In a self-managed enterprise, by contrast, there are no separate employers and consensus becomes more feasible.

Other types of conflict are just as difficult to deal with. Imagine a group of anarchists, Marxists and liberals (with a few conservatives tossed in for good measure) trying to reach consensus on a campaign for reducing crime. Even with the best intentions, the different perspectives on the world are likely to undermine attempts at consensus on more than the most superficial level.

The larger the group, the more likely there are to be fundamental conflicts of interests. Consensus is most likely to work in small, self-selected groups. But as a democratic alternative to elections it has severe limitations dealing with large groups. The problems of consensus are also the problems of self-management in large groups.

Small size. One solution to this dilemma is to keep group sizes small. Rather than centralization of power, decentralization is the aim. There is no intrinsic reason why education, health, investment and many other functions have to be administered at the level of many millions of people rather than, say, thousands or tens of thousands. Many of the most participatory polities, from ancient Greece to today, have been relatively small. Conversely, many of the ills of electoral politics seem to be associated with the enormous population in many countries.

Small size reduces the severity of many of the problems of decision-making. Even voting is not so limiting when the number of voters is so small that everyone is potentially known to everyone else. The use of consensus can be maximized.

Furthermore, small size opens the possibility of a plurality of political systems. Frances Kendall and Leon Louw propose a Swiss-like federation of autonomous political entities, each of which can choose its own political and economic system. With Kendall and Louw's system, the difficulties of trying new methods, and the costs of failures, are greatly reduced.

Small size may make governance easier, but there will still be some large-scale problems requiring solution. Global pollution and local disasters, for example, call for more than local solutions. How are decisions to be made about such issues?

More fundamentally, small size by itself doesn't solve the issue of how decisions are made. There can still be deep conflicts of interests which make consensus inappropriate, and there can still be problems of domination resulting from electoral methods.

Finally, in all but the very tiniest groups, the basic problem of limits to participation remains. No everyone has time to become fully knowledgeable about every issue. Consensus assumes that everyone can and should participate in decisions; if substantial numbers drop out, it becomes rule by the energetic, or by those who have nothing better to do. Representative democracy, by contrast, puts elected representatives in the key decision-making roles; the participation of everyone else is restricted to campaigning, voting and lobbying. In both cases participation is very unequal, not by choice but by the structure of the decision-making system.

Delegates and federations. A favorite anarchist solution to the problem of coordination and participation is delegates and federations. A delegate differs from a representative in that the delegate is more closely tied to the electorate; the delegate can be recalled at any time, especially when not following the dictates of the electors. Federations are a way of combining self-governing entities. The member bodies in the federation retain the major decision-making power over their own affairs. The members come together to decide issues affecting all of them. In a "weak federation," the center has considerable executive power in specified areas. By having several tiers in the federation, full participation can be ensured at the bottom level, and consultation and some decision making occur at the highest levels

Delegates and federations sound like an alternative to conventional electoral systems, but there are strong similarities. Delegates are normally elected, and this leads to the familiar problems of representation. Certain individuals dominate. Participation in decision-making is unequal, with the delegates being heavily involved and others not. To the degree that decisions are actually made at higher levels, there is great potential for development of factions, vote trading and manipulation of the electorate.

This is why the delegate system is supposed to be different. If the delegates start to serve themselves rather than those they represent, they can be recalled. But in practice this is hard to achieve. Delegates tend to "harden" into formal representatives. Those chosen as delegates are likely to have much more experience and knowledge than the ordinary person. Once chosen, the delegates gain even more experience and knowledge, which can be presented as of high value to the electors. In other words, recalling the delegate will be at the cost of losing an experienced and influential person.

These problems have surfaced in the German Green Party. Although formally elected as representatives, the party sought to treat those elected as delegates, setting strict limits on the length of time in parliament. This was resisted by some of those elected, who were able to build support due to their wide appeal. Furthermore, from a pragmatic point of view (which is often hard to resist), those who had served in parliament had the experience and public profile to better promote the green cause. Thus the delegate approach came under great stress even though the green politicians had little real power. In a situation where the delegates are truly making decisions, the stresses will be much greater.

The fundamental problem with the delegate system, then, is unequal participation. Not everyone can be involved in every issue. With delegates, the problem is resolved by having the delegates involved much more in decision-making, at the expense oft others. This unequal participation then reproduces and entrenches itself. The more layers there are to the federation, the more serious this problem will be. Federations, as well, are not a magical solution to the problem of coordination in a self-managing society.

In this brief survey of some of the more well-known participative alternatives to elections, I've focused on their limitations. But these and other methods do have many strengths, and are worth promoting as additions or alternatives to the present system. Consensus has been developed enormously over the past couple of decades as a practical decision-making method. The potential of decentralization is undoubtedly great. Indeed, the greatest successes of consensus have been in small groups. In addition to the idea of federations, there is also much attention given to networks, which do not assume any set of levels for decision making.

Rather than dismissing these possibilities, my aim is to point out some of the problems that confront them. The most serious difficulty is how to ensure participation in a wide range of issues that affect any person. How can the (self-managed) activities of large numbers of people be coordinated without vesting excessive power in a small group of people?

I now turn to "demarchy," which is one answer to some of these problems. It is by no means the only or final answer. But it is an approach that holds potential and, in my opinion, is worth much investigation and experimentation.

John Zube advocates "panarchy," the peaceful coexistence of a diversity of methods for voluntary association. In this spirit, demarchy can be considered as one candidate for organizing society in a participative fashion.

Three: Demarchy

The most eloquent account of demarchy is given by John Burnheim in his book *Is Democracy Possible?* Burnheim begins by analyzing the state and bureaucracy, and concludes that they are central obstacles to the achievement of true democracy. He includes electoral politics as part of the problem. Since the word "democracy" is so tainted by association with representative government, Burnheim coined the word "demarchy" to refer to his alternative.

Demarchy is based on random selection of individuals to serve in decision-making groups which deal with particular functions or services, such as roads or education. Forget the state and forget bureaucracies. In a full-fledged demarchy, all this is replaced by a network of groups whose members are randomly selected, each of which deals with a particular function in a particular area.

For example, in a population of 10,000 to 100,000 there might be groups dealing with transport, health, agriculture, industry, education, garbage, housing, art and so forth, or particular aspects of such functions as rail transport. Each group would be chosen randomly from all those who volunteer to be in it. The groups could be perhaps 10 or 20 people, large enough to obtain a variety of views but small enough for face-to-face discussion. The groups themselves could use consensus, modified consensus, voting or some other procedure to reach decisions. They could call for submissions, testimony, surveys and any other information they wished to obtain.

Before going further, it is worth looking more closely at random selection (also called sortition). This was used in ancient Athens as a democratic selection device, but has been little used since. Of course, Athenian democracy was limited, excluding women and slaves. Nevertheless, there are many things that can be learned from it.

One of the values of random selection was to increase participation and prevent the formation of factions. When the assembly met, the chairman was selected by lot at the beginning of the meeting. In this there was no opportunity for pre-assembly plotting to push toward particular outcomes by putting pressure on the chairman.

The Athenians used voting too, for example in choosing military leaders. In fact, they used a variety of democratic devices, each chosen for particular purposes. Writers on liberal democracy today draw on the Athenian experience selectively. They use it to justify representation, but ignore or dismiss the use of sortition. Indeed, democracy is often defined today as representative democracy.

The major use of random selection for important decision making today is the jury, which itself prospers in only the United States and a few other countries. "Ordinary people" are randomly chosen to decide the fate of their fellow humans. The jury is embedded in a political framework which constrains its potential: the framework of laws which is biased toward the interests of the privileged; the selective enforcement of law; manipulations by lawyers, judges and media. Considering these obstacles, the jury performs remarkably well.

Many governments have dispensed with juries, arguing that professional judges are more suitable. The argument that juries are less capable of dealing with complex technical issues is a vexed one. Arguably, a jury of a dozen people is likely to contain one or two people more technically competent than the average judge.

It is certainly the case that juries are hated by repressive governments. Judges can be pressured more easily by governments than can juries.

From a decision-making point of view, the great advantage of the jury is its capacity for testing opinions. In terms of participation in decision-making, the jury is a form of policy making, though this is greatly discouraged by most judges.

Considering that most jury members are given no training in critical assessment of evidence and formation of conclusions, in consensus decision-making techniques or in the role of the jury itself, the decision-making record of juries is remarkably sound. Rather than attacking the failures of the jury system, it would be more appropriate to develop ways of making it function better.

Returning now to Burnheim's picture of demarchy, how does it handle the basic problems of participation? Because there are no elections and no representatives, the problems of unequal formal power, disempowerment of electors, regulation of participation and so forth do not apply — at least not in the usual way. Formal participation occurs instead through random selection onto "functional groups," namely, groups dealing with particular limited areas. Random selection for each group is made only from those who volunteer, just as politicians must volunteer,. The difference is the method of selection: random selection rather than election.

Few people would volunteer for every possible group. Most are likely to have special interests, such as postal services, art, manufacture of building material and services for the disabled. They could volunteer to serve on the relevant groups, and also make submissions to the groups, comment on policies and in other ways organize to promote their favored policies.

Demarchy solves the problem of participation in a neat fashion. Recognizing that it is impossible for everyone to participate on every issue in an informed fashion, it avoids anything resembling a governing body which makes far-reaching decisions on a range of issues. Instead, the functional groups have a limited domain. The people who care most about a particular issue can seek to have an influence over policy in that area. They can leave other issues to other groups and the people most concerned about them. This is basically a process of decentralization of decision-making by topic or function rather than by geography or numbers.

Leaving decision-making to those who care most about a topic has its dangers, of course: self-interested cliques can obtain power and exclude others. That is what happens normally in all sorts of organizations, from governments and corporations to social movement groups. Demarchy handles this problem through the requirement of random selection. No one can be guaranteed a formal decision-making role. Furthermore, the terms of service are strictly limited, so no permanent executive or clique can develop.

Another problem then looms. Won't there be biases in the groups selected, because only certain sorts of people will volunteer? Won't most of the groups, for example, be dominated by white middle-aged men? This poses no problem, given a suitable adaptation of how the random selection is carried out. Suppose, for example, that 80 men and 20 women volunteer for a group of 10, for which it is desired to have an equal number of men and women. The method is simply to select 5 men randomly from the 80 male volunteers and 5 women from the 20 female volunteers. In this way, the gender balance in the group can equal that in the overall population even with different rates of volunteering. The same principle can be applied to characteristics such as ethnic origin, social class, age, occupation and religion.

This may sound logical enough, but who is to make the decisions about what groups are represented in what ways? After all, if a group decides on its own criteria for selection, this is open to abuse. Burnheim's solution to this is what he calls second-order groups. These are groups which act analogously to a judicial system for the operation of demarchy. The second-order groups deal only with procedural issues, such as what (first-order) groups should exist, how the random selection should be carried out, and any other disputed point.

Obviously, members of the second-order groups should have had experience in the first-order groups. How should they be selected? Burnheim suggests that first-order groups should select from among their members those most suitable for second-order groups. Bob James argued to me that this really goes against the guiding principle of demarchy, which is random selection of interested people rather than selection on the basis of performance or popularity. He suggests that second-order group members be chosen randomly from first-order group members. My guess is that the differences between these two procedures would not be so great. Even with a random selection, it is likely that members seen to be performing well would be strongly encouraged by their colleagues to stand for send-order group membership, which would probably not be all that sought after anyway. Finally, the limited term of office on the second-order groups will prevent entrenchment of power.

Several features distinguish demarchy from representative democracy, including random selection, functional groups, limited tenure of office, and elimination of the state and bureaucracy. Some of these could serve as reforms to representative democracy, but there is also a coherency in the entire package.

For example, a limited term of office, say, two years, would help prevent entrenchment of power in representative systems. Why should demarchy be better able to sustain such a requirement for turnover of members of decision-making groups? One difference lies in the legitimacy attached to the selection principle. Representatives justify their position in terms of repeated majority preference for their personal selection. Randomly selected individuals have no special legitimation except the random process itself. The legitimacy of random selection lies in regular replacement rather than popular mandate or acquired experience, and this type of legitimacy more easily allows challenges should those in office attempt to extend their term. A similar difference can be seen in the often lengthy tenure of judges, whether appointed or elected, compared to jurors.

There is not the space here to go into many of the issues raised by the concept of demarchy. Suffice it to say that there are many unanswered questions and many areas where further elaboration is required. I'll mention only a few here.

First, implementation of decisions. Burnheim has rejected the state and bureaucracy, so there won't be any permanent staff to carry out decisions made by the demarchic groups. Burnheim says that the groups will carry out the decisions themselves. That sounds fine in theory, but what will it mean in practice?

Second, how will decisions be enforced? Remember, there is no state and hence no military. Essentially, decisions will be effective if people abide by them, and this depends on the overall legitimacy of the system. Actually, this isn't too different from many aspects of present society. Most people accept the need to act in a sensible manner toward babies, public parks and (for that matter) private property, even when the possibility of legal sanctions and apprehension by the police is remote. Force plays only a limited role in the routine operation of society. In a more participatory society, force could play an even more limited role. The corollary of this is that unpopular decisions by demarchic groups would simply lapse through nonobservance. The groups would have to take into account the willingness of the population to accept their decisions.

Without the state, there would be no military. How would a community defend itself against external aggression? One possibility is arming the people. However, the most participatory alternative to military defense is social defense, based on popular nonviolent resistance. Demarchy and social defense have many compatible features.

Third, a big unanswered question is the nature of the economic system associated with demarchy. In principle, a range of systems are compatible with demarchic decision-making. A group could make a contract for recycling services either with a privately owned company or with a self-managed collective. Demarchy, though, is not compatible with bureaucratically organized economic systems, either socialist or capitalist.

Burnheim argues for extension of the principles of demarchy to economics. For example, there would be demarchic groups to make decisions about particular areas of land. Rents could be charged for uses of the land, and the rents would take the place of taxation, since there is not a state to collect taxes. This is an adaptation of Henry George's ideas. The random selection for groups making decisions over portions of land would prevent vested interests from gaining a stranglehold over the political-economic process. Burnheim would also extend this idea to control over labor and money as well as land. These ideas are in a very preliminary form.

One other important problem is the basic one of participation. What if people don't volunteer? What if certain groups don't produce enough volunteers for their quota? In some cases this would be a sign of success. If the way things are operating is acceptable to most people, then there would be no urgency about becoming a member of a decision-making group. By contrast, in controversial areas participation is not likely to be a problem. If topics such as abortion or genetic engineering generated passionate debate, then concerned individuals and groups would find it fruitful to educate as many people as possible about the issues and encourage them to stand for random selection. Indeed, any unpopular decision could generate a mobilization of people to stand for selection. Furthermore, the people mobilized would have to span a range of categories: men and women, young and old, etc. As a result, participation and informed comment would be highest in the areas of most concern. In other areas, most people would be happy to let others look after matters.

It would be easy to carry on at length about the hypothetical features of demarchy. But what's the point if it's all just a vision?

Burnheim's vision is a very decentralized and participatory use of random selection. By contrast, others have advocated random selection for the US Congress, for example, replacing the elected House of Representatives by a randomly selected "Representative House." These proposals have many merits but leave intact the power of the state.

Of special interest are those who have tried random selection in practice. One such person is Ned Crosby, a political scientist from Minnesota in the United States. In the 1970s, Crosby developed his own idea of a political alternative involving random selection, with a much more centralized system than Burnheim's. But failing to find a publisher for his book, he decided to work on practical implementation.

Crosby set up an organization which is now called the Jefferson Center for New Democratic Processes. It has devoted most of its energy toward practical experiments in random selection for policy-making.

One project concerned the question of whether to introduce school-based clinics to deal with teenage pregnancies and sexually transmitted diseases, a very contentious issue in the state. The Jefferson Center convened a number of groups of randomly selected people which they call policy juries. A 12-person policy jury was organized for each of the eight congressional districts in the state of Minnesota. Using the telephone directory, 100 people in each district were selected randomly and contacted and surveyed about their basic views concerning school-based clinics. Then a jury pool was set up from those contacted by ensuring that the demographic characteristics (ethnic origin, sex, social class) of those in the pool matched those in the overall population. Then people from each pool were elected randomly and invited to be policy jurors, until 12 jurors were obtained. In this process, it was ensured that the jurors' preliminary views about school-based clinics of the jurors matched the percentages found in the overall survey. Thus, the resulting policy juries very nearly matched the overall population both in demographic characteristics and in preliminary views on school-based clinics.

The policy jury in each district held "hearings": they listened to various experts, heard testimony from partisans on each side of the issue, and discussed the issues among themselves. At the end of four days of deliberation, each policy jury took a vote concerning various policy alternatives. As well, each jury gave reasons for its view, made additional policy recommendations and evaluated the experience of the policy jury itself.

In addition to the eight district-based policy juries, a statewide policy jury of 24 people was set up with three members from each district jury. This statewide jury went through a similar process. The recommendations of the policy juries were made available to Minnesota state legislators, and also widely publicized in the media. Through all this, the Jefferson Center provided the essential support for the process. It carried out the surveys, the random selection, convening of the juries, arranging for expert witnesses, coordination of the jury deliberations, and writing up and publicizing the recommendations. To carry weight, it was essential that the Jefferson Center be perceived as committed to a fair process and not to any partisan view on the issue being discussed.

In the above description, I've given only the basic outline of the process. There are many more details for those interested. The basic question to be asked is "how well did it work?" In terms of democratic processes, the answer must be "remarkably well." The key test here is the response of the jurors themselves. They quickly became very committed to the process, taking it extremely seriously. They demonstrated a good grasp of the issues and made sensible recommendations. They also evaluated the process very positively.

From the outside, the policy juries were also well received. They were given favorable reviews by the media and taken seriously by politicians, who recognized the grassroots origin of the views expressed. The Jefferson Center has had similar experiences and success with policy juries on topics such as pollution of water supplies by agricultural chemicals.

The policy juries are not the equivalent of the decision-making groups in demarchy. Policy juries have no formal power, which remains with elected representatives. The policy juries can only influence policy on the basis of the persuasiveness of their views and the process which led to them. But then, in one sense, this is not so entirely different from demarchic bodies, which would gain most of their power from community acceptance.

There are several lessons for promoting demarchy from the Jefferson Center projects. First, random selection can be seen as a legitimate basis for a process leading to policy recommendations. Second, participants become strongly involved in the decision-making process; policy juries are practical experiences in participation which may whet the appetite for more. Third, extensive and careful planning is essential to the success of policy juries. It should be remembered that enormous preparation and energy is put into making elections "work" in legitimating a certain policy process. To be fairly judged, the same preparation and energy must be devoted to demarchic alternatives.

Finally, policy juries represent a practical intermediate stage for advocates of demarchy. Crosby sees random selection as a means for reforming and revitalizing democracy in the United States, making government truly responsive to the will of the people. Demarchy, as presented here, is a more fundamental restructuring of society, eliminating the state altogether. This difference in goals need not cause any special problem. After all, there is a great need for practical steps which are valuable in themselves but also the basis for more fundamental change. Cooperatives can be an experience and a step toward an economy based on production for use rather than profit or control. Similarly, policy juries can be an experience and a step towards demarchy.

Quite independently of the Jefferson Center, similar projects were being undertaken in West Germany beginning in the 1970s, led by Peter Dienel at the University of Wuppertal. The groups of randomly selected citizens brought together for these projects are called "planning cells." The cells have dealt with issues such as energy policy, town planning and information technology. The cell members are typically brought together for four days of talks, discussions and evaluations, and are compensated for wages foregone.

Planning cells have many similarities to policy juries. Here I'll mention just a few highlights, focusing especially on differences. First, the planning cells have usually been given wider briefs. Rather than focus on particular policy options on a well defined issue such as school-based clinics, a broader range of scenarios is dealt with. For example, in looking at energy policy, several options were canvassed, ranging from a heavily nuclear future to a soft energy path based on energy efficiency and renewable energy technologies. These widely divergent futures are part of conventional political debate, to be sure. But seldom are they confronted in direct fashion in the normal course of policy-making, which deals for the most part with the issues in terms of particular urgent decisions on particular projects — a waste disposal site, a regulatory decision, a funding decision. The planning cells are able to deal with broad social issues and take a long-term view, certainly far longer than the typical politician concerned about the next election.

Second, the planning cells make more use of small-group techniques. Much of the time of members of a 25-person planning cell is spent in groups of five, discussing the issues. Whereas the policy jury seems to be modeled on an actual jury, hearing testimony and discussing the issue in the full group, the planning cells are somewhat more oriented to mutual support and building up the participation and understanding of the cell members.

But these differences are minor compared to the major similarities: random selection of group members to deal with policy issues. The striking result is that most of the randomly selected volunteers quickly become quite knowledgeable about the subject matter and committed to the decision-making process.

Toward Demarchy

Between the few experiments with policy juries and planning cells and Burnheim's vision of demarchy is an enormous gulf. What strategy should e used to move towards demarchy?

Burnheim has some ideas. He thinks that as various government bodies become discredited, they may be willing to switch to demarchic management in order to maintain community legitimacy. For example, a health service might be wracked by disputes over salaries, conflict over provision of high technology medicine or community support services, severe budgetary crises and claims of mismanagement and corruption. This wouldn't be unusual. In this crisis situation, management by randomly selected groups might be seen by state managers as a way of resolving or offloading conflict and re-legitimating the health service.

These and other similar scenarios may sound plausible, but they really provide little guidance for action. After all, there are plenty of unpopular, discredited and corrupt institutions in society, but this has seldom led to significant changes in the method of social decision-making. More specifically, how should demarchy be promoted in these situations? By lobbying state managers? By raising the idea among the general population? One thing is clear. The idea of demarchy must become much more well known before there is the slightest chance of implementation.

The experimentation with policy juries and planning cells is vital in gaining experience and spreading the idea of participation through random selection. The limitation of these approaches is that they are not linked to major social groups which would be able to mobilize people to work for the alternative.

Among the "major social groups" in society, quite a number are likely to be hostile to demarchy. This includes most of the powerful groups, such as governments, corporate managements, trade union leaders, political parties, militaries, professions, etc. Genuine popular participation, after all, threatens the prerogatives of elites.

In my opinion, the most promising source of support is social movements: peace activists, feminists, environmentalists, etc. Groups such as these have an interest in wider participation, which is more likely to promote their goals than the present power elites. Social movement groups can try to put demarchy on the agenda by the use of study groups, lobbying, leafleting and grassroots organizing.

Demarchy, though, should not be seen only as a policy issue, as a measure to be implemented in the community as a result of grassroots pressure. Demarchy can also be used by social movements as a means. In other words, they can use it for their own decision making.

This may not sound like much of a difficulty. After all, many social action groups already use consensus either formally or de facto. Also, the system of delegates is quite common. It would not seem a great shift to use random selection for decision-making at scales where direct consensus becomes difficult to manage.

Unfortunately, matters in many social movements are hardly this ordered. In many cases, formal bureaucratic systems have developed, especially in the large national organizations, and there are quite a number of experiences and sometimes charismatic individuals in powerful positions. These individuals are possibly as unlikely as any politician to support conversion to a different system of decision-making. (This itself is probably as good a recommendation for random selection as could be obtained. Any proposal that threatens elites in alternative as well as mainstream organizations must have something going for it.)

Nevertheless, social movements must be one of the more promising places to promote demarchy. If they can actually begin to try out the methods, they can become much more effective advocates. Furthermore, the full vision of demarchy, without the state or bureaucracy, stands a better chance within non-bureaucratized social movements than amid the ruins of bungled government enterprises.

One of the most promising areas for promoting demarchy is in industry. Workers are confronted by powerful hierarchical systems on every side: corporate management, governments and trade union bosses. There is plenty of experience in cooperative decision-making at the shopfloor level; difficulties arise at higher levels of decision-making. It is here that random selection presents itself as a real alternative. Workers councils, composed of both workers and managers selected randomly to serve a short period, provide a basis for communication and coordination. This approach overcomes the defects of all forms of representation. Workers' representatives on boards of management have served to co-opt workers, while representatives in the form of trade union delegates have often become separated from the shop floor. Demarchic groups proved a way to maintain shop-floor involvement in large enterprises.

The key point here is that demarchy should not be treated as a policy alternative, to be implemented from the top, but rather as a method of action itself. The ends should be incorporated in the means. It is quite appropriate that groups promoting demarchy use its techniques.

Needless to say, the future of demarchy cannot be mapped out. It is stimulating to speculate about solutions to anticipated problems; Burnheim's general formulations are immensely valuable in providing a vision. But as democracy by lot is tested, promoted, tried out, enjoys successes and suffers failures, it will be revised, and refined. That is to be expected.

The message is that the process of developing and trying out alternatives is essential for all those seeking a more participative society. True enough, some worthy reforms can be achieved through the old channels of electoral politics, but that is no excuse for neglecting the task of investigating new structures. Demarchy is one such alternative, and deserves attention.

Demarchy is unlikely to be the final word in participative politics. No doubt it has flaws. But it is certain that present electoral methods provide no final solution.

Electoral methods — that brings me back to the greens. They may be one of the most exciting political developments in decades, but in entering electoral politics they may have limited their potential for bringing about radical change. Ironically, it is the popular, charismatic green politicians who provide the least threat to established power structures. Their electoral success will ensure continuing reliance on the old system of politics.

This volume was designed
by a.h.s boy and typeset by dada typo
in Baltimore, Maryland.

The cover image depicts cover art from
issues of the journal *Social Anarchism*
since its inception. Titles are set in
ITC Officina Serif and ITC Officina Sans.

The interior titles are set in Syntax, designed by Hans
Eduard Meier . Body copy and notes are set in the
OpenType format of Robert Slimbach's excellent Minion
Pro from Adobe.

Produced with Adobe InDesign from CS6
(in the future that will be funny).

For info on See Sharp Press see
www.seesharppress.com

Our anarchist titles include:

African Anarchism: The History of a Movement
by Sam Mbah & I.G. Igariwey

Cuban Anarchism: The History of a Movement
by Frank Fernandez

Free Radicals
by Zeke Teflon

The Heretic's Handbook of Quotations
Chaz Bufe, editor

**Hungry for Peace: How You Can Help End Poverty and War
with Food Not Bombs**
by Keith McHenry

Venezuela: Revolution as Spectacle
by Rafael Uzcategui

Social Anarchism is still publishing, twice a year.
Subscriptions are available online at

http://www.socialanarchism.org/

or by writing to

Social Anarchism
2743 Maryland Ave
Baltimore, MD 21218

There is a website for this book at

www.bestofsocialanarchism.org

where we welcome your feedback and discussion
on topics related to the material found in the current volume.

Email the editors at editors@socialanarchism.org.